Islam and the West
THE MORISCOS

Islam and the West
The Moriscos

A CULTURAL AND SOCIAL HISTORY

ANWAR G. CHEJNE

STATE UNIVERSITY OF NEW YORK PRESS
Albany

Published by
State University of New York Press, Albany

Printed in the United States of America

For information, address State University of New York Press, State University Plaza, Albany, N.Y., 12246.

Library of Congress Cataloging in Publication Data

Chejne, Anwar G.
Islam and the West.

Bibliography: p. 216
Includes index.
1. Moriscos. I. Title.
DP104.C45 306'.089927046 82-703
ISBN 0-87395-606-0 AACR2
ISBN 0-87395-603-6 (pbk.)

Contents

Preface

Shortly after the conquest of Granada in 1492 by the Catholic kings, their Muslim subjects in Spain became known derogatorily as Moriscos (little Moors), Moros, Muhammadans, Hagarans (bastards or descendants of Hagar), and Saracens, despite the fact that they were forced to accept the sacrament of baptism. Such appellations remained in use throughout the sixteenth century, applied indiscriminately to all Moriscos regardless of the degree of their devotion to Christianity. The appellations differentiated between the new converts and the Old Christians, believed to be of pure Spanish stock and possessing purity of blood (*limpieza de sangre*).

Born and reared in the Iberian Peninsula of mixed ancestry (Spanish, Jewish, Berber, Arab, and other ethnic groups), the Moriscos were considered aliens in their own land, heretics who presented an imminent danger to both church and state. Edict after edict reinforced this attitude and relegated the Moriscos to the margin of Christian society. In turn, the Moriscos developed their own attitude, accompanied by passive resistance and sporadic revolt, and expressed in an extensive clandestine literature—the Aljamiado literature—which was written in Romance in Arabic script. Although they preserved a sentimental attachment to Arabic as their own language, the Moriscos were no longer able to use it, speaking native Romance dialects that were given the derogatory designation of "foreign" (Ar. *'Ajami*—hence, *'Al-jamiyyah, Aljamia, or Aljamiado).* This literature was for the most part inspired by Arabic models that not only expressed defiance toward the oppressor, but reiterated Islamic values. At the same time, the Moriscos could no longer write in Arabic or recite the Qur'ān in the Arabic original. A new perspective had developed, causing the Morisos to draw closer to their Christian neighbors despite disavowal and reservations on their part and despite Old Christians' rejection.

It is for these and other reasons that the Moriscos and their literature are significant for the study of cultural change, offering valuable data for the historian, religious scholar, sociologist, anthropologist, philologist, belletrist, and civil and human rights advocates who would gain insight into the fate of a deprived and persecuted minority living in a hostile environment. Aljamiado literature, written mostly during the fifteenth and sixteenth centuries, supplements much of the external documentation in the form of edicts, official correspondence, memoranda, records of the tribunals of the Inquisition, and contemporary histories.

The present work is the outgrowth of several years of research. A substantial amount of material was gathered in Spain. Contemporary histories, archival material, modern scholarly books and articles, and a variety of published and unpublished Aljamiado manuscripts, found largely in the National Library of Madrid, the Institute of Asin Palacios, the Royal Academy of History, and the Royal Palace. Morisco writings are classified here into such broad categories as religious works, polemics, history and legends, divination and the sciences, epic, wisdom sayings, and poetry. In view of publication costs, the available data have been treated as concisely as possible without sacrificing the essentials of the literature.

This book is intended to survey and analyze the self-expression of the Moriscos as contained in their own literature, the Aljamiado literature. Simultaneously, it assesses the status of a minority struggling for survival, with reference to ideological conflict, the clash of religions and cultures, and differing mutual perceptions. It is hoped that this work will be of use to Hispanists, Arabists, comparativists, medievalists, and other students. The author would be amply rewarded were it to inspire the reader to pursue further research and reading from the bibliography.

A. G. C.

Minneapolis, 1980

Acknowledgments

I wish to express my gratitude to the John Simon Guggenheim Foundation for granting me a Fellowship during 1979-80 which enabled me to finish this work at this time. I also wish to thank the Graduate School and the Office of Research and Development of the College of Liberal Arts at the University of Minnesota for their financial assistance during the preparation of the manuscript. A special word of thanks goes to my good friend Ann Harbour for her assistance in editorial matters. I am equally indebted to the officers of the National Library of Madrid, the Royal Academy of History, the Institute of Asin Palacios, the Royal Palace, the Escorial, the National Archive of Madrid, the Archive of Aragon, the Central Library of Barcelona, and the Archive of the Alhambra for their generous assistance in supplying me with the necessary material and help during my several trips to Spain. Finally, I wish to thank my colleague Asaad Busool for reading the galley proofs and for his valuable suggestions. I also wish to thank my daughter Cecilia for the preparation of the index. It is of course understood that these people are in no way responsible for whatever defects or inadequacies may be found in this work.

1

The Moriscos in a Hostile Environment

For centuries the Moriscos have had apologists and critics, the former pointing indignantly to the Moriscos' inhumane treatment from Christian masters[1] and the latter attempting to show that however harsh, such treatment was dictated by the necessity of securing the unity of church and state.[2] From the time of Mármol Carvajal in the sixteenth century to Boronat y Barrachina in the nineteenth century, the former approach to the Morisco question was often advanced by foreigners, who might be expected to view the situation with some detachment, whereas the latter was traditionally held by Spanish scholars, often influenced by national, ethnic, and religious considerations. However, modern Spanish scholarship has approached the subject of the Moriscos with great objectivity, thereby contributing to its better understanding.[3] Nevertheless, the Morisco question still evokes emotional views, often passionate, and philosophical speculations and moralistic judgments whose consequences are reflected in similar situations affecting minorities in every time and place.

However interpreted, the ultimate solution of the Morisco problem is amply documented, giving a pattern over centuries of an ascendant majority of Christians and a declining minority of Muslims attributable to complex and multiple causes. The imbalance prevailing between the two societies with respect to power tempts the researcher to accumulate data favoring a given interpretation or simply to moralize on what should have been. This parallels the imbalance between Europeans and Indians or between whites and blacks in the United States in the similar complexity of reconciling Christian doctrine with the attitudes and practices of Christians.

This kind of parallel perhaps may explain why the Moriscos received scholars' attention from the time of their emergence as a minority at the mercy of a powerful majority. The abundant literature consists of contemporary or near-contemporary histories, archival materials in various major Spanish cities, and numerous scholarly studies and monographs. However, this literature is based largely on Christian sources; until recently, little attention was paid to the Moriscos' own, Aljamiado literature. The present study will look at the Moriscos from within, drawing upon their experiences recorded and viewed in Aljamiado literature.

The Moriscos must be viewed within the broad context of the Arab conquest of the Iberian Peninsula in 711 and the subsequent reconquest by Christians from 1085 to 1492. These processes of conquest and reconquest, lasting almost eight centuries, had enormous repercussions on the two contending societies, affecting attitudes, religious affiliations, language, customs—indeed, a whole identity and way of life. These fluctuated with politico-military ascendance and accompanying institutions. The Arab conquest of Spain and consolidation of the occupied areas superimposed Arabic as the language and Islam as the religion of the majority, replacing Latin and Christianity in Spanish society. Arabization and Islamization included other sociocultural changes which made Arab Spain, known as al-Andalus, a cultural sphere quite different from that of Christian Spain to the north, thus presenting a challenge to be met in the battlefield in centuries to come. The challenge to Latindom and Christendom transcended the Iberian Peninsula: the struggle between Islamic and Christian Spain was but part of a wider struggle between Christianity and Islam, producing the Crusades and many casualties, among them the Moriscos.

To Spanish Christians, Muslims in general were known as Moros, or Saracens, whether living under Christian rule or outside it. Although this usage did not cease even after their forced conversion to Christianity, the term *Mudejar* (Ar. *Mudajjan*),[4] "the one allowed to remain" became current in the fifteenth century. Mudejars were Muslims living under Christian rule while preserving many Arabic customs along with their religion. The history of the Mudejars began in 1085 with the fall of Toledo to Alfonso VI. Thereafter, a large segment of the Islamic community lived under Christian rule. Christian rulers grew accustomed to their presence during the Reconquest, which made great headway with the conquest of Saragossa in the twelfth century, and that of Cordova, Valencia, Seville, and other major cities over the thirteenth century. The fall of Granada in 1492 marked the culmination of the Reconquest, ending Muslim rule in the Peninsula. Only a few years after the fall of Granada, the history of the Mudejars can be said to have ended, giving rise to the history of their descendants, the Moriscos.

The Mudejars inhabited cities, towns, and rural areas throughout the Peninsula—Aragon, Castile, Valencia, Estremadura, and Andalusia. They lived in separate communities as protected minorities whose status was determined by the terms of capitulations contracted upon surrender. These capitulations were similar to those granted by Muslims to non-Muslims living under their rule and often guaranteed the freedom of worship, freedom of movement, and the use of language and customs in return for tribute paid in money or in kind. In cities, the Mudejars lived in ghettos, or *morerías*, having jurisdiction over their own affairs, maintenance of their quarter, and places of worship. They associated with their Christian masters daily through commerce, agriculture, administration, industry, and other pursuits.[5] The Mudejars' fortune and role in a Christian environment may be compared to a degree with those of the Mozarabs[6]—Christians living under Muslim rule who were protected by the religious law (*sharī'ah*) that designate them as the people of the Covenant (*ahl al-dhimmah*) or "people of the Book" (*ahl-al-kitāb*).

Religious sanction guaranteed the Mozarabs freedom of worship and jurisdiction over their own affairs in return for the payment of a poll tax (*jizyah*) and a land tax (*kharāj*). These provisions emanate from the religious law; only a heretic or an unjust ruler deviated from their implementation. In consequence, the Mozarabs as well as the Jews were able to preserve their religious identity within a spirit of tolerance allowing them to interact with Muslims, to become arabized in language, customs, and taste to the point of becoming indistinguishable from their Muslim neighbors. Although Christian policy toward non-Christian subjects in Spain appears to have been inspired by the Islamic model, there was, however, a major difference in the contractual nature of minority protection with respect to durability and implementation. This difference may have been the major cause leading to the ultimate tragedy of the Moriscos. Protection of minorities in Islam was conferred by God through his *Sharī'ah*—that is, it was immutable and inviolate, binding for all times, and beyond all human power to amend. Except for occasional aberrations, the provisions of the law regarding religious minorities have been upheld even to the present day. In contrast, the protection of minorities in a Christian environment was conferred by a treaty whose provisions were often influenced by political and military expediency and by other circumstances. Treaties were apt to change, and actually did, subject to the whims of rulers or to the ever-changing politico military situation. Moreover, agreements between the Christian conqueror and the subject people were more often than not opposed by the clergy, which endeavored to annul them by all available means. Among numerous instances of such interference is the conquest of Valencia by James I of Aragon. James I, who had ambitions of conquering the eastern shores of Spain, showed magnanimity toward the subject people by entering into treaties guaranteeing their safety, freedom of movement and of worship, and protection of individual rights in return for payment of a tithe on wheat, barley, and other produce.[7] However, this seemingly benign treatment had its disadvantages, as Burns points out in a thorough study of the Kingdom of Valencia: "Where two exclusive systems exist, this dilemma is native to the concept of tolerance, no matter how sympathetic its framers may be toward the minority; the tolerance that fully preserve an alien group's existence also condemns that group to a life apart, inverted, and undernourished, so strange to the other community as to seem repugnant and even inimical."[8] In fact, even this uneasy accommodation was soon altered through restrictions, pressures, and confiscation of property at the behest of the local clergy and the papacy. Upon the conquest of Murcia in 1265, James was congratulated by the Pope, who added: "It is necessary that you exterminate all Saracens."[9] This policy became almost a pattern throughout the Peninsula, carried out through the office of the Inquisition.[10] The policy became official upon the accession of the Catholic kings, Isabella (1474-1504) and Fernando (1479-1516), who, after consolidating their power in Aragon and Castile, decided to pursue the goal of total reconquest of the Peninsula.

This notwithstanding, the Spanish monarchy often resisted the pressure of the clergy and allowed the Mudejars to participate in economic life, contributing their skills and labor in the crafts, agriculture, and other professions. The Mozarabs and Mudejars served as intermediaries between Islamic and Christian societies, contributing to the integration of many Arabic elements. Estimating their numbers is difficult, since many of them either emigrated at the time of the Reconquest or underwent the process of latinization and Christianization, making them almost indistinguishable from the rest of the Christian population. A sizable segment of Mudejars retained Islam as their religion and were attached to Arabic and Islamic values as long as circumstances allowed, but gradually became latinized—like their counterparts the Mozarabs, subject to the ever-increasing change of language, customs, and even religious practices. Many Mudejars may have adopted Christianity out of conviction or convenience. There is no indication that they were coerced before the policy of forced conversion that was instituted early in the sixteenth century. They were labeled Christian Mudejars, to distinguish them from Old Christians. This differentiation grew more pronounced as the Reconquest gained impetus. The Mudejars were placed in a vulnerable position during the thirteenth century when the major Muslim cities—Cordova, Valencia, Seville—and others—fell to the Christian kings. Their importance, along with that of the Jews, gradually declined as Christians assumed the skills and functions hitherto associated with them. In fact, they remained separated from the mainstream of Christian society, whether they converted to Christianity or adhered to Islam. This segregation increased in the fifteenth century. In 1476 the Courts (Cortes) de Madrigal petitioned the monarchy that Jews and Mudejars be obliged to wear distinctive clothing.[11] At the same time, the role of the Inquisition was expanded for the purpose of punishing heretics,[12] who often were newly converted Jews and Mudejars. The Inquisition had been established in the thirteenth century to prosecute heresy and "did not care to impress the minds of men with magnificence, but rather to paralyze with terror."[13]

During the fifteenth century, the Spanish monarchy and church appear to have had a united policy for their conversion, differing only in timing and approach. Influenced by politicomilitary circumstances, the Catholic kings often found it expedient to enter into contracts that promised a great deal to the subject people, but they, like the clergy, were pledged to eliminating Muslims.[14] Thus, their contractual pledges to Jews and Mudejars were temporary, rescinded as will. Before the conquest of Granada, enormous pressure was placed on the Jews, who were expelled in 1492. The explusion of the Jews was to be reenacted with respect to the Moriscos.

An international dimension exacerbated the status of the Mudejars. The zealous monks of Cluny in the south of France, reinforced by papal bulls, added more pressure on the Spanish monarchy to resolve the Moorish problem through more radical means. They called for sweeping crusades to eliminate the infidels, accompanied by bitter polemics against Islam and its founder. The double-edged war of pen and sword appeared inconclusive to Bishop Juan Segovia (ca. 1400-1458), who perceived a stalemate in the struggle between Islam and Christianity and proposed peace and open forum with Muslims (*per viam pacis et doctrinae*) to reach a modus vivendi.[15] However, his peaceful approach was unheeded; the Mudejars remained vulnerable to the ever-changing conditions. The decisive moment came in 1481, when the Catholic kings attacked Alhama, a fortress in Granada, looting, pillaging, and putting many to death:

Hombres, niños y mujeres	Men, children and women
lloran tan grande pérdida	lament such a great loss.
lloraban todas las damas,	All ladies lamented
cuantas in Granada había	As many as were in Granada.
Ay de mi Alhama!	Alas, my poor Alhama!
Por las calles y ventanas	In the street and windows
mucho luto parecía	Great mourning was seen
y llora rey como fembra	And the king crying like a woman
que es mucho lo que perdía	For the much he had lost.
Ay de mi Alhama[16]	Alas, my poor Alhama!

The fall of the Alhama led to the capture of other Granadan towns—Ronda, Marabella, Almería, Málaga, Baza, and others—followed by the siege and surrender of the capital city of Granada in 1492. The fall of Granada had enormous religious signficance, described vividly in the following poem:

En la ciudad de Granada	In the city of Granada
grandes alaridos dan	Great outcries are heard.
Unos llaman a Mahoma	Some invoke Muhammad

otros a la Trinidad	Others invoke the Trinity.
Por un cabo entran las cruces	Crosses enter from one end
de otro sale alcoran	And the Qur'ān leaves from the other;
donde antes oían cuernos	Where horns were heard before
campanas oyen sonar.[17]	Now the sound of bells are heard.

The fall of Granada added the last independent Muslims to the body of Mudejars and had grave implications for their future status. The Granadans were granted generous terms guaranteeing their safety; the preservation of their law, mosque, and religious foundations; respect for their privacy; general amnesty for all prisoners; freedom to emigrate; freedom of travel and worship; and the use of their language and customs.[18] However, they were soon subjected to strictures in violation of the terms of capitulations granted under solemn oath.

The procedure of the Catholic kings may be viewed as part of a pattern that dated from the beginning of the Reconquest. In similar, earlier surrenders, the Catholic kings had proceeded cautiously, with all the appearance of implementing the terms of capitulations. They appointed over Granada two fair-minded men: Iñego López de Mendoza as its governor and Hernando de Talavera as archbishop. These were men of goodwill who appeared to understand the sensitive situation within two communities long at war. Although Talavera was committed to converting Muslim subjects, his peaceful and persuasive method was to establish communication and to attain conversion through education. Talavera encouraged his subordinates to learn Arabic in order to facilitate the process of conversion. He enlisted rural priests of mixed, Moorish-Christian ancestry who were familiar with the language and customs of the subject people. Arabic catechisms were to be used, and to facilitate the task of the priests, Pedro de Alcalá composed his *Art for Learning Rapidly the Arabic Language,* a grammar of the colloquial language whose purpose, stated in the prologue, was "to bring these recent converts out of the darkness and many errors induced by that evil, vile, and accursed Muḥammad."[19]

Talavera's approach appeared too slow to the Catholic kings, who sent Francisco Ximenez de Cisneros, Archbishop of Toledo, to Talavera's assistance.[20] Cisneros came prepared with expensive gifts for Muslim leaders whom he hoped to employ in converting the masses. He succeeded in baptizing some of them and three thousand other Muslims in a single day (December 18, 1499).[21] Emboldened by initial success, Cisneros pushed on with mass conversion, arousing great protest from staunch Muslims. He imprisoned many, among them their proud leader, Zegri, who was starved until he begged for conversion under the name of Gonzalo Fernández Zegri.[22] Zegri was rewarded with a pension of fifty thousand maravedis. Cisneros ordered the main mosque of Albaicín to be converted into a church, had all Arabic religious books burned, and transferred Arabic books in philosophy to the University of Alcalá de Henares, which he had founded.

Cisneros's high-handed methods of conversion constituted a gross violation of the terms of capitulations.[23] Granadans reacted violently, precipitating the revolt of Albaicín and the murder of one of Cisneros's agents. The revolt was harshly quelled in 1501, and revolt gave the monarchy an excuse for declaring the terms of capitulations null and void, thus placing the Granadans and Mudejars elsewhere at the mercy of the authorities. In 1501 a royal ordinance was issued calling for the conversion of the Muslims of Granada, followed by another in 1502 calling on the Muslims of Castile to choose between baptism and exile.[24] These and similar ordinances were followed by harsher measures leaving no doubt about the direction of state policy toward Granadans in particular and Mudejars of the Peninsula in general. In 1516, Cisneros not only insisted on forced baptism, but instituted an ordinance calling for the abandonment of Moorish dress and customs. Although the ordinance was rescinded through the intervention of influential people, it had enormous repercussions among the Mudejars of Castile, Arágon, Valencia, Estremadura, and elsewhere, starting a cycle of mutual resentment and suspicion which lasted until the final expulsion in 1609-1614.

After the forced conversions of 1501, the neophytes—whether baptized by force or free will—came to be called Moriscos (little Moors), placing them in a special category within the Christian faith. They were differentiated from Old Christians not only by the recency of their conversions, but also by race. The label "Moriscos," or sometimes "Christian Mudejars," placed them at a great disadvantage vis-a-vis their Christian fellows in that they were considered Arabs or Berbers and, thus, inferior to "Old Christians," who enjoyed "purity of blood" (*limpieza de sangre*).[25] These claims could not, of course, be justified, since Old Christians were as much a mixture as the Moors. In fact, it was almost impossible to distinguish one from the other at this juncture of history, notwithstanding claims to the contrary. The Arab conquest of Spain had been achieved by a small band of Berbers and Arabs who intermingled with the overwhelmingly larger native population steeped in Christianity and Latin culture. Subsequent to the conquest, this native population underwent linguistic, religious, and cultural changes, but hardly an ethnic or racial transformation. The neo-Muslims, mostly of Spanish stock and known as Muladíes (Ar. *Muwalladūn*), constituted the bulk of the Muslim population of the Peninsula preserving Islamic values and culture. They were the ancestors of the Mudejars and Moriscos, whether of Spanish, Berber, Jewish, or Black ancestry. Castro, who has been criticized for his Moorish-Jewish sympathy, may be close to the mark when he says: "The Moriscos constitute a part of Spain and an extension of its people."[26] In fact, they were as Spanish as Indians are American.

Be that as it may, the Moriscos came into the spotlight following the establishment of forced conversion. Subsequently, they were at the mercy of church, state, and Old Christians, and were subjected to all sort of strictures with regard to their persons, family life, and associations. The Inquisition punished any infraction or any appearance thereof severely with long imprisonment, confiscation of property, exile, or even death.[27] For example, Moriscos could be brought before the tribunal of the Inquisition on charges of not eating pork or not using bacon in a frying pan.[28]

Finally, the Moriscos were singled out as a thorn in the side of Spanish society. Moriscan utterances, deeds, behavior, customs, dress, food, and very manner of doing things were abominable and ought to be eradicated. Edict after edict was issued to correct or eliminate all features associated with Moriscos. As a people, they not only lacked purity of blood, but were crude and ignorant.[29] They were often ridiculed as peasants, peddlers of figs, almonds, and other produce.[30] Although they were considered industrious, hard working, thrifty, and family men, these virtues were read as competitive, greedy, avaricious, with a fecundity that would eventually upset the population balance.[31] Except for some Frontier Romanceros where he appears cavalier, loving, and courageous,[32] the Morisco was generally represented in the literature as *mezquin* and ridiculous.[33] In sum, he was an undesirable stranger in his own land, denied the opportunity to adjust within the new religious order. Furthermore, church and state were alarmed by the Morisco's practice of divination, use of amulets,[34] and beliefs in prophecies that foretold the doom of Christianity and the ultimate triumph of Islam.[35] These attitudes and images made any future accomodation between Old Christians and Moriscos almost impossible.

While much of this antagonism toward the Moriscos may be attributed to internal factors resulting from a long contract marked by conquest and reconquest, religious friction, and conflict of language and culture, there were other external factors that exacerbated Christian—Morisco relations. The Moriscos were considered a fifth column, not only an obstacle to the unity of Spain but also potentially a force colluding with North Africans, Egyptians, French, Turks, pirates, Lutherans, and other Christian heretics.[36] This was part of Spanish national posture during the fifteenth and sixteenth centuries. The discovery of America and the subsequent Spanish expansionism with designs in Italy, the Mediterranean, and North Africa brought Spain face to face with France, England, and the Ottoman Empire, resulting in expensive wars and humiliating defeats. Wars between France and Spain were recurrent throughout the sixteenth century, and France did not fail to exploit Morisco discontent. Spain also had encounters with England, which defeated its Great Armada in 1588. But the Turks were the most fearsome and formidable enemy, not only to Europe in general, but to Spain in particular. After their conquest of Constantinople in 1453, the Turks threatened Europe, besieging Vienna in 1529 and making inroads into Egypt and North Africa, where they conflicted directly with Spain, which had established its presence in Oran, Bougie, and Tripoli as early as 1509-1511. The Muslim Turks were regarded by Christendom as the scourge of God for Christian sins,[37] to be fought by all means possible, including an all-out Crusade. They were of immediate concern to Spain as a potential conqueror, who would be aided by the oppressed and disaffected Moriscos. In their desperate situation, the Moriscos entertained the hope that their fellow Muslims, the Turks, would sooner or later deliver them from oppression. In fact, they appealed to both Turks and North Africans for assistance,[38] thus giving some substance to the concern that the Moriscos constituted a fifth column set to destroy both church and state. Concomitant with the ever-increasing presence of the Turks in the Mediterranean was the increasing piracy that long ravaged the eastern shores of Spain and other coastal areas of the Mediterranean. The pirates were well organized and indulged not only in intercepting and robbing ships on the high seas, but in taking men, women, and children to be sold as slaves. Their excesses were more manifest in coastal areas where a large number of Moriscos lived, in a position both vulnerable and suspicious.

Finally, the rise of Protestantism in the first half of the sixteenth century also had its adverse effect on the Moriscos. Spain viewed Protestantism as the gravest threat to national unity and was committed to eliminate it. As Protestantism spread into southern France and Spain, Spain saw the danger of collusion between Moriscos and Protestants, and set the Inquisition to deal severely with any religious deviation, whether inspired by Muslim traditions or Christian reformers. Though the Moriscos remained faithful to their own traditions, they saw in Protestantism certain elements that conformed with some of their religious thinking—such as the denial of the supremacy of the pope, the frowning on images, and the freedom of the individual to scrutinize the Scriptures. Furthermore, the Moriscos had hoped through their contact with France to shake off the yoke of oppression along with the persecuted Protestant minority. In sum, Spanish international involvement with France and Turkey, concern with piracy, and preoccupation with Protestantism compounded the already tenuous position of the Moriscos.

The attitudes toward the Morisco and his ancestors, a long time in the making, became articulated in the course of the sixteenth century. The Catholic kings had achieved the territorial unity of spain, but still ruled over many Muslim subjects, a legacy of several centuries of granting generous terms of surrender and rescinding them as circumstances permitted. They acquiesced in Cisneros's policy of forced conversion, which remained in effect during subsequent reigns.[39] Charles V (1516-1558) of Austria was faced with the disadvantage of being a foreigner amid the internal and international pressures surrounding the Morisco question. In 1519, he had to cope with the controversy over whether forced conversion actually turned Moriscos into Christians.[40] After some time, it was decided that forced converts were Christians and, hence, subject to the Inquisition, which could sentence them for any religious infraction. In 1524, Pope Clement VII requested Charles V to end the Moorish question by means of baptism, upon which the monarch gave the Moors of Valencia and Aragón a choice of conversion or exile. Shortly thereafter, an edict was issued prohibiting the Arabic language, clothing, amulets, jewels, circumcision, manner of slaughtering animals, and Morisco practices.[41] The edict was rescinded in return for a payment of ninety thousand ducados.[42] These and similar measures provoked the Moriscos of Valencia to revolt in

1526. The revolt ended in an agreement guaranteeing Moriscos' rights.

However, the agreement was soon revoked on charges that some Moriscos were flirting with Lutherans, while others were aiding and abetting pirates in the Levant, led by the brothers Barbarossa. Piracy remained rampant for decades in the Mediterranean, on eastern shores of Spain inflicting enormous damage and taking Christian and Morisco captives for sale as slaves in Algeria. Another grave concern of Charles was the actual or imagined Turkish threat to the Peninsula, thought to have been encouraged by Moriscos. All this led to further restrictive measures on the Moriscos, believed to be as Arabic as ever. As late as the nineteenth century, a Spanish scholar could state: "This was a war of religion and race, making a fusion impossible. Thus, it was futile for the Monarchy to offer the Moors any benefit."[43]

After the death of Charles V, his successor, Philip II (1555-1598),[44] attempted to pursue a policy of moderation toward the Moriscos but could hardly afford to antagonize the local clergy and the papacy, which often pointed to the persistent piracy, the danger of Protestantism, and the threat of the Ottomans. The papacy had invested the Inquisition with enormous power. The Inquisitor General could condemn to death anyone who confessed error or was involved in the Protestant movement. In 1559 sentences (auto-da-fé) were issued in Valladolid, Saragossa, Seville, Valencia, and Murcia against heretics of Protestant and Muslim persuasion. The Moriscos were charged with not taking Christianity seriously, practicing their Muslim religion, observing circumcision, assuming Arabic names, fasting in Ramaḍān, working on Christian holidays, and in general, showing contempt for Christian sacraments and practices, along with the usual charges about Moriscos' involvement in piracy and intrigue with Turks and North Africans. These charges emanated mostly from clerics, who demanded swift, corrective actions.

In 1563 the authorities disarmed the Moriscos of Valencia and sentenced nine Moriscos. In 1564 the Courts of Monzón petitioned the monarchy to institute indoctrination of the Moriscos through teaching, constructing new churches, and appointing honorable and capable priests to guide and instruct them. The petition was a fresh attempt to persuade the Moriscos, but asked also that no mercy be accorded to religious scholars (*alfaquies*) and proselytizers (*dogmatizadores*).[45] However, this peaceful approach did not last long and led to stiffer measures in the ordinance of 1566, prohibiting the Moriscos the use of the Arabic language, annulling of all contracts written in Arabic, surrendering all Arabic books within thirty days, and prohibiting any Moorish rite, Moorish clothing, and the use of Arabic names and customs. The edict also called for destroying all public baths, requiring Moriscos to leave the doors of their houses open, unveiling women and requiring Castilian dress, and ceasing to dance the zambra and sing.[46] The decree created great consternation among the Moriscos, who attempted to have it repealed, without avail.[47] The Moriscos of Granada launched the Revolt of the Alpujarras (1568-1570), ending in disaster and grave repercussions for Moriscos throughout the Peninsula. The Revolt of the Alpujarras was savage on both sides, demonstrating the intense animosity between Old Christians and Moriscos. The Granadans burned churches, forced people to secede from Christianity, and killed clerics and innocent people. The government response was equally intense, characterized by pillage, rape, indiscriminate killing, and enslaving of people whether implicated or not in the revolt.[48] Some fifty thousand Granadans were rounded up and redistributed throughout the Peninsula among Christians in Seville, Cordova, Toledo, Castile, León, and Aragón, who kept them under surveillance.[49] Their presence resulted in acute mistrust and tension between Old Christians and Moriscos. Many Moriscos in fear or despair chose the road of self-exile (*monfies*), and indulged in brigandry in Andalusia, Castile, Aragón, and elsewhere, leading to unrest and recriminations.[50] This antagonism was exacerbated by the fear of an imminent Turkish invasion, which persisted despite the Turkish defeat at Lepanto in 1571[51] and increased when Tunis fell to the Turks in 1574.[52] Moreover, the defeat of the Spanish Armada in 1588 and the subsequent coalition of France, England, and Holland placed the Spanish monarchy on edge, and contributed no small share to endangering the position of the Moriscos.[53]

Throughout the reign of Philip II and that of his successor Philip III (1598-1621), the Morisco question remained alive, producing a deluge of complaints not only against the religious beliefs and customs of the Moriscos, but against the danger they presented to church and state. For example, a report about the Moriscos of Valencia, Aragón, and Cataluña was presented to Philip II complaining, among other things, that the Moriscos circumcized their children, erased the Christian sacrament of baptism through washing, and gave their children Arabic names. Further, it was charged that the Moriscos continued to observe their holidays; failed to go to church, did not confess, did foolish things during mass in contempt thereof, disrespected rectors and preachers, ate meat on forbidden days, were polygamous, and said blasphemous things about God and the Catholic faith. More grievous still, they conspired with Turks to come and conquer Spain.[54] Gregorio de Miranda, Inquisitor General of Valencia, complained in 1561 that the Moriscos continued to live as Moors and presented a great danger to church and state: the Moriscos were as Moorish as their brethren in Algeria, in practicing their rites and customs, possessing mosques where they met to offend God; they were traitors and rebels, took Christians into captivity, hid pirates, and spied for the Turks.[55]

Such charges contributed to an image that time and conditions translated into reality in the mind of Old Christians. It became clear in time that the policy of forced conversion instituted at the beginning of the sixteenth century had failed—not so much from the stubborn resistance of the Moriscos as from the many obstacles placed on its way by the Christians themselves, whose anxiety, perhaps, did much to make it fail. Pressures on all sides were mounting, while the Inquisition multiplied its trials of Moriscos on frivolous charges that resulted in harsh sentences. Pleas for Christian charity and understanding proved unsuccessful in face of more powerful forces calling for a speedy and radical solution. The Moriscos were often unreceptive to overtures of "clemency," since they had more than once been betrayed by broken promises and violated treaties. Thus, following the Alpujarras revolt, the two communities could no longer function, and a call for explusion was set in motion.

A memorandum by the bishop of Segorbe dated July 30, 1587, testifies eloquently to the mood of the day. The bishop reviews the Morisco question from the time of the fall of Granada, pointing out: (1) the Moriscos were told from the outset to embrace Christianity, or leave the country; (2) they refuse to confess their sins, preferring instead to wash their heads, hands, and feet for the remission of their minor sins while believing that their major sins will be forgiven through repentance; (3) they practice polygamy and divorce; (4) they believe killing Christians will secure them salvation; (5) they commit murder, theft, and other illicit acts; (6) they have complete contempt for the church and its rites; (7) they circumcize their children and, when questioned, answer that they were born that way; (8) they use Moorish names after being given baptismal names; (9) they refuse to receive the sacraments of confirmation, unction and penitence, and mock them; (10) they perform their own prayers, ablution, and other rituals; (11) they refuse to bury their dead in consecrated ground, preferring virgin land in the Muḥammadan custom; (12) they do not contribute to the church, work for its improvement, in spite of the fact that they are rich and powerful; (13) they abhor representations of saints and refuse to have them in their homes; (14) they do not drink wine or eat bacon; (15) they do not pursue Christian professions at the university; (16) they abhor Christianity; (17) they conspire with Turks and north Africans for the conquest of Spain; (18) they kill priests, profane sacred places, and organize revolt; (19) they take jobs away from Christians; (20) the church and state did much for them, but this has been of no avail, since they persist in following the abominable sect of Muḥammad; (21) the evidence is overwhelming that conversion did them no good: they remain as Moorish as the north Africans; and (22) distributing them among Christians also failed, since they remain as Moorish as ever.

The Bishop concludes that the Moriscos are indeed heretics, enemies of the church, and blasphemous against the Trinity and all the articles of the Catholic church. They are worse than the Jews, who were expelled for lesser crimes. Thus, they should be expelled, thereby cleansing these kingdoms from this abominable sect of Muḥammad. He is calling the king's attention to this problem as a matter of duty to God and to His Majesty—although such expulsion may mean the loss of more than three thousand ducados to the archdiocese.[56]

Philip II was by now used to these complaints about the Moriscos and to the suggestion of expulsion, but he was unwilling to settle the Morisco question by this means. Philip III, who lacked the ability and the leadership of his father, also appears to have been reluctant at first to implement such measures. However, he fell under the influence of his courtiers, and especially his wife and the Duke of Lerma, who pushed for expulsion. Expulsion had been discussed as early as 1582,[57] and was delayed by considering alternatives, such as settling Moriscos in ghettos and forbidding intermarriage, or castration for preventing increase in Morisco population.[58] More humane proposals were also advanced, some calling for patience and charity and for a better attempt at educating the Moriscos.[59] Their advocates pointed to the exemplary conduct and devotion of some neophytes and to those who had intermarried with Old Christians. The push for expulsion was renewed at the accession of Philip III in 1598, and in 1609 he issued a royal decree calling for explusion.[60] The order of expulsion exempted only a small number of farmers, children under four provided that their parents consented, children of Old Christians married to Moriscos, and other bonafide baptized Moriscos, who had given proof of their faith and who never had any political association with Moriscos.[61] The order was kept secret to avert serious obstacles, and was to be carried out piecemeal in Valencia, Granada, Murcia, Jaén, Andalusi'a, Hornachos, Castile, Mancha, Estremadura, Aragón, and Cataluña. Orders were issued to landlords *(señores)* to deliver Moriscos working for them to the port of departure, allowing them to carry portable things. Although they were guaranteed a safe conduct to the port of departure, many Moriscos were robbed, injured, or killed on the way. Except for such mishaps, the expulsion was carefully organized and proceeded until 1614.

The Moriscos of Valencia were of immediate concern by virtue of their numbers and geographical position on the Mediterranean, vulnerable to pirates and a potential Turkish invasion. Moreover, the Moriscos of Valencia had been restless and in constant conflict with Old Christians. Valencia and its surrounding areas had a population of about half a million, of which 160,000 or thirty-four percent were Moriscos.[62] Of this number, it is estimated that 125,000 were sent to North Africa in boats prepared for them, while a small number had managed to flee to France.[63] It may be assumed that some 35,000 managed to remain according to the terms of expulsion or simply went into hiding. Similar conditions prevailed elsewhere. It is estimated that 110,000 left Andalusía, Murcia, and Hornachos;[64] some 50,000, Cataluña,[65] 120,000, Aragón;[66] 250,000, Castile, Mancha, and Estremadura. Altogether, it is estimated that the number of exiles was about half a million, although there is no general agreement upon the exact number.[67]

The orders of expulsion had, for all intents and purposes, been accomplished by 1614. However, there remained the preoccupation of cleansing the land of the remaining infidels and those who managed to return from exile. The Duke of Lerma, on the sideline until the final vote for expulsion, became a staunch exponent of eradicating the last Moriscos, "so that all the kingdoms of Spain will remain pure and clean from this people."[68] This sentiment was echoed by his contemporaries, as reflected in the works of Aznar Cardona, Marcos de Guadaljara, Gaspar de Aguilar, and others, who saw great benefit in the expulsion.[69] Even the word *Morisco* was decreed to be forgotten, for its use would constitute bad taste.[70] Furthermore, Salazar de Mendoza exclaimed: "In order for Spain to stay clean, it remains to do the same with the

Gypsies."[71]

Nevertheless, it appears that an unspecified number of Moriscos remained clandestinely, some of them hiding, others returning from exile. Orders for bringing them to justice were issued, but the frenzy subsided, allowing them to settle down peacefully and integrate with a society that had persistently rejected them. Although there is no agreement among scholars concerning the number who remained on Spanish soil, contemporary accounts suggest that many stayed. This is corroborated by later travelers, such as Swinburne,[72] Townsend,[73] Ford,[74] and Irving,[75] who felt the presence of their culture still permeating the landscapes of Spain.

The exiled Moriscos were scattered throughout the Mediterranean basis: the Balearic Islands, France, Sicily, Italy,[76] Constantinople and other Eastern cities, but with the greatest concentration in Morocco, Algeria, and Tunis. Their fortunes varied from place to place with their numerical strength. They were quite visible in Morocco, Algeria, and Tunis,[77] which had hosted large numbers of Andalusians from the beginning of the Reconquest. In these countries they participated actively in administration, agriculture, crafts, art, and architecture, leaving an imprint of their culture. Those who settled elsewhere appear to have become fused, by virtue of their small number, into their host countries, leaving little or no trace of their legacy. By and large, the Moriscos were not welcomed, even in the Islamic countries of North Africa. They endured great hardship and alienation. Their North African hosts labeled them "Spanish Christians"—the same who only recently had been called "little Moors" by the Spanish. They were ill treated and robbed in Algeria, making many of them wish that they were back home.[78] Their lot was more tolerable in Morocco, where they could be seen in large numbers in Ceuta, Tangier, Tetuan, Fez, Rabat, and Salé. In Tunisia, they appear to have enjoyed an atmosphere conducive to a cohesive community life and established several towns that still bear Andalusian names.[79] Some Tunisians' Andalusian names still indicate their place of origin. Although they have been fused into North African society, a few can still be found who look nostalgically to the land of their ancestors in Spain, preserving the keys to their old homes with the expectation of returning one day.

The Morisco question has given rise to a number of studies concerning their treatment by Christians, the manner and causes of the expulsion, and its impact on the economy of Spain. Because of the complex implications of the question for history, religion, culture, and language, there are no simple answers. Although the Moriscos faced different problems in different regions, there appears to have been a general pattern in their treatment, molded by church and state almost from the time the Reconquest began in earnest at the fall of Toledo in 1085. Even the staunchest critics agree that the Moriscos received harsh treatment at the hands of their Christian peers. On the reasons for such treatment, there is no general agreement. Braudel,[80] who views the Morisco question in a Mediterranean context, is inclined to think that lack of assimilation and continued adherence to Morisco customs and beliefs are at the root of the harsh solution. For him, the question is basically a clash of two cultures, the oriental and occidental. Lapeyre[81] studies the geographic distribution of the Moriscos, comparing the relationship between Moriscos and Old Christians with that between French Colonials and native Algerians. Caro Baroja[82] in an incisive study of the social structure of the Moriscos of Granada emphasizes their occupation and customs and, at the same time, shows the conflict in policy between the Spanish bureaucrats and clergy, on the one hand, and the aristocrats, on the other. Regla[83] examines the differences between the Moriscos of Castile and those of Aragón, discussing the Morisco problem at the international level with respect to the French and the Turks.

These and other modern views contrast with some earlier interpretations. Writing in the nineteenth century, Dánvila[84] speaks of the incompatibility of the Christian and Moorish races. While admitting the harsh treatment of the Moriscos and the negative consequences of the expulsion on the revenues of church and state, he considers their treatment as "part of . . . a religious war, a war of extermination of the opposite race."[85] Moreover, their expulsion was favored by Spaniards and was justifiable and unavoidable. He states elsewhere:

> The expulsion of the Spanish Moriscos was carried out without regard to young and old, fit or unfit, guilty or innocent. The question of political unity was a sequel to the necessity of church unity. It was initiated by the Catholic kings. Charles V and Philip II attempted to accomplish it, but had to fall back in face of its consequences. Philip III, exercising the power through his favorites, made it easy through the combination of religious and political power. The religious war was much alive against the Moorish race, and the sweetest sentiments of the soul came face to face with the political question. Humanity and religion fought, but religion emerged victorious. Spain lost its most industrious sons; children were separated from the lap of their mothers, and from paternal love. There was no pity or mercy for any Morisco, but religious unity appeared radiant and luminous in the sky of Spain. Happy is the nation that is united in all its sentiments.[86]

The economic consequences of the expulsion have also received the attention of scholars. Relying on contemporary accounts and recent research, Domínguez[87] gives a balanced assessment of the situation. He states that the expulsion constituted a "human hemorrhage" and "an impressive loss of vitality"[88]; he considers that the effect must have been enormous, particularly where there was a high concentration of Moriscos, as in Granada, Valencia, and Aragón—entire villages depopulated, irrigation and cultivation of rice and other produce neglected, not to mention the loss to industry and crafts. Church and state lost considerable revenue; there was shortage of manpower, and drainage of currency. He concludes that the impact was disastrous in Valencia and Aragón, and appreciable in Castile.[89]

In sum, the Moriscos must be viewed within the context of the long history of Muslim Spain, marked by interminable conflict between two societies vying for religious supremacy, territorial hegemony, and economic advantages. The internal confrontation characterized by conquest and reconquest was further compounded by religion and international politics. Clerical and papal intervention from beyond the Peninsula led eventually to crusades and *jihāds* involving the major powers of the Mediterranean. The initial success of the Reconquest following the fall of Toledo inspired an all-out crusade, which in turn animated the process of Reconquest, making Spain the center of crusade and countercrusade. The Moriscos became the casualty of this situation, particularly after the fall of Granada in 1492. The Granadans, who had preserved an Islamic entity in the Peninsula and were proud of their Islamic heritage, were caught in the web of international politics as had been the Mudejars elsewhere in the Peninsula. Events moved very fast. Following the humiliation of defeat, they were confronted with forced conversion, with no choice other than almost total effacement of their identity overnight. Little time was allowed for accommodation that could lead to assimilation; instead, differences of religion, language, and culture were accentuated. The end result was alienation, with grave sociopsychological consequences that led to the tragedy of the Moriscos.

It would be misleading to attribute all the bitter antagonism toward the Moriscos to rulers and the clergy. The populace had deep feelings, though these may have been manipulated from above. On the other hand, the landowners, who counted a large number of Moriscos in their service as peons and farmers, showed sympathy for the Moriscos to the point of overlooking some of their religious practices. In addition, a good number of highly placed people, including clergymen, objected to the harsh methods employed against the Moriscos, preferring a more moderate and humane approach for the total latinization and Christianization of the Moriscos. Indoctrination through education was believed to accomplish the goal of total and sincere conversion; manuals were even written in Arabic to facilitate such a task, as attested by the works of Alcalá, Ayala, Ribera, and others. Other methods of social fusion through intermarriage and social conviviality were often suggested, but failed, as did the many edicts of "grace" calling upon the Moriscos to confess and repent, whereupon all their past sins would be forgiven. Such approaches were advocated by a concerned minority and never constituted an established policy of either church or state. However well intentioned, these efforts were sporadic and often intended to ameliorate grave injustices. Moreover, even the policy of moderation appears never to have deviated from the main objective of eradicating the whole Morisco personality in both external and internal aspects, giving little or no option of preserving the Morisco's identity as an individual or as a member of the social group to which he had been bound by history, religion, and culture. In addition, occasional humane overtures were insufficient to dispel Moriscos' fear and mistrust after long repression. The Morisco could never be sure that any act, however innocent, would not lead to grave consequences, including trial before the tribunal of the Inquisition. The conflict between the two societies, powerful Christians and suppressed Moriscos, had reached a point of no return.

2

Morisco Reaction: A Self-Image

To complete the general picture of the Moriscos in a hostile environment requires an evaluation of the Morisco's view of himself and the world, his problems and hopes for their solution, basing this evaluation whenever possible on his own writings and expressions. Whether living in Granada, Andalusía, Valencia, Aragón, Castile, Estremadura, or Cataluña, the Morisco and his forerunner, the Mudejar, had historical consciousness about his past Islamic ascendancy and, by extension, about his place in history. This produced not only strong pride in past Islamic accomplishments and faithfulness to Islamic values and practices, but also the unshakable belief in the Morisco's ultimate deliverence. This consciousness of a glorious past and present tribulations strengthened belief in a future redemption through the triumph of divine power over the deeds of man. Untutored and relegated to a low place in society, aware of his shortcomings and difficulties, the Morisco's hope for a brighter future did not falter. This unshaken confidence and its underlying expectations emerge from his literature on religious matters, polemics, history, legend, and even novels. The writings are for the most part didactic and often deal with the theme of hopelessness and despair which end in triumph and bliss within a divine plan.

The Morisco, like his Mudejar ancestors, witnessed abrupt and shattering changes within a lifetime. His mosques were destroyed or converted to churches; his estates and homes were taken away and occupied by military commanders, noblemen, and church leaders under whom he served in a status below a slave.[1] He worked in the fields with little or no return, under "the Christian bossing him with an ecstacy of self-magnificence."[2] He was conscious of the perfidy of his Christian oppressor, who reneged upon the terms of capitulation accorded to him under solemn oath. Moreover, when he was forced to embrace Christianity, he was rejected even within the fold of Christianity, and placed in the position of upholding a religion that from the outset denied him any hope now or in the future. Hence, the Morisco felt a strong sense of betrayal and, inspired by his heritage, resisted. The Granadans, in particular, had a vivid memory of their past. Although it was demeaning to them to live under christian rule, they had little choice but to accept terms in 1492 that were both generous and benign, hoping to coexist peacefully among Christian compatriots with whom they were bound by history and geography, besides other, linguistic and cultural factors. No sooner had the peace terms been concluded than they were revoked, leaving Granadans frustrated and humiliated.

Following the conquest of Granada, the Moriscos became increasingly alienated and ultimately ostracized. They lacked local organization and had little or no rapport with fellow Moriscos living elsewhere in the Peninsula. This lack of social cohesiveness made them more vulnerable and contributed to their inefficacy in crisis. The landowners among them were fearful of confiscation by greedy secular adventurers and clerics; they often would sell their property at bottom prices and emigrate to North Africa. Those who remained had to settle for whatever they could get. Some became domestic or menial workers, often as slaves purchased in the free market or captured during wartime; others were a migratory group of merchants, peddlers, transportation workers, and civil servants; a third group was engaged in the crafts and industries as bakers, butchers, goldsmiths, carpenters, weavers, tailors, dyers, and similar kinds of work;[3] and a fourth group manned agriculture as small farmers or as vassals of the Christian nobility. To these may be added the scholars and religious men, who appear to have presided over the religious life of the Moriscos. All together, the Moriscos constituted a social group separate from Old Christian society. They lived for the most part in rural areas and in *morerías* on the fringes of towns and cities.

To the lack of social cohesiveness may be added the internal dissension within the Morisco communities. This fragility was inherent in Muslim society of al-Andalus, where loyalties were ethnic and regional rather than national or religious. This can be seen repeatedly during the Reconquest, when town after town fell to the Christian conquerors with little or no help from neighboring Muslims. This vulnerability is expressed eloquently by Burns, referring to the situation in Valencia: "Religion so rented with cliques and factions always rested on unstable equilibrium. It might fragment in a dozen different patterns according as the winds of new doctrine or political opportunity blew . . . No common bonds, no deep political allegiance, bound this diversity into more than an accidental unity. Religion could not always be counted on to rally these forces."[4]

This divisive, traditional pattern evident throughout the Reconquest was visible also during the siege of Granada in 1491, the Morisco revolt in Valencia in 1526, and the Alpujarras revolt in Granada in 1568-1570. Factionalism following tribal affiliation or blood relationship[5] played havoc in Morisco ranks and was a major factor in their ultimate downfall. The edict of 1566 calling practically for the self-effacement of the Moriscos might be imagined to have caused them to unite and meet the challenge by any or all means, yet the course of the Revolt of the Alpujarras indicates malaise in the social structure. The Alpujarras revolt was beset by serious problems from the outset. Response to the call of arms was lukewarm; the heterogeneous army of some 15,000 was made up of exiled brigands (*monfies*),[6] corsairs,[7] and other groups with little support from town dwellers. Moreover, the struggle for leadership revived old animosities based on genealogical affiliation: Hernando de Valor, known as Ibn Umayyah, and Faraj Ibn Faraj of Banū Sarrāj contended during the revolt until both were assassinated. Besides, popular support was lacking and treason was rampant,[9] placing the Morisco population at the mercy of the Christian army. Moriscos were aware of the malaise, as is attested by this complaint: :"Some Moriscos boasted of being descendants of the Helpers;[10] others of being émigrés;[11] a third group of being descendants of 'Abd al-Manāf.[12] They also boasted of other exuberances and ambitions decomposing and causing them to fall into error."[13]

Moreover, the Morisco was aware of other shortcomings, among them the erosion in his beliefs and customs, lack of education, neglect of the Arabic language, and diminution of his social, economic, and political power. The exodus of many intellectuals during the Reconquest had left the Mudejar community without leadership. Arabic culture had been declining in al-Andalus at the time of the Reconquest, and intellectual leaders found new horizons in the Muslim countries of North Africa and the East, leaving their fellow Andalusians intellectually impoverished. Muḥammad al-Rāqilī, who lived in Aragón at the turn of the fourteenth century, lamented that he had to live among polytheists and coreligionists who were ignorant and ill equipped to defend their religion against vilification.[14] Another complained that al-Andalus "had become a dark Island because of the loss of scholars to maintain the Islamic religion . . . Those who continue residing there by the grace of the Almighty God have lost the light, schools, and the Arabic language."[15] Another Morisco scholar complained that not even one of his co-religionists knew Arabic, in which the Qur'ān was revealed, or understood the verities of the Islamic religion, which are not explained in the language of the Christian tyrants. He felt it demeaning to write in Aljamía (Romance), apologizing for expressing what is in the heart in such a vile language.[16] Morisco scholars (*'ālimes*), rare and with limited education, had to function in secrecy under the constant surveillance of secular and ecclesiastical authorities who regarded them as troublemakers deserving no mercy.[17]

In spite of Christian strictures, the Mudejars continued to practice their religion, to use the Arabic language, and to practice their customs.[18] Visiting Spain in 1494-1495 shortly after the fall of Granada, the traveler Munzer gives glimpses of the Muslim presence in the call of the muezzin at the time of prayer.[19] In 1499, things changed swiftly, particularly when forced conversion was put into practice, silencing once and for all time the voice of the muezzin. The Islamic community in Granada and elsewhere in the Peninsula went underground. Moriscos' protests that such action violated the terms of capitulation were ignored, and the Moriscos had to accept a religion considered inferior to their own, for which they had neither inclination nor conviction. On this account alone, the new imposed religion was doomed to failure. Yet the choice was this or exile. As a result, the Morisco began to lead a dual life, one appearing to be what he was not and the other, in secrecy, conforming to his inner feeling and real being.

Imposed Christianization did not stop at adopting external religious observances and rituals, but aimed at eradicating all visible differences in the Morisco, which required changes in his customs, language, vestments, food, and entertainment. Decree after decree called for these radical changes, and met with passive resistance and, occasionally, open revolt. Appeals were often made to repeal the decrees, resulting in some success until 1567, when both the monarchy and the church had apparently decided to implement them. The last plea to rescind the edict of 1567 was made by Francisco Núñez Muley, a Morisco of great sensitivity and insight, who appeared to inspire respect as a loyal Christian. Núñez, who had deep knowledge of Islamic customs and religious observances of the Moriscos, questioned the wisdom of the ordinance of 1567, which called for the summary abolition of Morisco customs and Arabic.[20] Núñez systematically reviewed and refuted the terms of the edict, arguing that the measures affected only customary and regional practices and, thus, placed a great burden on unhappy people. He implored the governor to rescind them, reminding him of precedents of tolerance. He also pointed out that the measures of the ordinance not only violated the terms of capitulation of 1492, but also the edicts of conversion, which did not obligate the Moriscos to abandon their language, customs, feasts, dancing, singing, and the like. He claimed such measures were the doing of clerics, who advocated them since 1501. He then takes up the measures of prohibition one by one:

> 1. Our women's clothes follow local traditions (*traje de provincia*), as Castilians and other provincials wear their own traditional clothing. Our women keep their dresses from year to year, and cannot afford to buy new ones. On the other hand, men dress modestly á la Castilian, yet they are set apart as well and abused to the point that if a Morisco were caught with a knife, he would be sent to the dungeon. Moreover, not all

Muslims dress alike; the Turks dress in one way, and other Muslims in another. This is true of Christians, who dress according to their nationality and speak local languages without knowing any Latin or Romance—yet are Christians, nevertheless. Such measures are simply persecution of people who have been loyal vassals and obedient servants of His Majesty, always ready to serve him, and therefore deserving of his consideration and esteem.

2. Wedding ceremonies, singing, dancing, and other entertainments are not obstacles to being good Christians, nor do they constitute Moorish ceremonies. In fact, pious Muslims and learned men (*alfaquies*) frown upon them. The zambras (dancing) are provincial customs, not found in Turkey or North Africa. Thus, it follows that they cannot be considered the peculiarity of any particular denomination.

3. Requiring the doors of homes to remain open is unfair since that invites thieves and molesters. If the purpose is to prevent performing Moorish ceremonies, it will not work because people could perform them at night.

4. The allegation that public baths are used for Islamic rituals is without foundation since public baths are full of Christians. Moreover, they are filthy and not suitable for Moorish rituals that require cleanliness and privacy. More important, they are places for washing—and if they are closed, where do people wash?

5. The veil is not required by religious law, but has customarily been used to prevent moral laxity and inequity in marriage. Without the veil, men would only choose the beautiful women, leaving the ugly ones unwed.

6. Prohibition of the use of old Arabic names is unreasonable, since names are used for ascertaining the genealogy of people. Thus, what good does it do to forget them?

7. Exiling *gacis* (unbaptized Moors) presents a great problem, since the majority of them are natives and married. Thus, it is a matter of conscience. The same can be said of the prohibition of having black slaves, whose number has been exaggerated beyond recognition.

8. On the Arabic language, he inquires, "How is it possible to take away from people their native tongue with which they were born and brought up? Egyptians, Syrians, Maltese, and others speak, read and write Arabic, and are as Christian as we. Moreover, no writing, contracts, or wills have been executed in Arabic from the time of conversion. There are many people in towns and places from within and outside the city who cannot use the Arabic language correctly and speak in so many dialects that one can identify a person from the Alpujarras by his accent. Many were born and reared in small places where Aljamía (Romance) was never spoken or understood, except by priests or sacristans, who also speak Arabic. All Moriscos wish to learn Castilian, but it is difficult, if not impossible, to learn Castilian in their remaining years even if they

were to spend all their time going to and from school. In any case, there is no one available to teach Aljamía. In sum, the ordinance was contrived to ruin us. Imposing it by force causes pain to those natives who cannot meet such a burden: they flee the land as self-exiles (*monfies*) in fear of penalty.[21]

Núñez's analytical and reasonable approach to the Morisco problem went unheeded, and the edict of 1567 was implemented. Vociferous protests followed, and old and new grievances were aired. Leaders incited people to revolt, and one of them, Muḥammad Ibn Muḥammad Ibn Dāwūd, composed a provocative ballad not only expressing the injustices to which the Moriscos had been subjected but ridiculing Christian beliefs and practices. After praising God and exalting his attributes, Ibn Dāwūd tells his audience about the once peerless Andalusia now dominated by heretics, who sent Jews to force Moriscos to practice the unclean rites:

To adore their painted idols,

mockery of the Great Unseen

When the bell tolls, we must
gather to adore the image foul;
In the church the preacher rises,
harsh voiced as a screaming owl.
He the wine and the pork
invoketh, and the Mass is wrought
with wine;
Falsely humble, he proclaimeth
that this is the Law divine.

Yet the holiest of their shavelings
nothing knows of right or wrong,
And they bow before their idols,
shameless in the shameless throng,
Then the priest ascends the altar,
holding up a cake of bread,
And the people strike their bosom
as the worthless Mass is said.

All our names are set in writing,
young and old are summoned all;
Every four months the official
makes on all suspect his call.
Each one of us must show his
permit, or must pay his silver over,
As with inkhorn, pen, and paper,
on he goes from door to door.
Dead or living, each must pay it;

young or old, or rich or poor;
God help him who cannot do it,
pains untold he must endure.[22]

The authorities' refusal to rescind the edict heightened tension among the Moriscos. Hitherto leaderless, disorganized, and without military training and ammunitions, they opted for revolt, expecting to receive the general support of the populace and support from North Africa and Turkey. Ibn Dāwūd wrote to North Africa for help but his letter in Arabic was intercepted.[23] The Moriscos amassed an army of fifteen to twenty-five thousand, among them were included Berbers and Turks,[24] but the army was ill equipped and beset by divisions. At a meeting in Granada, contention for leadership arose between Hernando de Valor and Faraj Ibn Faraj. Hernando was elected and assumed the genealogical name of Ibn Umayyah.[25] The rebels did not receive the expected help from the urban dwellers and had to gather around them villagers, self-exiles (*monfies*),[26] corsairs,[27] brigands,[28] and vagrants (*gandules*). The undisciplined army burned churches, forced people to secede from Christianity, and killed clerics and innocent people.[29] The great damage alarmed Philip II, who entrusted the campaign to his brother, Juan of Austria. The royal army quelled the revolt after enormous loss in life and property, unleashing fury as intense as that of the Moriscos, manifested in pillage, rape, killing innocent people, and enslaving many others indiscriminately.[30]

The Moriscos lost the Revolt of the Alpujarras through internal conflicts, and lack of genuine popular support, not to mention the indifference of fellow Muslims in North Africa and Turkey.[31] The aftermath was disastrous not only for the Granadans but for Moriscos throughout the Peninsula. The savagery of the war rekindled old suspicions and led to an impasse between Old Christians and Moriscos with attendant hatred and unwillingness to compromise. The repatriation of some fifty thousand Granadans in the northern provinces merely acted as a reminder of how distant and separate the two communities were. The Moriscos, who had hoped to regain their lost position through the help of North Africans and Turks, continued to entertain such expectations—becoming more vulnerable to attacks from Old Christians, who clamored for the elimination of the Moriscos by any means available, including mass expulsion.[32] Christian mistrust of the Moriscos was so deep and generalized that it did not spare even those who had accepted Christianity in good faith. The term *Morisco* evoked perfidy in the mind of Christians, and similarly, the Moriscos equated *Christianity* with calamity, widening the polarization between the two communities. Each group was convinced that God was on its side.

The Morisco was in a predicament. Were he to say that he was truly a devout Christian, no credence would be given to him; were he to say that he was a staunch Muslim, he would be put to the stake. Thus, he had scarcely any choice except resignation and passive resistance, adhering covertly to old religious beliefs and customs that were under constant attack. Adhering to them at least gave him a sense of belonging. In an uncertain environment, he shared his hopes and beliefs with his family and was instructed in the true faith by romanized scholars (*alfaquies*), who kept the Islamic traditions alive through an extensive literature, the Aljamiado literature. Through this literature the Morisco found solace and hope for the future, and discreetly but defiantly, he continued to observe fasting, prayer, ablution, and other religious obligations. As a convert, however, he felt obliged to attend church, to have his children baptized, and to participate in Christian feasts. This dual behavior only accentuated the difference between him and Old Christians. He perceived Christianity as the religion of his oppressors, and Islam as that of hope and salvation. He mistrusted priests as his persecutors and avoided confession, believing that God alone is the Confessor.

The Morisco found ingenious ways of annulling or washing away Christian rituals. After the child was baptized, he could be taken home, washed with hot water to remove the oil and annul the sacrament of baptism.[33] Similarly, a Church wedding was nullified by having the bride undressed at home, and given a Moorish dress and Moorish nuptials.[34] Nevertheless, this dual life presented a problem of conscience for the Morisco. He felt in limbo, neither genuinely a Muslim nor a confirmed Christian. As a result, appeals were made to Islamic authorities requesting a legal decision on the validity of such conflicting religious practices. They ruled that a double religious life was condoned by religious law under the umbrella of *taqīyah* (disguise or simulation), permitting a Muslim to dissimulate his religion under duress or threat to life.[35] This dispensation is attributed to the Prophet Muḥammad, allowing a Muslim to forego religious obligations under compulsion as long as the faithful continues to entertain true belief in the heart and to make up his religious obligations at a more appropriate time or in secrecy.[36] Such dispensation was contained in a legal decision (*fatwā*) by the Mufti of Oran in reply to an inquiry of 1563 made by concerned Moriscos.[37] The Mufti's response, originally in Arabic, was soon translated into Aljamiado.[38] The good Mufti suggested ways of altering the manner of religious performances but nevertheless upholding them, recommending the maintenance of prayer even if made by signs; almsgiving; performance of the required ablution; glorification of the name of God in the heart when compelled to pray in churches and face idols; imbibing wine if compelled but with the intention of not committing a vice; this also applies when eating pork or being forced to do other forbidden things. Most significantly, if the faithful is forced to believe in something other than Islam, it could be said with the tongue but denied by the heart, and the same when asked to denigrate the Prophet Muḥammad. However, this facile way of avoiding reality was denounced by another North African jurist, al-Wansharīshī (d. 1508), who charged those who remained in Spain as infidels for living under Christian rule instead of returning to the land of Islam.[39]

The ambivalent posture under the *taqīyah* was difficult both for the Morisco's peace of mind and for his relationship with Christians within the Peninsula and with fellow Muslims overseas. His Christian neighbors were aware of his religious dualism[40] through espionage and frequent accusations among quarreling neighbors, including the Moriscos themselves, as attested by reports to the authorities and numerous trials before the Inquisition. As for Muslims overseas, al-Wansharīshī wrote that North Africans considered the Moriscos "Spanish Christians" rather than bonafide co-religionists. In response, the Morisco developed his own attitude amid lawlessness, defeat, and rejection. Jose Venegas, a farmer in Andalusia, lamented to the Mancebo of Arevalo: "In my view, no one bewailed such calamity as the sons of Granada. Don't doubt my saying, for I am one of them, and an eyewitness. I saw with my own eyes noble ladies, and married women naked, and three hundred girls sold at auction. I do not cry for what had happened, for nothing can be brought back, but I cry for sensible men . . . And if the conquering king does not observe an oath, what do we expect of his successors?"[41] This state of despondency is reflected also in a poem by the exiled Morisco Juan Alfonso, who resided in Tetuan:

Cuerbo maldito español	Accursed Spanish raven
pestifero cancerbero	Pestiferous Cerberus
q'estas con tus tres cabezas	With your three heads
a la puerta del infierno[42]	Stands at the gate of Hell.

In the Morisco's world view, not only were kings and people in general cruel and evil, but the chief prelates of Spain had violated an oath, as had the pharaoh of Egypt.[43] Spanish priests were wolves, merciless thieves, characterized by haughtiness, vanity, sodomy, laxity, blasphemy, apostasy, pomp, vainglory, tyranny, brigandry, and injustice.[44] Christians were mere infidels, "worshippers of the Cross and eaters of pork."[45] The Inquisition inspired fear and was considered the tribunal of the devil, "where the demon presides having deceit and blindness for council."[46] The inquisitors were infidels, who, "in their diabolical way and prompted by the demon, wanted to be judges of souls, forcing people to follow their accursed, bedeviled, and unfounded sect."[47] A Morisco refugee in Tunis recalled that the Christians brought prison, torment, and death to al-Andalus, making us firmly sustain the true faith (Islam) by beholding it in the heart while making display of Christianity and laughing at their lies and weak sect.[48] Spurious prophetic traditions were invented regarding the consequences of being associated with Christians. It was said on the authority of Muḥammad that if a Muslim associates himself with a Christian for forty days by virtue of friendship, and dies during that period, he will die an unbeliever and will go to Hell.[49] Finally, Muḥammad Alguazir, a refugee in North Africa, stated confidently that the Christians had failed during more than one hundred years to make the Muslims abandon their religion in spite of the threat of being burned at the stake by the Inquisition.[50]

In spite of despondency and despair, the Morisco had the conviction that his trials and tribulations were part of a divine plan beyond human power to alter or control. Thus, he placed his fate in the hands of God and the stars, developing certain messianic ideas about the future and attributing his desperate plight to divine punishment for past sins. He was comforted in the belief that the day of redemption would come when God will inflict retribution on misguided and cruel Christians. Even the forced exile was part of the divine plan by means of which God delivered them from pharaohs, accursed heretics, and inquisitors.[51] In addition to reliance on God and the stars, the Morisco made profuse use of amulets and figurines for chasing away bad spirits and attracting good ones. These expectations were expressed in writing in the form of anecdotes, legends, divination, and prophecies.

The expectation of the Morisco's ultimate deliverance and triumph was inspired by his unshakable belief in Islam as the only true religion. One polemic treatise[52] refers to a secret letter kept by a pope which reaffirms Islam as the true faith. Upon the pope's death, the letter was discovered by the king of France, who became concerned and summoned the clergy to give them the ominous news that the Muslims would conquer the land unless Christians threw them out along with the Jews. The anonymous author of the treatise concludes triumphantly that though the Christians succeeded in expelling the Jews, they have not been able to do the same with the Muslims, who one day will be victorious.

Furthermore, the Moriscos were reassured by a number of traditions going back to Muḥammad which extol the merit of remaining in al-Andalus and the reward accruing therefrom.[53] Examples of such traditions are: Blessed is the one who maintains Islam (*el-dīn del alisallām*) in al-Andalus, for he will always have an angel beside him. He who maintains a frontier in Tortosa for one hour will receive pleas for his forgiveness from all creatures, dead and alive. He who stays in Saragossa for one day is better than the one who seeks penance for his sins in Mecca or Jerusalem. He who does two prostrations of prayer in Tortosa is more meritorious than the one who does them in Mecca or Jerusalem. God will forgive all those in Tortosa and al-Andalus for just knowing and confessing that there is no God but God and Muḥammad is His messenger. Finally, God will protect all Muslims from any evil, and those living in al-Andalus are better than those living in Mecca.[54] However spurious, these traditions had the dual purpose of legitimizing Moriscos' stay in Spain even under Christian rule and of answering the criticism of Muslims overseas, who maintained that it was demeaning, if not heretical, to live under such conditions.

The planets were also thought to be on the Morisco's side. In *The Book of Omens*,[55] which deals with physical phenomena—rain, thunder, eclipses, motion of the stars, the zodiac, dreams, and so on—there are some interesting predictions that favor the Moriscos. It is maintained that if an eclipse of the sun takes place in June, there will be many wars among the unbelievers and God will facilitate the victory of Muslims over Christians.[56] The same will happen if an eclipse of the moon falls in July.[57] If the New Year falls on a Tuesday, many Christians will die.[58]

The strength of Moriscos' belief in a future deliverance is based on a number of prophecies that foretell not only their desperate plight, but the ultimate triumph of Islam over Christianity.[59] Some of those prophecies became known to the Inquisition, giving an added pretext for harsher measures against the Moriscos.[60] It is of great significance that two prophecies are attributed to San Isidoro, which give added strength to Morisco expectation. One prophecy[61] says that one cannot change what Allah has ordained: In the year 1501[62] Spain will be so chaotic that no one will know whether he is coming or going; there will be great evil and corruption. In that year the Muslim faith will decline and will be followed by conversion of Muslims into Christianity. However, Christianity will soon be overtaken by evil and will be finished at the hands of Moors, who will conquer all of Spain. A destructive war will continue until the will of God is fulfilled. The second prophecy[63] of Isidoro is filled with admonition and lament: Spain is depicted as boiling in the passion of its evil deeds, beyond salvation because of the enormity of its sins. It will become like a herd without a shepherd, a corpse without a head, and widows and people without a leader.[64] Its governors will be thieves; famine, war, and death will overwhelm it; knights will be hypocrites, and the clergy vainglorious, sinful, and lecherous. Religious men will lack conviction, truth, and charity; and the anger of God will fall upon them. All this will come about after the fall of Constantinople, when the Moors will give the final blow.

A third prophecy[65] is attributed to Muḥammad himself, and may have formed the basis for other prophecies. It is related that Muḥammad was asked about the end of the world and what would happen thereafter to his community. Muḥammad replied that the world will come to an end when the most perverse and worst people appear at a time when a part of his community will still be in an island situated in the extreme west which is called Andalusía. The people of his community will be the last of its inhabitants. All calamities will befall them because of their neglect of the religious law and their worldliness, neglecting prayers and indulging in luxury. The minors among them do not respect the elderly, nor do the elderly have compassion for the minors; injustices and false oaths abound among them; merchants purchase and sell with usury and deceit and covet properties. These and other evil things will become manifest, and God will subject them to people worse than they. They will be tormented; cruel governors will rule over them; their property will be confiscated for no reason; they will be captive and subject to killing and conversion and will worship images and idols; they will be obligated to eat bacon, and will endure other oppressions to the point of hopelessness and despair. God will punish their sins, but He will also have pity on them and will forgive them when those evils are eradicated and when they return to the practice of the religious law. The cruelty imposed will be so intense that the angels will become vexed and will appear before Almighty calling His attention to their plight. It is then that God, the Avenger, will send someone to rescue them from their miserable condition. This will take place when the New Year falls on a Saturday. God will then send a sign consisting of a cloud of birds, two of which will represent the angels Gabriel and Michael. The first cloud of birds will be followed by other birds of the earth to announce the coming of the king of East and West, who will take Andalusía. The conflict between Islam and Christianity will end with a return to the law of the Moors. There will be much cloud in that year, scarcity of water, trees bearing extra fruits, and other signs.

There is a fourth prophecy[66] which reiterates the same points but is more specific with respect to names and dates when the calamities befalling the Moriscos will begin and end. The prophecy bears the title "Scandals" (*los escandalos*) and consists of a dialogue between two men in Damascus. The scandals or calamities will take place when people abandon prayer, fail in almsgiving, neglect fasting, and lose faith. The result will be that "people will sow much, but harvest little, and will work hard but with little benefit."[67] Elsewhere in the world "there will be little shame, much adultery, and brothers will not know brothers."[68] Nor do sons recognize parents, nor minors respect elders. Great animosity will prevail among people in cities and towns; and God will send them rain when it is not needed. In 902 A.H. (1514) there will be discord between two Christian kings, "worshippers of the cross and eaters of pork."[69] They will fight each other, and they will fall under the Muslims when God will send a king named Aḥmad, who will become the lord of land and sea.[70] The sign of his coming will be a star, when the Turks will rise against Christians and overtake them. This will coincide with the suffering and tribulations of Spanish Muslims at the hands of Christians. Men, women, and children will be homeless; their mosques will be burned or converted into churches; and they will be forced to become Christians. Then God will move the hearts of Muslim kings, who will engage in battle under the leadership of the Turk and will defeat the Christian enemy at sea, recouping Sicily, the Balearic Islands, Valencia, and other towns. It will be a sweeping victory over the worshipers of idols, who, great and small, will become Muslims.[71] The Qur'ān will then be read in public, and peace will prevail. The anonymous author concludes: "Have good hope, for the time is near."[72]

For their part, Christians had parallel prophecies which foretold the fall of the Ottomans and the ultimate expulsion of the Moriscos from Spanish soil.[73] Such attitudes in the two communities contributed to continued strife. The Morisco prophecies did not materialize. Instead, mass expulsion was carried out in 1609-1614, forcing the Moriscos to leave their homeland and settle wherever they could. To their former suffering was added exile in inhospitable lands. They could see the folly of events, but not without bitterness and a sense of betrayal:

Razon duerme	Reason sleeps
Trayzion bela	Treason Vigilant
Justicia falta	Justice falters
Malicia reina[74]	Malice reigns

In fact, there were common factors that could have facilitated the peaceful coexistence of two communities bound by blood relationship, intermarriage, common interest, and similar outlooks on life—notwithstanding their differences. Little was heard about the possible fusion of the Moriscos into the mainstream of Spanish life, except scattered calls for moderation, understanding, and tolerance. It is futile to point to mistakes or suggest how things should have been. On the other hand, one may be justified in bringing out some of the historical processes if only to illuminate the actual course of events. The vanquished Muslims, though not fully resigned to their defeat in the course of the Reconquest, were practical about having to live in a Latin Christian environment that was not wholly alien to them. Many of them actually did make the transition from an Arabo-Islamic to a Latin-Christian base, and in time probably more would have done so had it not been for the undue harshness of forced conversion and the obstacles to acculturation and assimilation. This process of cultural change, of acculturation and assimilation, was not unknown in the Peninsula, having occurred under the Romans and subsquently under the Arabs. Perhaps, the difference after the Reconquest lay in emphasis on a religious ideology, to which the factors of language, culture, politics, and economics were subordinated. The Moriscos were singled out as needing an instant, radical transformation. In this, church and state policies were doomed to failure; they were demanding a historical process and ignoring the sensitivity of a proud people steeped in a deeply ingrained tradition. The Mudejars or Moriscos, who had been reassured by solemn treaties preserving their legacy and traditions, could hardly conceive giving up everything—property, institutions, langauge, beliefs, customs—for nothing. Theirs was a bitter experience of broken promises and betrayal. Even when they were willing to make the necessary accomodation of becoming Christians, they were looked upon with suspicion and were exploited by clerics who appeared to be more concerned about acquiring the possessions of the Moriscos through levies and confiscation than about the purity of their souls. This raises the question whether church and state were genuinely desirous of facilitating the process of acculturation and assimilation which would bring about the eventual unity of the state. The authorities' policies of forced conversion and numerous prohibitions led to the Moriscos' open revolt and passive opposition. Passive resistance acquired a significance that can be gauged from the literature discussed in the following chapters.

Again, Morisco resistance was a reaction not only to the negative attitude of the Old Christians toward the Moriscos but also to the oppressive methods employed. Christianity was not an alien religion for the Morisco; it shares many common elements with Islam and could have been espoused in time under the proper incentives and circumstances. In this lies, perhaps, the great past success of Islam in attracting many Jews and Christians to its ranks. The reverse could have happened under proper conditions, and in fact, many conversions of Moriscos to Christianity were quite successful. Many examples of zeal in the adopted religion are known, and many others have escaped notice. Juan Andrés[75] was a neophyte who defended Christianity with zeal. Núñez Muley was another Morisco whose Christian beliefs were accepted and respected to the point that he took issue with the authorities on the injustices to other Moriscos.[76] Núñez shared this quality of courage with two other Moriscos, Alonso del Castillo and Miguel de Luna. Both were cultured men and knew Arabic and Romance well. They served at the court as interpreters and translators. Miguel de Luna, who appears to have led a good Catholic life, was appointed by Philip II as servant and interpreter at court, attaining the coveted rank of hidalgo, which conferred the privileges of nobility.[77] In such a sensitive position, he could not voice his concern about the Moriscos openly. However, he used the legendary, novelistic approach in his *History of the Conquest of Spain by the Moors*,[78] contrasting the conduct of Christians and Muslims toward the subject people and arriving at the implicit suggestion that Muslims were far more benevolent. It appears that Luna was not so much interested in writing a reliable history as in offering a lesson in tolerance and virtue: "Luna's book is something more than just a blatant attempt to foist a falsified Arab history on the public; it is a defense of *tolerance*, and as such, it belongs in the class of novels of the sort of the Abencerraje which also attempts to show how on the level of *virtue* and *tolerance*, both Muslims and Christians could coexist in perfect harmony."[79]

His contemporary and friend Alonso del Castillo (ca. 1520-1607)[80] was the son of a converted Morisco. He studied medicine at the University of Granada and knew Arabic well, becoming an interpreter and translator for the monarch and the Inquisition. He appears to have been a loyal Catholic with a sensitivity for the underdog. His writings include translation of some inscriptions of the Alhambra, documents, official correspondence, and a catalogue of the Arabic manuscripts in the Escorial Library. But his most interesting task was deciphering the *Libros Plumbeos* (*Leaden Books*) of the Sacro Monte discovered in 1588-1607.[81] These books written in Arabic comprise aprocryphal gospels and religious texts showing the great affinity between Islam and Christianity, supposedly genuine gospels allowing for a harmonious coexistence of Muslims and Christians. The question of their authorship and authenticity has engendered heated controversy, but it is generally admitted that they were the works of Moriscos, possibly of Luna and Castillo as Canabelas suggests.[82] This suggestion is quite plausible considering the situation, the role of the two men as a bridge between two cultures, and their familiarity with the two religions whose differences rather than common bonds had been accentuated hitherto. Their attempts came, perhaps, too late. The passion of reactionaries prevailed in causing the expulsion of a substantial part of Spanish society.

3

Morisco Education and Literature

After the Reconquest, the Christian community was able to express itself openly with the encouragement of the secular and ecclesiastical authorities, whereas the Morisco community was impelled to develop its education and literature clandestinely. Thus, there are no data about educational institutions, curriculum, educational goals, literary expression and its impact, and the professions in general. Only scattered statements remain from which the researcher may attempt to reconstruct a possible system of education. However, owing to the survival of manuscripts, he is on more solid ground in assessing Morisco literature and, through it, education and intellectual perspective.

Although education and literature are interrelated, and, in the case of the Moriscos, sufficiently intertwined to suggest the extent of their dissemination, it must be emphasized that Morisco education and literary expression were subjected to the harshest strictures and prohibitions. Thus, the Morisco's artistic and intellectual development was limited from the outset by the same historical circumstances that brought about a gradual dislocation of his total society, the loss of his traditional institutions of learning, and the loss of the intelligentsia. The intelligentsia, which had given shape and direction to Islamic society in the past, dwindled as the Reconquest progressed, moving at first to Granada and, after its fall in 1492, to north Africa and the East. This exodus of Andalusian talent—educators, poets, historians, religious scholars, grammarians, and scientists—is amply documented by Arab writers, who left an impressive list of talented people who sought new horizons elsewhere.[1] With their departure, educational institutions such as the mosque, private instruction, libraries, publications, and book-making came to a standstill and eventually stopped altogether through neglect or official measures. The major Islamic educational institution, the mosques, reduced in number by destruction or conversion to churches, were never replaced by educational centers.

Long before the prohibitions imposed on them by Christian rulers, the Mudejars, and later the Moriscos, were robbed of intellectual leadership, remaining basically untutored and struggling for subsistence as farmers, vassals, craftsmen, and workers in other occupations that left no leisure for study and literary pursuits. However, before the fall of Granada limited liberties allowed them to pursue a rudimentary education and to preserve some of their institutions, including the mosque. Furthermore, they were able to have some contact with Granadan and North African scholars who assisted them in preserving some of their cultural heritage. Men such as al-Rāqilī,[2] al-Qaysī,[3] and Turmeda[4] contributed their writings and even undertook to preserve the Mudejars' religious fervor through showing the superiority of Islam over both Christianity and Judaism. Their treatises written in Arabic had enormous impact on the Moriscos, who appear to have translated them into Romance.[5] The fall of Granada and the subsequent policy of forced conversion gave Morisco education and intellectual life a blow from which it never recuperated. Arabic education, rudimentary as it was, soon disappeared and was replaced by Romance education of a quality below that offered to Christians at established educational institutions. In sum, the exit of talent, lack of contact with the outside world, the limitations of the Moriscos themselves, and Christians' persistent attempts to eliminate cultural, linguistic, and religious traditions were all devastating factors against preserving the essentials of Morisco culture, let alone encouraging its resurgence. Further, the absence of an atmosphere conducive to the pursuit of learning and the concomitant decline of Arabic culture in general militated against the traditional quest of knowledge that was almost taken for granted in the great periods of Islamic culture.

One can scarcely name a Mudejar or Morisco who possessed the traditional encyclopedic education expected of an *adīb* (a cultured man), who would have studied lexicography, poetry, religious sciences, and the secular sciences and who would have written on them. Prolific Andalusian men of letters of the stature of the theologian Ibn Ḥazm of Cordova (1064), the philosopher Ibn Rushd (1198), or the historian Ibn Ḥayyān (d. 1075) could not be found among the Mudejars/Moriscos, indicating that Arabic culture was giving way to the process of latinization. Although the Mudejars/Moriscos appear to have followed Arabo-Islamic cultural traditions, they lacked literary productivity, even in writing regional histories, biographical dictionaries, and chronicles, all of which had been basic to Arabic literary production. Literary developments among the Moriscos in the fifteenth and sixteenth centuries were highly selective and slavishy dependent on Arabic materials, expressed in Romance dialect. In place of the totality of the traditional Arabic disciplines—Arabic grammar, lexicography, Arabic versification, Arabic poetry, Qur'ānic studies, prophetic traditions, jurisprudence, theology, the natural and speculative sciences, the ideal liberal arts curriculum expected of the *adīb*—came the study or memorization of selections of a discipline. This tendency toward selectivity rather than systematic study of a total discipline is quite apparent in Morisco literature, the Aljamiado literature.

The limitations in Morisco education must be viewed not only within the context of historical change, but within the immediate environment. Although Spanish literature was gaining a wider dimension, it was socially oriented and theocentric. Medicine was regarded as magic and left largely to Jewish *conversos* and Moriscos.[6] Education was limited mostly to clerics and the nobility, who were responsible for literary standards and intellectual perspectives. The establishment of universities such as those of Salamanca and Valencia did little to improve the education of the average Christian, and still less that of the alien Morisco.

The cultural traditions of the Morisco were inspired by and rested on Islam—a religion, a culture, and a way of life. Concomitant with Islam was the Arabic language, the instrument of religious expression and of a whole culture. Around these disciplines—religion and Arabic—the Morisco developed a hybrid culture and a peculiar outlook that clashed with that of his Christian neighbors. His education and outlook may perhaps be gauged from the content of a library discovered accidentally in 1884 in Almonacid de la Sierra, west of Saragossa.[7] The library, consisting of some hundred items, may have belonged to a bookseller or to a scholar. At any rate, the collection contains both Arabic and Aljamiado texts, dealing mostly with religious matters and including a bilingual translation of a famous Arabic grammar. The collection is significant in demonstrating that there were still people in Spain who could read Arabic as late as the sixteenth century.

The Morisco's obligatory closed society permitted him in some respects to live in an Islamic environment—using Arabic for daily communication, practicing Islam, and following his customs with respect to food, clothing, entertainment, and the like. Even after forced conversion he continued to learn rudimentary Arabic and the fundamentals of Islam. This haphazard education was received mostly at home or in a small group instructed by a religious scholar, commonly known as *alfaqui* or *'ālime*.

The significance of Arabic in education rested on its association with the divinely revealed Qur'ān, believed to have been written in a "clear Arabic" and preserved on tablets in Heaven.[8] Arabic has no substitute; it is unique and must be learned in order to understand the meaning of divine revelation. This conception was current among Muslims, including Mudejars and Moriscos. A sixteenth-century Morisco of Cuenca is reported to have said that not only is God a Moor and with the Moors, but He speaks Arabic, which is the language of salvation.[9] Another Morisco of the same region would admonish his wife, saying: "Stupid, learn Arabic (*algaravia*), for God will cause salvation in Arabic in the Day of Judgment, with Muḥammad close by saying: 'Lord, save these, because they have preserved our law, and send Christians to Hell.' "[10] Similar conceptions were echoed by exiled Moriscos in North Africa, who maintained that God had chosen the Arabic language as the vehicle of revelation and the instrument of His will and that Arabic was meant to serve as the language in the Day of Judgment since it has the superiority over all other languages that the sun has over the planets.[11] Finally, Adam, the first man, spoke Arabic at first,[12] but God caused him to forget it after his sin and made him learn Syriac instead.[13]

This conception of the Arabic language, however, did not conform to the actual situation of the Morisco, particularly when he was becoming more romanized and de-Arabized. The quasi-divine status of Arabic could not be measured by his competence in the language. Moreover, in Spain, as in the Arabic-speaking countries, classical and colloquial or spoken Arabic existed side by side, with the classical serving as the language of literature and the colloquial as the language of illiterates. The spoken language had numerous regional dialects which could be learned at home or in the street without formal schooling, whereas the classical or written Arabic required prolonged training, including study of Arabic grammar and Arabic lexicography, for its mastery. There is no evidence that such study was ever pursued on a large scale among the Moriscos. The fact that the Moriscos were forced by circumstances to use a "foreign language" (*'ajamiyyah*) may have precluded any deep study of Arabic grammar and Arabic lexicography.

In any case, the study of Arabic did not result in any appreciable publications in that language. Surviving materials classify Arabic letters according to their phonetic value or describe their points of articulation and pronunciation.[14] Other fragments consist of practice exercises for mastering the Arabic script,[15] spelling, and calligraphy.[16] Another set of documents contains exercises in Arabic script and some grammatical questions.[17] There are other fragments on Arabic grammar.[18] The most significant grammatical works among the Moriscos were al-Zajjāj's *Taqrīb*[19] and Sanhāji's *'Ajurrumiyyah,*[20] both available in Arabic and in Aljamiado translation.[21] Although al-Zajjāj's *Taqrīb* was not very popular, Sanhāji's *'Ajurrumiyyah* had enormous popularity in the East and was the object of commentaries. Both the grammar and the commentary were available to the Moriscos, who made interlineal Aljamiado translations of them.

Related to the study of Arabic grammar is the study of Arabic lexicography. The Moriscos appear to have composed no works, depending almost wholly on Arabic material. Inasmuch as the Moriscos had to translate a huge body of material from Arabic into Aljamiado, one would expect to find bilingual dictionaries facilitating the task. No comprehensive lexicons are known to exist. However, there are some brief glossaries attached to particular works, listing some Arabic expressions and their Aljamiado equivalents. One such glossary appears at the end of an Aljamiado commentary on some chapters of the Qur'ān.[22] The few expressions are listed at random; the commentator may have listed them to make sure their religious connotation was understood. Here they are in his order:

Arabic	*Romance*	*English*
al-'ālam	el-mundo	the world
bi-asrihi	kon-kuwanto ay	totally
mudabbir	rrigente	manager
al-thanā'	alabansa	praise
dāfi'	defendedor	defender
lā yarjū	no-aghuwarda	does not wait
'adl	justisiya	justice
matā	kuwando	when
kāna	era	was
wa-lā-makān	i-no-teniya lughar	not occupying a place
kawwana al-makān	hizo ser el-lughar	made the place
wa-dabbara	i-arreghlo	managed
lā yataqayadu	no-se jusmetiyo	not bound
wa-lā yatakhaṣamu *[sic]*	ni-se espesiyalo	does not quarrel
lā yalḥiqahu *[sic]*	no-lo-alkansa	does not encompass
wahm	piyenso	imagination
wa-lā tukayyifuhu	ni-lo-puwede edificar	cannot be fashioned
'aql	sentido	intellect
lā yatashakhkhaṣu	ni-se-puwede fighurar	cannot be represented
fī-l-dhihn	en-la-fantasiya	in the mind (fantasy)
al-wahm	memoriya o entendimiyento	memory or understanding
wa-lā yatakayyafu	ni-se-le puwede meter esensiya	cannot be given form
fīl-'aqli	en ninghun sentido ni juisiyo	in no sense
al-awhām	las imaginasiyones	imaginations
wa-l-ifkār *[sic]*	ni-pensamiyentos[23]	without reflections

This far from comprehensive glossary appears to be limited to those expressions which the commentators may have had difficulty rendering into Romance. In some translations Arabic and Aljamiado texts appear side by side, with the Arabic written in bold characters and the Aljamiado appearing interlineally above or under the Arabic version. This method may have been thought adequate, precluding the composition of bilingual lexicons.

It may be surmised that the study of the Arabic language was not pursued so avidly as the quasidivine conception of the language would require. That some study was attempted is corroborated by testimony in places such as Socuellamos in the region of Cuenca by about 1582. A Morisco admonished his wife, reared in a Christian home, for not knowing Arabic and for not being able to invoke God's praise in that language.[24] Another Morisco was brought before the Inquisition charged with teaching his wife Arabic at night against her will. He was declared guilty on her testimony.[25] Finally, edicts forbade the use of Arabic, which was a major deterrent to studying Arabic.

These same unfavorable conditions apply to the study of the religious sciences, including the Qur'ān, prophetic traditions, and law. As in the case of Arabic, these studies were limited to a small minority, who do not appear to have published works of their own. Their goal apparently was to learn the fundamentals of religious beliefs and practices, since fulfillment of the religious obligations was incumbent upon all Muslims in order to attain the goal of salvation. The Qur'ān constituted the basic education of the initiate, who was expected to memorize and recite it in the original Arabic at the age of eight and to refer to it in all matters affecting beliefs and rituals. This insistence on preserving the Arabic character of the Qur'ān is demonstrated by the enormous number of Qur'ānic copies that have come down to us, presumably used by the Moriscos. Even after the Moriscos lost sufficient command of Arabic to require translation of the Qur'ān into Aljamiado, the Arabic text appeared, more often than not, alongside the translation.

Next in importance to the Qur'ān were the prophetic traditions, meant to elucidate and elaborate upon the Qur'ānic verses and to give details on religious observances, legal questions, and all manner of behavior. As such, the traditions were sacrosanct and supposed to be learned in the original Arabic, but they were often translated, indicating a general lack of fluency in Arabic. The extensive literature in translation indicates the degree of de-Arabization and offers great insight into the education of the Morisco. This literature comprises instructions in performing the obligatory ablutions before prayer, prayer, fasting, almsgiving, and all aspects of law governing marriage, divorce, circumcision, sales, and contracts. Such regulations permeate Aljamiado literature, indicating that the education of the Morisco was basically a religious one—more often than not, conducted in Romance.

In the absence of religious and educational institutions, the task of educating fell on individuals who had reasonable familiarity with religious tenets and zeal for preserving and disseminating them first in Arabic and then in Romance when people had lost a working knowledge of Arabic. Such men, known as scholars (*sabiyos, alimes,* Ar. *'ulamā'*) or learned men (*alfaquies,* Ar. *fuqahā'*), were self-appointed, and their devotion to instruction earned them the respect and financial support of their communities. The Christian authorities feared them and considered them troublemakers and corruptors. It was they who perpetuated Islamic traditions through the selective compilation of Arabic texts and translation into Aljamiado. In addition, they preserved and transmitted into Aljamiado some of the Islamic notions about scholars and scholarship: The search for knowledge is incumbent upon every Muslim;

and the scholar who fails to disseminate or denies it to others not only will commit a mortal sin, but will suffer greatly in the Day of Judgment.[26] The true scholar (*sabiyo*) enjoys a preeminent position not only in this world but in the hereafter, as noted in the saying, God will choose for the seeker of knowledge (*sensiya*) and wisdom (*sabiduriya*) the road to Paradise;[27] and the angels will extend their wings for him and will intercede on his behalf seeking forgiveness. The scholar is acknowledged as the 'clarity and splendor'' (*la kalorar i-resplandor*)[28] of the moon by all creatures of heaven and earth. Scholars are heirs of the prophets, not in terms of gold and silver but in knowledge and wisdom. Being in the company of true scholars is aromatic, whereas being in the company of bad ones is like being with a goldsmith, who not only burns your clothes but causes you to smell of bad odors and smoke.[29]

These Aljamiado sayings are direct translations from Arabic, ordinarily found in *adab* works such as the famous *Unique Necklace* of the Andalusian bellelettrist Ibn 'Abd Rabbihi.[30] Such sayings no doubt had a great impact on the Morisco *alfaquies*. Whatever their intellectual limitations, the Morisco scholars were the leaders and teachers of their community, striving to preserve and disseminate Islamic values and mores. Their role was dangerous, closely watched by the Inquisition. Bilingual in Arabic and Romance dialect, they served as intermediaries between Islamic and Christian cultures. Likewise, the Mozarabs continued the use of Arabic long after the Reconquest.[31] In fact, both Mozarabs and Moriscos used Arabic during the fifteenth and sixteenth centuries.[32] This bilingualism became valuable when the Mudejar/Morisco community underwent the process of latinization whereby Arabic was no longer current among the majority of Moriscos. The *alfaquies* undertook the difficult task of paraphrasing and translating Arabic texts into a Romance dialect, making them accessible to a large audience. In so doing, they remained faithful to the substance of the original Arabic texts and preserved the minutiae of religious beliefs and practices in a language they considered foreign (*al-'ajamiyyah*, Sp. *Aljamīa* or Aljamiado).[33] The use of a foreign, vulgar language was regarded as demeaning if not a betrayal of Arabic linguistic tradition, but was justified as a necessary expedient in the face of rampant illiteracy in Arabic. A Morisco laments that none of his co-religionists knew the Arabic language in which the Qur'ān was revealed, nor understood the truth of Islam contained therein except in a foreign language (*'ajamīa*), the language of the Christian dogs, the tyrants and oppressors. He asks forgiveness for communicating by such a vile means, stating that he does so only to open the road of salvation to the faithful Muslim.[34]

The practice of rendering Arabic texts into a Romance dialect became current in the fifteenth and sixteenth centuries, during which the bulk of the Aljamiado literature was written. At first, Arabic and Aljamiado translation appeared side by side, particularly for Qur'ānic texts, Traditions, prayers, and sermons. Later, only Aljamiado translations were given—even for the Qur'ān, which was not supposed to be translated into any foreign language according to the dictum of Muslim theologians. Translation became standardized with respect to transliteration, wording, and preservation of certain Arabic terms that were considered untranslatable by virtue of their religious connotations. Translations were usually literal, accompanied by explanatory notes whenever the text was obscure or involved a religious concept needing elucidation. The names of translators are rarely mentioned, so that most of the authors remain anonymous. Moreover, most of the Arabic works translated are given no title or author, except for a few such as al-Samarqandī's *Ghāfilīn*, Bakrī's *Book of Light,* and Quḍā'ī's *Book of Stars.*[35]

The fact that translating or paraphrasing of Arabic texts into Aljamiado was imperative as Moriscos' knowledge of Arabic decreased is acknowledged by various contemporaries. The author of the *Guidance and Maintainance of the Faith* states: "Many of my friends begged me to put the Qur'ān and legal texts in Aljamiado (*'ajemi*) the best I can so that our holy law and *sunah* can be pursued."[36] In the introduction to his *Brevario Sunni*, the fifteenth-century 'Īsā de Jābir states that he undertook to explain the divine grace of the Qur'ān from Arabic (*gharabiya*) in Aljamiado at the request of some chiefs (*kardenales*) who were concerned that the religious law was hidden from the people and who impressed on him that those who knew it must convey it to others in the language they understood to avoid doubts and difficulty. His explanation of the Qur'ān was written for those who did not know Arabic, particularly for Muslims of Segovia who were overtaxed and overworked and who had lost their wealth and their Arabic schools.[37] Similarly, the Mancebo of Arevalo states in his *Tafsirs* that some scholars in Saragossa lamented the state of Muslims and requested him to write a brief commentary of the Qur'ān to remedy the situation.[38]

'Īsā de Jābir and the Mancebo de Arevalo are important since they are two of the few Moriscos whose works bear their names and about whom there are some clues not only about their persons but about the Morisco perspective in general. The majority of Aljamiado authors, translators, or paraphrasers chose anonymity by design to avoid the wrath of the secular and ecclesiastical authorities. Aware of the important position of the *alfaquies*, the authorities often tried to seek their help in carrying out forced conversion but also mistrusted them as dangerous elements in society and instituted stringent measures to limit their activities. Various documents attest to this concern. A document issued in Monzon in 1564 states, among other things, that some mercy should be accorded to misguided neophytes but not to *alfaquies*, proselytizers (*dogmatizadores*), or midfives.[39] In 1567, a good number of scholars were brought before the Inquisition of Valencia to answer for their disruptive influences.[40]

'Īsā de Jābir appears to be among the first Moriscos to undertake translating or paraphrasing of Arabic materials into Aljamiado. He lived in the fifteenth century at a time when some Islamic practices were still tolerated. In fact, he was the Mufti of Segovia on whom the Mudejars depended for advice and legal decisions. He was bilingual in Arabic and Aragonese. In 1462, he wrote his *Brevario Sunni*,[47] a comprehensive work dealing with the major religious obligations expected of a Muslim. The treatise is significant for its impact on the development of Aljamiado literature, serving as a model for future works. ʿĪsā's scholarship was highly esteemed, and his knowledge of Arabic, Latin, and Aragonese made him an ideal intermediary between Arabic and Latin cultures. Bishop Juan de Segovia (ca. 1400-1458), who desired to reach a practical compromise with Muslims through peace and understanding, commissioned him to translate the Qur'ān into Castilian. ʿĪsā added to the translation a summary of the genealogy and life of Muḥammad.[42] It is of significance to point out that ʿĪsā's *Brevario* bears the name of the author and the date of composition, which is rare in Aljamiado works: "This book, *Brevario Sunni*, was completed in 1462; planned, compiled and collected in the Mosque of Segovia by the honorable and discreet alfaqui Ikshadil,[43] the Great Mufti of the Moors of Castile, and Imām of the community of Moors in Segovia."[44]

While ʿĪsā de Jābir lived in a time and place where the Mudejars were still allowed to practice their religion, the Mancebo of Arevalo[45] (ca. 1510-1550) lived in a period so intolerant that the Moriscos hardly dared to express their religious sentiments openly. He followed in the footsteps of ʿĪsā, but was beset by a life of uncertainty and persecution. This notwithstanding, he acquired a broad education in history, religious studies, Islamic mysticism, philosophy, Arabic, Hebrew, Greek, Latin, and Romance. He traveled widely in Valencia, Saragossa, Granada, Cordova, and other Spanish cities, leaving valuable impressions. On traveling in Andalusia, he remarks nostalgically: "Each step I undertook pained my soul, seeing such a sweet and delicious land, moderate weather throughout the year, fertility, rich towns with bread and oil, many rivers with sweet water and a land with silk and gold—more gold and silver than in all Spain put together."[46] Equally interesting is his reference to the Moorish lady of Ubeda whom he met in Granada. She is described as a ninety-three-year-old woman of great natural gifts who never married and who led an ascetic life in the manner of the great mystic al-Ghazālī (d. 1111). Although she was not literate, she had a wide knowledge of history, the four legal schools, and the major grammarians. She had a sharp mind, and her word was heeded in all Granada, exerting an enormous influence on all things pertaining to the religious law. She wished never to leave her native land, because she felt that it was lofty to remain and fight a holy war *(aljihād)* to disseminate the Islamic religion. Though she spoke a coarse dialict, she made so much sense that her utterances were equal to the language of grammarians. She possessed a substanital collection of Arabic books belonging to former kings of Granada.[47]

But the merit of the Mancebo lies in his literary legacy. He is known to have written three major works dealing with Islamic doctrine and rituals which exerted an enormous influence on his contemporaries and succeeding generations of Moriscos, including Muḥammad Rabadan.[48] His *Tafsira* in some 472 folios contains the fundamentals of religion and an explanation of Islamic rituals. His *Compendium of Relation and Spiritual Exercise*[49] has depth and originality, giving the mystical reflections of the author in addition to profuse instruction in religious matters, including the manner of conduct within the sanctuary of Mecca during the time of pilgrimage.[50]

To the voices of ʿĪsā and the Mancebo may be added that of Juan del Rincon, a Morisco of Huesca in the kingdom of Aragón, who explains his reasons for writing his *Guide to Salvation* for his Muslim brethern. Juan states in a fatalist vein that it is God's will to have the Moors afflicted and suppressed, and to have them neglect their religious duties to an abject extreme:

> All this is owing, first of all, to the circumstances which have placed the Moors for so many years far from any spiritual advice; and secondly, to the tyranny of the Christians, who have caused them to be forcibly baptized through fear and terror. Their books are all lost, and scarcely any remembrance remains of them; the doctors of the law are no more, some are dead, others lie in prison; the Inquisition displays against us its utmost fury and oppression, so that few parts of the kingdom are free from fire and faggot; the newly baptized Moors are everywhere seized and punished with galleys, rack and fire, and other chastisement best known to God, the master of all secrets . . . Some people among us do not know what prayer is, nor by whom it was instituted; if you ask them when our lord and prophet, Muḥammad, was born, they will not answer you; and if you happen to mention in their presence Mecca, that mother of cities and cradle of our religion, they will stare in your face and shrug up their shoulders. Therefore I, who profess to be a good Mussulman, although the number and depth of my sins God only knows, have undertaken the meritorious task of writing this *Guide to Salvation* and have composed it in Spanish: may God forgive me for using any language other than that in which the sublime Koran was revealed.''[51]

ʿĪsā, the Mancebo, and Juan del Rincon represent the body of anonymous Moriscos who under adverse conditions produced a large new literature, a remarkable achievement under highly unfavorable circumstances. Aljamiado literature remained clandestine. Its two principal features—first, Arabic script used for writing a Romance dialect and, second, an Islamic content based on Arabic sources—deserve further consideration.

There is no definitive answer for when Arabic script was first used to write Romance, nor is there a single answer for the motivation of the Moriscos for such a use. One can speculate that the Arabic script, current for centuries in the Peninsula, may have been used by the Mozarabs for writing in Romance at an early date, but no concrete evidence attests to this practice. When Aljamiado literature was discovered in the eighteenth century, scholars were surprised and even baffled that Romance literature in Arabic script could have ever been possible. At first some scholars thought the manuscripts were written in either Persian or Turkish. When they were identified as Romance or Aljamiado, scholars pondered on the reasons behind the use of Arabic script for writing in Romance and speculated that it was used to conceal the content of writings from the watchful eye of their oppressors. In his insightful lecture before the Royal Historical Academy of Madrid, Saavedra proposed some reasons in the form of a question: "Was it due to the strength of a rancid custom, to a superstitious veneration of characters that looked holy by virtue of a divine revelation, or was it due to a clever artifice for concealing the secrets of conscience from a vigilant and powerful enemy?"[52] Saavedra did not elaborate an answer except to suggest it may have been due in part to all three—custom, reverence, and fear—according to different circumstances. More recently, Hegyi examines the motivation behind the Moriscos' use of Arabic script within the general context of its use in various countries having had exposure to Arabic and Islam at different junctures of history, concluding that the Moriscos used it principally because of the sacred character of the script.[53]

However, another explanation follows from the Moriscos' being deprived of a Latin education: they had no choice other than continuing to use Arabic script, acquiring in the process consciousness of its significance as a symbol in their struggle for identity under heavy strictures. This explanation, on the whole, meets Saavedra's unanswered query, except using the Arabic script for "concealing the secrets of conscience." Such concealment does not fit into the historical framework, since the Moriscos were forbidden to use Arabic or any form associated with it under severe penalties. The Moriscos, for whom a Latin education was out of reach, continued an Arabic education based on Islamic content that could hardly be separated from the Arabic language and script, which had acquired a halo of sanctity in Muslim traditions. Also, the necessity of using Arabic script for languages that did not possess a traditional one cannot be discounted altogether. This often occured when historical circumstances revived national languages that came to supersede the predominance of Arabic. Thus, the use of the Arabic script for writing in languages other than Arabic had wide currency in the Middle Ages: Persians, Afghanis, Pakistanis, Indonesians, Somalis, Hausas, and for a time, Turks, Maltese, and others made use of the Arabic script. In these cases, the use of the Arabic script by people who were largely Muslims was motivated in part by pragmatic considerations arising from prolonged cultural intercourse and religiocultural ascendance.

This aspect of cross-fertilization is, perhaps, more pronounced in the Iberian Peninsula than elsewhere owing to the presence of three well-established scripts—Latin, Arabic, and Hebrew—each with a long tradition and a wide currency within the respective religious community. With long-standing interaction at all levels, it was not uncommon to use Arabic script for writing Hebrew and Romance, Hebrew script for writing Arabic and Romance,[54] or Latin script for writing Arabic.[55] This phenomenon can be seen today among Lebanese emigres in Latin America who, for lack of literacy in Spanish, use Arabic script for writing Spanish.[56]

Finally, Arabic script had ideological significance among the Moriscos, who strove to preserve their identity within the framework of Islam long after they had been latinized. To them, Arabic script was important as an integral part of their Arabic education, as a symbol of cultural heritage, and as a means of preserving the association with the revealed Qur'ān and the quasidivine source of the Arabic language. These factors were interwoven and constitute some of the basic elements of the Morisco perspective.

In spite of his limited Arabic education and Arabic language, deteriorating in the process of latinization, the Morisco had deep-rooted attitudes inspired by an equally profound historicoreligious consciousness. His whole literature attests to this posture. Consequently, the motivation for using Arabic script for writing Romance must be sought in the Islamic background of the Morisco and in stubborn resistance in face of constant, often inhumane Christian harassment. The Morisco had always considered himself a member of the Islamic community, with which he identified himself in religion, culture, and language. This attachment is rooted in the history and development of Islamic culture in the Iberian Peninsula, its ascendance and eventual erosion. Arabic script symbolized the earlier cultural change from a Latin to Arabic base, with the attending linguistic and cultural supremacy. During the peak of Spanish Islam from the eighth to the thirteenth centuries, Arabic reigned supreme among Jews and Mozarabs, who used it in areas such as Toledo and Huesca long after the Reconquest, and no doubt the lingering presence of Arabic among non-Muslims contributed to the preservation of Arabic script.

In any case, Arabic script for the Moriscos, as for Muslims in general, possessed a halo of sanctity as a part and an extension of the divinely revealed Qur'ān. The divine conception was not the invention of the common people, but the formulation of grammarians, theologians, and jurists, who placed a high value on Arabic and its script. Arabic script was conceived as possessing symbolic values, each letter having a religious meaning. *Alif*, the first letter of the alphabet, means the name of God; *Bā'* (b) signifies the domain of religion; *jīm* (*j*) God's nobility; *dāl* (*d*) God's law; *hā'* (*h*) repels sins; *ṭā'* (*ṭ*) is a tree in Paradise; *yā'* (*y*) is the hand of God extended to His creatures; *kaf* (*k*) is God's words to Moses; *lām* (*l*) represents evil people who do not believe in eternal suffering; *ṣād* (*ṣ*) signifies the blessed people and invokes the formula "There is no God but God"; *fā'* (*f*) means the Lord is above His People; *ḍad* (*ḍ*) means *lex talionis* (*medida por medida*), that is, he who sows evil will harvest bitterness; and *qāf* (q) represents the sinner during the Day of Judgment.[57] In addition, the Arabic script was used by the Moriscos for divination, amulets, and talismans. These religious and divinational considerations,[58] however subjective, cannot be discounted as important factors in the preservation and dissemination of Arabic script among the Moriscos. They were compelling reasons for an Arabic education, even if it meant learning only the alphabet. The task of using Arabic script for writing Romance presented difficulties, which the Moriscos resolved by devising a system of transliteration conforming to most of the phonetic values of the Latin characters, both consonants and vowels.[59]

However great its religious significance, the use of Arabic script may be viewed as a pragmatic means for the non-Arabic-speaking Morisco to learn the fundamentals of Islam in a "foreign language"—*'Ajamiyyah*, derived from the Arabic *'ajam*. Originially, the term *'ajam* was applied to people of non-Arabic ancestry, mainly Persians. The Moriscos, who considered themselves as belonging to the Arabic linguistic tradition containing Islamic tenets, viewed a Romance language (even though it may have been their own native tongue) as foreign and demeaning to use. The expression Aljamiado was extended to mean the literature written in a Romance—be it Castilian, Aragonese, or others. The development of such a literature is of the utmost significance religiously, culturally, and linguistically. It was written by an oppressed minority during the fifteenth and sixteenth centuries when Arabs in the Peninsula were subjected to great persecution. Nonetheless, Aljamiado literature escaped the vigilance of the authorities and came down to us in a quantity that conveys its nature and scope. All indications are that Aljamiado literature was written by devotees to Islam who wanted to preserve their Islamic heritage and to teach it to those who had forgotten the Arabic language. Further, Aljamiado literature mirrors the Moriscos' innermost thought and feeling and eloquently reaffirms their beliefs and observances—and, at the same time, presents a challenge to the numerous Christian edicts of restriction and persecution. As such, the literature is a valuable document for understanding not only the plight of the Moriscos, but their psyche, indomitable endurance in face of heavy odds, hopes, aspirations, and manner of resolving the conflict between retaining self-identity and escaping persecution.

Although the status of the Morisco in a hostile environment has been the object of numerous studies based on contemporary histories and a wealth of archival documents in Simancas, Toledo, Aragón, Valencia, Gaudix, Cuenca, and other Spanish cities, little attention has been given to the self-expression of the Morisco as found in Aljamiado literature. Being clandestinely written in Arabic script, Aljamiado literature was rarely a source for contemporary historians. Awareness of its existence came only in the eighteenth century, when some scholars still assumed that it was written in an Oriental language, perhaps Turkish, Persian, or Berber.[60] By the end of the century, scholars had determined that it was written in Romance by the oppressed Moriscos. Its discovery aroused the interst of nineteenth-century scholars, who began to call attention to its importance as a source material. Estabañez Calderón referred to it as "a real America needing discovery."[61] But Gayangos, an avid collector of Arabic and Aljamiado manuscripts (now housed in the Royal Academy of History and the National Library of Madrid), was already at work. In 1839, he published an article on the language and literature of the Moriscos, describing the nature and content of Aljamiado literature and explaining for the first time the system of transliteration used for writing in a Romance dialect.[62] Subsequently, he published two Aljamiado treatises dealing with the fundamentals of Islamic religion, one by an anonymous author[63] and the other by 'Īsā de Jābir, the earliest author known.[64] Gayangos also made available to Ticknor some material consisting of a poem in praise of Muḥammad and another about Joseph, which Ticknor included in his history of Spanish literature.[65]

About the same time, Fernández y González referred to it and used some Aljamiado documents in his valuable work, the *Mudejars of Castile.*[66] Aljamiado literature attracted the attention of scholars outside of Spain as well. In Germany in 1860, Müller published three poems based on Escorial manuscript no. 1880 dealing with a praise of Muḥammad, an invocation to God, and a sermon,[67] and Morf made known the *Poem of Joseph.*[68] In England, Stanley delved into the poetry of Muḥammad Rabadan[69] at Gayangos's urging.

But the man of the century most notable for studying the Moriscos through their own literature was Saavedra, an able Arabist and an engineer by profession. A disciple of Gayangos, he pursued Aljamiado literature where his mentor left off. His *Discurso* of 1878 before the Royal Spanish Academy has not been superseded in its account of the form and content of Aljamiado literature. The *Discurso* is further enhanced by an invaluable appendix describing some one hundred thirty-six Aljamiado manuscripts found in private collections, in the National Library of Madrid, the Escorial, the Provincial Library of Toledo, the Library of the Pilar Church in Saragossa, the Bibliothèque Nationale in Paris, the Library of the University of Uppsala, the British Museum, the University of Bologna, and the Royal Academy of History, which houses the collection of Gayangos. Saavedra's *Discurso* was followed by two other studies: *The Narration of the Bath of Zarieb*, a love novel, and the "Story of the City of Alaton," a legend depicting the heroism of 'Alī, a cousin of Muhammad, in a city haunted by strange creatures.

In his *Discurso*, Saavedra sympathetically recognizes the Moriscos' plight and evaluates their intllectual outlook and attitudes through some discerning quotation. He classifies Aljamiado literature as consisting of: (1) religious materials, (2) didactic and entertaining stories, (3) love stories, and (4) poetry of religious character and laments of exile. He characterizes the Aljamiado literature as ordinarily poor, having a common style but acquiring at times delicacy, freedom, and eloquence.[70] Its mostly anonymous authors thought in Arabic; what they wrote in Romance preserves Arabic idioms, technical terms, and Arabic syntax. He concludes that the Moriscos portray themselves through the literature, conveying their customs, beliefs, thought, and suffering; they were good men with lofty understanding who did not indulge in licentiousness. "And if the blind popular passion had not wasted away this important segment of the nation demanding inhuman amputation, the Moriscos, as the old Mudejars, would have been incorporated in every respect with the rest of the Spaniards, thereby contributing with their strength and vitality to the greater glory of the homeland."[71]

Gayangos and Saavedra set the stage for the study of Aljamiado literature. They were followed enthusiastically by Guillén Robles, whose *Leyendas Moriscas* in three volumes was drawn from several manuscripts.[72] Although his system of transliteration is inconsistent, the work is still valuable for the general reader. In the introduction, Robles recognizes the importance of Aljamiado literature: the linguist will find in it part of the foundation of the

Spanish language besides idiomatic expressions, expressive terms, and Arabic expressions used among the Spaniards; the archaeologist will find explanations of symbols and mythology used among the Muslims; the artist will find beautiful, original, and even grand inspirations; and the historian will find documentation of the moral, religious, and intellectual life of thousands of Spaniards over a long period.[73] The *Leyendas* amply reflects the tenor of Aljamiado literature, consisting of legends and stories about religious and epic characters, the prophets of old, Muḥammad and his ascension to the seven heavens (*mi'rāj*), and the heroes of early Islam. The *Leyendas* was followed by the publication of the *Legend of Joseph* and the *Legend of Alexander the Great*.[74] Robles also compiled a catalogue of Arabic manuscripts in the National Library of Madrid, which includes a description of Aljamiado manuscripts in that library.

In 1888, Gil, Ribera, and Sánchez published their anthology of Aljamiado texts on a variety of topics[75]: the reward of the scholar, astrology, the legend of Alexander, sermons, couplets of the Pilgrim Puey de Monçon, the novel of the bath of Zarieb, marvellous sayings, private letters, and three chapters of the Qur'ān in Arabic and Aljamiado translation. By virtue of paleographic variety and content, the anthology constitutes excellent instructional material. Subsequently, Gil published a description of his private collection of Aljamiado manuscripts.[76] Just before the close of the century, Pano y Ruata published the *Coplas* (couplets) of the pilgrimage of Puey de Monçon to Mecca.[77] Finally, Codera gave a brief acount of the discovery of a large collection of Arabic and Aljamiado manuscripts in the Almonacid de la Sierra,[78] later catalogued under the supervision of Ribera and Asín; these manuscripts are now housed in the Institute of Asín Palacios in Madrid.[79]

The pioneering works of Gayangos, Saavedra, Guillén Robles, and others opened new horizons and gave promise of continued interest in Aljamiado literature. However, the initial enthusiasm waned, followed only sporadically by works that added little to the knowledge already available. In the first decade of this century, Menéndez Pidal published his *Joseph Poem*[80] with copious linguistic annotations, and Meneu wrote a general article on Aljamiado literature which drew on material published by Gayangos and Saavedra. In the 1910s, Zettersteen published some chapters of the Qur'ān, followed by a manual on religious obligations and another dealing with Muslim rituals.[82] González Palencia called attention to some Arabic and Aljamiado manuscripts in Madrid and Toledo,[83] and Longás made use of Aljamiado texts in his valuable work, *Religious Life of the Moriscos*.[84] In 1924 Asín traced the novel of the bath of Zarieb to Arabic origins.[85] In 1929, Nykl published the legend of Alexander.[86] In the 1930s, Lincoln published Aljamiado prophecies[87] and, in 1945, some religious and legal texts dealing with marriage contracts.[88] In the 1940s and 1950s, Aljamiado literature was almost relegated to oblivion, except for Harvey's publication of the BNM 245 manuscript about Yuse Bānegas,[89] followed by his doctoral dissertation in 1958 on the literary culture of the Moriscos.[90] Harvey has also published articles dealing with some Aljamiado manuscripts at Cambridge University and the Godolphin Collection at Oxford; the Aljamiado version of the Mufti of Oran's letter to the Moriscos; and other studies of the Mancebo of Arevalo.[91]

In the 1960s a renewed interest in Aljamiado literature among Spanish, French, German, British, and American scholars resulted in the publication of numerous articles, books, and editions of Aljamiado texts. This interest has continued, showing a genuine commitment to Aljamiado literature. Pareja gives a Morisco account about the life of Jesus and Mary.[92] In 1965, the German scholar Hoenerbach published a substantial number of documents, consisting of a variety of marriage and business contracts and other legal matters and miscellanies dealing with amulets, prescriptions, private letters, prophecies, and divination.[93] As an outgrowth of this study, Hoenerbach published an incisive article dealing with the Moriscos in the light of their literature in which he brings out important elements of the literature: Arabic script, faulty Arabism, the gradual preponderance of Romance, writing Arabic with Latin script, instructional material in Arabic, decoration of manuscripts, manner of translation, and some of the content of Aljamiado.[94] In the United States, Manzanares de Cirre published three Aljamiado texts of religious nature,[95] and is preparing the important legal work of al-Samarqandī. The Spanish scholar Vernet has concerned himself with the translation of the Qur'ān with a view of ultimately achieving a complete Aljamiado translation. He collaborated with Moraleda,[97] who edited an Aljamiado text of the Qur'ān for a master of arts' degree, and supervised López Lillo,[95] who wrote a master's thesis on the same subject.

The dean of Aljamiado literature is, perhaps, the Spanish scholar Galmés. His careful editions of the novel *Paris and Viana* and the *Book of Battles* are profusely annotated. His articles deal with linguistic and literary aspects[99] of Aljamiado literature. Like Vernet, he has encouraged his students to work on Aljamiado texts. He has also organized colloquia on Aljamiado literature and arranged for subsequent publications of the papers.[100]

Labib published the interesting BNM 5301 manuscript dealing with a dialogue between two friends, followed by an article on the role of Aljamiado literature in influencing the Aragonese dialect.[101] Hegyi edited the BNM 4953 manuscript dealing with some legends, homilies, and orations; it was followed by an article presenting a rationale for the use of Arabic script for writing in Romance, and another discussing the presence of Arabic expressions in Aljamiado texts.[102] L. Cardaillac has published a number of articles as well as an important work dealing with the confrontation between Christians and Moriscos.[103] D. Cardaillac edited the BNM 4944 manuscript dealing with anti-Christian polemics.[104] Kontzi also edited some ten Aljamiado texts on a wide range of topics—religious and legal texts, the life of Muḥammad and a poem praising him, an invocation to God for securing water, magical formulas, the ascension of the Prophet to the seven heavens, and instruction for guiding the faithful in the performance of his religious duties. Kontzi has also studied some aspects of Aljamiado texts.[105] Klenck dealt with the Legend of Joseph.[106]

Chejne devoted a chapter to Aljamiado literature in his *Muslim Spain* describing its inception, nature, and content; he also edited a bilingual Arabic and Aljamiado text dealing with an invocation to God.[107]

On the basis of these modern studies and examination of some sixty manuscripts in Madrid at the National Library of Madrid, the Royal Academy of History, the Royal Palace, and the Institute of Asín Palacios, I have arrived at the following characterization of Aljamiado literature. Even from a cursory inventory of available manuscripts, one is struck by the large number of religious materials. The Qur'ān, prophetic traditions, legal manuals, instructional materials directing the faithful to perform his religious obligations, catechisms, and religious admonitions could safely be said to constitute the bulk of Aljamiado literature. This religious perspective permeates even profane stories, such as those dealing with love and battles which, more often than not, draw a moral or show the role of God in human affairs. The aim of the literature is to guide the faithful and prepare him for brighter days on earth and ultimate salvation in the hereafter. It is basically didactic, offering hope for redemption when God and His angels will, sooner or later, intervene and rescue the faithful from an impossible situation. Historical tracts, legends, and secular stories are given a religious dimension: the hand of God will eventually determine the outcome. The career of the Prophet was a model of suffering and despair, but also of hope and deliverance at the hand of God. This theocentrism constitutes the major element in Morisco perspective and permeates all his thinking. The Morisco used his literature not only as an outlet and means of self-edification, but as an instrument of self-defense against the Christian threat to his beliefs, dignity, property, and very being.

Aljamiado literature was inclusive in that it could satisfy all the emotional, spiritual, and social needs of the Morisco. It encompassed Islam as a whole way of life—customs, daily conduct, food, drink, marriage, burial, and other practices—and was nourished and inspired by a strong historical consciousness of Islam as a religion, a state, and a culture. In other words, Aljamiado literature started from an Arabo-Islamic base and adhered to the fundamental values of Islam, notwithstanding the change in language from Arabic to Romance. Moreover, the bulk of its subject matter is Arabic material, either paraphrased or translated into Romance. With the gradual decline of arabization, paraphrasing and translating into Romance increased to provide Moriscos a variety of subject matters: Qur'ān, orations, sermons, prayers, prophetic traditions, and a host of legends and stories.[108]

The process of cultural change from arabization to latinization appears to have affected the form rather than the content of the literature. Although most of the manuscripts are anonymous and undated, they reveal the gradual linguistic change. In a number of manuscripts of religious character instructions are given in Romance, and the rest of the text in Arabic.[109] Those manuscripts may have been written at a time when Arabic was still being used in religious functions such as prayers, Qur'ān recitation, and even in the study of grammar, where bilingualism prevailed.[110] Ordinarily, the Arabic text is written in bold characters with interlineal translation in Romance in small letters. This bilingualism appears to have waned over time until even Qur'ānic chapters and commentaries thereof appear in Romance, with only certain technical terms in Arabic.[111] Such manuscripts were presumably written during the later part of the sixteenth century when Arabic was no longer understood. This contrast—Arabic along with Aljamiado, on the one hand, and the absence of Arabic, on the other—may be helpful in dating manuscripts as belonging to either the fifteenth or the sixteenth century. However, Arabic script was maintained for the most part and, interestingly enough, was replaced by Latin script by Morisco refugees living in North Africa such as Ibrahim de Bolfad, Juan Alfonso, Muḥammad Rabadan, and others who wrote in Romance using the Latin script in an Arabo-Muslim environment.[112] This is, perhaps, one of the reasons that those Moriscos were resented by the North African population and often accused of being Spanish Christians.

In conclusion, bilingualism in Arabic and Romance was common in the Peninsula for centuries. Christians such as the Mozarabs were at home with both languages, as were many Muslims, whose mothers were often of Spanish stock. Thus, a change from one language to another may have not presented much of a hurdle, particularly when it accompanied change in state policy as territory fell under Arab and Christian rulers during the Conquest and Reconquest. Significant elements of interchange are perceptible and have enormous importance for the philologist and sociologist. Aljamiado literature occupies a middle ground between Christian and Islamic cultures. It contains numerous archaic Spanish expressions—such as *cibdad* (*ciudad*), *fazer* (*hazer*), and *kerades (querays)*—as well as a variety of local expressions, dialectal variation, and other linguistic features of Spanish.[113] Conversely, Aljamiado texts also contain a host of arabisms of lexical and syntactical nature. The Moriscos appear to have resisted translating Arabic expressions with religious connotations. Thus, the words *prayer* (*ṣalāh*), *fasting* (*ṣawm*), *ablution* (*waḍū'*), *pilgrimage (hajj), almsgiving (zakāh), prophet (nabī), God (Allāh), Creator* (*khāliq*), and many others preserved their Arabic origin. Some of these expressions were integrated into Spanish, and formed the basis for new verbs and nouns in the Arabic manner. From the Arabic *khalaqa* (to create) was formed the Spanish *khalaqar* (to create) and *khalaqador* (creator). These are also instances of literal translation of Arabic idioms and profuse use of participles of Arabic origin.[114] Preserved Arabic words, although written in Arabic script, are often misspelled or given a Romance pronunciation.

As a hybrid literature with a strong Arabic base, Aljamiado literature is important for reflecting action and interaction between two societies in confrontation. However strong the Morisco's commitment to Islamic values, he could not escape the influences surrounding him. Conversely, his Christian neighbor who had long coexisted with the Mudejar/Morisco in peace and war could not escape some of the literary, artistic, and cultural heritage of Islam.[115] In this connection, Aljamiado literature represents a valuable tool for appreciating the interaction between medieval Spanish literature and the Arabic legacy, valuable to the Arabist for its content and to the Hispanist for both content and form. Aljamiado literature should be studied with special attention to its antecedents and with a comparative approach, which would ultimately lead to a deeper understanding of the self-expression of a minority and the process of interaction between two disparate societies.

Besides being anonymous and untitled, Aljamiado manuscripts are frequently composites of a variety of unrelated items. This may have been not the original format, but a late combination of subjects under a single cover. This practice would lead one to assume that such composite manuscripts were owned by individuals who wished to have an encyclopedia of religious materials for performing daily ritual obligations and other needs. In some respects, Aljamiado literature resembles the Genizah documents written by the Jewish community living in various parts of the Mediterranean basin. Preserving the vestiges of a great Arabic legacy, it presents Arabic materials in abridged or expanded form. Moriscos developed a technique of translation from Arabic into Aljamiado and a fairly standardized system of transliteration and religious terminology. This apparent uniformity would imply the existence of a bureau of translation or close consultations among those scholars involved in the transmission of Arabic lore into Romance. The Moriscos do not appear to have been much concerned about innovation or the linguistic dexterity that is so important in classical Arabic literature, where eloquence and correct syntax characterize good style. Unlike Arabic literature, addressed to the erudite, Aljamiado literature was meant for the common man. Its simple language lacks ornamentation of style, complicated similes, and metaphors. Its artistic merit rests in simplicity, directness, and an often lofty and intense feeling, which has great dramatic effect. No Aljamiado authors achieved the stature of such Islamic figures as Ibn Ḥazm, Averroes, or al-Jāḥiẓ, but they excelled in their purpose: instructing in simple, straightforward language rather than innovating. To fulfill this purpose, they exercised discerning selectivity of materials not so much for intellectual stimuli as for self-edification and regulating one's conduct in this world in preparation for the hereafter. These spiritual and pragmatic needs called for religious materials dealing with beliefs, religious observances, and legislation pertaining to marriage, divorce, birth, burial, inheritance, and contractual obligations of all sorts. History, legends, stories, wisdom sayings, poetry, divination, prophecies, astrology, and the like were ancillary to and almost inseparable from the religious purpose of the literature.

The occurrences of these themes and their frequency are interesting and revealing in themselves for an insight into the perspective of the Morisco. It is doubtful that the Morisco had any consciousness of the division of the sciences into categories, common in classical Islam. His interest in a particular discipline was subjective rather than scientific, suiting the need of the moment. The Morisco was scarcely aware of the Islamic controversies separating the religious scholars and the philosopher or the question whether the religious sciences or the secular sciences should take precedence. He followed his Andalusian predecessors by adhering strictly to a simplified orthodox doctrine without considering complicated theological questions.

4

Religion, Beliefs, and Observances

The external documentation of the Inquisition, accounts of contemporary historians, and the internal evidence of Morisco writings testify to the Moriscos' deep commitment to Islamic beliefs and values. These beliefs and values are prescribed in the Qur'ān and prophetic traditions and codified in legal and theological texts. Thus, it is no surprise that Morisco writings should have been largely religious, cherished and hidden from watchful authorities in hollow walls and false ceilings.[1] The following paragraphs describe the religious writings that serve as the basis for evaluating the religious beliefs and observances of the Moriscos.

The religious sciences known among the Moriscos were: (1) the Qur'ān; (2) Qur'ānic commentaries (*tafsīr*); (3) prophetic traditions (*ḥadīth*); and (4) jurisprudence (*fiqh*). The Moriscos simply drew from their Muslim predecessors the material to meet their religious and emotional needs without contributing much to the further study or elucidation of these disciplines.

THE QUR'ĀN

Muslims consider the Qur'ān the Book of God, uncreated or co-eternal with God Himself. It is the most revered document in the Arabic language, permeating Muslim thought throughout the ages as the truest and most authentic of all revealed scriptures, including those of Judaism and Christianity. Its language and content are inimitable, a miracle that is the base of Islam, the best testimony of its validity as a revealed religion, and the proof of the veracity of the Prophet and Messenger Muḥammad. As the container of God's truth, the Qur'ān is eternal and can never be superseded. It embodies all the religious obligations that prepare the faithful for an upright life in this world and for the hereafter. Because of its enormous significance, every Muslim must learn it in the original Arabic, understand its content, and be guided by it. The Qur'ān is like a tree that bears fruit throughout the year, from which people can take all they want with plenty left.[2] Reciting or reading it carries enormous rewards, as conveyed in this Aljamiado tradition: "Muḥammad—may God's prayer and peace be upon him—said: he who reads the Qur'ān in his prayer, God will register for him a thousand good deeds *(alḥasanas),* and will elevate him a thousand degrees in Paradise, will marry him to a thousand angels of Paradise, will give him the rewards of a thousand martyrs, and will register for each hair of his body the reward accruing from a thousand major pilgrimages *(alḥajjes)* and minor pilgrimages *(al-'umras).*"[3]

The doctrine of the divine origin of the Qur'ān connotes the divine origin of the Arabic language itself, making it a unique language whose expressions cannot be duplicated in any other tongue—hence, the prohibition of committing the Qur'ān to any foreign language on the ground that such translation would distort not only the beauty and sonority of Arabic, but the actual meaning of the Qur'ān itself.[4] This prohibition presented a dilemma for non-Arabic-speaking Muslims and particularly for the Moriscos, unwilling to compromise their faith and yet unable to maintain knowlege of Arabic. An examination of some manuscripts containing Qur'ānic chapters indicates that the Moriscos were reluctant to violate the religious injunction against translation; they attempted to preserve Arabic wordings whenever feasible and to learn them by heart. This pious resolution proved impractical during the process of sweeping latinization, and interlinear Aljamiado translation of the Qur'ān was gradually introduced. By force of circumstance or under the dispensation of *Taqīyah,* the Moriscos had imperative need of translating the Qur'ān for the dual purpose of maintaining their religious convictions and of responding to the Christians, who already possessed a Latin translation of the Qur'ān which formed the basis of anti-Muslim polemics.

In this connection, it is significant to point out that the first translation of the Qur'ān into Latin was made on Spanish soil during the twelfth century under the auspices of Peter the Venerable (1092-1156) of Cluny in southern France who, visiting Spain in 1141, commissioned the translation of the Qur'ān into Latin.[5] It was followed by the translation of Mark of Toledo in the thirteenth century,[6] and by others during the fourteenth and fifteenth centuries.[7] Juan Andrés,[8] originally a Muslim, embraced Christianity in 1487, becoming an ordained priest and critic of Islam. He joined Martín Carcía (ca.

1441-1521),[9] Inquisitor General of Aragón, in translating the Qur'ān as part of a bitter attack against Islam, hoping to persuade the Moriscos to abandon Islam. Their attempt failed and may have had the opposite effect of influencing the Moriscos to translate their own version of the Holy Book into their own dialect.

In their translation of the Qur'ān, the Moriscos proceeded rather cautiously. Sensitive to the religious injunction against translation, they preserved the Arabic text of the Qur'ān in bold letters and added paraphrasing or translation into Romance in small letters above or below the Arabic text. Portions of the Qur'ān and verses thereof were translated this way by different hands; there is no indication that a systematic translation of the whole Qur'ān was made by a single individual or group.[10]

More often than not, translations were a literal and faithful reproduction of the Arabic original. When the rendering made little sense, it was often accompanied by explanatory annotations that are actually Qur'ānic commentaries.

The Qur'ān occupies such a prominent place in Aljamiado literature that one can hardly find an Aljamiado text without an invocation of the Holy Book. Its enormous religious significance also included its magical power, often used for divination. Reading the Qur'ān is not only meritorious, but carries reward for both the reader and listener. Numerous manuscripts exist containing one or more chapters of the Qur'ān, and verses are spread throughout the literature.[11] Some manuscripts deal with the excellence of the Qur'ān,[12] its benefits,[13] and the reward accruing from reading, copying, or carrying certain verses thereof.[14] There are manuscripts exalting a certain chapter,[15] and others demonstrating the manner of uttering (*tahlīl*)[16] or reading it.[17] Finally, some manuscripts of the Qur'ān are in Arabic;[18] others in bilingual Arabic-Aljamiado;[19] while others are in Arabic written in Latin script[20] or in Aljamiado in Latin script.[21]

QUR'ANIC COMMENTARY *(tafsīr or sharḥe)*

Qur'ānic commentary, an established discipline in Muslim scholarship in both East and West, does not appear to have been pursued as an academic discipline among the Moriscos. The extant manuscripts bearing the title of commentary (*sharḥe*)[22] constitute bare explanations of the Qur'ān to convey the essential meaning for the initiate rather than long scholarly explanations that would have been meant for erudites. Such commentators, if they can be called this, appear to have given the gist of a verse on the basis of an old Arabic commentary, without giving the source from which the explanation was derived. The term *sharḥe* as used by the Moriscos appears to correspond to translation rather than commentary (*tafsīr*) in the classical conception of the word. This is attested by the extant manuscripts, which are concerned mostly with conveying the meaning of the original Arabic. The long commentary in Aljamiado[23] for several chapters of the Qur'ān conforms to this suggestion. A translation of the opening chapter of the Qur'ān (*fātiḥah)* may be contrasted with a commentary thereof:

Aljamiado Translation	*English Translation*
en-l-nonbere de-Allah, piyadoso de piyadad	In the name of God, the Merciful the Compassionate;
1. las loores a-da Allah senor de todas las cosas.	Praise be to God, the Lord of the worlds.
2. Piyadoso de piyadad	The Merciful, the Compassionate.
3. Rrey del-diya del-judisiyo	King of the Day of Judgment,
4. A tu adoramos, i-ya-tu demandamos ayuda.	Thee we worship, and in thee we seek succor.
5. Ghiyanos a-la-karrera deresada	Guide us to the right path
6. A-la-karrera de-akellos ke faziste gharasiya sobre-llos,	The path of those whom you graced;
7. No de-los-ke tensanes sobre-llos ni-de-los yerrados.[24]	Not those who angered thee Not those who are astray.
En-el-nonbere de-Allah, piyadoso de-piyadad	In the name of God, The Merciful the Compassionate
1. Las loores son a-da-Allah senor de todas las cosas khaleqadas,	Praise be to God, the Lord of all created things,
2. El piyadoso de-buwenos i-malos en este mundo i-de-piyadad a-los buwenos en-elotro mundo.	The merciful over good and evil in this world, and of mercy for the good ones in the hereafter.
3. Rrey del-diya del-judisiyo el-diya ke ghuwalardonara Allah a-las gentes por sus obras.	The king of the Day of Judgment the day in which Allah will reward people according to their deeds.
4. A-tu adoramos kon obidensiya yumillansa ya-tu demandamos ayuda.	Thee we worship with obedience and humility, and in thee we seek help.
5. Ghiyanos a-la-karrera adresada	Guide us to the straight path
6. A-la-karrera de akellos ke hiziste gharasiya sobre-llos kon-el alislām.	The path of those on whom you bestowed grace with Islam
7. no-de-los ke te ayres sobre-llos ke son los judiyos ni-de-los yerrados ke son los kiristiyanos.[25]	Not those who made you angry who are the Jews nor those astray, who are the Christians.

This straightforward commentary does not delve into complicated theological questions. This procedure continues throughout the manuscript, entitled, "This is the Explanation and Elucidation of the Documents."[26] In fact, the commentary does not differ much from a straight translation of the *Sūrat altīn*:

Arabic	*English*
wa-l-tīni wa-l-zaytūni wa ṭūrī	By the fig, by the Olive, by

Sīnīna wa-hādhā al-baladi al-amīni	Mount Sinai and by this safe city
Aljamiado	*English*
Juro Allah-por el-monte de watīn, i-por el-monte de azaytūni i-por el-monte de ṭūrsinā	I swear by God, by the mount of fig, by the mount of olive, by the mount of Sinai
i-por esta villa de-seghuridad kes Maka[27]	And by this city of safety, which is Mecca

It may not be farfetched to suggest that in the light of the religious injunction against translation, the Moriscos thought that rendering the Qur'ān in the form of explanation rather than straight translation would do less violence to the Holy Book. Thus, for them translation and commentary may be one and the same thing.

PROPHETIC TRADITIONS (*ḤADĪTH*)[28]

The Moriscos also resisted translation of prophetic traditions without the inclusion of the original Arabic texts. Next to the Qur'ān, prophetic traditions constituted the source of the religious law (*sharī'ah*). Authenticated traditions reporting the sayings and deeds of th Prophet were considered perfect in wording and meaning and, furthermore, more specific for adjudicating all sorts of cases not fully spelled out in the Qur'ān itself. Consequently, they were revered as much as the Qur'ān and rendered in the same manner into Aljamiado with the Arabic text in bold characters and the Aljamiado translation or explanation in small letters placed above or below the Arabic lines. Being the major source of religious law, the traditions were extensively used for theological, legislative, historical, and eschatological purposes. The Moriscos relied on the established traditions contained in collections based on the accepted Six Canonical Books.[29] Although they did not attempt specific studies of traditions in terms of their authenticity or classification in a hierarchical order, they selected those traditions that best met their needs and added some of their own traditions that do not appear in the established Six Canons.[30] This simplification and selectivity of traditions can be seen in legislations, religious observances, God's attributes, the ultimate deliverance of the Moriscos, the triumph of Islam over Christianity, and so forth. Traditions were considered above scrutiny, and nowhere is there any tendency toward nonconformism or question of their validity. Traditions were often traced back to the Prophet Muḥammad without establishing a full chain of transmitters (*isnād*), as is the case in most Arabic collections of traditions; rather, the authority of old traditionists was cited, such as 'Abdallah Ibn 'Abbās,[31] 'Abdallah Ibn Mas'ūd,[32] Abū Hurayrah,[33] Anas Ibn Mālik,[34] and the four Orthodox caliphs.[35] In spite of their importance as the second pillar of the religious law, no complete or comprehensive manual of traditions has come down; traditions are interspersed throughout Aljamiado literature in commentaries, religious regulations, history, legends, and maxims.[36]

JURISPRUDENCE (*FIQH*)

As with the Qur'ān and traditions, the Moriscos appear to have been less concerned with the theoretical aspect of the law than with its immediate application. It was generally understood that the law comprises the Qur'ān and traditions and is inseparable from them. As such, the religious law (*sharī'ah*) is all encompassing, including not only the articles of faith, beliefs, and observances, but all manner of behavior. Thus, prayer and fasting are as much a part of the law as purchase-sale or any other contracts. Therefore, the Moriscos provided themselves with comprehensive legal material, abridging texts written by Eastern legalists or translating them into Aljamiado. For example, the Eastern scholar al-Samarqandī's comprehensive Arabic work, *Awakening the Negligent and Illuminating the Road of the Novice*,[37] was translated into Aljamiado, known as the *Book of al-Samarqandī* (*alkitāb de Samarqandī*). Samarqandī's work covers a wide range of subjects: fear of death, etiquette of the tomb, fear of the Day of Judgment, people of Hell, people of Paradise, good and bad deeds, repentance, obedience to parents, rights of children, envy, silence, suffering, the merit of the month of Ramaḍān, adultery, piety, good habits, cleanliness, ablution, prayer, fasting, pilgrimage, holy war, purchase-sale, marriage, divorce, what is permissible and what is forbidden in food, drink, and other matters. Equally comprehensive is the *Tafria* (Ar. *tafrī'ah*),[38] a translation in Latin script of the work of the Eastern scholar Abū-l-Qāsim 'Ubaydalla Ibn al-Ḥusayn Ibn Jallāb. This stout work in some forty-two books deals with ablution, prayer, almsgiving, fasting, burial, holy war, oaths, slaughtering, hunting, contracts, and other religious and secular matters. It is similar in content to the *Brevario Sunni* of 'Īsā de Jābir, which was intended to meet the general needs of the Moriscos.[39] Other works with the same purpose included the *Tafsira* of the Mancebo de Arevalo in some 472 folios.[40] The *Tafsira* covers a wide range of subjects, including not only the precepts of the faith and the religious obligations expected of the faithful, but also an exhortation of the jurist Mālik Ibn Anas,[41] the order of creation, admonitions, home management, Creation of Adam and the fall of the angels, Job's patience, the excellence of Mary and that of other biblical personalities.

In addition to these comprehensive works, numerous composite manuscripts have one or more items bearing on religious duties. In fact, the great majority of the extant manuscripts contain such seemingly disparate items. The massive work, *Advice for People*,[42] contains reflections on Islam and the opinion of the jurist Mālik on the fundamentals of Islam. Similarly, the *Book of Admonitions and Examples*,[43] diversified in content, meant as a cure for the soul by teaching it to love the hereafter and abhor this world. Other treatises were intended to guide the ignorant to the true faith and to urge him to comply with his religious duties, for which he will attain eternal rewards.[44] Finally, one may add the large number of manuscripts bearing the title of *devocionario* explaining God's unity, His beautiful names, and other religious matters.[45]

As already indicated, the Moriscos did not show much concern about the politicoreligious controversies that had divided Islam in the past. However, a brief treatise[46] deals with some Muslim heresies which lead to perdition. Aljamiado manuscripts record the ninety-nine beautiful names of God,[47] God's unity as found in thirty-seven passages of the Qur'ān,[48] and the like. While avoiding any contentiousness, the Moriscos were quite aware of the differences separating Muslims from Christians.[49] Although they held views about Christ and Mary conforming to Islamic doctrine, they were forced by circumstance to respond to attacks against their own religion, thereby producing a relatively abundant polemical literature offering broad refutation against Christianity and Judaism.[50]

The Moriscos followed in the footsteps of their Andalusian ancestors and adhered closely to the legal school of the Medinese legalist Mālik Ibn Anas (d. 795), whom they regarded as "our doctor and the best among other Muslim legalists."[51] He was created from the blood of Muḥamad, whose bleeding by the angels was witnessed by Mālik's father (d. 711), who drank the blood instead of letting it seep into the ground.[52]

RELIGIOUS PRACTICES

Materials on the Qur'ān, prophetic traditions, and the law were abundant among the Moriscos, and enjoyed great currency for instruction in the basic beliefs and observances of Islam. It was perhaps these religious practices and not the writings in themselves that placed the Moriscos outside Christian society. The religious manuscripts and other evidence suggest that the Moriscos took their religion seriously and abode by its tenets, persecution notwithstanding. Numerous treatises for instruction on the religious duties have survived.[53] One treatise elucidates all the duties expected from the faithful:

> If you are asked what are the five pillars of the Islamic religion (*del-adīn del alisalām*) you shall say that they are these: the first pillar is believing in no other God (*senor*) but Allah, Who has no partner (*sin abarsonero*), and in Muḥammad as the servant and messenger of Allah; the second pillar is maintaining the five prayers (*aṣalaes*) night and day; the third pillar is payment of almsgiving (*l-azake*); the fourth pillar is fasting during the month of Ramaḍān; and the fifth pillar is performing the pilgrimage (*alḥaje*) to the house of Mecca, if possible.[54]

Brevario Sunni,[55] Mancebo de Arevalo's *Tafsira*,[56] and other treatises that deal with one or more pillar. In his *Religious Life*, Iongás has given a detailed account of those pillars based mostly on 'Īsā's *Brevario*; only broad outlines are given here.

Belief in God and Muḥammad. The first pillar, or confession of faith, is a simple recognition of God's Oneness and of Muḥammad's Prophecy. Religion requires belief, defined by 'Īsā as "the beginning of reason whereby human understanding shows us that faith is something that guides man to know what thing is God, to believe in Him, and to be convinced that there is no ultimate good without Him."[57] God created man from nothing and gave him life; He will reward or punish him according to his deeds. Thus, it behooves man to believe in and trust Him. Although it is not possible to see Him, He can be known through His creation. 'Īsā de Jābir lists thirteen articles to be followed: (1) belief in the heart, utterance with the tongue, and affirmation with the will that the Almighty God is one without a partner, creator of the universe, did not beget and was not begotten; (2) belief that God sent the blessed Muḥammad as the Seal of his Prophets with the divine law of the Qur'ān through which he revoked other laws and removed all doubts and errors in them, thereby guiding people to everlasting good; thus, it is incumbent to follow Muḥammad's deeds and ways and those of his companions and give up those of past or future generations; (3) belief that all God's creation will come to an end except God, and that the soul of man will be received by the angels to be judged at the time of death; (4) belief that two angels will ask the dead who was his lord, his prophet, and the law; if he gives the right answer and his deeds prove to be good, he will be elevated to the most high; (5) belief that all beings—including men, angels, and demons—will die at the end of the world, except God; (6) belief in resurrection in which souls return to their bodies; (7) belief in the Day of Judgment in which each nation will be judged in the presence of its prophets, and the good ones will see the face of God; (8) belief that the honored Muḥammad will intercede in the Day of Judgment on behalf of people when other prophets will fail to do so, and belief that God will heed Muḥammad's invocation to withdraw members of his community from Hell; (9) belief that man is expected to render an account of his deeds on earth, and that Muslims will do that first because they will serve afterward as witnesses over other nations; (10) belief that deeds will be weighed on a balance to determine whether the person should be sent to Paradise or Hell; (11) belief in crossing a bridge during the Day of Judgment: the blessed ones will cross it like a ray, and the infidels and blasphemous will fall into Hell; (12) belief that the blessed believers will end in Paradise; and (13) belief that evildoers and the blasphemous will end in Hell.[58]

These beliefs are those of traditional Islam, presented clearly to leave no doubt that Islam and its community of believers (*aluma*, Ar. *al-ummah*) are God's favorites. But beliefs alone are not sufficient to attain salvation. Elsewhere,[59] belief (*kereyensiya*) is defined and linked to deed (*obra*). Belief must be felt with the heart (*kon el-korason*), uttered with the tongue, and carried out by the limbs. Belief is meaningless if it is not accompanied by deeds, which are subject to will (*voluntad*), and this is, in turn, meaningless if it does not conform to the *Sunnah* (*asunna*) as commanded by God in the Qur'ān and enunciated by his Messenger Muḥammad. Obviously, God and Muḥammad occupy a preeminent place in Aljamaido literature.

A number of treatises deal with God's attributes in both Arabic and Aljamiado. The attributes consisting of ninety-nine names known as the beautiful names of God (*los buwenos nonberes*, Ar. *al-asmā' al-ḥusnā*)[60] are based on a prophetic tradition indicating that God's names are one hundred minus one. Among these are: "Creator," "Lord of the Hereafter and of This World," "Sovereign," "Merciful," "Great," "Magnanimous," "Generous," "Everlasting," and "Victor."[61] These names are recited in prayer, commented on,[62] and exalted in sermons.[63] Similarly, God's unity was emphasized and elucidated on the basis of thirty-seven passages of the Qur'ān.[64] His Prophet Muḥammad is the greatest of His creatures and receives the widest attention with respect to his birth, mission, miracles, journey to the seven heavens, and death.[65] Muḥammad's preeminent position among the prophets is unquestionable. When a Jew asked Muḥammad why God placed him above all prophets, Muḥammad is said to have given the following seven reasons: God would not have made Paradise and Hell, heavens, earth, and the throne had it not been for him; He made him ascend to the seven heavens (obviously in reference to the Mi'rāj); He responded to his plea on behalf of the sinners of his community; He instructed angels, prophets, and all nations to invoke his name; he will be the first to be received at the end of the world; all prophets and pious men of his community will be saved and the rest tormented; and he will be the first one to enter Paradise in the Day of Judgment.[66]

Prayer and Ablution. Prayer is minutely prescribed in general works as well as in special treatises.[67] It is commanded by God and his Prophet, enabling the faithful to enter Paradise. Numerous traditions exalt the virtue of prayer and the reward accruing therefrom. A prophetic tradition compares prayer with a sweet river passing five times a day in front of a house; who can resist drinking from its water and cleansing himself with it?[68] Prayer eliminates sins as water eliminates coarseness from the body, and if performed on time it will devour sin as fire will devour dry wood.[69] Prayers are the key for facing the Lord without an audience. The worshipper is nearer to God when he prostrates (*alsajdado*); and when he dies, the land on which he prayed will cry to the heavens and all onlookers.[70] But for prayer to be valid, it must be preceded by ablution (*aṭahor)*. A major ablution is tantamount to a full bath with clean water, and a minor ablution (*alwaḍu* Ar. *wuḍū')* consists of washing the extremities of the body: hands, feet, face, nose. Their object is to wash away error and sin.[72]

The significance of the minor ablution is explained in a prophetic tradition as follows: Each drop of water that falls in the hand makes the devil (*el-ashshayṭān)* flee; ten merits (*alḥasanas)* eliminate ten sins and bring in ten degrees (*gharadas)* in Paradise (*aljanna)*. When the face is washed, sins will leave through the eyelids. When the hands are washed, God will give a letter in the right hand and sins will fall from the left hand through the tips of the fingers. When he wipes off (*masha*, Ar. *masaḥa*) his head, God will forgive his sins and the hairs of his head will be illuminated (*kalaridad*) in the tomb as well as in the Day of Judgment. When he washes his feet, he will be able to cross the bridge (*aṣṣirāṭ*) without fear or difficulty, and his sins will be forgiven.

When he rinses his mouth, God will forgive what the tongue said and the forbidden things that were eaten. When he rinses his nose, the smell of Paradise will enter his nostrils.[73] Equally, the major ablution (*ṭahur*) has enormous rewards. God will have his angels as witnesses for the great reward awaiting those who performed it: a thousand merits for each hair of the body, elimination of a thousand sins, and a thousand degrees high in Paradise.[74] In short, minor and major ablutions are "the weapons and garrison with which the faithful prepares himself to make prayer."[75]

Ablutions were ordinarily performed at the mosque or the public bath adjoining it. After prohibition of such institutions, ablutions were performed at home or in the fields in utmost secrecy to avoid the watchful authorities. The performance of the minor or major ablution did not consist of mere washing but followed strict rules for reciting specific formulas when washing each part of the body. Also, the place of ablution and the water used are subject to conditions of cleanliness. The water ought to be running, clean, odorless, tasteless, and untouched by an unbeliever, a dog, a wolf, or any other animal. When water is scarce, sand or unpolluted soil may be substituted.[76]

These religious rituals of ablution formed an integral part of prayer which was to be performed five times a day. The Inquisition took firm steps to abolish ablution, to the point of forbidding bathing to the Moriscos even for hygienic purposes. Various edicts against public baths were instituted, and clerics viewed any form of bathing as a heretical act—complaining to the authorities that the Moriscos were so incorrigible as to take a bath in December!

The Morisco was expected to pray five times a day, a number commanded by God Himself during Muḥammad's journey (*mi'rāj*) to the seven heavens. Traditionally, prayers are conducted in a mosque, preceded by a call to prayer (*adhān*) by a trained person known as *almu'adane*, Ar. *mu'adhdhin*, who will stand high in the Day of Judgment because of having exalted God's name.[77] Once the believers are congregated in the mosque, the *imām*, or leader of prayer, makes the initial convocation (*iqāmah*), which is repeated by the congregation.[78] The worshiper faces the Qiblah toward the Holy City of Mecca. The first chapter of the Qur'ān or verses from other chapters are recited.[79] There are prostations for each prayer: two for Dawn prayer (*el-ṣubḥ);* four for the Midday prayer (*alẓuhar);* four for Midafternoon prayer (*al-'aṣṣar);* three for Sunset prayer (*al-'aṭoma);* and four for Night prayer. Each prayer is minutely described step by step in the formulation of the Seven Pillars of Prayers (*Los siete el-haykeles*).[80]

Prayers are prerequisites to salvation, for the Prophet will recognize His community (*aluma*) in the Day of Judgment by the traces of ablution and by the marks of prostration, which will shine as the ray of the sun.[81] The five prayers constitute minimal obligations. In addition, numerous prayers are expected from the faithful during the day for each activity: when awakening, dressing, going to the mosque, before and after meals.[82] These prayers are short utterances invoking or exalting God's name. The Moriscos also had invocations (*addu'a,* Ar. *du'ā)* for forgiveness,[83] for rain, and for seeking a favor.[84] There are litanies[85] and various sermons, some of which were translated from the Arabic. These sermons (*khuṭbah*) are broad in content and may include current affairs, social or political matters, and edifying or moralizing materials. They were ordinarily delivered from the pulpit (*minbar*) during the Friday prayer. Inasmuch as the Moriscos could not gather openly, let alone in a mosque, they availed themselves of old sermons, preserving the Arabic content and form along with the Aljamiado translation.[86]

Although deprived of his mosque and center of worship, the Morisco appears to have performed his regular prayers, which did not actually require a mosque. Islamic law has been quite accommodating in this respect, allowing prayers to be performed anywhere, at home or in the open fields. The Morisco was also allowed within the prescription of the law to circumvent the time of prayer. Thus if circumstances beyond his control prevented him from prayer at a given and precise time, he could make up for it at a more suitable time. This kind of dispensation applied to the rest of his religious obligations, and the Inquisition appears to have been aware of these options. Thus, the Morisco remained vulnerable, particularly on Friday, the Muslim Sabbath, when he would be suspect were he to have clean clothes.

Almsgiving (azake, Ar. *zakāh).*[87] Charity taxes are prescribed in the Qur'ān as a duty incumbent upon every Muslim for the purpose of aiding the poor. They were paid in currency or in goods proportionate to possessions. They are collected by a special office in a Muslim state. Among the Moriscos, however, they were collected by a local chieftain or a trustworthy person who would see that they went to the needy. Although some 2.5 to 10 percent was expected, it is not certain to what extent people complied, the whole question being a matter of conscience. In addition to almsgiving, which is obligatory, there is no limit to charitable donations (*aṣṣadaqa*), which are voluntary on festive occasions such as weddings, birthdays, or other social events. The practice of *aṣṣadaqa* was so current as to be as obligatory as the payment of *azake*. Muḥammad is reported to have said, "The *aṣṣadaqa* is a defense against misfortune (*albela*, Ar. *al-balā*)," and the Almighty said, "I shall give innumerable rewards (*ghuwalardon*) to those who make it."[88] Avoidance of such payments, however, was not uncommon and may be illustrated by the following story, which shows the enormous penalty awaiting those who fail to give alms to the poor as prescribed by religious law.

A Muslim went to a religious scholar and informed him that the following day was the Feast of Lamb and that he had nothing to eat. He asked the religious scholar to tell him where to seek help. He was told to go to the mayor, who upon seeing him, ordered his servants to send him away. He returned to the religious scholar and informed him what had happened; then he was sent to a Christian for help. The Christian received him well; gave him ten bundles of wheat, a lamb, and two gold coins, and told him to come back every year to receive the same things for the rest of his life. The Muslim was so delighted that he informed the religious scholar, who was well pleased. Meanwhile, the mayor dreamed of a palace of gold with precious stones housing beautiful ladies and a palace of fire filled with torment and punishment. An angel told him that the palace of gold had been reserved for him but had been given to a Christian who gave alms to a Muslim denied by the mayor. Now he was left with the palace of fire. The mayor went to the Christian on the following day and asked what he had done the day before. The Christian replied that he had done nothing unusual, but the mayor persisted inquiring until he found out about the donation to the Muslim. The mayor then proposed to buy the almsgiving, offering him half his property, but the Christian would not agree; the mayor then offered all his property, his children, and himself, but the Christian refused, and the mayor dropped dead and went straight to Hell. Thereafter, the Christian informed the religious scholar what had happened and was asked to become a Muslim; he accepted. He went home and informed his wife that he could no longer live with her; however, the wife knew his reason and confessed to him that she had herself been a Muslim since their marriage forty years before.[89]

On another occasion giving *aṣṣadaqa* influenced God to reconsider a promise He had made. "The Story of the Tree and the Birds" relates that twelve birds living in a tree were harassed by a man who killed their offspring every year until they appealed to God for justice. The next year the man was climbing the tree to kill the offspring when he heard a man at his door asking for charity (*aṣṣadaqa*). The man descended from the tree and complied with the poor man's wish; then he returned and killed the little birds. The birds then reminded God of His promise, to which God retorted, "How could I do wrong to a man who did good for the love of me? Go elsewhere, for my land is ample."[90]

Fasting.[91] Obligatory fasting was observed during the ninth lunar month, Ramaḍān, starting as the new moon appears and ending at the beginning of a new moon, at the start of the tenth month of Shawwāl. The significance of fasting can be inferred from that given to the month of Ramaḍān, considered by Muḥammad as "The month of my community (*aluma*), the month of benediction and blessing (*albaraka*), and the month for the remission of sins, besides being the month in which the Qur'ān was revealed."[92] Moreover, it was the month in which Adam fasted after he had eaten the forbidden apple, and the fast helped to expurgate the fruit. Thus, the rewards accruing from fasting are many: elimination of sins from birth; expurgation of the forbidden; granting God's mercy; granting a palace (*alqaṣar*) in Paradise; absence of hunger and thirst in the Day of Judgment; immunity from all horror and torment in the Day of Judgment; and no entry into Hell (*jahannam*).[93]

Fasting is obligatory on all Muslims, male and female, with ample dispensation for the sick, pregnant women, old people, travelers, Muslims working for Christians, slaves whose owners do not observe fasting, and others because of physical conditions or extraordinary circumstances. These exemptions, however, do not release the individual from fulfilling his obligations at a later or more suitable date either through fasting or donating food to the poor in quantity equal to the amount of food ordinarily consumed during the fasting days. Fasting consists of total abstinence from food and drink during the day and is invalidated by any food, drink, or sexual intercourse. However, food, drink, and sex are allowed at night. Ordinarily, meals are taken after sunset and before dawn. The conclusion of the fasting during the month of Ramaḍān is often celebrated by a small feast, followed, forty days later, by the grand feast celebrated by slaughtering a lamb—hence, its Spanish designation, "Pascuas del Carnero."[94] In addition to the obligatory fasting of Ramaḍān, other voluntary fasting is recommended, particularly during the third and tenth days of the month of Muḥarram, and the twelfth day of Rabīʿ I, which is Muḥammad's birthday.

Pilgrimage[95] *and Jihād.* Although obligatory and an integral part of religious belief, pilgrimage to the holy cities of Mecca and Medina in the Arabian Peninsula was at best limited, if not beyond the reach of the Morisco. However, provisions were made for pilgrimage in the manuals dealing with religious duties and obligations. No doubt, the Morisco did hope one day to make the pilgrimage to the holy city, though he was unlikely to go. Puey de Monçon was a rare exception in undertaking such journey and recording it in couplets that must have been recited by Moriscos.

Finally, the Moriscos followed their Muslim ancestors in adding a sixth pillar, known as *jihād* (holy war),[96] to the prescribed religious beliefs. This consisted of advancing oneself on the path of God through performance of good deeds, including war against the infidels and enemies of religion.

A number of other practices and ceremonies were viewed by the Inquisition as heretical and grounds for bringing participants before the tribunal. Among those customs and practices were those related to birth and circumcision, wedding and burial ceremonies, the slaughtering of animals, and some aspects of dietary law.

The birth of a child was a joyful occasion attended by festivities. When the child reached seven days old, a special ceremony of consecration (Ar. *ʿaqī qah*) was held in which the child was purified with water and an amulet bearing Qur'ānic verses was placed around his neck. He was given an Arabic name, his hair was clipped, and its weight in gold was distributed to the poor. This practice known as *fada*,[97] Arabic *fidā'*, or *fadā*, meaning ransom. In some respects, the *fada* was the equivalent of baptism and served as its counterpart to erase or nullify it. The practice of *fada* was quite common among the Moriscos, who were impelled to have their children baptized and who found in *fada* a way of annulling the baptism. Music, dancing, and singing were part of the ceremonies of the *fada*. A more significant ritual was the ceremony of circumcision, an obligatory religious practice in Islam. When done openly, circumcision was attended by a procession of dancers, musicians, singers, and a large gathering of relatives and friends. Such practices were outlawed by the Inquisition, so they had to be performed covertly and with the utmost discretion. During circumcision, it appears that the Moriscos sacrificed (*aḍaḥeas*) an animal, which was ordinarily slaughtered in the morning. Some of its meat was eaten, and the rest was distributed (*aṣṣadaqa*) among the poor.[98] If the family could not afford an animal, grain or fruit was given to the poor.[99] Circumcision was done by the time the child was eight years old and often escaped the inspection of priests since it was done long after baptism.

Marriage[100] was also a memorable family event attended by friends and relatives with ceremonies and fanfare: singing, dancing, feasting, and distribution of food among the needy. A wedding was basically a civil ceremony, but regulated by religious law with respect to conjugal contract, property ownership, the couple's relations, divorce, and other aspects of marital life. As Christian converts, the Moriscos were, of course, compelled to be married in church, but this did not prevent them from having a Muslim wedding ceremony at home after the church nuptials. This seemingly prevalent practice often aroused the suspicions of Old Christians, who brought it to the attention of the Inquisitors. Also, accusations of practicing polygamy were often made against the Moriscos, but there is no solid evidence that the Moriscos availed themselves of such a practice, notwithstanding that the religious law permitted them to have as many as four wives and that Muḥammad himself had several wives. However, Muḥammad's polygamy is explained as having been beyond his control: perfect, clean, and humble women pleaded with God to have Muḥammad as their husband, and God responded to their plea through the angel Gabriel, who relayed to Muhammad God's will.[101]

Death and burial[102] were sad occasions attended by elaborate rituals according to the prescriptions of the law. These rituals appeared to be widespread, causing Old Christians to complain about their heretical nature. These rituals involve purification of the corpse, tantamount to a total ablution. The corpse is then shrouded with white cotton cloth, and the face of the dead is turned toward the *qiblah*. It is carried to the cemetery in a procession of relatives and friends uttering religious formulas. At the cemetery, a formal prayer is given, and burial proceeds in a prepared grave on virgin land. The practice of providing the corpse with jewels, clothing, and food existed among some Moriscos, although there was no legal prescription requiring or condoning such practice.[103] The Moriscos also attached great importance to a letter of death (*karta de la muwerte*),[104] which accompanied the corpse. It acted as a passport identifying the dead as a believer before the angels of death, Munkar and Nakīr, who were created by God for the purpose of testing all creatures in the tomb as to their former religious beliefs.[105]

Finally, mention should be made of dietary law among the Moriscos.[106] Inasmuch as Islam regulates every aspect of life, the law books contain a variety of regulations on general etiquette as well as prohibitions of all sorts. These regulations have a sacrosanct character, becoming part of the obligatory religious duties expected of the faithful. With respect to food, particularly meat and fish, the law books ordinarily stipulate in detail which animals are suitable for eating and which are not. There are strict rules as to the manner of slaughtering an animal, which is done by decapitation while God's name is being invoked. The animal's head must face the *qiblah*, and the slaughtering is to be done by a Muslim, who is clean—although it may be permissible at times to eat meat slaughtered by a Jew or Christian provided that the animal is killed according to the prescriptions of the religious law.[107] Hunting is not condoned as a pastime, but if indulged, prey must also be killed following the rules of animal slaughtering.[108] Accordingly, the Moriscos appear to have resisted purchasing meat in Christian markets, for which they were brought before the Inquisition.

Altogether, the Moriscos appear to have followed the spirit and letter of the religious law with regard to edible or inedible animals. They abstained from eating carnivorous animals such as wolves, tigers, lions and from eating domesticated animals such as donkeys, horses, cats, dogs, and pigs. Inasmuch as the consumption of pork and bacon was common among their Christian neighbors, the Moriscos were often impelled to demonstrate their Christianity or lack of it be eating or refusing to eat them. Nonconsumption of pork was often cause for appearing before the tribunals.

Beverages of all sorts were also regulated by the religious law. Even certain licit beverages were subject to regulations in that they should not be mixed—for instance, the juice of dates should not be mixed with that of raisins. If a rat or similar animal falls in honey, water, oil, or other liquid, it should be discarded.[109] The stiffest regulations were imposed on alcoholic beverages, which were totally prohibited. Prophetic traditions were invoked with regard to the seriousness of imbibing wine and the danger accruing therefrom. A tradition attributed to a scholar says: "Wine remains in the body of its imbiber for forty days; and if he dies during that time, he will die as an unbeliever and will go to Hell."[110] Another tradition states that God will curse the cultivator of a vineyard for the purpose of making wine, will curse the one who cares for the vineyard, and will curse the vendor, the carrier, the treader of grapes, and others who are involved in making and selling wine. The whole act of making wine is a major sin, and the income derived therefrom is forbidden (*ḥarāmes).*[111]

Didactic stories were built around the danger of imbibing wine. "The Story of the Wine Drinker'[112] shows the gravity of imbibing wine. It is related on the authority of the traditionist Mālik Ibn Dīnār (d. 748), who says that after he performed the rite of pilgrimage (*elḥajje*), he heard a voice saying that all who performed the pilgrimage would be forgiven by God except 'Abd al-Raḥmān Ibn Muḥammad al-Balkhi, with whom God is angered and displeased. This aroused Ibn Dīnār's curiosity and he vowed not to leave Mecca until he had identified 'Abd al-Raḥmān. After inquiry, he was informed that 'Abd al-Raḥmān was a good servant of God (*buwen servidor de-Allāh*), who observed prayer, fasting, and almsgiving, besides being wholly devoted to God. Ibn Dīnār became the more puzzled and inquired where he could find him. He was informed and went searching for him. He found a youth (*mansebo*) with his hands tied around his neck (*peskuweso*) screaming and saying, "This is the reward of those who disobey their parents." Ibn Dīnār was the more surprised when the youth addressed him by his name; when Ibn Dīnār inquired how he knew it, the youth said that he saw it in a dream. Ibn Dīnār then asked him to tell his story, and the youth said that when he was young, he imbibed wine and was irreligious and disobedient. Once in a state of drunkenness, he hit his father, who had tried to make him a Muslim through the confession of faith—that is, through the utterance of the formula, "There is no God but God, and Muḥammad the Messenger of God." After that incident, he left home in remorse and devoted himself to God for the following twenty years, pleading with the Almighty to forgive his sin, to no avail. Ibn Dīnār persuaded the man to go to his father, who forgave him after he uttered the confession of faith. The youth died thereafter, and was given a Muslim burial.

Other reasons are given for not drinking wine. It is related that a man asked a scholar, "Why does not the Moor drink wine?" The scholar responded, "What is the best jewel of the body?" The man said, "The judgment of a person." Then the scholar answered, "The Moor does not drink wine in order to preserve that jewel."[113]

Finally, games of chance were interdicted by religious law, and the Moriscos took warning against games such as chess (*asedrese*) and poker (*porkes*). They invoked Muḥammad as saying that any person who plays any game for profit or pleasure is unbeliever in the eyes of God and of His Prophet. His good deeds are neither received nor acknowledged by God. Furthermore, if a gambler were to go home and use water for ablution (*alwaḍu*) as a prelude to prayer, his ablution be as invalid as if he had used the blood of a pig. Even onlookers of games and gamblers are sinful and are like those who desire their own mothers.[114]

The Moriscos aspired to a life of austerity, devotion, and strict social behavior. The best man is the one who is kind to people and whose tongue and hands can be trusted.[115] The best deed by a Muslim is the one done in secret, in fear and love of God.[116] Right conduct resides in the avoidance of seventeen mortal sins: not believing in Allah; disobedience to parents; killing a fellow Muslim; eating dead animals; eating blood; eating pork; committing adultery; gambling; usury (*loghoro*); acting as procurers for unbelievers; false testimony; lying; falsehood; drinking wine; usurping orphans' property; doubting God's mercy; and cheating fellow Muslims.[117] God forgives major sins if the person repents and desists from evil.[118] But in the last account, good deeds will prevail in the meticulous performance of prescribed religious obligations, which will count in the Day of Judgment when all creatures will be called by their names.[119]

Judging by the number of manuals for instructing the religious obligations, it is reasonable to assume that the Moriscos were deeply attached to Islamic practices and that neither forced conversion nor the harsh measures imposed by Christian authorities deterred them from their religious convictions. On the contrary, it appears that both forced conversion and the harsh measures made the Morisco more determined to preserve his religious and cultural traditions. Religion permeates every aspect of his life, making it difficult if not impossible to differentiate between the secular and the religious behavior of the Morisco. This fusion of secular and spiritual posed a seemingly insurmountable problem for the Morisco vis-à-vis his Christian neighbors, who hardly appreciated his stand. Determining whether the Morisco always acted religiously with full consciousness is problematic since daily actions are usually performed routinely without much reflection or awareness of their symbolic value or religious significance. This is exactly what the Morisco Núñez Muley tried to convey to the Christian authorities in expounding the unreasonableness of their measures against the Morisco's whole way of life. Thus, whether bathing is a religious or a hygienic act in a setting such as that of the Morisco is a moot question. This is true of food and drink and other areas of life where the line between religious habit and custom is very fine. Thus, it was a matter of attitude and willingness to understand. To the Christian, as much a victim of history and circumstance as the Morisco, every exterior manifestation of the Morisco was suspect. If the Morisco, for instance, were to put on a clean shirt on Friday, this simple act of wearing a clean shirt or taking a bath evoked heresy in the mind of the Christian, who construed the whole act as a challenge to Christian doctrine.

In this connection and as part of Morisco basic beliefs, it is relevant to add that the Moriscos, like their fellow Muslims everywhere, conceived both Judaism and Christianity as revealed religions, with Islam assigned the mission of fulfilling God's covenant. This conception is articulated in the Qur'ān, the prophetic traditions, theology, jurisprudence, and religious polemics. For this reason Moriscos devoted ample space in Aljamiado literature to biblical figures—Abraham, Noah, Job, Moses, and others, including Christ and the Virgin Mary[120]—who were not only revered but considered bonafide Muslims, though they preceded historical Islam by centuries. The qualified recognition of both Judaism and Christianity includes, however, a difference with regard to their evolution or departure from the original divine plan. This firm doctrinal matter was opposed vehemently by Jews and Christians to the point of denying any validity to Islam and its founder.

Some of the issues separating Muslims, Jews, and Christians became almost an integral part of the faith of the Morisco. The Judeo-Christian denial of Islam as a revealed religion and of the prophecy of Muḥammad is rebutted by Muslims and Moriscos on charges that both Jews and Christians have not only deviated from the true Scriptures but adulterated them almost beyond recognition, adding and omitting things to suit their whims.[121] The Jews not only failed to recognize the prophecies of Jesus and Muḥammad whose coming was foretold in the Scriptures,[122] but continued the pretense of being the heirs of the earth by virtue of their descendance from Isaac, when actually the descendants of Ismā'īl—Arabs and Muslims—are the true heirs of mankind.[123] This is so because the Jews disobeyed God; as a consequence, they broke the Covenant with God and became accursed.[124]

Similarly, the Christians have committed many enormities in belief and practice. They failed to recognize the Prophet Muḥammad, whose coming as the Paraclete was announced by Jesus himself[125] and the prophets of old. Moreover, Christians were divided into many sects, each one contradicting the others. They did a great violence to God's unity by upholding the Trinity in which they made Jesus, a mere mortal and prophet, a god incarnate with the appellation of Father, Son, and Holy Spirit at one and the same time. This conception is a blasphemous innovation that has no foundation in either the Gospels or the Qur'ān—all of which give ample evidence of Christ's humanity as an apostle born miraculously to the Virgin Mary[126] and who, as a prophet, performed many miracles, as had other prophets and messengers.[127] Contrary to Christian conception, Christ was neither crucified nor killed even as a prophet, let alone as a god.[128] All this and other conceptions make the whole Christian doctrine and practices mere innovations of Paul, unbelievers, popes, and monks.[129] Moreover, Christian church ceremonies are noisy and irreverent, and the priests corrupt and adulterous.[130]

In sum, Islam is the one and only true religion, and the Qur'ān is God's Book (*alkitāb de-Allāh*),[131] admitting no other. Unlike the Judeo-Christian Scriptures, the Qur'ān is the Word of God and free from adulteration in any shape or form; further, it contains true beliefs and clear prescriptions of the religious obligations that will guide the faithful in this life and will prepare him for a life of bliss in the hereafter. These complex doctrinal matters are brought into sharp focus in the Morisco polemics.

5

The Polemics of the Moriscos

The confrontation of Islam and Christianity has had multifaceted dimensions from the seventh century to the present. This confrontation has at times been intense, resulting in vast destruction, loss of life, and great animosity. Religious differences were heightened by other considerstions—expansionism, politics, economics, and conflicting cultures. At first Islam expanded at the expense of Christianity, adapting to the culture and institutions of the conquered areas and forming a new and vigorous civilization, while Christianity was torn by religious controversies and political divisions which led ultimately to a theocentric view of the world and, finally, to cultural stagnation. This disparity between the two societies had enormous consequences, but these began to even out from the eleventh century onward when Western Christendom started a vigorous expansionist move into Islam, resulting in another process of adaptation to new realities. The issues separating the two religious groups remain much alive, the object of unending wars and debates adversely affecting such minorities as the Moriscos. One need merely outline the tense relations between Christianity and Islam in order to appreciate the position and temper of the supressed Moriscos as expressed in their polemics; such an appreciation must be understood within the larger context of the relationship between Christianity and the Islam under the following headings: Western image of Islam, Islamic image of the West, and the Morisco polemics.

WESTERN IMAGE OF ISLAM

Wars of the sword were fought concurrently with wars of the pen, which produced abundant polemic literature.[7] Polemic literature dates to the very inception of Islam and reached a peak in the Morisco period of the fifteenth and sixteenth centuries. Both Muslims and Christians were convinced of the righteousness of their cause and promoted it with every rhetorical device at their disposal. Evidence was often distorted beyond recognition. Both refused all compromise and ultimately sank into a polemic of self-righteousness characterized by flagrant double standards and arbitrary criteria. By this process, the differences separating Islam and Christianity were accentuated, and reconciliation became unattainable. No attempt was made to reach a balanced and detached judgment of the actual position of the other side. Thus, each group formed its own image of the other with fallacious arguments and with little or no regard for the truth.[2]

No doubt prolonged wars, attended by destruction and humiliation, contributed to this attitude, which began to take shape the moment Islam made its first inroads into Christian territory in the seventh century. Although Islam at first had the upper hand politically and militarily, expanding widely at the expense of Christianity, it labored from the outset at a disadvantage in defending itself against Christian and Jewish polemicists, who refused to concede any validity to Islam despite its contention that it was the continuation and culmination of the Judeo-Christian traditions, emanating from the same God and resting on the same foundations. Although Muslims held that the Scriptures of the Jews and Christians were adulterated by misguided adherents, they agreed nevertheless that these were important documents containing the essentials of Islam. This was persuasive enough for many Christians and Jews to embrace Islam. On the other hand, those who remained faithful to Judaism or Christianity denied Islam any validity, condemning it as a forgery perpetrated by a sensual man, an impostor, who could never be elevated to the rank of a virtuous man, let alone to that of a prophet. Moreover, the basic Islamic doctrines—belief in one God, the admission of Prophecy, and belief in the Day of Judgment—were dismissed as pretentions. Misrepresentation of facts, misinterpretation, and bitter attacks were the norm among Christian polemicists, even among those who knew much more about Islam than they were willing to admit. They represented Islam as an idolatrous worship or pernicious heresy. Its founder Muḥammad was an impostor who fabricated the Qur'ān, claiming that it was revealed to him by God. Whether acquainted with the Qur'ān or not, they dismissed it as a miscellany including abominable licenses that lead to perdition in this world and in the hereafter. In short, a pattern of vilification of Islam based upon preconceived notions had been set for centuries to come. Even when attempts to translate the Qur'ān were made in the twelfth century, they served to aid in the articulation of deep-rooted established views rather than to facilitate any new understanding. As an unwelcome minority, the Moriscos continued, long after their conversion to Christianity, to suffer the handicap of having descended from an enemy religion.

The genesis of Christian polemics against Islam is often traced to Saint John of Damascus (d. 749), a cleric and theologian who, interestingly enough, served at the Muslim court of the Umayyads of Damascus (661-750). Saint John appears to have enjoyed the confidence of the Umayyad ruler, who permitted him to speak openly. It is reported that in a dialogue with Muslims, Saint John defended Christianity, upholding it as the true religion vis-à-vis Islam, which he considered a Christian heresy at best and its founder a man far removed from prophecy. Although his assessment could not have been pleasing to Muslims, it included the generous admission that Islam was not alien to Christianity. In his *Chronicle,* the Byzantine Confessor Theophanes (ca. 758-818) expressed similar views and called Muḥammad "the ruler of the Saracens and a pseudo-prophet."[3] Another Eastern Christian named 'Abd al-Masīḥ Ibn Isḥāq al-Kindī (ninth century)—not to be confused with the philosopher al-Kindī—supposedly served the 'Abbāsid caliph al-Ma'mūn (813-833), defended Christianity, and attacked Islam in violent terms, maintaining that Muḥammad was a sensual and murderous man and that his religion was a forgery which had spread through violence and deceit. The attribution of such a statement to a man who served a Muslim caliph can be discounted altogether, although possibly other such statements may have been common among some Christians, who may have argued, further, that the Qur'ān had nothing new to offer.[4]

The attitude toward Islam reportedly enunciated by Saint John of Damascus, Theophanes, and al-Kindī may have shaped Christian thinking in the East and presumably reached the attention of Western Christians, particularly in Spain and Sicily. Western Christians built upon those derisive accounts of Islam and added their own diatribes. A treatise virulently attacking Islam is reported to have been written in the eighth century in Pamplona in northern Spain. Such a treatise became the basis for Christian attacks against Islam and may have been used by the Martyrs of Cordova in the ninth century.[5]

As far as can be ascertained, the Martyrs of Cordova represent an unusual case of clerical revolt under Muslim rule. Their complex story has all the earmarks of a pogrom at a time when Muslim-Christian relations in the Iberian Peninsula were undergoing some tensions. The process of arabization and Islamization was making headway to the point of exerting pressure on those who remained Christian. Furthermore, the relentless wars between Muslims and northern Christians contributed their share to the strain between the two communities. These factors, along with the underprivileged position of Christians and neo-Muslims in the state structure, were causes for both alarm and resentment—alarm for the potential loss of Christian identity and resentment at being deprived of the privileges and wealth of the country. These frustrations led eventually to an emotional explosion. What was significant about that explosion, however, was the fact that it was ignited accidentally by individual clerics who had neither a preconcieved plan nor the organization to engender a widespread revolt. As a result, those individuals remained isolated and even opposed by fellow, arabized Christians, who objected to their radical method in the face of heavy odds. Rightly or wrongly, these clerics were convinced that Christianity not only was being eroded by the arabization of its own adherents, but was threatened with extinction by the ever-increasing number of converts to Islam. This deep concern came to the fore when two clerics were put to death after they had denigrated Islam and its founder in public. The crisis began in about 850 when the monk Perfectus, who apparently knew Arabic, was asked by a group of Muslims what Christians thought of Christ and Muḥammad. Perfectus asserted the divinity of Christ, but suspended judgment on the Prophet Muḥammad. Pressed for a more direct answer, he implied that Muḥammed was a false prophet. This created a frenzy among the Muslim mob, which accused him of cursing the Prophet and for this he received the death penalty. In 850, a similar episode took place involving the Christian merchant John, who was accused of swearing by Muḥammad when selling his goods. His rival merchants accused him of ridiculing and invoking the name of the Prophet in vain, and the court decreed his death amidst a cheering and unyielding crowd.

These episodes created a convulsion among some Christian clerics and led to the rise of the Martyr Movement, whose members would insult and denigrate Islam in public, knowing that such defamation carried the death penalty. Some fifty individuals, including the two Christian girls Flora and Marí'a, perished. They greeted their own deaths with the strong belief that their end would earn them martyrdom, sainthood, and a certain place in Paradise. Members of the clergy, among them the cleric Eulogius (d. 859), encouraged such beliefs and sought more candidates. Finally, the government, in cooperation with leading bishops, introduced stern measures to put a stop to such conduct. Eulogius himself was asked to desist from his suicidal course, but refused, leaving the government no choice by enforcing the death penalty. With the death of this ringleader and under the pressure of the Christian clergy, the Martyr Movement died out, leaving a legacy of recrimination.

Eulogius and his friend Alvaro perpetuated that legacy in various writings. Both men justified the martyrs' behavior, arguing that to face death for combating the evil of Islam was a sacrifice praiseworthy in the eyes of God.[6] Their writings reflected the belief that Muḥammad was a false prophet and Islam a false religion. Eulogius relates that the disciples of Muḥammad watched for angels to descend after his death and carry his body away but, instead dogs came and devoured it. He also maintains that Muḥammad's life was mundane and could not possibly meet the requirements of prophecy and that his teaching as embodied in the Qur'ān was no more than spurious stories. Eulogius was supported in this by his friend Alvaro.[7] This kind of attack appears also in the French epic *La Chanson de Roland*, where Muhammad's death is attended by swine and dogs: "Mahomet, where foul swine rend him and dogs hale to and fro."[8]

The martyrs may have aroused the feeling of neo-Muslims (the Muwallads, born Muslims of Spanish ancestry), who felt that they were deprived of their rights and privileges by fellow Muslims. They rose in open revolt. One of their leaders, Ibn Ḥafṣūn, who rose in the South and threatened Cordova itself, reverted to Christianity and continued to challenge the government until the second decade of the tenth century. This significant erosion in the Muslim ranks would have continued had it not been for the intervention of the caliph 'Abd al-Raḥmān III (912-961), who succeeded in forging a homogeneous society in which the old guard and converts joined to determine the destiny of al-Andalus.

But local accommodation did not resolve the problem of universal antagonism between Islam and Christianity. Old traditions reappeared again and again in the writings of Western authors during the Crusades and Renaissance, down to recent times. The works of Daniel, Southern, and Schwoebel, among others, clearly convey Western attitudes toward Islam; only some of the highlights can be mentioned here. The eleventh century, which witnessed political disarray in Muslim ranks in both East and West, also saw the emergence of Western forces that struck at the very heart of Islam. Muslim reverses in Spain, the success of the Normans in Sicily, and the launching of a successful Crusade in the Holy Land were great blows to Islamic predominance in the West and, at the same time, gave credence to old myths about Islam and the Arabs, to which many new ones were added. People who participated in the Crusades and clerics who visited the Holy Land went back to Europe with accounts about the savagery and infidelity of the Muslims. They mixed fact with fiction to denigrate the Prophet Muḥammad and his religion. Muḥammad was said to have married Khadījah of Khurasan; she was actually a Meccan. He was further said to have been a commoner, an astrologer, musician, and magician, who could never have attained the stature of a prophet.[9] These and similar distortions were incorporated into contemporary writings, accepted by the twelfth- and thirteenth-century authors of the *Chanson de Gesta, Gesta Francorum,* the *Chanson d'Antioche*, and other works. In Spain, where the confrontation between Islam and Christianity had been relentless for centuries and where the crusading spirit was nurtured and brought to fruition, a number of new works attempted to prove the invalidity of Islam. Some of these were written by men "knowledgeable" in Islam who used their knowledge to denigrate it on the basis of textual evidence—the basis used by Ibn Ḥazm of Cordova (d. 1064)[10] to defend the superiority of Islam over all world religions. A converted Jew probably quite knowledgeable about Islam, Pedro Alfonso (12th c.), refused Islam on the basis of internal evidence. His near contemporary Peter the Venerable, Abbot of Cluny in southern France, visited Spain and in about 1142 commissioned Robert of Ketton, Herman of Dalmatia, and others to translate the Qur'ān into Latin.[11] Peter's purpose became apparent when a summary of the Islamic doctrine served as the basis of his *Summa totius haeresis Saracenorum* and his *Liber contra sectam sive haeresim Saracenorum*, in which he attempted to show textual inconsistencies and contradictions in the Islamic scriptures.[12] In the thirteenth century, Mark of Toledo translated the Qur'ān for similar purposes.[13] This kind of refutation in "documentary evidence" was continued by Jiménez de Rada,[14] Alfonso X,[15] Peter Pascual,[16] Ramon Marti,[17] and others.[18] Their works included pejorative stories about the Prophet and Islamic doctrine.

This was done at a time of Western awareness of the cultural superiorities of Islam and at a time when a considerable number of Arabic scientific works had been translated into Latin. But even while Arabic scientific lore was exerting an enormous impact on Western thought and effecting the outlook of Western man toward the physical and metaphysical worlds, there was little change in Western attitudes toward Islam and its adherents. On the contrary, the blurred Western image of Islam was being distorted further through the intellectualization of its preconceived demerits. Although leading Western writers studied and quoted the works of Muslim scientists and philosophers, invoking their authority on this or that point, they still gave full credence to stories and anecdotes reviling Islam and its followers. Even a cursory look at the works of some leading authors shows this unmistakable tendency. Alfonso X (1252–1284), a king and scholar who lived in an environment permeated by Arabic culture and whose numerous writings were translations and imitations of Arabic works, exemplifies the general Christian attitude toward Islam. In his *Crónica General de España,* Alfonso considers the Arab occupation of Spain as marked by horror, pillage, destruction, and slavery, and the "moros" as vile, cruel, and deceitful people.[19] The prophet Muḥammad "was well-versed in the art of magic," and learned from the monk Juan all those things that were against God; he deceived by means of charms and magical tricks, he wrote many falsehoods in the Qur'ān, and was followed by unhappy and bedeviled people. When he died, his resurrection was expected within three days, but this never took place; on the eleventh day, his body was found eaten by dogs.[20] Similarly, Thomas Aquinas, who accepted much of the thinking of Islamic philosophers, saw no validity in Islam, and no legitimacy in the prophecy of Muḥammad. The same attitude is conveyed by Roger Bacon (ca. 1210-1294), whose *Opus Majus* frequently invokes the authority of Arab scientists and philosophers such as al-Kindī, al-Fārābī, Ibn Sīnā, Abū Ma'shar, Ibn al-Haytham, al-Ghazālī, and Ibn Rushd.[21] Equally interesting is the attitude of the great Florentine poet Dante (d. 1321), who in *The Divine Comedy* and other works displays an awareness and recognition of the merit of Arabic culture and at the same time a great aversion to Islam and its founder. Dante considers Averroes, al-Ghazālī, and Saladin to be virtuous men in Limbo, but Muḥammad and his son-in-law are assigned to the Ninth Circle of Hell for having been "the sowers of scandals and schisms."[22]

This aversion toward Islam intensified after the Ottoman Turks' conquest of Constantinople in 1493. References to Moros, Saracens, or Arabs were replaced by the generic term *Turks*, the object of such familiar pejoratives as "villianous," "barbarous," and a visitation from God for the sins of Christendom.[23]

The Turks' subsequent advance into eastern Europe and siege of Vienna in 1529 generated fervent rhetoric for an all-out crusade against the infidels. Anti-Islamic traditions found a place in Spanish, French, Italian, German, English, and other European literature. Christian Spain, in particular, was alarmed at Turkish ascendancy and vented its concern against its Morisco minority in the belief that they were in collusion with the Turkish infidels.

Discussion of Islamic elements and themes in European literature would fill several monographs; space permits only some broad references here. Early English literature contained the tradition that Muḥammad did not actually have the Angel Gabriel as an intermediary with God; rather, he had trained a white pigeon to sit on his shoulder, pick grains from his ear, and pass for an angel.[24] The English poet John Lydgate (d. ca. 1451) refers to Muḥammad as a false prophet who was devoured by swines while drunk.[25] Shakespeare inquires, "Was Mahomet inspired by a dove?"[26] In fact, the dove received the appellation of maumet or mammet, a corruption of the word *Muḥammad*, which came to mean puppet.[27] Francis Bacon refers to Muḥammad as a miracle monger and was responsible for the proverb, "If the mountain will not come to Mahomet, Mahomet will go to the mountain."[28]

In France, in addition to the attitude reflected in the *Chanson de Roland*,[29] other traditions denigrated Islam and its founder. As late as the eighteenth century, Voltaire portrays Muḥammad, in *Mahomet, ou le fanatisme*, as an imposter, tyrant, and libertine. This image of Islam and its founder was not limited to an intellectual elite, but filtered down to all levels of society. If this was true among Europeans who had scarcely any contact with Muslims, one would expect it to be more passionate among the Spanish. When the Spanish Reconquest was completed, the remaining Muslims—known first as Mudejars and then as Moriscos—were oppressed by the forces of religion, ideology, politics, and economics and became pawns in the settlement of old and new accounts. Clerics and writers of the period kept the religious controversy alive and added to it a racist philosophy, implying that Moriscos lacked purity of blood (*limpieza de sangre*). They considered the Moriscos worshipers of an evil religion, paying more lip service to the Christian faith after conversion by force.

ISLAMIC IMAGE OF THE WEST

The Morisco had his own prejudices borne out of a long history of self-defense. He was faced with a double-edged sword presenting two unlikely alternatives: he could assimilate into a society that did not accept him or he could live in expectation of a return to the golden days of Islam when his ancestors enjoyed supremacy in Spain. The Moriscos opted for adherence to old traditions on the strength of history. For an appreciation of their position, it may be helpful to point to some of the factors underlying their attitude.

Historically, relations between Christians and Muslims were characterized by feelings of mutual antagonism. After the almost categorical Christian refusal to accept Islam as a religion and its founder as one among the prophets of old, Islam—although accommodating some Christian beliefs—assumed in practice a less tolerant attitude toward Christians and Christianity. As a rule, Christians living in East or West were designated as *Rūm*, and on occasion Western Christians were known as *Ifranjah, Firanjah,* or *al-Firanj*. Both terms—*Rūm* and *Ifranjah*—invoked repulsion in the mind of a Muslim.[30] A Christian ruler, whoever he might be, was the king of the *Rūm* (*malik al-Rūm*) and a tyrant (*ṭāghiyah)* from whom no virtue could be expected.[31] Christians were infidels (*kuffār)* living in the Abode of War (*dar al-ḥarb),* as opposed to the Abode of Peace (*dār al-islām),* which is the locus of Islam. As ingrates representing a danger to peace, they ought to be fought as a matter of communal duty (*farḍ 'alā al-kifāyah*).[32] This attitude toward Christians evolved and was widely articulated during and after the Crusades.

It should be emphasized that this general antipathy toward non-Muslims, and particularly toward Christians, did not prevent a modicum of peaceful coexistence. More often than not, Christian communities lived unperturbed under Muslim rule in both East and West and had the full protection of the law in return for the payment of a poll tax (*jizyah*) and land tax (*kharāj*). However, the prolonged confrontation between Christianity and Islam, particularly in the western Mediterranean, polarized the two religious communities, creating prejudices that went beyond juridico-theological considerations. Appellations of savagery, barbarism, and cruelty were hurled by members of one group at the other regularly, notwithstanding the long and intimate relationship that should have established fairer views. No doubt the psychology of war made it expedient to deny humanity to each other. Muslims, conceiving the earth as divided into seven zones, invoked the climatic factor to show the baseness and crudity of Western man, particularly the *Firanji* of France, Germany,, and northern Europe, who appeared on the scene during the Crusades. Ibn Khaldūn (d. 1406) of Tunis, who derives his knowledge from the works of previous geographers, articulates the notion that regions in the extreme north and south are unsuitable for civilization due the excessive cold in the north and excessive heat in the south. Their inhabitants are crude, closer to animals than civilized beings. These regions include the first zone running along the equator, hot and intemperate, inhabited by black people with little or no civilization.[33] The opposite climatic extreme includes the seventh zone—comprising England, Poland, Finland, Russia, and Bulgar[34] —and the sixth zone—containing France, Germany, Saxony, Hungary, part of Poland and Russia, portions of the Black Sea, and the Khazars, Bulgars, Turks, Gog and Magog.[35] The remaining zones—the second, third, fourth and fifth, inhabited mostly by Muslims—have been the site of great civilizations. The fourth zone is the most temperate and cultivated region; the third and fifth zones bordering in the fourth are relatively temperate; the sixth and second zones are far from temperate, however; and the first and seventh zones are least so. Ibn Khaldūn concludes: "Therefore, the sciences, the crafts, the buildings, the clothing, the foodstuffs, the fruits, even the animals and everything that comes into being in the three middle zones are distinguished by their temperate character. The human inhabitants of these zones are more temperate [well proportioned] in their bodies, color, character, qualities and general conditions."[36]

Such notions may have been a factor in influencing Muslims' attitude toward northern Europeans. Muslims had felt superior to the *Ifranjah* (Franks), or northern Europeans, long before their encounters in the Crusades. Muslims in both East and West recruited a large number of slaves from northern and eastern Europe, such as the Ṣaqālibah (Slavs) in Spain, who served their masters as eunuchs, praetorian guards, and servants. The great historian-geographer al-Mas'ūdī (d. 956) lumps together the Franks, Slavs, Lombards, Spaniards, Gog and Magog, Turks, Khazars, Bulgarians, Galacians, and others by saying simply that they are descendants of Japhet and are white as opposed to the black people, who are descendants of Ham. He notes that the Franks and the Galacians are warlike people, well-disciplined, and loyal to their kings.[37]

The historian-scientist Ṣā'id of Toledo (d. 1070), who was influenced by geographic determinism, declared that northern Europeans were more like animals than human beings owing to extreme cold making their temperaments chilly and their humor rude; he describes them as having huge bodies, lacking sagacity, and evincing ignorance and stupidity. Slavs, Bulgars, and other neighbors share these characteristics.[38] His near contemporary, the geographer and philologist al-Bakrī (d. 1094), describes the Galacians as inhabitants of an "arid land; they are treacherous, dirty, and bathe once or twice a year; then with cold water. They never wash their clothes until they are worn out because they claim that the dirt accumulated as the result of their sweat softens their body."[39] He dismisses Brittany by saying that the language is unpleasant to the ear; the people are ugly, have bad character, and include many who steal from the French and die on the cross when apprehended.[40]

One of the most interesting portrayals of Westerners is that of Usamah Ibn Munqidh (d. 1188), an Eastern official and historian, who met Crusaders in the Holy Land. He saw the Franks as like animals possessing courage and fighting prowess. He refers to the new immigrants to the Holy Land as having rude character, and provides illustrations drawn from his own observation of the crude state of medical knowledge among the Crusaders. He relates that a Frankish physician cut a leg on which an abcess had grown, causing the man's death. A woman afflicted with imbecility was diagnosed as possessed by the devil; the physician recommended for her cure the shaving of her head, and as her case worsened, he made a deep cruciform incision on her head, presumably to chase the devil away, but the woman died in the process.[41]

But acrimony was most intense at the religious level. Islamic polemics against Judaism and Christianity began with the founder of Islam, and were expressed in the Qur'ān and the prophetic traditions (*ḥadīth*). They were expanded by Muslim theologians and jurists over the centuries, resulting in an abundant literature[42] with a dual purpose: (1) self-justification, claiming Islam as a revealed religion whose place in history is to complement, if not to supersede both Judaism and Christianity, and (2) self-defense against Christians who not only denied Muslim claims to superiority but the very validity of Islam. Only a few highlights of this controversy relating to Morisco polemic can be noted here.

When, beginning in 610, Muḥammad announced his revelations, he became involved in controversies not only with his fellow pagan Arabs but with arabized Jews and Christians. In response to Muḥammad's claim that he was the Seal of the Prophets announced in the Old and New Testaments and that his new revelations constituted the continuation and culmination of past prophecies, Christians and Jews argued that there was no justification for these claims in Scriptures. They argued, further, that many Qur'ānic statements were not in consonance with Scriptures. For his part, Muḥammad insisted on the divine nature of the Qur'ān and referred repeatedly to the basic issues between the new monotheistic religion and its two sister religions, Judaism and Christianity. Speaking through the angel Gabriel, Muḥammad considered Jews, Christians, and Sabaeans as deserving God's reward as long as they believe in God and the Day of Judgment and they do right.[43] He went on to say that Paradise is not limited to Jews and Christians[44] and that the conflicting claims of Jews and Christians are false, since Allāh alone will be the ultimate judge in the Day of Resurrection.[45] Muḥammad noted that God appeals to Jews and Christians to recognize the new Prophet, "O people of the Scripture! Now has our messenger come unto you to make things plain after an interval of messengers."[46] God shows His displeasure when He warns the true believers, "O ye who believe, take not the Jews and Christians for friends."[47]

Prophetic traditions *(ḥadīth)* and Qur'anic tenets reiterate that both Judaism and Christianity are revealed religions possessing true scriptures, even though their adherents have deviated from both the letter and spirit of Holy Scriptures. In so doing, they have become unbelievers *(kuffār),* but they are not barred from redemption. Christians and Jews were assigned an intermediary status between belief and unbelief and tolerated in the Islamic community as "people of Covenant" *(ahl al-dhimmah)* or "people of revealed Scripture" *(ahl al-kitāb).* Jurists defined their legal status, and theologians determined their place in the hierachy of potential but misguided believers.[48]

The rationale of the jurist-theologian Ibn Ḥazm (d. 1064) of Cordova illustrates the attitude of a European Muslim who had witnessed the intense confrontation between Christianity and Islam. Ibn Ḥazm was the ablest polemicist not only in Western Islam, but in the whole Muslim world. In his work *Denominations and Sects,*[49] he used logic and scriptural documentation to refute the major philosophical systems and other world religions; his aim was to assert the validity of Islam and its superiority over all other world religions. An outstanding feature of his method was the systematic use of Judeo-Christian scriptures, showing their inconsistencies, contradictions, and lack of authenticity and veracity are deemed unquestionable in the light of history and internal evidence. He wrote at a time when Spanish Islam was in a state of disarray following the fall of the Umayyad dynasty in 1031. Elsewhere, he laments the erosion of the Islam of his day, complaining that Muslim rulers allow the tongues of infidels and polytheists to be free.[50]

Ibn Ḥazm attacked both Judaism and Christianity, maintaining that their scriptures were hopelessly adulterated. The Jews had been scattered and their scriptures destroyed; Christians had lived in secrecy for almost four centuries.[51] The result of this dislocation and cultural turmoil was adulteration, forgetfulness, omissions, and additions. He collated some seventy passages of the four Gospels to show textual discrepancies. He argues that such a religion cannot have a continuous and authentic tradition and surely contains untold distortion.[52] Many Christian beliefs and practices—the doctrine of the Trinity, the divinity of Christ, the mixing of divinity and humanity, the incarnation, and sacrament—are innovations; and the four Gospels are full of contradictions and lies.[53] Furthermore, the Christians' version of the Old Testament (Torah) is different from that of the Jews,[54] a fact which Ibn Ḥazm demonstrates through numerous examples relating to the different ages given to several biblical characters.[55] He concludes that discrepancies and contradictions such as these could not have emanated from God or His prophets or even from well-informed, truthful persons.[56] It follows that one or both versions of the Torah are false, which places the very bases of Jewish and Christian doctrine in grave doubt. Moreover, both versions contain shameful lies, thus reducing Judaism and Christianity to nothing. He ends by praising God for the great gift of Islam, whose doctrine is devoid of any lie or error and which was transmitted by a continuous and authentic tradition through His truthful Messenger Muḥammad.[57]

This is tantamount to a dismissal of both Judaism and Christianity, but Ibn Ḥazm goes on to a more detailed scrutiny of the Gospels, showing the various discrepancies found therein with regard to Christ's genealogy, his temptation by the Devil, and humanity. Matthew's version of the geneaology of Christ departs in various points from that in the Old Testament.[58] Luke contradicts Matthew.[59] Ibn Ḥazm compares Matthew and Luke concerning Christ's encounter with the Devil and the reported temptation of Christ.[60] Finally, he objects to such reports, saying that Christ could not have allowed himself to be taken from one place to another by the Devil, particularly if one grants, as Christians do, that Christ is God—even for a prophet, temptations to worship the devil or to grant him the power of creating a king of the world are not feasible.[61] The Christian argument to the effect that the Devil was addressing himself to the humanity in Christ is rejected by Ibn Ḥazm, who maintains that the divinity and humanity of Christ cannot be split arbitrarily.[62] Moreover, Matthew (4:12–22), Mark (1:14–20), Luke (5:1–11), and John (1:35–42) differ among themselves in reporting these incidents with respect to time, place, and conditions; these inconsistencies cannot be attributed either to God or to true prophets.[63]

The same contradictions occur in the Gospels in the treatment of such subjects as abrogation or no abrogation, circumcision, and sabbath.[64] The attribution of divinity to Christ is traditionally abhorrent to Islam; Ibn Ḥazm refutes this notion on the basis of the same scriptures which he considers adulterated, stating that Christ refers to himself as a mortal being and the son of man, and thus it is absurd to equate Jesus with God and to conceive him as representing Father, Son, and Holy Spirit simultaneously.[65] It is also absurd to maintain that God died.[66] It was the apostles who perpetuated the notion of the divinity of Christ and who arrogated to themselves divine authority, thereby corrupting the reality of Christ's religious mission.[67]

Essentially, Ibn Ḥazm reaffirms established Islamic doctrine with respect to the state of the Judeo-Christian scriptures, the permissibility of abrogation, and the denial of Christ's divinity and the whole concept of the Trinity. However, what is novel in his treatment is his textual analytic method. He draws on deep familiarity with the writings of his adversaries to reach conclusions often filled with acrimony and irreverence. Christian polemics adopted such an approach against Islam only after twelfth-century translation of the Qur'ān at the behest of Peter the Venerable.[68] Thereafter, the use of scriptural texts became the chief method in religious arguments, an example of which is Alfonso X's biography of Muḥammad and his ascension to heaven (*mi'rāj*)—both of which no doubt paraphrased Arabic sources.[69] After the success of the reconquest in the thirteenth century and the subsequent preponderance of Christians over Muslims, it may be assumed that Christians, in their eagerness to convert Muslims to Christianity, undertook the task of familiarizing themselves with Islamic scriptures if only to show to potential converts the fallacy of their religion. Thus, clerics learned Arabic to assist them in the task of conversion. Conversely, Muslims who resisted conversion found themselves obligated to defend their belief and to retort in kind, using the method of textual criticism inaugurated by their compatriot Ibn Ḥazm in the eleventh century.

Evidence of such an approach can be seen in some Arabic works that appear to have served as models for Aljamiado literature in approach and content. Discovery of such writings would have comprised their very existence. The Moriscos appear to have responded to presistent attack not only by defending themselves but also by disseminating basic Islamic beliefs. Muslims had always conceived their religion to be a continuation and culmination of the Judeo-Christian traditions, Islam being the third and last cycle of a divine plan and abrogating Christianity in the same manner the latter was revealed to abrogate Judaism. In spite of the general belief that Jews and Christians tampered with their own scriptures to a point of unbelief, there is still specific reference in their scriptures attesting to the validity and mission of Islam in the divine plan. Only through misinterpretation of those texts, not to mention omissions and additions, was Islam denied its rightful place as a true religion superseding both Judaism and Christianity.

Disputation of this nature gained currency in Western Islam. Abū-l-

Walīd al-Bajī (d. 1081), a friend of Ibn Ḥazm, defended the Islamic religion in response to a letter written by a French monk to al-Muqtadir (d. 1082), the Muslim ruler of Saragossa. He was followed by Qāḍi 'Iyāḍ (d. 1149), who wrote a book on the merit of Muḥammad on the basis of supposed refences to him in the Old and New Testaments, emphasizing his miracles and concluding with an assurance of the superiority of Islam over other religions.[70] The work influenced subsequent authors, including Morisco writing.[71] Of equal importance are the work of the Cordovan al-Khazraji (12th c.),[72] *The Triumph over the Cross (Kitāb maqāmi 'al-Ṣulbān),* and that of the mystic Ibn Sab'īn (d. 1271), who wrote an anti-Christian treatise.[73] The Moriscos relied heavily upon the polemical tradition.

The Confirmation of Religion (ta'yīd al-Millah) is significant in this connection. It is an Arabic treatise against the Jews written in 762/1360 by Abū Zakariyā Yaḥyā b. Ibrāhīm b. 'Umar, known as Muḥammad al-Rāqilī, who lived in the province of Aragón and died about 1405.[74] This treatise shows great affinity in form and content to the Aljamiado manuscript BNM 4944, which will be analyzed, (see below). Defensive in character, the treatise attempts to nullify what the author conceives to be the distortion and lies of the Jews of his day against Islam. He draws his documentation from the Torah, the Psalms, and the Book of the Prophets in order to show not only the distortion of the scriptures, but the revocation of the covenant entered into between the Jews and God. In the introduction to the *Confirmation of Religion,* the author laments that since he must live among polytheists and his own ignorant and ill-equipped co-religionists, he is compelled to study the scriptures of his adversary in order to silence and dispel any doubt about the validity of Islam. From internal evidence in the scriptures, the author deduces that the Jews rebelled repeatedly against God, failed to fulfill sacred promises, and were ungrateful for divine bounty, after which God punished them by voiding the covenant He earlier made with them. The body of the treatise is divided into five sections, each containing several chapters devoted to specific issues.

The first section[75] is devoted to the question of whether the descendants of Isaac or those of Ismā'īl are the actual recipients of God's favors and blessings. This question was an issue not only between Muslims and Jews, but between Muslims and Christians as well. In the Judeo-Christian view, Muslims were the descendants of the concubine Hagar; hence they were bastards, or "agarenos."[76] Thus, Moriscos took a special interest in this questions.[77] Muslims maintained that it was Ismā'īl, the son of Hagar, and not Isaac, the son of Sarah, who was favored by God despite the fact that Hagar was a slave given by Sarah to Abraham. He was the first offspring and the legitimate descendant of Abraham. The Jewish argument that Sarah, the mother of Isaac, is better than Hagar by virtue of her status is contrary to God's promises, which were fulfilled by the descendants of Ismā'īl and not by those of Isaac, as both the history and the territorial situation of the day demonstrate: Ismā'īl's descendants, the Arabs, and not the descendants of Isaac, have domain over the Holy Land and other vast territories.

The second section[78] examines the Jewish denial that there was any divine revelation subsequent to that given to them. The author attempts to show the fallacy of such views, maintaining that God revealed himself to various people over a long period of time, abrogating some decrees and replacing them with others. Such changes are construed by the Jews to indicate that God changed His mind, thereby compromising His Divine Will, but such a construction is false.

In the third section,[79] the author demonstrates that the coming of Muḥammad was foretold in the Jewish scriptures. He invokes the authority of Deut. 18:16–19, saying that those verses refer specifically to Muḥammad and Muslims and not to Job and the Jews.[80] He also calls attention to the prophecies of Daniel (Psalms 71:12) and those of Jesus (John 14–16) foretelling the coming of the Holy Spirit, which is Muḥammad.

To give credance to this interpretation, the author takes up in the fourth section[81] the miracles of Muḥammad, contrasting them with those performed by previous prophets. Among those miracles are the inimitability of the Qur'ān, the splitting of the moon into two halves, supplying ten thousand men with water which flowed from his fingers, making the sun stand still, and others. All of these were extraordinary feats, greater than any performed before, and they demonstrate the obvious superiority of Islam and Muslims over Judaism and Jews.

In the fifth section,[82] the author continues his diatribe against Jews, pointing to their infidelity and their rebellion against God, who relegated them to perdition, servility, and humiliation until the Day of Judgment. This is why God did not speak to them about Paradise, Hell, the Day of Judgment, resurrection, rewards, and punishment in the hereafter. Jews have been incapable of adhering to the prescriptions related to worldly affairs, committing many sins—such as failure to observe the Mosaic Commandments, fornication, transgression of the Sabbath, assassination of prophets, worship of the golden calf and other idols, adultery, incest, and other crimes. Al-Rāqilī concludes *The Confirmation of Religion* by calling upon the Jews to repent and believe in Christ and Muḥammad as the messengers of God, reiterating the biblical warnings ordaining their doom and reaffirming that Muslims alone are heirs to divine legacies as foretold in the scriptures.

Of great historical relevance also to the Aljamiado polemic contained in BNM 4944 are the works of Muḥammad al-Qaysī and that of Fray Anselmo Turmeda, known as 'Abdallah al-Tarjumān. Al Qaysī is described in the manuscript as a cultured man (*sabidor*) from al-Zaytunah Mosque in Tunis who served as secretary in Lérida,[83] where he came into contact with Moriscos and Christians and the religious issues separating them. He wrote an anti-Christian polemic[84] in which he appears to have relied on a certain 'Abdallah al-Kātibo or 'Abdallah al-asīr,[85] who in all probability was Fray Anselmo Turmeda (d. 1424), a renegade who served at the Tunisian court and wrote *Tuḥfah*, consisting of an autobiography and a refutation of Christianity.[86] Al-Qaysī's manuscript consists of three folios limited to refuting the Christian view concerning the divine and human natures of Christ. Al-Qaysī maintained that Christ was mortal being and a prophet, not a god. His birth from a virgin, his miracles, and his other endowments were no more extraordinary than those of other prophets. The births of Adam and Eve were as extraordinary, if not more so than that of Christ; yet neither one was considered God.[87] Furthermore, should it be allowed that Christ is God, it is inconceivable that God should constitute a trinity or a compound existence (*wujūd)*, science (*'ilm),* and life (*hayāh)*—which correspond to father (existence), son (science), and Holy Spirit (life).[88] For Al-Qaysī, to say that divinity is science and humanity is the body of Christ and that these can be combined in the same way water, milk, and wine are combined is fallacious, constituting an abomination that only an ignoramus can accept. Al-Qaysī elaborates on these points: Science is a quality that cannot be transferred from one thing to another. Moreover, the whole concept of mixture of science and body is absurd since mixture is a propriety while science and body are not. Al-Qaysī concludes that Christ was one of God's creatures in whom the power of God was made manifest through extraordinary deeds such as resurrection, the power of healing, and other miracles.

Turmeda may have served as a bridge between two warring religions by virtue of his dual Islamic-Christian background, his bilingualism, and his extensive travels through and exposure to both Christian and Islamic cultures. Born in Mallorca, Turmeda traveled to Lérida in Aragón, Barcelona, Lombardy, Sicily, and finally, Tunis, where he became a Muslim and a staunch defender of the new faith. His *Tuḥfah* reveals his early curiosity about the identity of the Paraclete mentioned in John (14:16, 16:7), identified by Islamic tradition with Muḥammad or Aḥmad since the Greek *Paraclete* and the Arabic *Aḥmad* both mean "praised" or "laudable." Turmeda relates that his elderly mentor, a priest, acknowledged that Muḥammad was the Paraclete, making Islam the true religion guaranteeing salvation on earth as well as in Heaven.[89] His mentor added that he would embrace it himself were it not for his advanced age.[90] Following this advice, Turmeda became Muslim at the age of thirty-five, married, and had a son whom he named Muḥammad.[91] He entered the service of the Tunisian ruler, becoming his translator (*tarjumān*). In 823/1420, he completed his *Tuḥfah*, the third section of which, using the gospels as a point of reference, is devoted to a refutation of Christianity. He follows Ibn Ḥazm's approach in both form and content, indulging in similar acidic attacks. Although he points to many corruptions and alterations in the holy texts, he does not hesitate to quote them profusely to illustrate the validity of Islam. He divides the work into the following nine headings.

1. Refutation of Christians.[92] In the manner of Ibn Ḥazm, Turmeda maintains on the basis of collation of texts that the Gospels are not in agreement and contain many lies and discrepancies. He condemns the authors for doing violence to Christ's religion, adding to, subtracting from, and modifying the work of God. They had hardly any acquaintance with Jesus; in fact, Turmeda notes that Matthew never met Christ, and Luke have become a

Christian at the hands of Paul, who was the enemy of true Christians.[93] The same is true of Mark, who was converted by Peter,[94] and John wrote in Greek.[95] Given all these factors, one can hardly rely upon them. Turmeda supplies examples of their distortions.[96]

2. Division of Christians into seventy-two sects.[97] Turmeda shows the inconsistency in Christian beliefs, accusing them of lies and calumnies. Some Christians conceive Christ as God and Creator, contrary to statements in Matthew 26:37–42 and John 11:41–42, which point out that Christ was a mortal who feared death and invoked the name of "his God." Other sects believe that Christ was both God and man—God on the part of his father and man on the part of his mother—and others claim such absurdities as his divine part descending to Hell and bringing Adam, Abraham, and the rest of the prophets to Heaven.

3. Corruption of Christian dogmas.[98] Turmeda condemns the five Christian articles of faith as false: (1) baptism as a prerequisite to Paradise questions the whereabouts of Abraham, Moses, and others who were not baptized; (2) the belief in the Trinity is an absurdity on general grounds and specifically also in the light of Mark's statements (13:4,32) recognizing Christ's limitations as a mortal being; (3) also absurd is the concept of incarnation, which claims that Christ is man on the part of his mother and God on the part of his Father—while his birth is a miracle, it is no more miraculous than the birth of Adam or the creation of angels; (4) the belief in the Eucharist *(qurbān)* is blasphemy for acknowledging bread as Christ's body and wine as his blood; and (5) confession of sin to a priest as a form of expiation is not mentioned by Christ or in the Gospels. This illicit practice allows priests and the pope to forgive sins, often in exchange for money or favors!

4. All in all, the whole Christian doctrine is a false one[99] and was written for the Christians by Peter. To say that God is one and yet that he has a son who is His co-Creator is a gross contradiction, constituting unbelief.

5. Turmeda proceeds to show that Christ is not God but a prophet.[100] The Gospels attest to his humanity in discussion of his genealogy. Turmeda wonders how he can be a god when God is primeval, does not beget, and is not begotten. How can he be Creator and created at one and the same time, particularly when Christ displayed such human qualities as eating, drinking, and cutting his nails and hair. He adds that intellectual proofs and textual evidence (*nuṣūṣ*) attest that God is not a body nor a substance nor an accident; He is indivisible and immutable. None of these qualities can be applied to Christ, who was born in a place and in time; time cannot have existed prior to the birth of its creator. In short, whoever is born in time and in a place is an animal and a son of animal being. Christ, a man and the son of man, is simply the noblest of the animal species.

6. Turmeda continues to show the enormous discrepancies in the Gospels with respect to events and their sequence, place, time, and other details.[101]

7. In sum, such statements attributed to Christ are lies and fabrications by the writers of the Gospels.[102]

8. Having demonstrated the fallacy of Christianity, Turmeda takes up Christian criticism of Islam.[103] To the argument that pious Muslims marry and monks do not, Turmeda answers that David had a hundred wives and Solomon a thousand, not to mention other prophets who were married and had children. Thus, Christians are in violation of the Scriptures and are followers of Paul (Corinthians 7:10–11), who ordered monogamy and celibacy for priests.[104] The same can be said about circumcision, which, according to Luke, was performed on Christ.[105] With respect to eating and drinking in Paradise, Christian objection is unfounded; according to Matthew 25:29 and Mark 16:25, Christ himself referred to much eating and drinking.[106] This does not preclude the existence of castles, jewels, and other things in Heaven.[107] Finally, to the Christian objection to Muslims' assuming names of prophets, Turmeda retorts that it is shortsighted and foolish for Christians to deny Muslims the names of mortals while they assume the names of angels such as Gabriel, Michael, and the rest.[108]

9. Turmeda concludes the *Tuḥfah* with the most important question—that is, confirmation of Muḥammad's prophecy on the basis of the Old and New Testaments.[109] This theme was reiterated by al-Qaysī[110] and the Moriscos.[111] He cites scriptures profusely, noting numerous references to the coming of Muḥammad. Among these were: when Hagar fled from Sarah, the angel ordered her to return, saying that her son Ismā'īl would become the most glorious of people and that one of his descendants, Muḥammad, would rule over mankind and spread his religion, Islam, through East and West among the most civilized people (Genesis 16:6–12); God told Moses that he would bring forth a prophet like him (Deut. 18:18); David said that such a prophet would come and would reign from sea to sea to the extreme point of the earth (Psalms 72:8); John (15:28) referred to the coming of the Paraclete, a Greek word which has the same meaning as Aḥmad (the Praised One).[112]

MORISCO POLEMICS: ALJEMIADO MANUSCRIPT BNM 4944

From such antecedents—Ibn Ḥazm, Rāqili, Turmeda, and al-Qaysī —one is able not only to gain insight into the cultural background and religious perspectives of the Moriscos, but also to understand the content and the method of the Morisco polemics, which preserve many of the traditional concepts.

An Aljamiado manuscript in the National Library of Madrid (BNM 4944) is a valuable document in this connection. The work was written in the fifteenth or sixteenth century and bears no name. An obvious explanation might be the enormous strictures imposed on the Moriscos. The work does refer to al-Qaysī[113] and to a certain 'Abdallah al-Asīr (the Captive),[114] who may be identified with Fray Anselmo Turmeda, known as 'Abdallah al-Tarumān.

BNM 4944 is a composite work consisting of two parts: the first an anti-Jewish polemic of some thirty-five folios,[115] and the second and longer,[116] a refutation of Christianity which appears to rely on al-Qaysī, who, in turn, appears to have relied on Turmeda and Ibn Ḥazm with respect not only to the points discussed but also to the method of argumentation—that is, stating the argument of the adversary, producing evidence to contradict it, and drawing the desired conclusion.

The anti-Jewish polemics are violent in tone, opening with an accusation that Jews attempted to kill Moses and in fact killed other prophets and pious men.[117] It continues with a systematic deliberation about Hagar, the mother of Ismā'īl, who had been given by Sarah to her husband Abraham; closely following Rāqilī, the Morisco argues that Hagar was as much a wife as Sarah; and that Ismā'īl and his descendants were the recipients of God's blessing and the legitimate heirs to the kingdom of mankind. Using the Torah as a basis, the author argues that when Sarah could not bear Abraham a child, she gave Hagar as a wife (*su-mujer*) to bear Abraham a child. When Hagar conceived and the damage (*injuriya*) was done, Abraham wanted to give her back, but Hagar fled, to be intercepted by the angel, who commended her to return to Sarah and to inform her that the angel of God had said that she would have a son, who will guide the people and will oversee them.[118] Subsequently, Ismā'īl was circumcised[119] and the angel told Abraham that he and his son would be the fathers of "many prophets."[120] When Sarah bore Isaac, at the age of ninety, God entered into a covenant with him which was far less binding than the blessing bestowed upon Ismā'īl; consequently, the Jewish pretension that Isaac's decendants are the heirs of the earth on the ground that God made a testament with Isaac and that Sarah was the wife and Hagar merely a servant does not conform to reality,[121] since a blessing has more force than a contract. The distance between God and the Jews was increased when the contract was violated through unbelief, killing of prophets, and other abominations.[122] Moreover, the Jews failed to acknowledge Christ[123] and committed a further enormity by not believing in Muḥammad.[124] The testimony of history supports the supremacy of the decendants of Ismā'īl, who occupy the Holy Land abandoned by the Jews and more recently wrested from the Christians.[125] All this disqualifies the descendants of Isaac as the heirs of the earth; only Muslims, the sons of Ismā'īl, are the true heirs.[126] The author returns to the legitimacy of Hagar, saying that her servitude does not diminish her dignity, for Joseph was made captive, but his position was not diminished thereby.[127] The allegation that a wife cannot give her husband another wife without blessing (*barakhā*) (sic) is false since Sarah herself married without blessing. Furthermore, the author notes biblical precedent in the case of Jacob, who also had children by servants, gifts of his sterile wives Rachel and Leah. Thus, the sons of Jacob, the forefathers of the Jews, were also the children of concubines.[128] In sum, the preeminence of the children of Ismā'īl was foretold. Ismā'īl had twelve children on whom God placed nobility and supremacy, through the Arabs ('arabes), over all people.[129] Once more, he reminds the Jews of the case of Jacob.[130]

The Jews committed many sins that would be hard to enumerate. In addition, their scriptures were destroyed by the Assyrian kings and rewritten later with many spurious passages. Moses himself broke the tablets containing the

Ten Commandments upon his return from the mountain after he saw his people worshiping the bull (golden calf).[131] As a result, their scriptures contain worldly things to satisfy their desire, omitting important things related to the hereafter such as the Last Day, Paradise, and Hell.[132] They were cursed by God, who bestowed His power, mercy, and grace on the descendants of Ismā'īl through Muḥammad and the Qur'ān, relegating the Jews to perdition until such time as they believe in Jesus as prophet and in Muḥammad as prophet and messenger of God.[133]

Now the author comes to the role of mission announced by the prophets of old. Moses was told about the coming of Muḥammad, whose followers would be the actual heirs of the earth.[134] God told Habaqūq that He would assist the children of Qaydar, descendants of Ismā'īl and ancestors of the Arabs, with angels, white horses, and arms and would submit people to Islam.[135] The author also mentions two knights: the one riding on an ass refers to Christ; the other, on a camel, to Muḥammad.[136] The miracles of Muḥammad—such as the splitting of the moon, supplying water from his fingers to ten thousand men and beasts, the closing of the cave in the face of his pursuers, making a barren sheep give milk, and other marvels—were not tricks or works of magic, but supernatural deeds that are the equal and even superior to any miracle performed by a prophet of old.[137] And there is the miracle of the spread of Islam.[138] Isaiah, Amos, and Jeremiah predicted the anger and curse of God upon the Jews.[139] Thus, the Jews have no hope of regaining their inheritance at the coming of the Messiah. Any Muslim should thank God for not having been made an infidel and a cursed Jew.[140]

This anti-Jewish polemic is a rendition of al-Rāqilī's *Confirmation of Religion*, which is closely followed with respect to form, tone, and content. The anti-Christian polemic proceeds with less harshness, appearing quite conciliatory in an attempt, perhaps, to find common ground with Christianity. Like the anti-Jewish polemic, it has the definite purpose of strengthening Moriscos' faith in the face of attacks by Christian polemicists. In fact, the author states, "I wish to demonstrate the blindness of the *goyim* for all those who will read this book so that they may know and understand how they should dispute with them and what is their belief."[141] An interesting feature of the polemic is a dialogue between a Muslim and a Christian, each of whom states his case and the point preoccupying him.

The anti-Christian polemic, transliterated by Cardaillac, consists of sixty-five folios[142] with the following major headings: a dispute with Christians,[143] discord among Christians (*dekonkordamiyento*),[144] the dispute of al-Qaysī with a priest,[145] a chapter dealing with the birth of Jesus,[146] a chapter on the Trinity,[147] and a letter of 'Umar Ibn 'Abd al-'Azīz to Emperor Leon.[148]

The treatise deals basically with traditional concepts concerning the person and nature of Christ, his resurrection, the Trinity, and other questions dealt with previously by Ibn Ḥazm and 'Abdallah al-Tarjumān. Further, it defends Islam and contrasts the two religions in beliefs and observances, attempting to illuminate the differences between the two.

In the dispute with Christians, the Morisco insists that Christ was a mere prophet as foretold in the old prophecies. He appeared in the Holy Land as bearer of a true religion and had some seven hundred true believers (*kereyentes*), whom Paul, the Jew, fought and expelled,[149] tricking some of them into believing that Christ was God.[150] Thus, Christians follow Paul, the Jew, and not Christ, the prophet. Paul was followed by Jacob and Nastur (Nestorious), who said that Christ was the son of God, and then by Malqūn, who said that he was three in one. Thus, gradually Christians went astray and only a few of them reached and embraced Islam.

The author then shows the falsity of Christian claims, basing his arguments on the Gospels. These clearly state that Christ is not a god. Christ referred to himself as a mortal being, and in the Sermon on the Mount, Christ said, "Your Creator sees and hears you," but did not say, "I see and hear me."[151] The author remarks, "What a great blindness this is. They read, but do not understand, like a donkey carrying books."[152] In Mark, Christ says, "I shall send my angels before you"; he did not say, "before me."[153] And the author notes, "It is a great wonder how they do not know, nor understand; they make false testimony against themselves knowing quite well that when Jesus resurrected the dead, he prayed to and pleaded with the Creator, stretching his hands toward heaven."[154] He relates the birth of Christ according to Luke,[155] showing the relation between Creator and created and concluding that God and not Christ is the Creator of all things, Knower, Powerful, Primeval, having no partner, or the Like of Him. Thus, it is an absurdity to say that Jesus, the son of Mary, is either God or a Trinity, which "God does not wish, nor we Muslims believe to be true, for we believe that God is the Lord without partner and that Jesus was the prophet, messenger, and servant of the Creator."[156]

The author delves into the humanity of Christ with various arguments and counterarguments:[157] (1) He discounts the contention that the Word, which is God and by which all things were created, could be Christ, saying that the Word is primeval and does not grow or decrease; Christ was a child and became big; thus, the contention that Christ is the Word is a "big lie."[158] (2) The author poses the question, if Jesus was God and man, who died and who was buried for three days, who managed the world on those days?[159] He answers that Jesus was created through God's power as Adam was created from dust.[160] (3) Moreover, Jesus was not the last prophet, for he himself announced the coming of the Paraclete who would bear witness to him and he urged his followers to believe in him. The Paraclete means "the praised one," corresponding to the Arabic names of Aḥmad or Muḥammad, the "spirit of the truth" that will bring all good tidings.[161] (4) If Jesus is God and the son of God, it follows that he is the son of his own self, an absurdity which no man of understanding could accept.[162] Moreover, the contention is false since it can be extended and applied to other creatures. Thus, if Adam is the son of God, then by the same token he would be considered God, and this would be a joke (*burla*) for God alone is the Maker of all things, which are subordinate to Him, not he to them. Christ is created of flesh and blood (*ya-l-masīḥ es kiriado de qarne i de sanghere*).[163] In sum, Christ was a man of flesh and blood, a prophet (*al-nabī*), and the son of God (*fijo de-Allāh*). There were hundreds of witnesses to testify to this, but two or four witnesses would suffice.[164]

The treatise is followed by excerpts from the book of al-Qaysī, who again appears to have relied on 'Abdallah al-kātibo.[165] It refers to "the monks of the Temple" (*farayeles de-l-tenpolo*) who followed a true believer (*al mūmin*). These monks had many villages and castles; they believed in God's unity and in the veracity of Jesus' sayings, which were distorted by later Christian infidels (*kāfires*),[166] some of whom maintained that God was three; others that Jesus was His Son; and a third group that Jesus was God.[167]

The excerpt proceeds in the form of an inquiry by a certain knight (*fulān kaballero*) who asks, "Are you not ashamed that you worship other than the Creator following the path of Paul, the Jew, and abandoning the wisemen, saints, and the admonitions (*kastigos*) of Jesus and other prophets?"[168] Then, on the basis of the Qur'ān (4:157), al-Qaysī examines the death of Christ, who was neither killed nor crucified—although it appears to have been so[169]—and reiterates the humanity of Christ, "servant of the Creator" (*komo servidor de-l-kiriyador*): "Know my brother, that there is no God but God—May He be praised—who is the Creator, the One, Alone, without a partner or semblance; powerful over and knower of all past and future things; and that the Prophet Muḥammad is His servant and messenger, who gave light to the blind in the world, and who showed the road and path of salvation. He is one of the two riders referred to by the Prophet Isaiah, . . . who announced the coming of two prophets: the one riding a donkey [Jesus] and the other riding a camel [Muḥammad].[170]

The treatise offers more arguments and counterarguments concerning the humanity of Christ: (1) Having been born in time, Jesus could not have been God: for if he were God, it would follow that God is created and made of different parts.[171] Furthermore, if Jesus is God, how is it possible that he died?[172] (2) God is all-powerful, knower, primeval Creator (*kiriyador antigo*), infinite, and perfect.[173] His unity cannot be compromised. But if the Christians say that knowledge, power, and will of the Creator are manifested in Christ, since knowledge, power, and will are one and the same thing and represent God, Son, and the Holy Spirit, respectively, one will retort, Why three parts and not more?[174] (3) Christians maintain that Jesus was tempted by the Devil; but how could this be so if he is God, who is all-powerful over all things?[175]

A very interesting part of the manuscript (BNM 4944) is a supposed secret letter discovered at the death of a pope, purported to refer to the true faith—that is, to Islam.[176] The letter was discovered by the king of France, who became concerned about its implications. He summoned the clergy and told them that the Muslims, who believe in one God, would conquer all the land unless they were expelled with Jews and monks. The narrator concludes that while the king managed to dispose of Jews and monks, he was not able to dispose of the Muslims.

Other hopeful signs for the future of Islam in Spain appear in the dialogue between al-Qaysī and a monk, who was accompanied by a knight (*kaballero*), who was an unbeliever. When they asked about his belief, al-Qaysī replied: "My belief is unity [of God]; my prophet is Muḥammad, who is the prophet of the truth whom Jesus mentioned in the Gospel as the Paraclete, or spirit. He is spirit in both the old law and the Gospel and you cannot deny it; that is all, and leave me alone and spare me your noise and polemics (*desputas*)."[177] The monk persisted, however; "Inform me about what you say regarding unity." Al-Qaysī replied: "I believe that God—may He be praised—is One, Power, Sovereign Lord, without beginning or end, and without form or semblance." To which the monk retorted that, according to the Qur'ān, you Muslims say one thing and believe in something else, providing God with body, hands, legs, members, the faculties of moving, descending and ascending.[178] Al-Qaysī appears reluctant to offer him a lengthy reply, reminding the monk of his confession of faith and pointing out that the monk does not understand the way things are expressed in the Arabic language; thus, discussion would be futile. Furthermore, al-Qaysī observes that the knight, failing to understand the terms of disputation, will be maddened by it and resort to hurling insults. Therefore, al-Qaysī concludes "Let your law be yours and my law be mine."[179] However, the knight reassured al-Qaysī that he had nothing to fear. So al-Qaysī took the offensive and asked the monk if he believed that Jesus is God, a trinity, or the son of God, to which the monk answered in the affirmative. Al-Qaysī offered his rebuttal, saying that such views were vain utterances (*dichos vanos*) and presenting arguments to demonstrate Jesus' humanity. He offered a Muslim conception of Jesus as the spirit of God (*rūḥ allāh*) who was blessed wherever he went, who received the grace and blessing of God and the gift of the self. [180] He noted that the events surrounding Christ's birth and other scriptural sayings offer ample evidence that Christ was a messenger of God.[181]

Al-Qaysī was here interrupted by the monk, who insisted on a reply to his early question concerning the anthropomorphic nature of God. Al-Qaysī, in turn, refused to reply until the monk offered his reaction to the discussion concerning Christ. Finally the knight interceded, saying to al-Qaysī: "By God, you have said a great truth and in a clear way that no one can contradict; you spoke about the faith using words that are heavier on me than the high mountains." As he was leaving, he turned to the monk and said, "This Muslim (*moro*] will give you advice [*avezara*] that your knowledge lacks; I am certain that you will not be able to defeat him with any rational argument [*razon nenguna*]."[182]

This marked a triumph for al-Qaysī, who in answer to the monk's question reiterated 'Abdallah al-kātibo:[183] the Qur'ānic verse (5:64) referring to God's hands being tied signifies "grace" while the verse, "We made the heaven with the hand" (51:47) signifies power.[184] In answer to the monk's skepticism about eating and drinking in Paradise, al-Qaysī invokes the words of Christ and the Gospels permitting such activities.[185] Finally, with respect to forgiveness of sins, al-Qaysī reiterates 'Abdallah, saying that the Almighty forgives all Muslims who read, listen, and understand the Qur'ān, regardless of their station in life.[186]

The treatise proceeds with an examination of the Christian conception of mingling (*el meskalamiyento*) of the Word (God) with the body in the womb of Mary, thereby creating Christ in the same manner in which water and milk are blended; al-Qaysī rejects this notion as arbitrary; why should the son be conceived in Christ and not in Moses, Abraham, or any other prophet?[187] To the Christian objection that this could not be possible since Christ resurrected the dead and performed miracles, such as converting a staff into a serpent and forging a road into the sea.[188] Al-Qaysī further argues that since Christians concede that Christ died, they must admit that God died also.[189]

Al-Qaysī concludes by refuting the conception of the Trinity, in which Father, Son, and Holy Spirit correspond to existence, life, and knowledge. He asks, "Why should Christ be made of three and not more than three that would include will, power, hearing, seeing, speaking and other similar things (*sembalanses*)?[190]

The final section of the anti-Christian polemic is the reported letter of 'Umar b. 'Abd al-'Azīz to the Byzantine Emperor Leon.[191] If authentic, the treatise is the earliest of its kind, setting down the basic Islamic conception of Christianity vis-à-vis Islam. 'Umar tells the emperor that religion is a serious matter and should be carefully pondered so as to follow the right path. He urges him to heed Christ's words, and turn away from distorted scriptures (*las eskirituras tarastornadas*),[192] the result of additions, omissions, and forgetfulness of people who injected into them their scandals, doubts, and unbeliefs (*sus eskandalos i sus dubdas i mal kerensiyas*).[193] This, sadly, is true for the Torah as well as the Gospels; for one thing, the Torah omits the notions of Paradise, Hell, and the Day of Judgment. The Gospels were written by various persons and contain changes and whims.[194] Only God's Book (*alkitāb d-Allāh*)—the Qur'ān—is one and true. It does not contradict the unadulterated Torah or the true Gospels, nor does it contradict God's commands or His religion.[195] In fact, Islam is the true religion; the true Torah and the true Gospels do not contradict this. Islam is the religion of His angels and the religion of His prophets, because our Lord God does not mislead His people not would He give them two religions to guide some with one and mislead others with another, for the Lord is one and His religion is one.[196] Angels and prophets worshiped and believed in Him—He is the Lord of the World and of all things. 'Umar observes that, unlike Christians, Muslims remained faithful to God's ordinances, and the true belief is that Christ was a man and not God, according to his own utterances, invoking God's name or praying to Him.[197] Furthermore, Christ anounced the coming of the Paraclete, of Muḥammad. In fact, the coming of both Christ and Muḥammad was foretold by the Scriptures, the one riding a donkey and the other riding a camel.[198] 'Umar's letter denies that Christ was tempted by the Devil and reiterates the humanity of Christ, who was sent by God to establish the right path.[199] However, he argues that Christ's mission was distorted by Christians, who thought of him as God, and by Jews, who expected him to sit on David's throne and rule the earth, when actually he did not.[200] Christ's humanity is attested to by his birth and by the fact that he ate, drank, grew, and experienced fever, hunger, and thirst like any mortal being.[201] All things considered, 'Umar concludes, the birth and formation of Christ were no more marvellous than those of Adam or those of the moon and other stars.[202] The same can be said of Christ's other miracles, which were no different or more marvellous than those performed by other prophets.[203]

In conclusion, manuscript BNM 4944 is a composite treatise, a collection of writings by persons who lived from the eighth (the letter of the Caliph 'Umar, 717-720) to the fifteenth century (Turmeda's *Tuḥfah*). As a result, basic doctrinal concepts are reiterated with almost boring monotony. Judging by the uniformity of style and the form of transcription, language, and script, one may assume that the treatise was by a single author, who may also have been the scribe. This author may be said to be the translator or paraphraser of the works, ideas, and methods of his Muslim predecessors. He is not an innovator in the art of polemics, although he discerns the important doctrinal questions and couches these in language intelligible to his less erudite co-religionists, who were apparently in need of defense against contemporary anti-Muslim polemicists.

Other polemical writings may have existed among the Moriscos, with a content similar to manuscript BNM 4944. Evidence of this may be found in Manuscript RAH-V7[204] which differs in script, form of transliteration, and language from BNM 4944, but parallels it regarding the basic controversial issues—such as the coming of Christ and his death; his seven hundred true followers persecuted by Paul, who also appears the villian in corrupting the true Christian doctrine; and the secret letter left at the death of a pope.[205] Although BNM 4944 hints at the laxity of Christians in the church, where women and men meet playfully and pray loudly,[206] RAH-V7 is more vocal in ridiculing Christians' prayers and religious practices. Men look at women in a sensual way and vice versa,[207] so their oration aims at serving the Devil instead of God. Such shameful conduct is rampant among monks, friars, and abbots, who are often tempted to have intercourse with women during confessions; thus, instead of alleviating a sin, they compound it for themselves and the penitent. To exacerbate the offences, the whole practice of confession is wrong; for God alone is the confessor and forgiver of sins.[208]

The purpose of such polemics appears obvious: to maintain the faith and reaffirm it against Jewish-Christian attacks. Those attacks, denying legitimacy to Islam and its founder, were made with impunity during and after the Reconquest by the populace, clerics, and intellectuals. While in Spain, the Moriscos were ill equipped to respond to such attacks and ridicule and had to rely on outsiders to defend and reaffirm their faith, often in diatribes similar to those of their adversaries. This mutual vituperation accentuated an already tense relation between Islam and Christianity, and became both more vicious and more sophisiticated as time went on. The novel method of combating the enemy through demonstrating error in the respective scriptures failed in that the contenders, whether Muslim or Christian, were unwilling to make any concession however persuasive the arguments. Thus, familiarity with the adversary's position did not necessarily facilitate understanding or willingness to understand in an atmosphere of tolerance. Raymond Lull (1235–1315) studied Arabic and urged the pursuit of oriental studies[209] not so much for humanistic purposes as for acquiring the tools to establish the legitimacy of Christianity at the expense of Islam and thereby to bring Muslim to the true faith. Lull's approach led him to martyrdom by attacking Muḥammad in a Muslim environment, which he finally achieved at the hands of an angry mob in Bougie.

But religious matters require a congenial and tolerant environment where people can communicate without fear of retribution. Such a peaceful approach of open discussion (*per viam pacis et doctrinae*) was suggested by Bishop Juan de Segovia (ca. 1400–1458)[210] as an alternative to emotional polemics, vituperation, and war. Segovia hoped to create an environment in which Islam and Christianity could coexist until one or the other prevailed on its own merit. Segovia was, of course, convinced about the ultimate triumph of Christianity. In order to attain his goal, Segovia proposed an accurate translation of the Qur'ān into Romance and Latin. He commissioned 'Isā de Jābir, Mufti of Segovia, to commit the Qur'ān into Castilian, from which Segovia himself made a Latin rendition, thus making the Qur'ān available in three languages and easily accessible to a wider audience for the first time.[211]

Segovia's peaceful intent remained unheeded, and the acrimonious polemics heightened in the course of the sixteenth century. Many polemicists used textual critique and dialectics to show the validity of Christianity and the falsity of Islam. Marti'n Garci'a, bishop and inquisitor, was convinced that the Agarenos (bastards) would sooner or later come to the fold of Christianity on the strength of scriptural evidence and demonstrative reasoning. He preached in Arabic, assisted by the neophyte Juan Andrés, who supplied him with first-hand information about the Qur'ān and prophetic traditions. This he used in his *Sermons*, in which he elucidated the Christian doctrine and pointed out, among other things, that Muḥammad was never a prophet and that his doctrine came from the Devil.[212] Similarly, Juan Andrés attacked Islam, pointing to the libertine life of Muḥammad, his bloody wars, and the impiety and contradictions and errors of the Qur'ān.[213] The most combative polemicist of the period was Pérez de Cinchon, whose *Antialcorán* attempted to convince his readers and listeners that Islam was an inferior religion; that Muḥammad was initiated by a heretic Arian and therefore was a liar who preached his doctrine by the sword[214]; and that if Jesus is the Word of God, Muḥammad is the Word of the Devil.[215] These and other notions were reiterated by other contemporaries and were refuted by Moriscos, who responded with equally harsh criticism of the whole Christian doctrine.

Morisco polemics in the Diaspora is of particular interest. Morisco polemicists in North Africa felt free to respond in kind with both textual critique and dialectics in vituperative language. Their attitude was as compromising as the Christians; and likewise, they approached the subject with closed minds and unwillingness to understand the opponent's position. As a result, the polemics resolved no differences but, rather, accentuated them. Though the Moriscos in the Diaspora added no new elements to the religious controversy, they appeared more knowledgeable about the issues and even used the rhetorical devices of poetry to ridicule their opponents' beliefs and practices and, at the same time, to reaffirm their own.

Such was the case of Muḥammad Rabadan, Juan Alfonso, Muḥammad Taylibi, Muḥammad Alguazir, and others whose views are ably analyzed by Cardaillac.[216] These men, like their Muslim predecessors, were anxious to establish the validity of Islam and explain their conception of Judaism and Christianity within an Islamic context. They adhered to the doctrinal concept that Islam was no more nor less than the continuation and culmination of the Judeo-Christian traditions, superior to both. Muḥammad Rabadan exonerates Islam and its founder in verse, showing that Muḥammad appeared in the form of light at the time of creating and that light continued to appear on the foreheads of the decendants of Adam until its full splendor in the person of Muḥammad.[217] Moreover, Muḥammad was the Paraclete already announced in the Old and New Testaments.[218] Rabadan—like his fellow Moriscos, Alfonso, Taylibi, Alguazir, and others—upheld the unity (*tawhīd*) of God and contrasted it with the Trinity, which was regarded as polytheism.[219] They followed the doctrinal concept that Christ was a venerable prophet born to a saintly and virtuous woman, Mary, but never God or son of God. Christ's deification and triplication into Father, Son and Holy Spirit is a contradiction and a heresy at best, and it attributable to the blindness, adulteration, and misreading of the scriptures by Paul and the popes, who added and subtracted things to their liking.[220] In sum, all the Christian creed and practices are mere fabrications unsubstantiated by true scriptures. Christ himself refers to his humanity in the Gospels, yet his followers regard him as God by virtue of his birth from a virgin and his miracles. This is refuted in that other prophets had extraordinary births (Adam) and performed miracles and yet they were not called gods. If such a thing is permissible, Muḥammad would be more deserving by virtue of his many miracles and by his being the Seal of Prophecy (*sello de la profecia*).[221] Belief in the crucifixion is an innovation, for Christ was never killed or crucified; a substitute was put in his place.[222] The veneration of the cross and statues is tantamount to idolatry. The whole Christian creed has no foundation, and is arrived at through the deletion of the first (belief in one God) and the second commandments (prohibition of worshiping idols). Furthermore, the popes arrogated to themselves the introduction of new religious prescriptions, such as prohibiting meat on Friday, not being eligible for salvation without membership in church, the supremacy of the pope, celibacy, purgatory, and other things for which there are no stipulations in the scriptures, even after their adulteration. All this makes the church a haven of lies, gossip, and deceit to the point of having the scriptures in Latin so that people are not able to read or understand them.[223] Other mockeries (*cosa de burla*) are the sacraments of baptism, confession, and the Eucharist.[224] Baptism is not a substitute for circumcision, which is prescribed by law[225]; God alone is the Confessor and Forgiver of sins; not a priest[226]; the Eucharist is no more than a piece of bread and a jar of wine brought from the tavern—thus, it is nonsense (*disparate*) to believe that God is in the host and is eaten.[227]

6

History, Legends, and Travel

Historical writings among the Moriscos were almost nonexistent. Even chronicles of contemporary events or sociocultural aspects of the Morisco life appear neglected, with only scattered documentation—mostly incidental and not reflecting the Morisco's historical perspective. However, the few documents that have reached us give some valuable glimpses of the Moriscos' activities. One set of documents[1] contains a memorandum to an individual stating the price of a home, draft of a petition, a receipt, a marriage license, and a dowry contract. Another set[2] consists of letters of dowry, a letter from an individual to his cousin, a request for a book, a marriage petition, and minutes of a court. A third set of documents[3] contains the testimony of two litigants, contracts of sale and dowry, and an inventory of property. There are birthday records using the Christian calendar, one of which reads: "My son 'Ali de Zeyne was born on Friday 17, 1578, following the calendar of the heretic Christians."[4] There are memos *(memoriya)* recording the purchase of a house,[5] a marriage,[6] litigation over a mule,[7] litigation over a will,[8] sale of inheritance,[9] marriage contracts,[10] division of property,[11] inventory of dotal possession,[12] litigation over the occupancy of a house,[13] and other correspondence,[14] bookkeeping accounts of loans, purchase, and sale.[15] Such documents occupy a very small portion of Aljamiado literature.[16]

Notwithstanding the absence of historical writings, the Moriscos had a strong historical consciousness, derived from religious history. The Moriscos chose to be guided by old Islamic historical traditions, omitting much of the political and intellectual history of classical Islam. As a result, the nearest thing to historical writings consisted of tracts written by Muslim predecessors in which history and legend were intertwined, which constituted an integral part of the religious writings that formed the basis of the education of the Morisco. In spite of such religious consciousness, the Morisco had lost awareness of secular history, even that concerning his ancestors' intellectual ascendance within the Iberian Peninsula. If the Morisco had any consciousness of his legacy in the various intellectual and scientific endeavors, it was certainly not manifested in his extant writings. Muslim men of letters, scientists, and philosphers were relegated to oblivion, as were the major and even brilliant periods of Islamic history, its great statesmen and generals. This limited the Morisco's perspective to presenting Islam the religion in its best light as a devine manifestation that would ultimately triumph over the seemingly impossible odds that confronted him. In short, the historico-legendary writings of the Morisco centered on the miraculous triumph of Islam, the personality of its founder Muhammad, and a few pre-Islamic and Islamic figures; these were conceived to be the instrument for bringing about the success of Islam in adversity against powerful evildoers and stubborn idolaters.

The Morisco had a theocentric view of the world. God, of course, is behind all things and always intervenes on behalf of Islam through His angel Gabriel, who would appear at the right moment to rescue Muslims from evil men and demons. The Qur'ān, the sayings and deeds of Muḥammad as contained in the traditions *(ḥadīth)*, and the utterances of venerable men of the past attested to the past, present, and future preeminence of Islam. This vision of history dates to the Creation[17]: Adam, Abraham, Noah, Moses, and other biblical figures were considered true Muslims, as was Alexander the Great, notwithstanding some of his deviations, and Jesus, the man and the prophet whom God sent as one among many other prophets to fulfill God's will on earth. The chain of prophecies ended with Muḥammad, "the Seal of Prophets" and "the best of God's creatures." The bulk of Aljamiado literature is based on this religious historical perspective. One may discern the following categories of historical themes in the order of their importance in the extant literature: biography of Muḥammad, Islamic figures, pre-Islamic figures, futuristic history, and travel.

BIOGRAPHY OF MUḤAMMAD

Muḥammad was the center of historical writings and the object of numerous treatises, each of which relates one or more aspect of his life. He was also the object of comprehensive works that related his presence from the

Creation down to the Resurrection and Day of Judgment. Among these are al-Bakrī's *Book of Light*[18] and Rabadan's *Discourse of Light, Descent and Limpid Genealogy of Our Blessed Leader the Prophet Muḥammad,*[19] in verse, which is based on al-Bakrī's work and relates Muḥammad are probably parts of larger works dealing with his birth,[20] death,[21] ascension to heaven,[22] advice and aphorisms,[23] testament to his son-in-law 'Ali,[24] relations with Jews,[25] and conversation with a lizard.[26] Also, praises of him and of his cloak (*burdah*) are found in poems. Finally, Moriscos wrote of his triumphs over false prophets[28] and his involvement in battles associated with early struggle of Islam, pointing to his miraculous triumphs over heavy odds.[29] He left a testament[30] before his death, which many looked upon with grief and consternation.[31]

The Book of Light (*Libro de las luces*) was a translation from Arabic of the *Kitāb al-anwār* by Aḥmad Ibn Muḥammad Abū-l-Ḥasan al-Bakrī (1493-1545), an Egyptian scholar. The work does not appear to be reliable, but it has the virtues of being written in a simple narrative with great display of devotion—two qualities that were probably behind its translation into Aljamiado and its apparent success among the Moriscos (Rabadan's *Discourse* appears to follow its main outlines). A summary of the work is of interest. The title itself, *The Book of Light,* is revealing: the author develops the doctrine of illumination whereby the coming of Muḥammad was made known at the time of the Creation of the world, manifested in a light (*luz,* Ar. *nūr*) that appeared on Adam's forehead and on those of his descendants down to Muḥammad. Al-Bakrī's account is quite expansive, emphasizing the presence of Muḥammad long before his birth; it also places great emphasis on Muḥammad's ancestors and the marvels attending his birth; mentions his stay with his uncle Abū Ṭālib; and tells of his journey to Syria where he met the hermit Baḥīra who announced his prophetic mission; his employment with Khadījah, whom he later married; and his revelations. All of this is narrated in readable style intertwinning facts with legends and marvellous accounts. The work consists of seven sections:

Section I. When God wanted to create (*khaleqar*) the world, He did it with limpid and clear dust (*tiyerra*) which he cleansed with the water of Tesnim, one of the fountains of Paradise. Angels and other creatures of Heaven and earth expressed their obedience, humility, and willingness to prostrate themselves before Muḥammad, whom they knew before the creation of Adam. At the moment of his creation Adam heard voices glorifying God (*alttasbiḥes*) and inquired about this; the Lord answered that the glorification was for the Seal of the Prophets (*sillo de los alnnabiyes*), who would be like the full moon and whose light would illuminate heavens, earth, and the courts of angels.[32] When Adam wanted to cohabit with Eve, he told her to make the ablution, perfume herself, and shave, for God would place a light in the purity (*limpiyeza*) of her womb. She begot Seth, in whom she saw the light of the Prophet Muḥammad, to which Adam paid homage and made Seth do the same. This light appeared on the foreheads of future generations, including Hāshim Ibn 'Abd Manāf, on whose forehead appeared a dazzling light. Al-Bakrī devoted ample space to

Hāshim, and to his marriage to Salma in Medina—a marriage that Satan (*iblīs*) and Jews attempted to foil, but Hāshim, the immediate ancestor of Muḥammad, fought and triumphed over them.

Section 2. Hāshim remained haunted by a conspiracy. When he begot 'Abd al-Muṭṭalib, Muḥammad's grandfather, he received a miraculous warning to guard and protect him against enemies, particularly Jews, whom he had to fight, as did 'Abd al-Muṭṭalib.[33]

Section 3. 'Abd al-Muṭṭalib emigrated to Mecca, where he settled, married, and vowed to God to sacrifice a child if he should ever have ten male children. Since he did have ten male children, he wanted to comply with his vows and went to the Ka'bah to consummate the sacrifice. His wife, Fāṭimah, opposed him as to which one to sacrifice; it was agreed to draw lots, and the choice fell on Fāṭimah's son 'Abdallah, the future father of Muḥammad. When 'Abd al-Muṭṭalib lifted the knife, a light spring from 'Abdallah's forehead and voices declared that 'Abdallah was under the protection of the angels. At the same time, armed men and relatives of Fāṭimah appeared on the scene and prevented the sacrifice over the protests of 'Abd al-Muṭṭalib.

Section 4. Determined to comply with his vows, 'Abd al-Muṭṭalib sought the advice of a soothsayer, who advised him to draw lots among his ten sons and ten camels. If the lot fell on one of his sons, he should add ten camels and repeat the process until all his children were spared. He followed the recommendation until he had added one hundred forty camels, which he sacrificed, sparing the sacrifice of a child. Then the light of the Prophet appeared over all the lords of Quraysh.[34]

Section 5. 'Abdallah grew handsome and was loved by women as Joseph had been. He married Āmīnah, over the protests and machinations of the Jews. He fought and defeated them. During the struggle, two branches of light appeared on his forehead: one radiating to the East and the other to the West.[35]

Section 6. All this was a prelude to the birth of Muḥammad, whose conception was preceded by ablution and perfuming; during it all the beasts of Quraysh spoke: 'Muḥammad is conceived by the Lord of Mecca, and will be the guarantee of the world and the candle of the people.''[36] It was the moment in which God took away knowledge from soothsayers, the earth trembled, mute kings spoke, and angels and the other creatures clamored in the waves of the seas and the abyss of earth counting the days to the time of his birth. His mother Āmīnah heard celestial voices by day and night. However, she lost her husband 'Abdallah during the seventh month of pregnancy, and the angels became concerned, reminding God that His Prophet would be an orphan. God replied that He Himself would take the place of 'Abdallah. Āminah remained slender and did not look pregnant, even during her ninth month of pregnancy. A voice commanded her to deliver, and she saw the white wing of a bird passing through her stomach; then a bright light illuminated her; she was surrounded by tall women smelling of musk, covered by veils of precious cloth from head to toe, and carrying vases of silver containing white water, like milk, from which she drank. They congratulated her. One said, "Good fortune for the leader of heavens and earth, the Seal of the Prophets, the chosen Muḥammad." A second said, "God has honored you among the people and made you a cell for having the most exalted creature." And a third said, "There is none like you, O Āminah, from whom emanates the perfect friend (*amigho akabado*), the resplendent light, and the supplicant for people in the Day of Judgment."[37] Āminah also saw other noble winged figures carrying silver cups and golden vases; birds with white wings covering all the house; people, trees, animals, beasts, and birds rendering congratulations.[38] When Muḥammad was born, the doors of Heaven opened; the angels extended their wings in the air; Paradise was embellished with blessings; and all idols fell to the ground. He was surrounded from dawn to sunset by the spirits of people and prophets.[39]

His grandfather 'Abd al-Muṭṭalib was not home when Muḥammad was born; when he went to see him, he was intercepted by a fierce man with a spear in his hand who told him that no one could see Muḥammad until the angels finished their visitation, which would last three days. Thereafter, people vied to see the Light of the Prophet, and voices were heard saying: "This is the friend of Allah, Muḥammad the Messenger of Allah."[40] Mountains, trees, animals, and clouds argued about which would rear him until they were interrupted by the angels, who said, "We are entitled to do so, since we get more honor, glory, and exaltation from God." But other voices were heard saying that God had already entrusted him to Ḥalīmah, daughter of Abū Du'ayb al-Asadiyyah, who was in the house of 'Abd al-Maṭṭalib.[41]

On the seventh day after his birth, his grandfather 'Abd al-Muṭṭalib gave a great feast, to which all the people of Mecca were invited; during it a large number of animals were slaughtered, and many people, birds, and animals ate of the meat for seven days.[42] No midwife or known being cut the umbilical cord, anointed him, or made up his eyes.[43] The year of his birth was marked by drought and famine except in Mecca. Ḥalīmah whom God chose as his future nurse was thin and weak, but soon rode to Mecca on a donkey and became beautiful and plump with breasts full of milk.[44] When she met the infant Muḥammad for the first time, he looked at her, and a light reaching the heavens emerged from between his eyes. She gave him her right breast, and he sucked, but refused to suck from the left breast "because Allah had shown him the right even in the manner of sucking."[46]

As he was playing one day, three men appeared and split him from the chest to the navel while he was looking without his feeling any pain. The first removed and washed his intestines; the second took out his heart, from which he removed black drops saying that they were part of Satan, and replaced it; and the third closed the incision. After this, they weighed Muḥammad, finding his weight to be greater than that of all the people of the world.[47] When a soothsayer heard about this phenomenon, he foretold the doom of the Arabs and urged that Muḥammad be killed. Ḥalīmah fled with him, but lost him at the gate of Mecca; and while an old man was interceding on her behalf before the idols, these fell down and were shattered, while a voice declared that Muḥammad was safe in the company of a nobleman in the Tuhama Valley, close by the Promised Tree.[48]

Section 7. His mother Āminah died when he was about six years old, and his grandfather 'Abd al-Muṭṭalib died when he was eight years, two months, and five days old. He went to live with his uncle Abū Ṭālib, who took him on a caravan journey to Syria, where he met the Christian hermit Baḥīra. Baḥīra warned him of the danger from the Jews, adding that Muḥammad would be the recipient of scriptures. This prediction was confirmed by another monk. When he was twenty-five years old, his uncle Abū Ṭālib urged him to marry the very rich Khadījah who employed him and then proposed marriage. Mention is made of their offspring and of the first revelation commanding Muḥammad to read in the name of the Lord.[49] Here concludes al-Bakrī's account.

The abrupt ending of al-Bakrī's account can, however, be supplemented by materials found in the *Book of Battles* and numerous other treatises dealing with one or several aspects of Muḥammad's life.[50] Of particular interest is the *Mi'rāj,* or *Ascension of Muḥammad to the Seven Heavens,* of which several Aljamiado versions are extant.[51] The *Mi'rāj* constitutes an integral part of Muḥammad's biography and was popular among Muslims everywhere. It made its way into Spanish, Latin, and French, perhaps influencing the theme in Dante's *Divine Comedy.*[52] The Aljamiado version of the *Mi'rāj,* based on early Arabic antecedents, offers interesting details and many embellishments that need to be studied carefully with a view to tracing them to an Arabic antecedent or to local Aljamiado innovations. The *Mi'rāj* begins with a prophetic tradition saying that while Muḥammad was sleeping on a dark night in which neither roosters crowed nor dogs barked,[53] he saw the angel Gabriel whiter than snow descending upon him, having on his face two veils *(dos astras)*; on one was written, "There is no God but God," on on the other , "Muḥammad is the messenger of God." Gabriel had six hundred wings on which were seventy thousand rubies, each of which had five hundred years distance *(andadura).*[54] He ordered Muḥammad to wake, to tighten his cloth, and to take courage, for he would come to speak with the Lord. Muḥammad was frightened, and then saw Burāq, an unususal beast of burden whose upper part was made of gold, neck of white silver, front legs of emeralds, and back legs of alikban. It had round feet, long ears, and the tail of ox. Gabriel ordered Muḥammad to mount, but Burā fled, inquiring about the man until Gabriel assured it that he was Muḥammad, the Seal of the Prophers, messenger of the Lord, the best of God's children, to whom all creatures will plead for salvation in the Day of Judgment.[55] Even then Burāq would allow Muḥammad to mount until Muḥammad promised that he would intercede on its behalf in the Day of Judgment. Then Muḥammad heard a voice from the right and another from the left, and saw a beautiful woman wishing to speak to him, but Gabriel told him to proceed without talking to any one. Since Muḥammad inquired about those voices, Gabriel said that the voice coming from the right was that of a Jew. Had he talked to him, his people would have become Jews after his death; the voice from the left was that of a Christian. Had he listened to it, his people would have become Christians; the beautiful woman represented the world. Had he listened to her, his people would have chose this world over the hereafter. Muḥammad then thanked God for saving him from these three scandals.[56]

During the journey, Gabriel ordered Muḥammad to dismount to pray before they reached the Holy House (*baytu almaqadis,* Ar. *Bayt al-Maqdis*) in Jerusalem. Gabriel stood at the door of the mosque (*meskida*) with three cups (*alqadaḥes*) in his hands, the first containing milk, the second wine, and the third honey. Gabriel asked him to choose, and he chose the first cup, from which he drank a little milk; then he heard a voice saying, "Had you drunk all the milk, oh Muḥammad, none of your people would have entered the fire of Hell."[57] Then he wanted to finish it, but Gabriel said, "The fate that is in the Mother of the Books (Qur'ān) is fulfilled."[58] They entered the mosque, where three hundred prophets were seated. Muḥammad greeted them, and they replied, "Welcome, good brother, the honored prophet of God and of all creatures."[59] They performed the prayer, then Gabriel took him by the hand and led him to a stair (*eskala*) that reached the heavens. The stair had steps of gold, silver, ruby, bronze, and amber, respectively.[60] Gabriel and Muḥammad left Burāq behind and ascended seeing "stars suspended like lamps, the smallest of which having the size of the biggest mountain in the world."

They reached the first heaven, which is separated from earth by five hundred year's journey and the width of which is equal to that number. They saw the angel Ishmael sitting on a chair (*alkursi*) of clarity with angels on his right and on his left praising the Lord.[61] Muḥammad greeted them, and they answered as "the most honored of God's creatures."[62] Moving forward, he saw an old man, Adam, also sitting on a chair of light, who smiled whenever he looked to the right where Paradise was located and cried whenever he looked to the left where Hell was. After the usual greeting, he performed the prayer with Adam and proceeded toward the second heaven.

In the second heaven, which is separated from the first by five hundred year's journey, Muḥammad saw innumerable angels in midst of whom sat a big angel on a chair of light, half made of fire and half of snow; he was praying: "O joiner [*ajuntador*] of fire and snow, join the hearts of your servants and believers."[63] As they advanced, they saw John and Jesus, with whom they prayed after the usual greetings.

They proceeded to the third heaven, made of silver, where they were received by an angel whose palm would contain all the world. An old man, Abraham, was sitting on a chair of light and surrounded by innumerable angels with whom they prayed after the usual greetings. In addition, Abraham asked Muḥammad to greet his community in his name.

In the fourth heaven, made of gold, they were received by an angel whose right thumb contained all the sweet seas and his left all the salty seas. There were some seventy thousand angels with hands of light praising the Lord.

There was also a gigantic angel, the angel of death, with a tablet on his right and a tree on his left. On the tablet were written the names of all Adam's children and on the tree's leaves were inscribed the names of all people, indicating the date of their death. Advancing, they saw Idris,[64] whom they greeted and with whom they prayed.

In the fifth heaven, made of white pearls, they were received by an angel with seventy thousand elbows, each of which had seventy thousand hands, and each hand had seventy thousand fingers; the angel praised God in seventy different manners. Inside, there were many angels with big wings covered with light surrounding an old man, Adam,[65] sitting on a chair of light.

In the sixth heaven, made of blue emeralds, they saw an angel with the figure of a rooster whose feet reached the lowest level of earth and whose neck reached the highest heaven. They saw another angel half of whose body was of snow and the other half of fire. He did not greet Muḥammad until Gabriel introduced him. They saw a third angel in the air, who was the gatekeeper of Hell. Inside they saw the biggest angel yet, which could swallow both heaven and earth; deep inside were other angels, each having seventy thousand horses adorned with pearls, sapphires, and golden reins.[65]

In the seventh heaven, made of colored pearls, they were received by an enormous and powerful angel, whom they greeted; advancing, they saw innumerable angels bigger than anything seen before. They saw a wall of Paradise made of gold, silver, and pearls; the soil was of musk and amber and irrigated with rose water. Neither angel, nor spirit (*aljinne*), nor Satan could pass through. It had never been seen by anyone before. Yet they entered Paradise and saw indescribable good things. An angel sitting on a chair of light and surrounded by other standing angels was Ridwan, the gatekeeper of Paradise, who rose and gave Muḥammad a tour of Paradise, enabling him to see its rivers, trees, and castles made of gold, silver, and pearls. Then Muḥammad was taken by Gabriel to a river called Life (*alḥayā*) whose width is five hundred year's journey, and on whose beaches lie green pastures, purple, silk, and sapphires. Thereafter, he was taken by an angel to a castle of Paradise where there were many beautiful things available to the believer. From there he was taken to *Sidratu almutaha* (ar. *al-muntahā),* a tree of pearls, near which was the fountain *alkawthar,* whose water was sweeter than honey and whiter than snow. That water was reserved for his community. He was soon facing the Lord, separated by a curtain of darkness. He heard a voice commanding him to draw near and place his hand on his head and saying that he would "know in one hour all things and will see my Lord with the heart and not with the eyes."[67] Muḥammad had a dialogue with God concerning the matter of faith, and was told to have the faithful pray fifty times a day. Heeding the warning of Moses, he asked for a reduction of the number of prayers to five, which was granted; also, fasting was reduced from sixty days to one month.[68]

Muḥammad returned happily, meeting the angel Gabriel and the gatekeeper of Paradise on the way. He continued with Gabriel and drank from a lake whose water was white and sweet, whose smell was better than musk, and whose taste was like milk.[69] Gabriel showed him Hell from the air, fenced with fire and iron as sharp as swords. He saw people taken by the hair and thrown into the fire. Among those people were the usurpers of orphans' property, those of discord, and the wealthy who had failed to do good and to perform prayers.[70] Finally, Gabriel put him on Burāq. At home he woke his wife and told her about his journey. She advised him not to tell people, for they would not believe him, but the following day he revealed his experience to an assembly of the Quraysh, who called him a liar (*mentiroso*) and demanded proof. Abū Bakr, his companion, pleaded with them to believe him, but they refused and had to be fought with the sword.[71]

The Aljamiado recensions of the *Mi'rāj* would make an interesting study—editing and collating the extant versions and tracing them to Arabic antecedents to determine the discrepancies between the Arabic and the Aljamiado versions. The Aljamiado version reveals that the *Mi'rāj* took place before the conversion of the Quraysh to Islam. This appears to be the case also in another Aljamiado version, which states that during Muḥammad's dialogue with God, he saw a sword suspended from the sky with blood dripping from it; Muḥammad felt uneasy at the sight and pleaded with God to have the sword removed, but God retorted, "I have sent you with the sword, for your people will never become civilized except with the sword."[72]

Thus, the *Mi'rāj* appears to presage a series of confrontations between Muḥammad and his numerous pagan enemies in the Arabian Peninsula. These enemies were overwhelmingly powerful and numerically superior, yet they were defeated by a small number of Muḥammad's followers with God's intercession through the angel Gabriel. The various extant stories have epical proportions, showing the succession of Muḥammad's triumphs over seemingly indomitable adversaries.[73] Moreover, his numerous miracles—the Qur'ān, the resurrection of a dead girl,[74] his curing of a scaldheaded man, making the blind see,[75] splitting the moon in two,[76] and others—were proof of his eminence and being "the best of God's creatures." This preeminance was acknowledged by God, angels, and prophets from time immemorial both in heaven and on earth.

These idealized notions of Muḥammad were not uncommon among Muslims elsewhere, but the Moriscos' restatements no doubt added some details not found in other Islamic countries. Moreover, Morisco assertions were straightforward, leaving no doubt about their intent. Notwithstanding his preeminence as "the best of God's creatures" to whom homage was rendered by a succession of prophets, Muḥammad was a mortal being. His death was attended by deep grief and consternation, even incredulity.[77] In his farewell address, he urged his followers to do the lawful and avoid the unlawful, reminding them that Allah would be watching over them and that succeeding generations would believe in his prophecy long after his death. Shortly before his death, he comforted his daughter Fāṭimah with a promise of Paradise, ordered his generals to continue the war in the north, and told his followers to gather in the mosque for the prescribed prayers, instructing Abū

Bakr to lead the prayer as Imām. He also summoned people to seek retribution for any injury he may have done them and instructed his followers not to bury him in the mosque.[78] This final moment was filled with emotion—his daughter Fāṭimah crying; his wives 'Ā'ishah and Ḥafṣa and his two grandchildren Ḥasan and Ḥusayn passed by him crying and bidding farewell. Finally, the angel of death was told to enter, and informed Muḥammad that the Lord had sent him to take his spirit if it was agreeable to him. Muḥammad responded that he should go away until the angel Gabriel appeared. Shortly thereafter, Gabriel appeared with the angel of death, informing him of God's wish; Muḥammad wanted to know what would happen to his people. He was reassured by Gabriel that his people would follow him to Paradise; he was pleased and asked the angel of death to take his spirit (*arrūḥ*).[79]

Muḥammad's birthday was on a Monday, the twelfth of Rabī 'I, fifty days after the Army of the Elephant (corresponding to the Ethiopian invasion of Mecca in 570) and his death took place in the full light of history (in 632), indicating that Muḥammad was a mortal being, but his spirit and person existed from the beginning of time. He was known and sought after from the time of Adam. *The Story of a Qur'ānic Commentary*[80] relates that Moses himself sought Muḥammad on a long journey, accompanied by his servant Joshua. As they were eating a salty fish on the edge of a river, half the fish inadvertently fell into the water. When they tried to retrieve it, they discovered that it became alive and headed toward the sea leaving behind a dry path which they followed until they reached an island where they found a youth who performed various miracles demonstrating God's power. Another story[81] relates that a Jew named Osri, a contemporary of Solomon, discovered in the Torah Muḥammad's grace and recorded it. His son Balūqīya found the information in his father's papers and set out for Syria in search of Muḥammad. He experienced extraordinary events and marvels on his way until he became a Muslim. He returned home and related his experiences, but no one would believe him until he performed some miracles by means of ointment that had been supplied him by a Muslim. Similarly, *The Story of Sarjīl Ibn Sarjūn*[82] contains "documentary evidence" about the coming of Muḥammad. It deals with the Christian Sarjīl of Syria, who searched for Muḥammad accompanied by fifty abbots and fifty friars in order to reveal a secret recorded in writing. When he reached Medina, Sarjīl was informed of the death of Muḥammad; he told Abū Bakr that he had in hand writings belonging to his grandfather attesting to the veracity of Muḥammad as a prophet and Islam as the true religion. However, he wanted answers to some questions before embracing Islam. Abū Bakr was amazed, but unprepared to answer Sarjīl's questions; he summoned 'Alī, who addressed Sarjīl by name, to the surprise of the visitor, who posed a number of questions and received satisfactory answers. He then embraced Islam. Such recognition of Muḥammad and his religion by Jews and Christians of old was important to the Moriscos as they strove to justify themselves and their religion to Jewish and Christian polemicists attempting to deny Islam any validity.[83]

ISLAMIC FIGURES AND EVENTS

Muḥammad's biography occupied most of the Moriscos' attention, overshadowing other epochs, leaders, and momentous events, which, if mentioned at all, were ancillary to Muḥammad and his religious movement. The Moriscos were interested in individuals only insofar as they could be identified as instruments of a divine plan or exemplary models of upright Muslims. This notwithstanding, there are a relatively small number of documents dealing with a variety of other subjects. One[84] is devoted to al-Ḥajjāj, the able viceroy of the Umayyad caliph 'Abd al-Malik (685-705). Another[85] deals with the Turks—their origins, conquest of constantinople, and future sway on Christendom as a part of the Moriscos' prophecies; it also contains a brief sketch of some Muslim rulers, including the Andalusian dictator al-Manṣūr (d. 1002); Mūsā and Ṭāriq, the Muslim conquerors of Spain; and the Reconquest by Christians. There is also a cryptic legendary account[86] of the conquest of al-Andalus. One would expect more historical tracts about al-Andalus, but this is not the case. Some information about al-Andalus is found incidentally in stories such as the love story *The Bath of Zarieb*.[87] Although the story had its origin in the East, it was given an Andalusian setting in the city of Cordova, described as having 9,609 mosques (*meskidas*), 10,000 ovens (*baberies*), 800 baths for men and 400 for women, 400 jails, and 100,000 homes. The story also describes al-Manṣūr's preparation for an expedition against the Christians, with figures about the composition of his army. There is also a sketch[88] dealing with some Arab tribes that settled in North Africa, and a poem[89] exalting the ancestry of 'Alī, Muhammad's cousin and son-in-law.

Morisco writings were mainly concerned with Islam as a religion, its pervasiveness in prehistoric and historic times, and its phenomenal success through pious figures who left their imprint on Islamic society. Those men, loyal supporters and faithful companions of the Prophet Muḥammad, were viewed as an extension of Muḥammad and as a manifestation of his religious movement. 'Umar is singled out, not as an able caliph (634-644) and founder of a vast Islamic empire but for his almost miraculous conversion[90] to Islam after having opposed it vehemently and even threatened Muḥammad's life. Hearing his sister reciting the Qur'ān, he was so overwhelmed by its wording and content that he rushed to Muḥammad to make the confession of the faith, becoming the fortieth Muslim to the delight of Muḥammad and his followers. 'Umar became a staunch defender of the new faith, killing seventy unbelievers and converting a thousand men.[91] His new faith led him to a strong sense of justice which he applied even with his own son, who had dishonored a Jewish woman and received severe punishment.[92] 'Umar's piety was so sincere that he asked and was granted his wish to see the souls of the dead in his dream.[93]

But the man who received the most attention was 'Alī, Muḥammad's cousin and son-in-law, not so much for his relationship to the Prophet as for his role in the Islamic movement. 'Alī emerges not only as the personification of pagan chivalry and heroism[94] but as an instrument in the fulfillment of God's will, always guided by Muḥammad's direction through the revelation of the angel Gabriel. He defeated the great champions of his day and thousands of men singlehandedly. Muḥammad depended on him whenever the Muslims were threatened by powerful and seemingly undefeatable forces.[95] He was selfless and fearless; only once did he request to engage the enemy in order to show his military prowess on the battlefield in order to impress and gain admiration of his future wife Fāṭimah, Muḥammad's daughter.[96] He was the ideal knight, working at Muḥammad's behest and in fulfillment of his mission. He fetched a man who had buried his daughter, thereby facilitating her salvation through the miraculous intervention of Muḥammad.[97] He freed many Muslim captives after defeating their oppressors[98] and proved himself the great champion not only over the proved champions of his days, but also over spirits and strange, enormous creatures.[99] Even the great general Khālid Ibn al-Walīd —entitled "the sword of Allah," the conqueror of Syria and Palestine, hero of many battles during the lifetime of Muḥammad—could not match him.[100] Finally, there was Bilāl,[101] Muḥammad's messenger, who was elevated to high esteem by virtue of his loyalty and devotion to Muḥammad despite his black background and low origin. He grieved at the death of his master and remained loyal to Islam to the end; he converted a Jewish woman.[102]

The notions surrounding the life of Muḥammad and the individuals connected with him and his religious movement form part of the Morisco's conception of Islam as an eternal religion, not subject to time and place. Islam made its historical appearance in the seventh century, but it is conceived in Muslim traditions to have existed from the Creation. As such, Islam defies any reckoning or chronological order. In consequence, preIslamic personalities of different persuasion are as Muslim as those appearing after the historical rise of Islam in the seventh century. Muslims in general and Moriscos in particular perceived no inconsistency or contradiction in this: existence began with the Creation and will end in the Day of Judgment, which leads either to eternal life of bliss or to damnation. The historical process cannot alter this reality or interfere with the ultimate goal and destiny of man, however history is told or arranged. Certain phenomena associated with inspired or gifted individuals will be settled in the final accounts. Noah and his Ark,[103] Job's suffering, and Joseph's tribulations are examples of how men obey and fulfill a higher order of things as an integral part of the divine plan.

PRE-ISLAMIC FIGURES

Following Islamic traditions, the Moriscos had great reverence for biblical characters, including Christ as a prophet and mortal being. Such men were instruments of God's will, upholding His covenant in consonance with a series of revelations. The Qur'ān and traditions contain numerous stories about them which are quite prominent in Aljamiado literature, indicating their importance among the Moriscos as part of the religious writings. There are tracts glorifying them,[104] and numerous treatises devoted to them. Abraham[105] and his son Ismā'īl[106] by his concubine Hagar are God's favorites and the true ancestors of the Arabs, who were destined to spread Islam. Abraham, "the friend of God," was a true Muslim to whom God showed many miracles and marvels, among which were walking on water, reviving a lamb after it had been eaten, and his recognition by a frog and a bird as the "friend of God."[107] His son Ismā'īl, and not Isaac, was the heir of the earth and occupies a preeminent position by divine grace, despite having been the child of a former servant of Sarah, who gave her to Abraham to perpetuate the race. The story of Job[108] pictures him among God's chosen people and a prophet, who from great power and affluence became poor and afflicted by horrible diseases until he was outcast by all but his beautiful wife, who cared for him and remained chaste to the end. Despite his tribulations, suffering, and humiliation, Job remained faithful to God, who ultimately sent him the angel Gabriel, who gave him back his youth, health, and wealth. Joseph's betrayal by his brothers and his subsequent saga in Egypt are celebrated in both prose[109] and verse[110] in a moving language conveying that good will ultimately triumph over evil. Joseph, the personification of virtue and beauty, overcame his hardships and met with success. His old blind father, who had grieved for him, was reunited with him by God's grace, regaining his sight.

Various stories are devoted to Moses,[111] communicant with God and possessor of the secret of nature. One[112] relates the events in Sinai, his dialogue with God, and his return to Egypt, where he performed miracles before the Pharaoh to free his people; a second[113] deals with a conversation he had with a dove; a third[114] describes how a despised butcher from Damascus named Jacob became his close companion; and a fourth[115] relates his death, the fate of all mortals. Solomon[116] was another biblical figure who received the attention of the Moriscos. He is pictured as superhuman, but devout and obedient to Allah. He had enormous power over nature, man, and beasts; enormous wealth; a unique sword; and a ring that would predict the future and recreate the past. Because of a moment of vainglory, God caused his ring to vanish and compelled him to walk forty days as a mendicant.[117]

Of special interest is the inclusion of Alexander the Great[118] in the biblical galaxy and almost as a true Muslim. Alexander the Great is referred to in the Qur'ān and the traditions as the "Two Horned" (Dhū-l-Qarnayn)[119]; he became the object of embellished stories from which the Moriscos derived their Aljamiado version. General historical notions are intertwined with legendary deeds in which his extraordinary power, military prowess, wisdom, knowledge, and virtue would qualify him to be a Muslim. Alexander had to wrestle with the question of good and evil, emerging in the process as the arbiter of goodness, the punisher of evildoers, and the rewarder of righteous people. He was an invincible hero. In his childhood, the Devil tried to poison him, but failed. He showed special endowments from an early age, and was educated by Aristotle, who taught him the merit of virtue.

Though following the traditional Islamic conception of Christ, the Moriscos appear to have devoted proportionately more space to him, owing to the Christian environment in which they lived and to the need to give ample proof of the truth of Islam vis-à-vis Christianity.[120] To Moriscos, as to

Muslims in general, Christ was a mortal for whom God had chosen a prophetic mission. Christian claims that he was God, tempted by the Devil, and crucified were mere fantasies of misguided followers. Christ's virtues *(eselensiyyas)* reside in having established just norms by which all sins are forbidden and in having taught a new law given to him by the Creator. He was just, performed miracles, preached splendid things, and ascended to Heaven—leaving his doctrine, which will remain until the coming of the Paraclete, the Prophet Muḥammad.[121] He will emerge before the Day of Judgment and will put the Antichrist to the sword, opening the way for all people to become Muslims.[122]

In addition to born Muslims, there were pagans who were compelled to desist from their cruelties and evil deeds in the light of extraordinary signs that foretold the coming of Muḥammad. *The Story of Tabi'u*[123] shows the futility of tampering with the work of the Almighty. Tabi'u was a king and the supposed founder of Yathrīb (Medina), who lived just before the birth of Muḥammad and who attempted to destroy the Ka'bah, destined to become the holiest shrine in Islam. Tabi'u mustered an army of some four hundred thousand, with ten thousand wisemen to advise him. As he was about to attack the Ka'bah, God gave him a headache and running nose. He summoned scholars, astrolgers, and physicians, but they failed to diagnose or cure his illness. Finally, an old wiseman told him that his illness arose from his intending to destory the Ka'bah; he could be cured if he desisted. He agreed and was cured. In gratitude he built Medina and named it after Muḥammad, whose coming was announced. Furthermore, Tabi'u made the confession of the faith to Islam, leaving a message written in gold for Muḥammad, who received it during his flight to Medina in 622. King Tabi'u died the day Muḥammad was born!

FUTURISTIC HISTORY (ESCHATOLOGY)

Morisco historical perspective extends to the world beyond, perceived as more real than this ephemeral world. Like their Muslim ancestors, the Moriscos believed in the Day of Judgment and had a clear conception about the fate of the soul in the hereafter. These beliefs appear to be of great concern to the Moriscos, recorded with expectation. The coming of the Antichrist, a prelude to the Day of Judgment, is marked with deceit and injustice until Christ emerges and puts an end to the Antichrist and the evildoers. He does it, however, as a surrogate of Muḥammad and in the path of Islam until all people become Muslims. During the Day of Judgment,[125] people will ask in vain for Adam, Abraham, Moses, and other prophets to intercede on their behalf. Then Christ will send them to Muḥammad, who will respond to their pleas, and who will prostrate himself before God imploring Him to forgive and redeem them.

Relevant to the life in the hereafter is *The Story of Two Friends.*[126] This dialogue on the fate of the dead describes how the dead man is surrounded by bad and good angels in two groups, each of which tries to bring the man to its side. The good angels win when the confession of faith is made, and the body is transported to Heaven, from which it is taken to Paradise to contemplate the

Lord. Muḥammad's ascension (*Mi'rāj*)[127] to the Seven Heavens is another view of life after death, showing Muḥammad's preeminent position in the celestial hierarchy. There are exhortations[128] reminding people of their religious duties and the consequences accruing from noncompliance: bitter death, suffering in the tomb, and failing to cross the bridge, thus ending in Hell. In short, he who obeys God and his Prophet will be rewarded in Paradise, and he who disobeys is punished in Hell. Hell is described as an awesome place. According to a prophetic tradition,[129] there will be ten kinds of people in Hell, each in a form corresponding to a sin on earth: (1) those in the form of monkeys, who were usurpers of people's possessions and who did the forbidden things; (2) those in the form of pigs, who were evildoers or accomplices of mischief; (3) those in the form of branches of fire, who were preachers who did not practice what they preached; (4) those without hands, who were the thieves; (5) those smelling like putrid meat, who were adulterous; (6) those clothed with fire, who were delinquent in almsgiving (*elzike*); (7) those with tongues stretched down to their chests, who were false witnesses; (8) those with faces turned downward, who bore false witness and broke oathes; (9) those with their hands tied around their necks, who judged without regard for the Holy Book; and (10) those in the form of fire, blind, mute, and deaf, who were scholars and readers who read but did not act according to what they read.

Another version[130] associates the penalty of Hell with earthly sins, relating that Christ resurrected a youth who had the face of a pig, his brain coming out of his ears, his tongue hanging over his chest, and a belly protruding over his legs made of fire. Christ inquired how he acquired these features and the youth replied: for failing to perform ablution and prayer, not heeding admonitions, converting lies into truth and vice versa, and usurping orphans' possessions.

Reportedly based on a prophetic tradition, *The Story of a Worshiper* (*'ābid*)[131] relates the extreme devotion of a worshiper who upon examination in the hearafter was sent to Hell. On earth, he was the ideal devotee, living on a mountain top for five hundred years, drinking sweet water from a fountain nearby, and eating fruits from a Mengharana (pomegranate) tree at the bottom of the mountain. He fulfilled all the religious obligations, including ablution (*alwaḍu*) and prayer (*aṣṣala*). In prostration (*asajdada*), he asked the Lord to take his soul, and his wish was fulfilled. When he faced the Lord in Paradise, he was asked whether he was in Paradise because of his devotion or God's mercy (*piyadad*). He said he was there because of his devotion; God ordered him to Hell. The worshiper began to scream, pleading that he be put in Paradise by God's mercy. He was brought back for further questioning, and was asked who was the Creator of things. Since he answered that all things were created by God's mercy, he was allowed to remain in Paradise. The moral of the story is that belief in God's mercy is worthier than five hundred years of complete devotion.

From this broad survey of the historico-legendary literature, a clear vision of history emerges. This vision is pregnant with religious significance, guided by belief in a divine plan in which God makes Islam the ultimate manifestation of His Will and the consummation of his Revelation. God selects His people, tests, punishes, or rewards them. In the final days, Islam will emerge as the best religion and Muḥammad as His Prophet, with Christ as an assistant for bringing people to the true faith.

TRAVEL

Inasmuch as travel and travel works were traditionally associated with historical writings and occupy no small place in Arabic literature, the Moriscos would presumably have cultivated this genre or taken an interest in earlier travel works so as to enable them to have a broad knowledge of the world of Islam. This appears not to have been the case. Unlike their Muslim predecessors in East and West, who traveled far and wide in their capacity as merchants, pilgrims, and students, leaving accounts of their journeys, the Moriscos had little mobility and lacked the sophistication to record impressions of their surroundings in the manner of Ibn Jubayr (d. 1217), Ibn Baṭṭūṭah (d. 1377), or other Andalusian travelers. Moreover, travel literature, as it existed in Arabic, does not appear to have interested them—if indeed, it was known to them. Indications are that some Moriscos traveled within and outside the Iberian Peninsula as merchants or missionaries, or out of curiosity, leaving few records of their journeys. Those which have come down to us contain valuable insights and nostalgic impressions. One such record is left by the Mancebo of Arevalo, who seems to have visited most Spanish cities; he gives glimpses of places and people, such as Andalusía and the old lady of Ubeda.[132]

International travel among the Moriscos was limited, although there are indications that Moriscos sailed the Mediterranean with acces to both North African and European ports. Two itineraries are relevant in this connection: one[133] giving a chart of travel from Spain to Turkey, and the other[134] overland from Venice to Spain. The best known and most unusual international traveler is the pilgrim Puey de Monçón,[135] who went by sea along the North African coast to Mecca. He celebrated his journey in couplets, which contain important and interesting impressions. Puey de Monçón undertook the trip during the sixteenth century, at a time when Moriscos were beset by prohibitions of any religious undertaking, let alone a pilgrimage to the Holy City of Mecca. Puey embarked in Valencia heading southward to the north African coast, where he continued eastward, stopping at various ports. He minutely describes the hardships and excitement of the trip—storms and lack of provisions. After a tedious journey, he arrived in Cairo (*alqahara*), marveling at its monuments and mosques. Arriving in Mecca, he describes in glowing terms his emotions upon seeing the Holy City, whose gates are "benediction" (*albaraka*), whose walls are piety (*piyadad*), and whose roof clarity. Merely being there is a great reward: "For whoever goes there will surely have gained forgiveness."[136] Mecca (Maka) is indeed indescribable—neither words nor writing will ever do justice to it. He felt heartbroken upon leaving it, and it pained him greatly not to have visited Jerusalem, where Moors and Christians alike go to ask for forgiveness.

Although normal travel and pilgrimage were beyond the reach of the Moriscos because of economics and restrictions on freedom of movement, the voluntary or forced exodus from Spain required basic information about routes, cost, destination, and other relevant facts.[137] One work meeting these needs bears the appropriate title, *Advice for the Traveler (Avisos para el caminante)* and contains valuable information and instructions about provisions, routes, places, cities, and other details.[138]

Other material of historical interest could have been included here, such as the epic narratives inserted in the Arabic historical writings which are treated elsewhere[139] because of their literary aspects. However, in reviewing the historical literature of the Moriscos, one can hardly speak of a Morisco historiography; rather, the Moriscos possessed a historical perspective, based on and inspired by careful selection of materials from Arabic sources in the form of translation or paraphrasing, preserving much of the integrity of the original with respect to form and content. Considering the plight of the Moriscos in a hostile environment, one may be justified in inquiring the reasons for their selectivity. A careful scrutiny of historical material against the background and the social setting of the Moriscos shows that the Moriscos made calculated selections to meet their social and religious needs. In so doing, they followed, consciously or unconsciously, the Islamic traditional conception of history as a discipline whose main purpose is to instruct and edify, with experience of mankind as a model. One can learn even from evildoers, but the Moriscos preferred heroic figures whom God chose and tested to lead mankind into the right path.

The Moriscos also adhered closely to the traditional Arabic form of narration known as *ḥadīth (*Alj. *el-alḥadīth)*, or information (*khabar,* pl. *akhbār). Ḥadīth* was handed down over the ages by reputable men and is above scrutiny, however doubtful it may appear to outsiders. An explicit vision of history emerges, conveyed through the compilation of suggestive items from the rich sacred history of Islam in which men and events are subordinated to divine will and in which legends and history are so intertwined. This appears to be true of the historical literature of the Moriscos.

Thus, the Moriscos were far from innovative in their approach to history. On the other hand, their literature conveys great insight into their psychological and religious needs through a discerning selectivity of material and presentation that can be read or listened to with the desired effect of impressing the mind and convincing the skeptic. These historical writings had the purpose of indoctrinating; they were written not by scholars for scholars, but by pedagogues who had a full appreciation of the needs and problems facing their fellow Moriscos. Each historical item, whether dealing with an individual or event, has significance for a particular need. The biography of Muḥammad is a case in point. This simple and straightforward narration is not based on the authoritative biography of Ibn Isḥāq (d. 767) in a later recension of Ibn Hishām (d. 834),[140] but on a version by the obscure scholar al-Bakrī (d. 1545), who wove a simple account of the life of Muḥammad deleting the long chains of transmitters (*isnād*) and other scholarly details found in Ibn Hishām's work. Al-Bakrī developed the theme of illumination, in which the existence of Muḥammad was preordained at Creation in the form of light, a theme which particularly suited Morisco spiritual needs in a time when their Prophet was not only denied the role of prophecy but villified. Also, the belief in Muḥammad's existence from time immemorial in the form of light conforming to God's design served the purpose of maintaining the faith and rebutting Christian and Jewish charges of unbelief.

Other historical literature emphasizes the spiritual and religious at the expense of worldly pursuits. Morisco treatment of some Islamic leaders often obscures their actual role in history, overemphasizing religiosity. For example, 'Alī (r. 656-661) was unsuccessful as caliph in coping with state affairs, but the Moriscos gave him the role of an undefeatible knight working for the eternal glory of Islam.[141] Their treatment of pre-Islamic figures follows a similar line, emphasizing their role in the growth and ultimate triumph of the Islamic movement conceived to have begun at the time of Creation. Traditional Islam recognized hundreds of pre-Islamic "believers" or prophets; the Moriscos selected (without disavowing the rest) only those who by word and deed reflected the best Islamic virtues and at the same time, Morisco preoccupations and aspirations. Even in this limited selection of prominent pre-Islamic figures, the Moriscos chose material which best conveyed religious perspective.

A review of *Biographies of Prophets (Qiṣaṣ al-anbiyā')* by the bellelettrist al-Tha'ālibī (d. 1038) bears this out. Using the Qur'ān, prophetic traditions, Qur'ānic commentaries, and works of his predecessors, al-Tha'ālibī gives sketches of an array of prophets, including some who were not prophets but revered for special endowments, such as Alexander the Great as a world conqueror and Luqmān as a wiseman whose counsels ought to be heeded.[142] Al-Tha'ālibī systematically treats each prophet's birth, career, and death. When the Moriscos wrote of prophets—though they may have drawn information from works such as al-Tha'ālibī's—their selectivity hinges on potential for an edifying lesson to strengthen and prove the validity of their religion. They did not deviate from Islamic orthodox norms, but singled out a particular feature of the extraordinary exploits of Alexander or the wisdom of Luqmān.

Abraham, "who was the first whom God called true Muslim,"[143] was also the actual ancestor of Muslims through his son Ismā'īl. They were both instrumental in building the Zamzam well and the holy shrine of the Ka'bah in Mecca. Such roles were significant to the Moriscos at the theological and polemical level for establishing the legitimacy of Islam vis-à-vis both Judaism and Christianity. The story of Joseph was regarded in the Islamic tradition as "the best story," embodying the qualities of patience, forgiveness, continence, God's divinity, right conduct, and interpretation of dreams[144]—with all of which the Moriscos could identify, especially Joseph's shattered life and ultimate triumph. Hope could also be derived from Job's deliverance from suffering after unshaken belief in the Lord and from Moses' deliverance of his suffering people from tyranny. Solomon, who rode the clouds and ruled over spirit, man, birds, beasts, and devils,[145] had particular interest for the Moriscos, who had a great propensity for magic and superstitions.[146] Finally, Christ was presented as a prophet and collaborator of Muḥammad but could not be worshiped as God, as Christians wished. In sum, the Moriscos remained faithful to traditional Islamic conceptions of history and the hereafter.

7

Sorcery, Talisman, and the Sciences

Although the Moriscos succeeded in maintaining their basic beliefs through the compilation of rudimentary religious materials, they were unable to engage in creative scholarly and intellectual pursuits, which would have required Muslim education and institutions, as well as freedom of thought. The Christians' calculated policy extended far beyond religious concerns, with repercussions for the pursuit and cultivation of the secular sciences—mathematics, astronomy, pharmacy, medicine, and others. To these, medieval Muslims made distinct contributions, with which Europeans within and outside Spain became familiar through the translation of Arabic works into Western languages.[1]

Paradoxically, this receptivity to the secular Arabic sciences in Spain and elsewhere in Europe, which might have constituted a meeting ground between Christians and their subject people, coincided and flourished with the progress of the Reconquest. Christian edicts and restrictions led to the Moriscos' becoming increasingly educationally undernourished until they lacked even an elementary education. But this decline took centuries. At first, despite Christian Spain's being the home of the major centers for translation of the abundant Arabic scientific literature in astromony, mathematics, medicine, and other disciplines, attention appears to have been focused on religiosity rather than on the sciences. Alfonso X, who encouraged the sciences through translating and writing, was an exception; later Spanish monarchs left learning to clerics. Such clerics were more concerned with preserving the purity of the faith than with philosophical or scientific deliberations, which were often considered detrimental to religious belief.

Thus, the sciences, particularly medicine, remained the domain of Jews and Mudejars/Moriscos, who met the scientific needs of the country until the sixteenth century using Arabic scientific lore as found in the Arabic originals or in translation therefrom. However, the Jews and Mudejars were working under heavy strictures and constant accusations of being infidels ready to corrupt the faith and to harm Christians.[2] They were scarcely able to make new contributions to the sciences, and relied mainly on the school of Galen as transmitted through such works as Ibn Sīnā's *Qanūn,* al-Rāzi's *Ḥāwi,* Ibn Zuhr's *Taysīr,* and others in rather clumsy Latin translations. Pursuit of the sciences was tolerated to a degree among the Jews and Moriscos until the end of the fifteenth century. There are some indications that the Mudejars of Saragossa were allowed to have their own school (*madrasah*) where medicine was taught.[3] Such schools were found elsewhere—for example, in the *morerías* of Valencia and in Granada, where the Arabic scientific traditions were for the most part preserved until the conquest of the latter in 1492. Regulation of medicine was introduced during the fourteenth century, the state controlling licenses and practice.[4] A number of women—Jewish, Moorish and Christian —were licensed to practice medicine, and many others acted as midwives. This tolerant policy came to an end in the course of the sixteenth century, when Arabic and anything connected with it were prohibited. The Moriscos were denied admission to universities and often refused licenses to practice medicine. The result was to stifle the Moriscos' scientific knowledge. Deprived of formal training and forbidden to possess Arabic books, they had to rely more and more on oral traditions, direct experience, and superstitions derived from their Latin environment as well as from the Arabic cultural legacy. This is borne out by their own writings.

The extant Morisco literature indicates that sorcery and talisman fall between the realms of religion and the natural sciences, and it is difficult to separate them or to determine where religion ends and science begins.[6] In Morisco belief and practice, sorcery and talisman occupied a position of validity almost equal to both religion and science.[7] It is relevant here to refer to Ibn Khaldūn's treatment of both sorcery and talisman in Muslim traditions. Ibn Khaldūn calls them sciences, but adds that they are forbidden by religious law because their practitioners get their power from sources other than God.[8] As such, sorcery and talisman are different from miracles and have grave religious implications: unlike prophets, who exercise their influence with the help of God for good purposes, soothsayers and magicians exercise their influence through the aid of or devotion to the Devil, stars and other means, often for evil purposes.[9] Thus, the difference between the prophets' miracles and actions resulting from sorcery is the difference between belief and unbelief, between good and evil. Nevertheless, sorcery, talisman, and astrology were practiced in Islam, resulting in a wide literature. The sorcerer was said to be able to cast a spell on a cloud, causing rain to fall, or to point at a garment, causing it to disintegrate.[10] Whereas the sorcerer derives his influence from his psychic power, the practitioners of talisman make use of loving numbers, seals, magic squares, stars, the secrets of letters,[11] or the qualities of existing things. Ibn Khaldūn's characterization of sorcery fits quite well into Morisco practices. The extant literature indicates that the Moriscos were almost totally unaware of the religious implications of the practice of sorcery, talisman, and astrology. The presence of a relatively abundant literature on divination—alongside the Morisco's strong attachment to Islamic dogma and values—further indicates their lack of speculative theology and of intellectual or scientific knowledge that would have facilitated the production of philosophical or scientific works either through the process of paraphrasing and translating Arabic works or of making original contributions. The Moriscos appear to have retained some notion about astronomy, medicine, and pharmacology—but it does not appear that such notions were derived from readily accessible Arabic scientific works, either in the original Arabic or in translation. Scientific notions were often intermingled with divinations, horoscopes, magical formulas, amulets, magical seals, magical letters, and inscriptions. A rudimentary knowledge of astronomy existed among the Moriscos appear to have retained some notion about astronomy, medicine, and pharmacology—but it does not appear that such notions were derived astrological notions consisting of predictions based on astral influences often considered decisive in determining human actions.[12] Although medicine appears to have been practiced widely, it lacked the scientific works and the clinics and hospitals that marked medieval Arabic medicine.[13] In fact, medicine appears to have declined gradually into superstitions and magical formulas.[14] Pharmacy met a similar fate, the scientific preparation of drugs becoming overshadowed by amulets, seals, and other devices.

In short, although the Moriscos did have a grasp of the fundamental precepts of Islam, preserving purity of the faith and avoiding controversial theological aspects, they fell short in the espousal of the sciences known to medieval Islam, even in their most rudimentary form. This neglect owed much to the restrictions imposed on their educational institutions, but it would be erroneous to suggest that the Moriscos' propensity to superstitions and divination was solely the result of a peculiar ethnic quality. Their notions derived from both Arabic traditions and the folklore of Spain, handed down orally from generation to generation. Such formulas for all season and every occasion are interspersed through Aljamiado literature and in the same religious tracts containing excerpts of the Qur'ān. Each day of the week, each month, the New Year, the change of seasons—each has religious and astrological significance and may portend good or ill.

A number of works illustrate the nature and the extent of the use of magical formulas, charms (*anusara*, Ar. *al-nushrah*), amulets, (*elḥirze*, Ar. *al-ḥirz*), spells (*al-'azīma*, Ar. *al-'azīmah*), incantations, and invocations. The *Memoria*,[15] a composite work in fifty-four folios, deals with the four seasons and with the manner of attaining what is desired through utterance of a specific invocation for each season.[16] Also, it contains a number of spells, charms, methods of divination through the use of number, and amulets—in addition to a section devoted to five physicians; Galen, Avicenna, Hippocrates, al-Rzī, and Ibn al-Wāfir. Similarly, *The Book of Marvellous Sayings*[17] contains a mélange of superstitions, magical formulas, spells, charms, and amulets for every need and cure. This stout volume of some five hundred seventy-three folios, divided into chapters and sections, is a veritable encyclopedia of ready-made answers to questions such as how to cause the devil to flee the house, how to make married people love each other, how to know a wife's secrets, how to cure animals and humans, see others without being seen, see one's desires in dreams, get what one wants, learn the result of a future undertaking, and so on. All these things are possible through "knowing." For instance, knowing the marvellous properties of the head, eyes, and heart of a dove, raven, wolf, or hare will help to devise certain formulas for achieving good things or preventing bad ones. Similarly, knowing the effects of the stars on human acts at every moment, one could choose the propitious moment for action. Certain chapters of the Qur'ān have enormous power, permitting a person to remain stationary, to see the Prophet, to have God listen to one's prayer, and to cure many diseases. Magical signs are effective in getting a loan and for securing food and drink, clothing, and other necessities. Other magical signs have the power of getting rid of worms, helping to sleep, reducing fever, curing any ache; still others prevent women from committing adultery or allow the discovery of women's mischief. A variety of amulets will eliminate spirits and fever, determine whether a sick person will die or recover, cause all the family to love the bearer, keep away the evil eye, and repel spells and all sorts of evils. Other formulas and prescriptions will cure animals that cannot urinate and cure people having shaky hands, noise in the ear, and inflamation in the head or in any other part of the body. Prescriptions are also given for easing fear and heartache, knowing secrets, making a husband love or hate his wife, preventing women's fear of childbirth, and the like. There is also the magical effect of Arabic letters, which have the virtue of predicting the favorable or unfavorable result of an undertaking.

Some amulets and magical formulas illustrating the *Book of Marvellous Sayings* are shown below. *The Book of the Moriscos*[12] also contains various crude illustrations: a Muslim with a beard and a crown reading a book, two blacks facing a tomb, and an eagle with two heads. In addition, the work contains various sheets of scribblings that may have some magical value —perhaps simply exercises. There are also geometrical figures and some other crude drawings. Another manuscript[19] contains numerous cases (*kaso*) explaining and illustrating formulas in the form of inscriptions using Arabic letters or geometric forms for curing fever, headache, ailing eyes, boredom, bleeding, and fear; for protecting cornfields, and for many other situations.

The Book of Divination[20] makes use of Qur'ānic verses for every conceivable activity (walking, hunting, and other wishes) and ends with a formula for making black ink. This work appears to be different from another with an identical title, *Libro de las Suwertes*, inserted in the *Book of Marvellous Sayings*.[21] The latter contains numerous superstitions and prognostications based on astral and natural phenomena, with the underlying thesis that all human events and actions are influenced by natural phenomena, leading to either great expectations or imminent danger. These natural phenomena include weather conditions, thunder, eclipses of the sun and the moon, motion of the stars, the beginning of the new year, the signs of the zodiac (*elburje*), interpretation of dreams, and the fortunes of Alexander the Great. These phenomena will lead to accurate predictions if they occur on certain dates. For instance, rain can be predicted on a cloudy day, but rain will surely fall if clouds appear on October 1, November 2, or December 3.[22] Thunder in January during the high moon signals snow mixed with rain and wind; in any month during low moon, that many people will die; in May during high moon, good things—abundant provisions and the king's compassion.[23] Eclipses of the sun and the moon also determine the course of events. If an eclipse of the sun takes place on the twenty-eighth of a month, extraordinary things will happen. If it falls in March, some people will die, and pregnant women will lose their babies; if in April, there will be fear all over the land; if in June, there will be great wars among the unbelievers, and God will give victory to the Muslims.[24] Extraordinary things will also take place during the eclipse of the moon. If the eclipse of the moon is black, infirmities and violent deaths will occur, but if it is not so black, only cattle will die.[25] If the eclipse falls in October, there will be drought, famine, locusts, and a plague among the Jews.[26] And if it takes place in July, there will be great wars in which God will give victory to the Muslims over the infidels.[27] Other texts deal with invocations and formulas for rain.[28]

Still other manuscripts[29] deal with the historico-religious significance of the lunar months, which BNM 5354 characterizes as follows:

Al-Muḥarram (The First Moon) is the beginning of the New Year, as January is for Christians. The tenth day marks a day of voluntary fasting *(ashūra, Ar. 'ashūrā'),* which not only carries enormous rewards, but is also the day in which God created Heaven, Earth, the preserved tablet *(lallawhi el-maḥfūẓ*, Ar. *al-Lawḥ al-maḥfūẓ*), Gabriel, Eve, and Paradise. Abraham and Jesus were born on the tenth, and Joseph was freed from prison and joined his brothers. The Day of *'Ashūrā')* also marks the date on which Solomon's seal (*sillo)* descended to return to him after it had been lost.

Ṣafar (The Second Moon) has no special days except the "white days" (*los diyas balankos*): the thirteenth, fourteenth, and fifteenth, which have merit (*faḍīla,* Ar. *faḍīlah*).

Rabīʻ al-Awwal (The Third Moon) marks Muḥammad's birthday.

Rabīʻal-Thāni (The Fourth Moon) has no special days except the white days.

Jumāda al-ūlā (The Fifth Moon) has no special days except the white days.

Jumāda al-Thāni (The Sixth Moon) has no special days except the white days.

Rajab (The Seventh Moon) is the month of God (*mes de-Allah*)—a month of voluntary fasting for gaining great merits and rewards (*ghuwalardons*). It is the month in which Revelation (*waḥy)*descended upon Muḥammad.

In Shaʻbān (The Eighth Moon), the fifth is significant in that all human deeds are then presented before God. It is also the date on which the Kaʻbah desended from Paradise to Earth, the doors of Hell (*jahannam*) closed, and God spoke to Moses.

Ramaḍān (The Ninth Moon) is the month of obligatory fasting for every Muslim.

Shawwāl (The Tenth Moon) begins with the break of fasting (*ʻīd el-fiṭr*).

Dhi il-qiʻda (The Eleventh Moon) contains days of voluntary fasting. It has the further significance of being the month in which the Kaʻbah was taken by Adam to the House of Mecca.

Dhū el-Ḥijja (The Twelfth Moon) has the first nine days of voluntary fasting. The ninth is the day of *ʻarafa*, which precedes the Feast of Lamb (*paskuwa de karnero*).[30]

Also, each day of the week has significance, either through the influence of the stars or by association with an extraordinary event. Thus, Sunday is a good day for planting and building since that is the day God created the world. Monday is good for walking and merchandising. Tuesday is bad since Cain killed Abel upon it. Wednesday is bad since that it the day Pharaoh sank in the Red Sea. Thursday is good for making petitions and asking favors. Friday is good for weddings. Saturday is a day of artifice and deceit.[31] This evaluation of lucky (*saʻd*) and unlucky (*naḥis*) days is extended to all the days of the month in BNP 1163,[32] based on a prophetic tradition classifying the days on the strength of God's will or as the result of happy or unhappy events:

The first day of the moon, on which God created Adam, is a good day for attending to necessities, weddings, and other activities; the second day is good for weddings, business transactions, asking favors, and doing what one wants; the third day is bad for business and for asking favors, and one ought to fear God, Who will defend him from evil; the fourth day, on which Abel was born, is good for weddings and other activities; the fifth day, on which Cain was born and on which he killed Abel, is bad; the sixth day is good for weddings, hunting, walking, and satisfying other needs; the seventh day is good for getting the worldly things one wants; the eighth day is good as the seventh day, except for walking; the ninth day is good for asking and doing what one wants; the tenth day is good and blessed for getting one's needs; the eleventh day is good for gainful pursuits, and those born in it will have wealth (*arrizke*); the twelfth day is good for asking what one wants; the thirteenth day is bad, strong, and severe; the fourteenth day is good for all pursuits—those born in it will be loved and will be seekers of knowledge; the fifteenth day is good for everything, but those born in it will be mute; the sixteenth day is bad, and those born in it will be mute; the seventeenth day is good for all activities; the eighteenth day is good for what one wants; the nineteenth day is chosen for all that one wants, except walking; the twentieth day is similar to the nineteenth day; the twenty-first day is bad, for in it blood was shed; the twenty-second day is good for walking and various other pursuits; the twenty-third day is as good as the twenty-second day; the twenty-fourth day is bad, and nothing good can be expected of it, for it is the date of Pharaoh's birth; the twenty-fifth day is bad, and those falling sick on it will never recover; the twenty-sixth day is good, the day upon which God opened the sea to Moses; the twenty-seventh day is good for asking what one wants; the twenty-eighth day is good and the day on which Jacob was born—those born upon it will love and be loved by their families, will be rich, and will live long, but will become blind; the twenty-ninth day is good for walking and other activities; and the thirtieth day is good for seeking merchandise, bleeding, and other activities.

All told, there are eighteen lucky days, seven unlucky days, and five days that begin well, but end badly.[33] The question remains to what extent the Moriscos allowed their activities to be influenced by auguries that recommended suspending activities upon some days and doubling of them on other, favorable days. It is difficult to reach an answer that would do justice to beliefs and observances, particularly among people who had to struggle for the bare necessities of life. One cannot wholly discount the elements of fatalism and despondency among the Moriscos. The problem becomes more complicated when this predeterminism is reinforced by other beliefs based on such haphazard occurrences as the beginning of a new year, which was believed to have enormous influence on the course of human events and on natural phenomena as well.[34] Thus, if the new year falls on a Sunday, the weather will be moderate, there will be some rain during the summer, the wheat harvest will be fair, nice people will die, there will be dissension among kings and discord among people, but grapes and figs will be good.[35] If the new year falls on a Monday, there will be a good summer, good fruits, abundant rains, and abundant honey, but great wars and highway robberies. If the new year falls on a Tuesday, there will be scarcity of provisions and fruits, famine, lies, quarrels among kings, heavy snow, and deaths among cattle and Christians.[36] If it falls on a Wednesday, there will be abundant rain but few fruits; if it falls on a Thursday, there will be abundant rain, abundant provisions and fruits, but little wool and honey; if it falls on a Friday, there will be abundant fruit and water, less falsehood among men, and less mischief among women; and if it falls on a Saturday, there will be winds, scarcity of flowers and water, a major sea war, and a king will be dethroned.[37]

Some of the numerous other spells or incantations (*annushara*, Ar. *al-nushrah*)[38] are attributed to Muḥammad himself.[39] There are also magical formulas,[40] esoteric secrets for curing wounds,[41] and amulets[42] for all situations, some of which are inscribed in Greek, Hebrew, Arabic, and Aljamiado.[43] The following examples, only a few of many, illustrate this type of literature. Animal organs were used in several situations, allowing a couple to love each other, and even to see spirits (*aljines*). Thus, "Take the skin of a black cat and the fat of a white chicken, mix them, and rub your eyes with them. This will allow you to see them [the spirits] whenever you want—God willing."[44] Future happenings can be perceived in the following manner: "He who takes the heart of the hoopoe when warm and at the moment of leaving its body will see all future happenings in his dreams."[45] "He who carries the head of a dove will be loved by anyone who sees him."[45] "He who carries the right eye of a wolf will not be seen or vanquished by anyone."[47] "If you take the heart of a black cat, wrap it with the skin of a wolf, and tie it on your left thigh, no one will see you and you will see everyone."[48] If a person is overcome by jealousy, "give him the fresh heart of a black dog to eat, and all jealousy will die from his heart—God willing."[49]

Seals (*khawetimes*)[50] with strange writings on them were used for all sorts of things: for curing diseases, for animals rejecting their offspring, for women who cannot give milk,[51] for protecting cornfields from birds.[52] For instance, if certain inscriptions are written on a Wednesday on a leaf of sugar cane and hung around the neck of an individual with fever, he will by "God's permission" (*pon lisensiya-de-Allah*) be cured.[53] To expel worms from the stomach, seals are hung on the neck.[54] If a person cannot sleep, inscriptions should be written twenty-seven times and placed under his head; without knowing it, he will sleep well (see Fig. 1 and 2).[55]

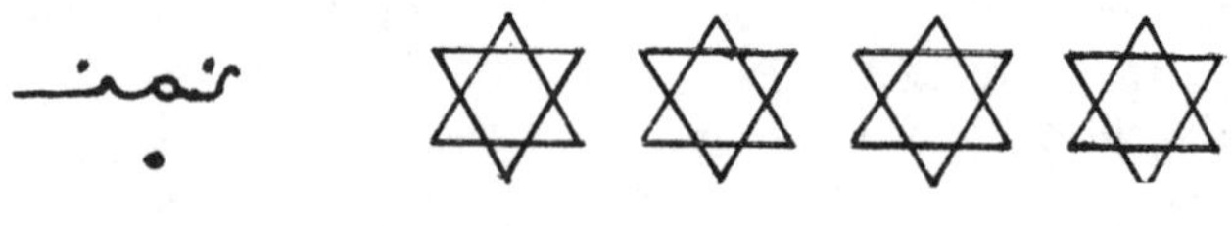

Figure 1

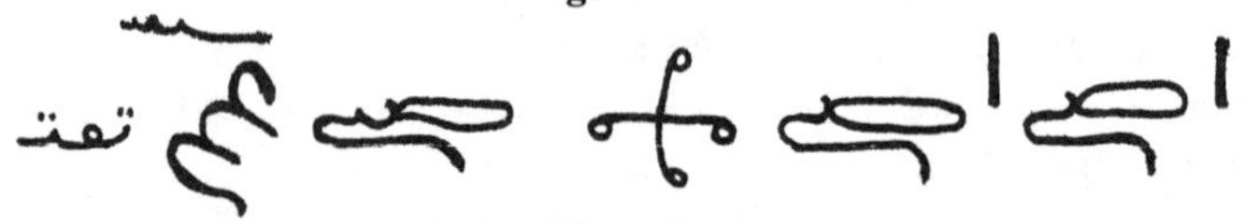

Figure 2

Herbs were also used for both medicinal and magical purposes. Two treatises[56] contain formulas for various diseases, giving remedies and instructions for their use. One such remedy and instruction for the woman who cannot have delivery consists of taking sesame (*el-salsamo*) with lukewarm water; then she will surely have it—with "the science of God."

Qur'ānic verses were considered to have enormous power for many situations. If carried by a person along with certain seals, they will eliminate fever, headache, and all sorts of disease.[57] Some such spells or charms are attributed to the Prophet himself. One spell consists of writing one or more verses of the Qur'ān in an empty glass; water is added afterward. Such a potion will accomplish wonders: "The Prophet—May peace be upon him—said, 'He who drinks this charm (*annushara*) will be safe of headache, toothache, and mouthache; it prevents all bad things: bleeding, mortality caused by unexpected and extraordinary situations, bedevilment, leprosy, hemmorhage, diathesis, deafness, muteness, and the like. Also, the individual will not be afraid in his sleep, nor will he faint; nor will he have any pain or twisting of the mouth; nor will he break wind; nor will he sleep or have any obstacle during prayer.' "[58]

The magical value of the Arabic letters[59] has wide application in births, marriages, diseases, and other situations. Arabic letters (*alḥarfes*) can be used alone, in their numerical value,[60] or in combination with something else. They can be used for removing obstacles (*Para desatar el-atado*), as: "Take these letters and an egg (*webo*) laid on Thursday; fry it until it is hard, clean it, and inscribe on it these letters as shown, and give it to the bound one to eat, and he will be untied—God willing."[61] They can also be used in combination with invoking God's name (*basmala*) three times for all sorts of ailment; thus:

Bismi Llāhi r-raḥmāni r-raḥīm
(In the name of God, the Merciful, the Compassionate)
Bismi Llāhi r-raḥmāni r-raḥīm
Bismi Llāhi r-raḥmāni r-raḥīm[62]

Illegible inscriptions are used alone or along with Qur'ānic verses for cures and other purposes. These inscriptions often take the form of seals *(sillos),* accompanied by geometrical forms or sometimes drawings. In order to be loved: "Write this and hang it in the air. These aer the names you ought to write."[63] (see Fig. 3) For the cure of fever a seal is used in the form of the inscription. "Take three eggs, boil them, remove the shell, write these seals on each one, and give them to the patient to eat."[64] And for night fever, "Write these seals, lay them on the patient, and he will be cured—God willing."[65]

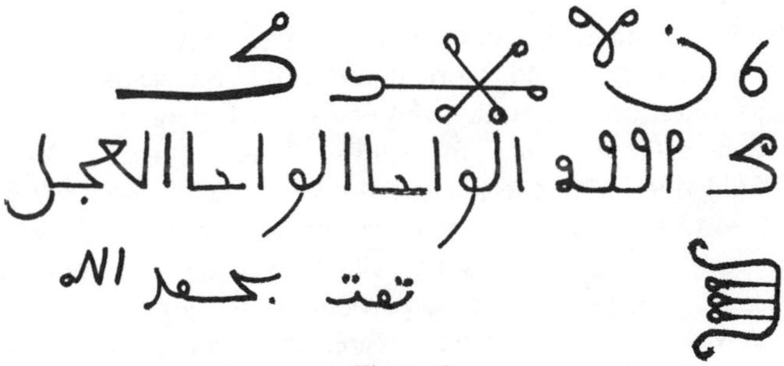

Figure 3

The *Book of Divination* (BNM 5300) makes use of both Arabic letters and Qur'ānic verses to predict the outcome of an enterprise, good (*buweno*) or bad (*naḥs*). The work has an answer for all human activities: buying, selling, marriage, walking, and all things within "God's obedience and will." The procedure follows: Write *alif* (*a*), *bā'* (*b*), *jīm* (*j*), and *dāl* (*d*) on a square dice (*poliko*)—one letter on each side. Throw the dice three times in order to get three letters; then look up the three letters in the chapter headings, often marked good (*buweno*) and bad (*naḥs*). If you throw the dice three times and get, for example, *bjj*, the result will be good; if you get *bdj*, it will be bad. One is warned not to throw the dice twice for the same question on a given occasion. The Qur'ānic verses are in Arabic, followed by explanations in Aljamiado.

In the presence of so many spells, charms, amulets, and other magical formulas for all eventualities, one can hardly speak of the sciences as established disciplines. Aljamiado literature indicates that the sciences fell, by and large, between the realm of religious superstition and folklore and that of undigested scientific knowledge from writings of Muslim predecessors. This appears to be the case with respect to medicine, which was highly developed early in Islam. Medical knowledge continued to be esteemed by the Moriscos, but its cultivation as a profession requiring rigorous training was in rapid decline, giving way to reliance on magic and on religious formulas, such as verses of the Qur'ān. Hospitals, dispensaries, and even physicians, all of which had been available during the classicial period of Islam, had disappeared. Such facilities were awaiting development in Christian Spain. Thus, the Moriscos had to rely on a mixture of superstitions, old folklore, and science.

Although the Christians had imposed heavy restrictions on the possession of Arabic books, particularly those of religious nature, scientific works were often spared—not necessarily in allowing the Moriscos to have them, but in confiscating them, as Archbishop Ximinez de Cisneros did when he ordered the burning of books in Granada except for scientific books, which he ordered taken to his recently founded University of Henares. Arabic scientific works had been translated into Latin beginning with the eleventh century and had currency throughout Europe and Spain in the following centuries; being quite available, these could have served as the basis for the continuation and advancement of the sciences, mainly, medicine. However, the Moriscos showed little or no interests in such works, both because they lacked the necessary background in the sciences and, more importantly, because they were obsessed with religious questions overshadowing other considerations. The sciences were of secondary importance for spiritual and physical well-being and relegated to oblivion. Moreover, science—like medicine, however pragmatic and relevant—was frowned upon by their Christian compatriots, who regarded even physicians as but a necessary evil, little better than magicians. This placed a great stigma on physicians, particularly if they happened to be of Morisco or Jewish ancestry. Christians feared that Morisco and Jewish physicians could not be trusted, employing them only as a last resort. Thus, a Morisco physician was always suspect—even if he were successful in attending and curing the sick, when he might be accused of receiving the aid of the Devil. Morisco physicians only had to account for their deeds before the tribunals of the Inquisition, which scarcely permitted medicine to flourish.

However, medicine could not be ignored altogether, and its practice, rudimentary and unscientific, continued. This is attested by the extant Aljamiado literature and also by archival materials reflecting the uneasiness of the church and Old Christians toward medicine in general and Morisco doctors in particular. The medical literature of the Moriscos was interspersed with religious texts, forming composite works of an overall religious or superstitious character. Moreover, there is no complete medical compendium in Aljamiado that could be said to have been based on earlier Arabic works, despite the fact that such works were readily available in Spain in both Arabic and Latin versions. Such negligence may be attributable to the Moriscos' profound religious perspective as well as to lack of education.

This notwithstanding, the Moriscos could hardly remain completely oblivious to the great names of Greco-Arabic medicine—however vague their knowledge. Dioscorides' *Materia Medica* appears to have been known among Moriscos in its Spanish version. The names of the great physicians al-Rāzī, Ibn Sīnā, Ibn Wāfir, Galen, and Hippocrates are mentioned, and to them are attributed prescriptions for a host of ailments. One treatise[66] on religious duties also has various medical prescriptions and advice attributed to Galen, Hippocrates, al-Rāzī, and Ibn Sīnā. The *Memoria*[67] and *The Book of Good Doctrines*[68] contain some one hundred prescriptions (*rresebtas*) capable of achieving "marvellous things" and attributed to the five wisemen and doctors (*sabyos dotores*) of medicine: Galen, Ibn Sīnā, Hippocrates, al-Rāzī, and Ibn Wāfir. Free from superstitions, these prescriptions are based on minerals, vegetables, and chemical compounds and are meant for the cure of headache, sciatica, evil eye, fever, sore throat, stomachache, liver, inflamation, colds, loss of weight, cough, bleeding, and other ailments. One set of documents[69] contains some medicinal notes. A second set[70] has a list of medical terms in Arabic, and notes on some drugs. A third set[71] includes magical formulas for curing every wound. An interesting treatise[72] of some thirty folios appears to be based on the medical work of Ibn Zuhr,[73] member of a prominent Andalusian family of physicians. The treatise refers to another medical scholar (*'ālime*), whose name is illegible, and contains three languages—Castilian, Arabic, and Latin. Another treatise[74] consists of a compilation of prescriptions for a variety of illnesses and instructions for administering them according to the dicta of past masters (*maestoro*) such as Galen, Dioscorides, Ibn Sīnā, and other contemporary Latin or Morisco physicians.[75] Some of the prescriptions are meant to cure infested wounds (*llagha*),[76] pimples of the mouth (*besighas de-la-boka*),[77] chestache,[78] swollen breasts,[79] and other ailments. These treatises, based on the works of physicians of the past, constitute the bulk of the relatively meager medical literature. It is supplemented by a larger number of treatises consisting of magical formulas, spells, and charms that were considered as effective in the art of healing as the medical prescriptions of ancient and medieval Arabic physicians.

In fact, amulets, sorcery, incantation letters of the alphabet, supplications, and the use of holy texts were so much used among the Moriscos as to be an integral part of the art of healing in both diagnosis and therapy. Amulets were particularly important, since their possession was a sign of being a good Muslim: "A good Muslim should always carry amulets, for he who does not is like a house without a door in which everyone who wants can enter: in the same manner, devils will enter all the parts of a person who does not carry them."[80] Letters were used in diagnosis, where their numerical value is taken into consideration. The Arabic writing symbol, the letter, *a* is given the value of one; *b*, two; *c*, three; *d*, four; and so on. To determine the sickness of a person, a numerical value is given to his name; this is added to the numerical value of the day in which the disease occurred, and the result is then divided by seven. If the answer is one, the disease is jaundice; if two, fever, if four, malign air from the devil; if five, melancholoy; if six, choleric humor; and if the division is zero, the sickness is mere vexation.[81]

This appears to have been the state of medicine among Morisco doctors, considerably reduced from the scientific medicine in which their Muslim ancestors excelled. Presumably, however, the Morisco doctor discharged his important function in society to the best of his ability, being accepted in his own community and sometimes by his Old Christian neighbors, who employed him as a last resort. The Morisco doctor enjoyed some prestige in his capacity as a healer (*sanador*) and may be regarded at the social level of the *alfaqui*, the religious *savant*, who himself may have been a practitioner or instrumental in making medical literature available to aspiring physicians. At any rate, the life of the Morisco doctor was not an easy one, despite the rewards of practice.

This general assessment of the study and practice of medicine based on the Moriscos' own writings is corroborated by external evidence—minutes of the Inquisition and other documents. In his studies of medicine during the Middle Ages, especially his *Social History of Medicine*, García Ballester surveys the decline of medicine among the Moriscos and the factors behind it, drawing upon archival materials in Valencia, Aragón, Cataluña, Granada, and Castile. He points out that "the physician of the Muslim or Morisco community went through the long and bitter road that began from the summit of the scientific and social respect of the thirteenth, fourteenth, fifteenth, and even part of the sixteenth century, to the deepest abyss of degradation as an individual and a member of society when the dominant Christian society converted him into an authentic marginal social being."[82] García Ballester's conclusion may be fully appreciated by a review of the factors that produced this state of affairs. The Greco-Arabic medical tradition in Spain declined as the Reconquest set in. At first Muslims pursued medicine freely. Immediately after the conquest of Granada in 1492, Muslim physicians contiued to receive professional training, after which a license (*ijāzah*)[83] was issued attesting to the competence of the candidate. Such a license was conferred in November 1506 upon a certain Abu-l-Ḥasan ʻAlī Ibn Muḥammad Ibn Muslim, a resident of

Albaicín; a number of witnesses/patients certified his expertise in healing wounds, administering drugs, and attending to fractures, luxatin, gout, and spine injury.[84] In 1531, the University of Granada was founded, with a faculty of medicine that was open to Moriscos such as Alonso del Castillo and Miguel de Luna,[85] who became an interpreter/translator at the court. However, Alonso may have been an exception in that heavy restrictions were placed on Moriscos' university training in medicine, though there are indications that Moriscos pursued medicine, whether at or outside a university.

Their prominence in the profession alarmed the authorities and university graduates, who attempted to restrict their number and even to prevent their practicing altogether. Such a complaint was made as late as 1607 by Pedro Vesga, who pleaded before the Cortes of Castile to stop Moriscos from entering medical schools and from practicing medicine since "many of them study and practice in the universities of Alcalá, Toledo, and other places; I plead that all this be remedied in case this should lead by default to all or most physicians being Moriscos."[86] Furthermore, Old Christians mistrusted the Moriscos, whom they considered to hate them and whom they could not trust with their lives. One such complaint stated: "There is evidence that many Morisco physicians whom the Holy Office punished after their own confessions had cured those of their own race and intentionally killed Old Christians, maliciously giving potions causing abortion."[87] It went on to ask why the Moriscos should enjoy the privileges of the profession when such privileges are forbidden to them by law? They cannot be trusted with patients; they are corrupt and are capable of killing subtly and secretly with drugs without being accountable—indeed, they could kill "more people in this kingdom than do the Turks and Englishmen."[88]

Whether self-taught or a university graduate, the Morisco doctor was known as *Medico* (physician), *cirujano* (surgeon), *sanador* (healer), or rarely, *alfaqui* (a learned man).[89] As admission to medical schools passed beyond his reach on both financial and socioreligious grounds, he had to rely more and more on oral medical traditions handed down to him by a member of his family or a friendly local practitioner, who may have learned the art of healing in the same manner. The Morisco Román Ramírez learned medicine from his mother, María, who learned it from her father, Juan de Luna. Very learned in things pertaining to medicine and herbs, María was sought by people miles away.[90] She was familiar with Dioscorides' *Materia Medica,* translated into Spanish in 1555 by Andrés Laguna.[91] She was one of a number of women licensed to practice medicine.[92] Román fell heir to her medical knowledge, becoming a successful practitioner. He was brought before the tribunal of the Inquisition on charges of having had experiences with demons and was jailed in Cuenca, where he died. This appears to have been the fate of other known Morisco doctors, who were often accused of incantation, sorcery and witchcraft.[93] Among severe penalties were life imprisonment and prohibition of practicing medicine. Gaspar Capdal de Bunol, accused of having had a pact with the Devil,[94] was sentenced to one hundred lashes, five years' exile, a fine of ten ducados, and prohibition from practicing medicine.[95] Jerónimo Pachet excelled in curing the sick when the "professionals" failed, gaining prestige, wealth, and the animosity of university graduates, who accused him of being in league with the Devil.[96] He was brought before the tribunal of the Inquisition in Valencia in 1580 and sentenced to life imprisonment. Such, too, was the fate of Román Ramírez in Cuenca and Francisco de Cordova in Toledo.[97] Jeronimo Jover of Valencia appears to have been qualified as a physician, but was refused the examination that would confer a license to practice. Faced with such difficulties, he emigrated to North Africa, where he practiced medicine with success.

Thus, even when successful, Morisco doctors had to cope with bitter and unsurmountable local prejudices, which García Ballester[98] attributes to four causes: (1) theological, concerning whether an infidel working for the Devil can cure; (2) religious, concerning how a Morisco could advise patients when to confess when he himself neither confesses nor takes communion; (3) social, keeping the Morisco at the bottom of the social ladder; and (4) professional jealousy, arising from competition between the Christian graduate and the Morisco nongraduate, particularly at times when Moriscos were able to serve upper classes, including the court. Examples of court physicians are the Morisco Pinterete,[99] who attended Prince Charles, son of Philip II, and Pachet, who cured Philip III when a child—the same Philip who signed and carried out the decree of the expulsion of the Moriscos.

In retrospect, it appears that sorcerers, magicians, and astrologers formed a class by themselves whose activities were condoned by the Morisco community. The extant literature indicates that the occult—sorcery, magic, incantation, spells, and astrology—occupied a significant place among the Moriscos, permeating both established religion and the bonafide sciences to the point where there was no appreciable distinction among them. Practice of the occult did not appear to present any contradiction despite the traditional controversy surrounding it—some supporting its validity, others disavowing it. This ambivalent attitude has a long history, but was heightened by religious implications, particularly among Jews, Christians, and Muslims who attempted to restrict practice of the occult but never succeeded in eradicating it.

Thus, belief in the efficacy of the occult sciences was not peculiar to the Moriscos, who fell heirs to a legacy whose roots can be traced to antiquity and whose practice was still common among Christians in Spain. Though persecuted, the Moriscos did not live in a vacuum, but shared much of their Christian environment. In this connection, Caro's valuable work, *Vidas Mágicas,* supplies ample documentation of the practice of sorcery, magic, and astrology among sixteenth- and seventeenth-century Old Christians.[100] The work, based on literary materials and on documentary evidence drawn from the tribunals of the Inquisition, not only reveals the pervasive practice of the occult sciences among Old Christians, but brings out many features that are similar if not identical with those of the occult as practiced among the Moriscos. Such practice was so extensive as to become a major concern of the

Inquisition, which viewed it as harmful to religious beliefs and accomplished through a pact with the Devil.

The Inquisition's view was similar in some ways to that held by a good many Muslims. Although Muslim scholars listed sorcery, magic, talisman, and astrology as part of the sciences, the occult was viewed by some as detrimental to the religious beliefs, if not altogether heretical. Ibn Ḥazm's views may be added to those of Ibn Khaldūn.[101] Ibn Ḥazm did not consider magic and talisman to be bonafide sciences; their practitioners could not possibly walk on water, create new bodies, or alter the nature of things.[102] Astrology is also false, since the supposed influence of the stars on man and his activities defies experimentation or proofs.[103] Ibn Khaldūn echoes these views, considering sorcery, talisman, and astrology to lack any scientific basis.[104] Both Ibn Ḥazm and Ibn Khaldūn conclude that God alone has power over nature and He alone can alter it through miracles. Thus, any action by man or spirit aimed at altering the nature of things is tantamount to the negation of Divine Power. Both men also disavow alchemy, and distinguish between astrology and the "noble" science of astronomy. Both were concerned about the impact of the occult sciences on the demonstrative sciences and theology, and were dismayed by the goodly number of fellow Muslims who not only looked upon the occult sciences as respectable but composed numerous works on them. Such works had wide currency among Muslims, and some were translated into Western languages, becoming part of the scientific literature of the Middle Ages.

This literature became a legacy common to Jews, Christians, and Moriscos. Old Christians were quite aware of its existence and considered the Moors to be expert in the magical arts.[105] The Moriscos themselves relied heavily on divination and astrology, using formulas, inscriptions, invocations, horoscopes, and the like. During the Granadan rebellion, leaders incited people to revolt on the basis of favorable signs in the air, land, and sea.[106] Similar phenomena swayed Old Christians, some of whom were strong advocates of the occult sciences while others opposed them on theological grounds. As in Islam, there remained an enormous contradiction between theological prohibitions and actual practice. This is reflected in early Spanish literature and that of the Golden Age, where the practice of the occult sciences might be either condoned or ridiculed.[107] Pact with the Devil was a common theme, having disastrous consequences for the individual.[108] However, astrology was regarded as both reliable and effective by Juan Ruíz, the fourteenth-century Archpriest of Hita, who says that the fate of all men is determined by the stars, that astrology is a good science, and that astrologers' predictions are reliable.[109] He adds that God can, of course, alter things as He wants.[110] Ruíz notes that he himself was born under the sign of Venus, which he describes as the beginning and end of love's journey, with Venus having great power over man and his fortunes.[111] Such beliefs were shared by contemporary and later clerics.[112] Furthermore, astrology was considered a necessary base for medicine,[113] required study for physicians.[114] As late as the end of the sixteenth century, Jerónimo Cortés wrote a work showing the importance of astrology for both agriculture and medicine.[115]

On the other hand, astrology and astrologers were frowned upon and even ridiculed. In 1585, Pope Sixtus V placed astrology in a class with divination, incantation, and magic, and urged clerics to persecute practitioners. Inasmuch as astrologers were still holding important places in the courts of rulers, the pope's appeal went unheeded.

Practitioners of the occult sciences did not, by and large, think that their skills contradicted religious tenets, though in some instances sacrilegious formulas were used for attaining the desired goal.[116] Too unsophisticated to realize the theological implications of such practice, they continued it in the expectation of gaining wealth and power, curing all disease, uncovering secrets, and predicting the future. The accompanying artifices—amulets, seals, inscriptions, herbal concoctions, animal organs, and invocations—were common to Jews, Christians, and Moriscos; their origin could be traced to venerable men of the past according to Muslim traditions. Among them was Solomon, honored by Jews, Christians, and Muslims alike. Solomon occupies an important place in Aljamiado literature, in which he is portrayed as having power over beasts and nature and having performed wonderous things by means of his ring.[117] To him is attributed an extensive work on divination, *The Key of Solomon (Clavicula Salomonis)*,[118] which appears to have enjoyed great popularity among Jews, Christians, and Muslims. The work contains many items that can be found in *The Book of Marvellous Sayings*,[119] such as prescriptions for satisfying desires, for gaining love, for uncovering secrets, and the like.[120]

Another work similar to *The Book of Marvellous Sayings* was composed by Amador Velasco, an Old Christian and a practitioner and teacher of the magical arts. Velasco's case illustrates the nature and practice of the magical arts in sixteenth-century Spain.[121] He was brought before the tribunal of the Inquisition on charges of sorcery. In his own defense, Velasco attempted not only to show the efficacy of his art, but to point out that its practice was quite common among the nobility, learned men, theologians, clerics, friars, and the common people. He protests that he is being used as a scapegoat.[122] His book constitutes a manual for the sorcerer, containing signs, symbols, formulas, and prescriptions for achieving love between a couple; protecting a wife or husband from mischief; preventing pregnancy; neutralizing venom; repelling spells; seeing good things in dreams; winning at games; discovering hidden treasure; making people happy, making men do ridiculous things; getting one's desires; preventing dogs from barking or biting; making pigeons multiply; understanding the language of birds; protecting the home from fire and theft; making oneself invisible; curing disease; covering one hundred to three hundred miles in a night; and more.[123]

Valasco's case is corroborated by others brought before the tribunals of the Inquisition. The charges varied, resembling practices or beliefs found in Aljamiado literature. It appears that sorcerers or astrologers became known for a particular talent or specialty. Some had the unique ability of covering an enormous distance in a short time. Such was the extraordinary journey of a bishop who was transported by a devil over a long distance to transact urgent business.[124] Dr. Torralba, a physician and a cultured man, was also brought before the Inquisition in 1528 on charges of having traveled from Valladolid in Spain to Rome in an hour and a half, accompanied and protected by a spirit named Zaquiel.[125]

Such occurrences are found in Aljamiado literature—as in the story of Tamīm, wherein a spirit transports Tamīm to a distant land from which he returns riding on the clouds.[126] Similarly, in the epic narratives, 'Alī covered enormous distances in a short time, although nothing is said about the means of transportation[127]; he also vanquished a haunted palace full of spirits and demons. Khālid b. al-Walīd, the able general of early Islam, not only understood the language of the birds but was able to do wondrous things with the aid of his ring.[128] Finally, Fāṭimah, Muḥammad's daughter, was able to see actual things in her dreams.[129] These and other phenomena were attributed also to Christian sorcerers who appeared before the Inquisition on charges of doing or undoing things,[130] making people fall in love, curing or killing people,[131] attracting men for erotic purposes,[132] summoning wolves to devour children,[133] and other bizarre things. These similarities of behavior and thought among Old Christians and Moriscos have significant implications for the degree of contemporary social interaction and integration of the two cultures.

8

Secular Literature

Since Aljamiado literature is permeated by religious sentiments, the spiritual and profane are intertwined even in the sciences, where physical phenomena are often inseparable from divine dictates. Thus, a secular literature must be assessed on literary grounds, such as the epic, novels, stories, and didactic literature. Aljamiado literature possesses not only significant religious, historical, and linguistic interest but also a literary merit of its own—in addition to being a hybrid literature drawing its inspiration and format from two worlds, the world of Islam and the world of Christendom, during their last encounter on European soil. The positive and negative nature of this encounter is reflected, illustrating an Arabo-Islamic society undergoing a radical change in language and mode of expression with the attending elements of borrowing and cross-fertilization. Essentially, the Moriscos tapped the resources of two antagonistic traditions, influencing and being influenced by them in all areas, including literature.

The Moriscos improvised a literature partly as an outlet for their spiritual and emotional needs with little or no consideration for the artistic merit of its form and content. Evaluating its style in the nineteenth century, Saavedra describes it as largely poor and vernacular, but acquiring delicacy, agility, and even eloquence at the hand of some authors.[1] He observes that the mode of expression indicates that the Morisco authors thought or studied in Arabic what they wanted to express in Castilian; then they translated, relying more on the vernacular of their provinces than on the strict observance of grammatical cannons, and preserving Arabic syntax in many instances, particularly certain idioms.[2] More recently, Galmés recognizes greater merit, as measured by current principles of linguistic and literary criticism,[3] adding that the style gives Aljamiado literature a special charm and artistic power that make it flexible and expressive, however elementary it may be: "We do not find in it either the stylistic variety or the complexity found in more erudite productions, but the expressive simplicity of Aljamiado writings constitutes its principal attraction."[4]

Considered from within and in relation to the Moriscos' circumstances, Aljamiado literature is remarkable, possessing two qualities: first, simple, straightforward language written to entertain and to instruct, and second, well-chosen plots in an easily followed narrative which evokes intense sympathy or admiration; the plots culminated in a moral lesson or affirmation of fundamental beliefs. Such plots fulfilled both the spiritual and the emotional needs of the Moriscos; they are well presented and there is no doubt that they were recited and enjoyed by the Moriscos.

Although largely derived from Arabic sources, the secular literature of the Moriscos is very different from classicial Arabic literature, which was written by crudites for erudites and in which eloquent language (*faṣāḥah*) and stylistic ornamentation, rhymes, imagery, and other devices were considered the essential ingredients of good writing. This was not the case among the Moriscos, who could scarcely emulate a classical Arabic no longer in use in their environment. Instead, they wrote in Spanish dialects, the dialect of the streets rather than the language of educated Spanish society. The Morisco writer generally conveyed his message clearly without literary device. Above all, he sought to share a religious belief or a moral lesson and the faith that God is omnipresent, probing and testing until he intervenes against unbelievers, spirits and demons, and against all injustices meted to his favorite people, the Muslims.

EPIC LITERATURE[5]

The *Book of Battles*[6] relates stories of heroism filled with the human qualities of courage, manliness, loyalty, truthfulness, magnanimity, gallantry to women, defense of the truth and the rights of the poor and the oppressed—all occurring through divine guidance and intervention. In other words, in spite of his superior human qualities, the hero appears as a mere instrument of the Creator. He is the Arab knight of pre-Islamic times, with symbolic horse, sword, and damsel named to inspire awe and admiration.[7] These heroic and symbolic qualities appear through the eight narratives in the *Book of Battles*, which is based on historical events as to time and place, supplemented by legend: interpolations and exaggerated actions of the hero which could only come about by divine guidance. Except for the religious aspect, this type of narrative was based on a pre-Islamic model, the saga of ʻAntar,[8] who always emerged victorious over nature, humans, and beasts. Like other pre-Islamic sagas, the saga of ʻAntar was preserved by narrators, (*rāwī*) and later codified by historians, becoming part of the general folklore up to the present. Pre-Islamic narratives emphasized the manliness of the hero, to which their Islamic counterparts added the element of divine intervention, while preserving the pre-Islamic heroic qualities.

ʻAlī, the cousin and son-in-law of Muḥammad, emerges as the Islamic hero par excellence both by virtue of his heroic qualities and by divine guidance. It is related that while Muḥammad was sitting with his companions and ʻAlī, they saw a beautiful horse descending from Heaven; it bore a saddle and a sword (*espada*) known as Dhulfiqar. ʻAlī was then young *(mansebo)*, thin, and sickly looking. When the companions asked Muḥammad who should have the horse, he said that it belonged to the best knight. One after another they failed to capture it. Muḥammad then asked ʻAlī to try. The knights interjected, saying, "How can he do it when we have all failed?" Nevertheless, ʻAlī approached the horse, which bowed before him and gave in without resistance. then the companions realized that the horse submitted to ʻAlī's knightly role in the nascent Islamic movement[9] despite his physical shortcomings.[10]

Henceforth, ʻAlī was destined to perform extraordinary things in the path of Islam, acquiring all the qualities associated with chivalry and guided by a divine power. This fusion of ʻAlī's secular and spiritual mission in Islamic tradition fitted very well into the perspective of the Moriscos, who adapted the Arabic narratives to their own needs not so much for entertainment as for conveying a message of hope in times of despair. This emerges quite clearly in the various narratives in the Morisco *Book of Battles*. In *The Battle of Ḥunayn*,[11] fought by Muḥammad against rebellious tribes in 630, the Muslims were outnumbered and almost defeated, only to be saved at the hands of ʻAlī, who subdued the unbelievers as if they were lambs. The angel Gabriel himself exclaimed, "Oh, Muḥammad, the angels of heaven marvel at ʻAlī."[12] Similarly, in *The Battle of Āṣyad and Mecca*[13] between Arab pagans and Muslims, ʻAlī once more showed his military prowess and the power of his sword Dhulfiqar, which decimated many of the enemy with a single stroke. In addition to his military prowess, ʻAlī showed his poetical gift when he proclaimed himself in the manner of the Arab bards to be "the knight of knights" (*kaballero de los kaballeros*).[14] He killed the tested champions of the enemy and captured their leader, al-Āṣyad, to whom ʻAlī boasted in a poem: "I am the killer of millions with license from my Lord . . . and I am the hero and shedder of the blood of unbelievers."[15] Al-Āṣyad was brought before Muḥammad, accepted his defeat, and became a Muslim.

In *The Battle of Muhalhil*,[16] Khālid Ibn al-Walīd, the great general of the Islamic conquest known as "the Sword of God," shares some of the glory with ʻAlī, but never equalled ʻAlī's heroic stature, notwithstanding his great military accomplishments during encounters with the Byzantines in Syria-Palestine. In the traditions, Muhalhil is an indomitable Arab hero who was preparing an expedition against the Muslims consisting of 100,000 cavalrymen, 50,000 infantrymen, and 40,000 Black soldiers. When Muḥammad announced his coming from the pulpit, it was agreed to send Khālid with a message to Muhalhil asking him to embrance Islam or face the consequences. Khālid undertook the long journey through dangerous mountains and valleys, fighting many people on the way. Before reaching Muhalhil's headquarters, he met Muhalhil's servant, described as a giant "with hands like windmills and legs like walls," who barred the way. Khālid subdued the giant and went on to find Muhalhil praying before an idol. Khālid presented himself, but refused to deliver the message from Muḥammad until the idol was removed from sight. When this had been done, Muhalhil read the message and became angry, particularly at the warning that Muḥammad had five knights who could dispose of all of Muhalhil's army. He ordered Khālid's horse to be skinned and Khālid to be wrapped in the skin and made ready for the fire the following day. The angel Gabriel intervened, informing Muḥammad of Khālid's fate and urging him to send 'Alī to the rescue. 'Alī rushed to the scene, covering in one night a distance that had taken Khālid twenty days. He freed Khālid, and together they confronted the enemy, inflicting terror upon Muhalhil's army and killing many, including champions and Muhalhil himself, sparing only those who accepted the call to Islam.

Clearly, most of the credit in the confrontation with Muhalhil goes to 'Alī as a part of divine will made manifest by the angel Gabriel. Although Khālid may have displayed extraordinary feats against Muhalhil's army, his heroic role is reserved for his encounter with the Christian Byzantines at the Battle of Yarmūk in 636.[17] Outnumbered by the Byzantines, Khālid won a decisive victory, which placed him next to 'Alī as the hero of nascent Islam. Khālid's victory over the Christians appealed to the Moriscos, who regarded the victory as a sign of the ultimate triumph of Islam. The Battle of Yarmū earned for Khālid the designation of the "Sword of Allah"; for the Moriscos the battle took on miraculous proportions, marking the victory of the true faith over tyranny, injustices, and worshipers of the cross (*fuwe desipadora de los servidores de la kuruz*).[18]

Notwithstanding, 'Alī remains the great hero, whose magnanimity, bravery, and fearlessness are shown in broad relief in other historico-legendary narratives. *The Legend of al-Ḥārīth*[19] deals with the Christian ruler of Yemen, showing both Muḥammad's determination to convert the Arabs to Islam and 'Alī's role in bringing this about. After the fall of Mecca to the Muslims, Muḥammad wrote to the Yemenite king, calling upon him to embrace Islam. Muḥammad's messenger reached the capital of Yemen and was taken to king al-Ḥārīth through many halls and luxurious palaces. After reading the message, al-Ḥārīth summoned his ministers for advice, but rejected conversion despite the warning of an old man about the consequences. War ensued between the Muslims and al-Ḥārīth, whose army was headed by the champion

'Amr. In the words of 'Alī, 'Amr was the strongest champion he had ever met.[20] In fact, 'Amr defeated several Muslim warriors in hand-to-hand encounters before 'Alī appeared, proclaiming: "I am the one who gives falls, decimator of squadrons, victor over champions, ejecter of knights to the ground, and the lion of Banū Ghālib, 'Alī Ibn Abī Ṭālib."[21] The two knights fought all day until sunset, inflicting deep wounds. When they met the following day, they inquired about each other's wounds. 'Alī suggested to 'Amr that he end the duel by simply making the confession of faith; 'Amr declined indignantly. The duel continued until 'Alī captured 'Amr and brought him before Muḥammad, who demanded that he become a Muslim. 'Amr swore he would not make the confession of faith under the threat of the sword. Muḥammad then ordered 'Alī to decapitate him, but rescinded the order and freed 'Amr. 'Amr rejoined his men, but later returned to Muḥammad and asked him whether Muḥammad or God had freed him, to which Muḥammad replied that he himself did but with God's will. This was sufficient reason for 'Amr and his men to embrace Islam; he succeeded later in persuading al-Ḥārith and his people to do the same.

The Muslims would have been defeated without 'Alī, who decided the outcome of a battle not only against powerful enemies but against spirits and idols. This is shown in *The Legend of al-Ashyab Ibn Ḥanqar*,[22] the leader of Tayma, a town north of Medina. Al-Ashyab is portrayed as a great champion (*barragan*) with enormous wealth and many followers; he had an idol in the form of a peacock housed in a sumptuous palace.[23] Al-Ashyab had turned down Muḥammad's invitation to embrace Islam, after which war ensued. 'Alī did not join the expedition, in which the Muslim army suffered defeat and was in a dire plight. 'Alī saw this development in a dream and rushed to the scene, covering a long distance in a very short time. He encountered the fearless champion al-Akhḍar Ibn Mashfūq, whom he captured, creating great consternation among al-Ashyab's army. Al-Ashyab then proposed to embrace Islam if 'Alī acceded, provided that he be allowed a thousand men. Arriving at the palace, 'Alī saw the idol surrounded by many spirits. His followers fled, but 'Alī remained undeterred, defeated the dinas (*eljines*), and crushed the idol with his sword Dhulfiqar, leaving al-Ashyab no choice but to embrace Islam.

'Alī defeats not only champions and spirits, but strange creatures as well. In *The Legend of the Golden Castle*,[24] an Arab convert to Islam complains to Muḥammad about an enormous serpent in a castle which ravaged the countryside, killing cattle, camels, and men. Muḥammad sent 'Alī and Khālid Ibn al-Walīd at the head of an army to the castle, well fortified with iron gates and high walls decorated with gold, silver, and precious stones. The palace was in smoke and from one of its gates emerged the head of an enormous serpent with an open mouth like a cave from which sprang enormous columns of smoke.[25] Pastures all around were in flames, causing the intruders to flee. 'Alī persuaded them to return, where they were overwhelmed by fire and smoke. His men could not withstand the fearful sight. Alone, 'Alī entered the castle shouting as if "the heavens were falling, the earth splitting, and the mountains moving."[26] At first the flames forced him to withdraw, but he soon returned with a determination defying nature and beasts. While his followers watched with suspense from a distance, he passed through fearful noise, fire, and smoke and fought fifty thousand champions from among the jinns (*eljines*) and devils (*el-saytanes*). His wife Fāṭimah saw the spectacle in her dream and informed her father, Muḥammad, who contacted the angel Gabriel. Gabriel reassured Muḥammad that 'Alī was fighting spirits, demons, and devils, he heard a voice advising him to kill the chief dragon. He heeded the advice and emerged victorious after having killed seventeeen thousand demons like "the wind hitting the sea and fire the dry wood."[27]

What is remarkable about these epic narratives is that each brings out a unique quality of the hero. In *The Battle of Khuzamah al-Bāriqiyyah*,[28] 'Alī had to fight a lady champion in the cause of Islam. The powerful lady, named Khuzamah, had seasoned champions among her followers, whom 'Alī had to defeat before his encounter with Khuzamah. 'Alī pulled these champions from their horses with a single hand. When the turn of Khuzamah came, he pulled her out of the saddle as if she were a bird. He was magnanimous with her despite her wickedness, requiring only that she become Muslim along with her tribe.

The Legend of Warā al-Hujūrah[29] not only shows another aspect of 'Alī's heroism, but tests whether God (Allah) or the godesses Allāt and 'Uzzad will prevail. One day the king of Warā al-Hujūrah appeared before Muhammad and told of his desire to become Muslim, since Allāh proved more effective than his female deities. He asked Muḥammad to send some of the companions to teach his people the new religion. In truth, the king had no intention of becoming Muslim, tricking the Muslims into coming to his capital in order to kill them. Muḥammad sent a party of four, including Khālid Ibn al-Walīd. On their way to the king's capital, the Muslims saw an eagle crying and pulling its feathers out, then disappearing. Khālid knew the language of birds and alerted his party to imminent danger, advising them to return home. However, they assessed their strength against that of the enemy and decided that they could triumph with the help of God and the grace of Muḥammad since each one of them was worth ten thousand horsemen and Khālid was worth forty thousand. So they proceeded to the king's capital, where they were given milk which contained a sleeping draught. While asleep, they were put in chains to be burned the following day. Soon Khālid awoke and woke his companions with the aid of his ring. The next morning, the king appeared before them and inquired satirically what had happened and what kind of knights they were. While they despaired, God sent His angel Gabriel to tell Muḥammad of their plight; Muḥammad sent 'Alī to the rescue. 'Alī always was ready to fight in the path of God and in honor of His messenger.[30] He rushed to the scene, freed the prisoners, and battled the king's army fiercely, defeating many; the rest pleaded with him that they were ready to embrace Allāh and abandon the goddesses Allāt and Uzzah.

The Legend of 'Alī and the Forty Girls[31] completes the list of 'Alī's extraordinary heroic qualities. For once, 'Alī would fight to prove himself before the lady of his dreams. The story is set in Medina during the Battle of the Trench in 627; the city was besieged by the Quraysh, then mortal enemies of Muḥammad. It conveys both gallantry to women and a great feat of heroism meant to compensate for some unattractive physical attributes. Forty beautiful girls attired in silk garments, pearls, and rubies accompanied by an old lady met Fāṭimah, Muḥammad's daughter, at a mill. The old lady told the ill-dressed Fāṭimah that with her looks and beauty she could marry a champion of the Quraysh and dress like these girls instead of being the wife of 'Alī, who had four defects: baldness, a large belly, thin legs, and no money. This made Fāṭimah unhappy. When he heard of it, 'Alī pleaded with God to send an army of unbelievers to besiege the city. No sooner had he made his plea than he was summoned by Muḥammad, who informed him that eighty thousand invaders surrounded the city. 'Alī was delighted. He asked Muḥammad to allow him to fight them alone and to have the forty girls, the old lady, and Fāṭimah watch the battle from the city walls. The hitherto poorly dressed Fāṭimah was provided with a beautiful dress sent from heaven with the angel Gabriel, and she joined the other ladies to watch 'Alī defeat one champion after the other until none was left; then he shouted, "Come out, oh enemies of God, for there is no name above mine."[32] No one dared to face him, so he plunged into the army, killing many and emerging drenched with blood. With victory achieved, he ascended the city walls, where he embraced Fāṭimah and kissed her on the forehead. Then he addressed the entourage, saying: 'Oh ladies, what do you think of the one who has little hair, a large belly, thin legs, and no money?''[33] Of course, the ladies were impressed and made the confession of faith, but the old lady refused and was split in half.

These narratives derived from *al-siyar wa-l-maghāzi (Biographies and Raids*) of early Islam combining history and legends around the person of 'Alī, the unrivaled knight (*fatā*), and his unique sword. They gave rise to the saying: "There is no sword like dhū-l-fiqār, nor any knight like 'Alī."[34] 'Alī's Shi'ite partisans in early Islam regarded him as infallible and quasidivine. This conception did not bother the Moriscos, who followed the orthodox path and displayed little interest in theological controversies within Islam. The historico-legendary accounts of 'Alī were directly relevant to their situation, showing the triumph of Islam over pagan and Christian enemies against heavy odds and providing a source of inspiration. 'Alī embodied their expectations of a deliverer, not only having the superior qualities of the ideal medieval knight with respect to bravery, honor, loyalty, selflessness, devotion, love, and defense of the true faith, but also serving as the instrument of God through Muḥammad and the angel Gabriel. This gave the hero superhuman qualities such as covering enormous distances in a short time, seeing things in dreams, and understanding the language of birds, not to mention extraordinary triumphs over whole armies, giants, dragons, serpents, spirits, demons, and devils. Yet 'Alī was quite human when it came to the fair sex and attempted to compensate his physical shortcomings through a heroic feat in order to gain the love of Fāṭimah.

Morisco epic narratives can be used profitably in a comparative study of Spanish epic. One should not be concerned about the dating of Morisco narratives, since all of them are traceable to early Islamic sources and were known for centuries among Spanish Muslims. 'Abd al-Badī',[35] Marcos,[36] and Galmés[37] have led the way in this area of scholarship, finding many elements common to both Arabic and Spanish epics.

NOVELLAS AND OTHER STORIES

The interaction between Arabic and Western literature can also be seen in other genres. Although some epic narratives clearly have a religious tenor, the Moriscos appear to have valued the profane aspects sufficiently to translate such material from non-Arabic sources. Such is the case of *The History of the Loves of Paris and Viana*,[38] a novella of chivalry which was widely read in the West and was translated into several European languages, including Aljamiado. The novella originates in France and develops around Paris's love for Viana, but the action extends to the Holy Land and incorporates many elements familiar to the Moriscos—mainly, the qualities of the hero and his determination to gain the hand of his beloved despite strong opposition. As in the 'Antar story, reciprocal love meets the opposition of the girl's father, in this case Viana's, causing the couple to elope. The elopement is foiled: Viana is apprehended and locked away; Paris escapes and travels incognito in countries bordering the Mediterranean, settling in the Holy land, where he learns Arabic and lives disguised as a Moor. In the meantime, Viana's father goes to the Orient as a spy for the Crusaders, but is discovered and jailed. Still in disguise, Paris manages through his influence to obtain the release of his would-be father-in-law, who promises to make his benefactor his favorite knight and his heir upon their return to France. Not only does he fulfill his promise, but Paris and Viana marry and live happily thereafter.

The theme of despair which ends in triumph had a particular attraction for the Moriscos, as seen in the epic narratives and the novel of Paris and Viana. It is also apparent in *The Bath of Zarieb*,[39] an Eastern love story[40] in the tenth-century Cordova. The story gives some glimpses of Cordova of that day and its powerful chamberlain al-Manṣūr (d. 1002), but its primary theme is the love at first sight of a playboy, who deceives a rich and beautiful girl into entering his house with the intent of seducing her. The girl, who had been lost in the street looking for the Bath of Zarieb, manages by clever means to escape from the young man's house and leaves her suitor deeply infatuated. He searches for her endlessly, to the point of madness. Finally, he finds her through the good offices of a friend, who intercedes on his behalf with the powerful al-Manṣūr. Al-Manṣūr arranges the couple's marriage.

In *The Story of Carcayona*[41] the cause of religion prevails at the end, along with true love, happiness, and miraculous happenings. Besides its religious focus, the story is full of suspense and drama and has various elements that occur in Western literature. The heroine embraces Islam and persists in her faith, to the rage of her pagan father, who amputates her hands and sends her into the wilderness to perish. Her faith in the new religion remains undiminished and is reinforced when a deer leads her to a cave and cares for her. She continues her religious practices. One day a prince appears and, dazzled by her beauty, falls in love with her. He takes her to his kingdom and marries her over the vehement protests of the queen mother. The couple lives happily and has a child. While the prince is away on a military expedition, the queen mother exiles Carcayona and her baby. Desperate and helpless, but keeping faith in Islam, she is again rescued by the deer, which cares for her, and the merciful Allāh causes her to regain her hands. When the prince returns from the expedition, the queen mother informs him that his wife had left him, but he remains faithful and seeks his wife. He finds her with great relief and renewed love. They return to his kingdom and live happily thereafter, removing the queen mother to a distant palace.

These tales of noble and true love may be contrasted with a tale of illicit love through seduction in *The Story of a Worshiper and the Naked Woman*,[42] where temptation is tempered by self-control and divine intervention. Its theme is similar in spirit to the one reported by Ibn Ḥazm in the epilogue of his *Dove's Ring* on love and lovers. The Aljamiado story centers around an ascetic known for his devotion. He lives in an isolated hut in the mountains, but often is visited by the king. One night, a woman knocks at his door; she claims to be very cold and insists upon entering. The ascetic reluctantly obliges. The room is dark. The woman pleads to have the fire kindled. When the fire is lit, he sees her completely naked and is taken by her extreme beauty. He asks her to leave his sight, but the woman refuses to cover herself and asks the ascetic to sleep with her. With the thought of Hell in his mind, he puts his finger in the fire. This was not enough, so God sends his angel Gabriel, who helps to burn all his fingers. At the awful sight, the woman screams and drops to the floor as if dead. The ascetic covers her with his cloak (*el-jaba,* Ar. *al-Jubbah*) and proceeds with his devotions. Meanwhile, Satan (*iblīs*) informs the king that the ascetic had slept with and killed the woman. The king rushes to the hut and finds the woman motionless on the floor. The ascetic claims innocence, but to no avail; the king puts him to death. Thereupon, the woman awakes and tells the true story, leaving the king and his entourage unhappy and pensive (*tiristes i-pensativos*).[43]

The Story of a Muslim Scholar[44] deals with love as an element in the long contest between Christianity and Islam. The Muslim scholar is able and pious, but is ruined when he falls in love with and marries a Christian woman, who compels him to embrace Christianity. The story has a happy ending when the couple embraces the true faith, Islam, through divine grace.

There are other stories of religious and human interest which have literary merit in their form, content, and manner of execution. In *The Story of Tamīm al-Dāri*,[45] a companion of the Prophet shows unshaken belief in Islam even when transplanted into the world of spirits and demons. The story, full of action and suspense, is written in the manner of the *Arabian Nights*, which probably inspired it. Muḥammad himself predicts Tamīm's trials as a test of faith. One night Tamīm was performing the ablution at home while his wife was waiting in bed. After long waiting, his wife searched for him but could find him nowhere. For days and weeks no trace of him was found. The demons had taken him away to a cave, where he lived among them but continued to believe in God and to read the Qur'ān—to the annoyance of the demons, who ridiculed and threatened him, insisting that he abandon his religion. This had gone on for almost four years when a good genie passed by the cave and inquired about Tamīm's fate and religion. The genie became interested in him as a tutor for his children, but the chief demon would not release him. This caused a war between the good genies and the demons, numbering in the millions. The good genies triumph over the demons, and Tamīm was taken to another mysterious world, where he lived in comfort for the next three years. Then the desire to return home overcame him. He was allowed to depart, passing through a fantastic world in which he witnessed many marvels: spirits, saints, great cities, believers, and other creatures with which he had dialogues concerning the virtue of the Islamic faith. While Tamīm is on his way home over a cloud, his wife decides to remarry after seven years' mourning. Her nuptials coincide with the arrival of Tamīm, who claims his wife. A quarrel between the two husbands is averted by the intervention of 'Umar, who allows the wife to choose between the two. She chooses Tamīm, saying that she has known no other man and will continue to be Tamīm's wife.

Mention should also be made of some of the stories about Muḥammad in addition to those in his biography. Like the epic narratives, these stories have literary merit and may be included among general stories despite their religious character. In the epic narratives around the person of 'Alī, Muḥammad appears almost without exception as the guiding spirit of all 'Alī's undertaking, watching over the triumph of Islam over heathenism and Christianity. Muḥammad is hardly an active participant, playing the sublime role of a spiritual leader endowed with the power of miracles beyond anything accomplished through the sword.[46] His is the glory of being in communion with the divine through the angel Gabriel.

While Muḥammad delegated 'Alī and his close companions to cope with armed opposition, he chooses to use miracles in his confrontations not only with fellow Arabs but also with claimants to prophecy. *The Story of a Prophetess and a Prophet*[47] reveals the miraculous power of Muḥammad. Two prophets, a male and a female, were contending for power. Although the prophetess was more capable and powerful than the prophet, she gave in to the male prophet through seduction, reducing the contenders to him and Muḥamad. The two now agreed to put their prophecies to the test through miraculous deeds. When Muḥammad put his hand on the head of a man who had been scalded, he cured him, but when the false prophet did the same, the patient caught leprosy. When Muḥammad made a blind man see, the false prophet made him blind again; when Muḥammad made salt water sweet, the other made the sweet water salty. In this way false prophecy was exposed for all to see. Similarly, in *The Story of the Miracle of the Moon,*[48] Muḥamad emerged triumphant when a Meccan leader pledged to embrace Islam if Muḥammad were to perform a miracle. Muḥammad met the challenge by changing the course of the moon and splitting it in two. But the most moving story in the production of miracles is *The Story of the Arab and the Girl,*[49] which deals with the unhappy fate of a girl who was buried alive by her own father in order to avoid a disgrace in the family. While the father was digging her grave, the beautiful and graceful girl became reconciled to her fate to the point of cleansing the sweat off her father's forehead. After the burial, the father was surrounded by an enormous fire from which a voice was heard commanding him to go to see Muḥammad if he ever wanted to be saved. In the meantime, Muḥammad brought the girl to life, and she greeted him by name. When Muḥammad inquired how she knew his name, she said that she learned it while she was in Heaven.

DIDACTIC LITERATURE

Much of Aljamiado literature is didactic in nature whether its form is epic, novellas, or stories, but some manuscripts consist entirely of wise sayings and admonitions meant to guide the reader toward right conduct. The sayings are often derived from utterances attributed to the Prophet, his companions, venerable leaders of Isiam, and pre-Islamic wisemen. This genre of teaching through concise statements on all behavior and general precepts is common to both Arabic and medieval Spanish literature.[50] The wise sayings may take the form of a father's counsel to his son, a wiseman's to a young ruler, or a teacher's to his pupil, placing wisdom derived from long experience at the disposal of the listener so that he may be guided and avoid pitfalls and needless mistakes.

Among such Aljamiado texts are the sayings of Muḥammad contained in BNM 5354,[51] untitled but dealing with counsels and manners (*kastigos i kostumberes*) translated from *The One Thousand and Two Hundred Words* of the Eastern scholar al-Quḍāʻī (d. 1062).[52] The sayings cover a variety of subjects relating to God, religious precepts, observances and reflections. The concise statements are arranged under chapter headings on attaining salvation, paradise, worldly things, and exhortations to follow the good path and to avoid the unlawful. Here are some of the sayings:

i-la-leghriya es ghanansiyah[53]
Joy is gain.

i-la-tiristora es perdida[54]
Sadness is loss.

La-rrogharya es obidensiya[55]
Supplication is obedience.

El-amoriyo es mediyo seso[56]
Love-suit is half-witted (madness).

El porovecho es kon vuwestoros mayores[57]
Benefit is with your elders.

La fuwersa del fecho es su kunpilimiyento[58]
The strength of a deed is its fulfillment.

El temor a-da Allāh es kabesa de toda sabiyeza[59]
The fear of God is the beginning of all wisdom.

Las mujeres son kuwerdas dela *shayṭān*[60]
Women are the halters of the devil.

El vino es suma de los pekados[61]
Wine is the sum of sins.

La fasiya es delas barasas de *jahannam*[62]
Falsehood is one of the embers of Hell.

El murmurar es de la obra de los *jāhiles*[63]
Gossiping is the work of the ignorant.

El-*azine* de los ojos es el mirar[64]
Adultery of the eyes is looking.

La tacha de la farankeza es la demasiya[65]
The blemish of frankness is excess.

El *aljanna* es kasa de los farankos[66]
Paradise is the home of the pious.

Los sabiyos son fiyeles de Allāh sobre sus *khaleqados*[67]
Scholars are the guardians of God over His creatures.

La kabesa de la sensiya es el temer a-da Allāh[68]
The beginning of wisdom is the fear of God.

El saber es amigho del kereyente[69]
Knowledge is the friend of the believer;

i la pasensiya es su *el-wazir*[70]
patience is his minister,

i el seso es su ghuiya[71]
and the brain his guide.

La soledad es mejor ke la konpaniya mala[72]
Solitude is better than bad company.

I dezir biyen es mejor kel hablar
To say good things is better than to talk;

i-el hablar es mejor ke hablar mal[73]
and talking is better than saying bad [things.]

A similar work entitled *The Book of Good Doctrines, Counsels, and Good Behaviors*[74] contains wisdom and moral sayings. One chapter exalts knowledge and urges the listener to act with wisdom and knowledge, offering numerous counsels about God's mercy and the rewards from adhering to religious tenets. There are other works aimed at instructing the soul, loving the hereafter, and loathing this world, together with advice about compliance with religious law.[75] *The Counsels for People*[76] is made up of miscellaneous sayings of Muḥammad, wisemen, traditionists, and the great theologian al-Ghazālī (d. 1111). Finally, there are *The Counsels of 'Alī*[77] and *The Counsels of a Wiseman to His Son*,[78] which are similar to *The Counsels of Dukama to His Son*[79] discussed here.

The identity of Dukama cannot be ascertained. He is presumably a legendary pre-Islamic figure like Luqmān,[80] prominent in Arabic literature as a man of great wisdom, some of whose sayings appear in Aljamiado literature. Dukama tells his son that there are five things in life which are nullified irreparably by their opposite: "O son, you will earn five things in life that are followed by another five: youth before old age; tranquility before fate; wealth before poverty; life before death; and health before sickness."[80] Dukama urges his son to be close to God, to know and beseech Him at all times, and to rely on Him, "for He alone allows things to happen."[81] He further urges him to live in this world as a stranger (*algharibu*), since this world is transitory.[82] Some of his other admonitions are: "O son of Adam, walk with your feet and hands on earth, for you shall end in the tomb."[83] "It surprises me to see someone becoming sad for the want of something, yet he is not sad for the diminution of life."[84] "It astonishes me when a person does not know which is better, increasing good deeds or decreasing life."[85] "O son of Adam, don't be sad for lost things, nor be merry for gained ones—for what is lost will never return and what is won has no permanence. It is certain that you will not escape death."[86]

Various sayings are attributed to Luqmān, who addressed his son: "O son, take of the world that comes to you, and keep the best for the hereafter . . . Don't accompany double-faced people . . . Don't laugh without cause or benefit . . . Don't walk aimlessly, or ask for what cannot be achieved . . . Happiness and sadness go hand in hand and do not last long."[87] "O son, have pity on three people: the honorable man who succumbs to meanness; the wealthy man who is overcome by poverty; and the scholar who is taken by madness."[88]

These and other sayings represent a faithful rendition of the Arabic original and have the virtue of being concise, expressive, and easy to retain, facilitating their dissemination among the population. This makes their study the more significant in terms of their Arabic antecedents and their disemination in areas beyond those inhabited by the Moriscos. Inasmuch as the Moriscos lacked a formal education and books, they relied more and more on memory to convey their thought as moralizers or entertainers. A whole neighborhood might gather around a storyteller to hear aphorisms and stories. The available literature gives a fair clue to the content of the storyteller's repertoire, which was both entertaining and edifying and could be listened to with pleasure and profit. In fact, it was through such a storyteller that Washington Irving wrote *Tales of the Alhambra.*

A few points should be emphasized with respect to the role and place of the storyteller, the nature and scope of the Arabic bellelettrists, and their affinity to their Spanish counterpart.

The role and place of the storyteller or narrator can hardly be overestimated in an illiterate society. The professional narrators played an important part in the early development of both Arabic and Spanish literatures, transmitting the wisdom and experiences of the ages in prose and poetry. Narrators were prolific, had the gift of good memory, and developed a technique of relating things in an interesting manner and an eloquent but simple language. In the process, they added and omitted things for effect and other purposes. In the evenings, they related stories of wars, love and lovers, fables, and historical events intermingled with exaggerated actions and legends. The tenth-century bibliophile Ibn al-Nadīm[90] lists a number of works dealing with night chats (*asmār*) and myths (*khurāfāt*).

In Muslim Spain, this kind of literature became the object of numerous belletristic works (*adab*), the most comprehensive of which is the *Unique Necklace (al-'iqd al-farīd*) of the tenth-century Andalusian Ibn 'Abd Rabbihi,[91] who included a variety of subjects of didactic and profane nature. The preceding survey conforms, on the whole, to this type of literature with respect to form and content, reflecting an Arabic tradition whose purpose is to instruct and entertain using examples in the form of epic narratives, stories, aphorisms, counsels, maxims, and proverbs. *Adab* constituted an integral part of Arabic literature, remaining popular throughout the ages and exerting an enormous influence on Hispanic literature from about the twelfth century onward through a long and intimate interchange between Christians and Muslims within the Iberian Peninsula.

Despite the fact that Arabic literature is replete with epic narratives that began in pre-Islamic times and continued through the Islamic period, of which the Aljamiado narratives constitute only a small part, nineteenth-century

Western scholars believed that epic narratives were nonexistent in Arabic and that Arabic writers dealt only with the tangible and the real, lacking the aspiration for the ideal and the unknown.[92] Even Spain was denied such a literary genre until the latter part of the nineteenth century.[93] Subsequent research revealed that both poeples had their own epics and that chivalry was known among the Arabs three centuries before it was known to Europe.[94] Although both Arabic and Spanish epic narratives were based on actual events with a real time, place, and protagonists, they contained most, if not all the elements that characterized European epics. In 1928, Ribera suggested an Arabic origin to Spanish narratives, but his suggestion remained dormant until 1964, when 'Abd al-Badī' published his *Arabic Epic and Its Influence on Castilian Epic*, surveying the literature on the subject from pre-Islamic times through the classicial period of Islam and down to its manifestation in Spanish literature, pointing to elements common to both Arabic and Spanish narratives. 'Abd al-Badī'compares narratives of early Islam, the biography of the pre-Islamic bard 'Antar (*Sīrat 'Antar*), and the epic narrative (*urjuzah*) by the tenth-century Andalusian Ibn 'Abd Rabbihi with their Spanish counterparts as found in *Poema del Cid, Los Infantes de Lara,* and *La Mora Zayda*, pointing to the affinity and common elements binding the two literatures. Meanwhile, Galmés took up the subject of epic narratives by first editing the Aljamiado texts contained in the *Book of Battles* with an incisive introduction and linguistic study; subsequently, Galmés brought out the major points in the *Book of Battles* in his short, lucid work, *Arabic Epic and Castilian Epic*. Then followed Marcos's *Arabic Narrative Poetry and Hispanic Epic*, expanding on some points and reaching similar conclusions.

The comparative approach of 'Abd al-Badī', Galmés, and Marcos amply documents not only the intimate relationship of Arabic and Spanish narratives, but the continuity of epic literature over the ages down to the Morisco period in the sixteenth century. It is relevant to mention that pre-Islamic times, known as the Days of Ignorance (*Ayyām al-Jāhiliyyah*) or the Days of the Arabs (*Ayyām al-'Arab*), were marked by intertribal wars that were celebrated in songs similar to later European *gestes*. These songs, fragments of which survived, were recited by narrators, who also used rhymed prose. Some of the narrations were extended into the Islamic period with many additions and embellishments. Such was the biography of 'Antar (*Sīrat 'Antar*) celebrating the heroism of the pre-Islamic bard 'Antar, who fell madly in love with his cousin 'Abla and undertook dangerous assignments in order to gain her hand. He was made to live almost five centuries into the Islamic period, performing extraordinary deeds beyond the confines of the Arabian Peninsula, in Syria, Iran, Byzantium, and North Africa.[95] He combined the pre-Islamic virtues of manliness (*murūwah)* with a crusading spirit against Christianity. Holy War (*Jihād*) became a common theme, finding full expression in the *Dhāt al-himmah wa-l-baṭṭāl*, a narrative relating the struggle between Islam and Byzantium.[96] These and other narratives exalting extraordinary heroic deeds were preserved by narrators and later by compilers.[97]

These narrations, known as *ḥadīth* (story, fable, or simply narration) or *Akhbār* (pl. of *khabar,* meaning "news") retained this designation among the Moriscos, who called them *el-alḥadīth*—which may correspond to the Spanish *nuevas* often used in *Poema del Cid.*[98] They formed part of Arabic historiography. Although their origin may date to pre-Islamic times, they developed under Islam, gaining religious meaning in the path of Islam and its encounter with Christianity. In addition to his secular role, the hero emerged as an instrument of a divine power. This can be readily seen in Aljamiado texts, in which the presence of the angel Gabriel is pervasive, always appearing at the right time and even participating directly in the action (a feature also found in *Poema del Cid*).[99] The epic narratives also contained spirits, omens, divination, and fantastic elements.[100] This notwithstanding, they became the heritage of Muslims everywhere, including Muslim Spain, which developed its own epic narratives celebrating the triumph of Islam in its confrontation with Christianity.[101] The poem in *rajaz* meter *(Urjuzah)* of Ibn 'Abd Rabbihi exalting the military expeditions of his patron the caliph 'Abd al-Raḥmān III (912-961) against the Christians is one such epic narrative.[102] Such compositions in both prose and verse formed part of the general history of al-Andalus and engendered a counterpart in Romance. These flourished during the border wars *(guerras fronterizas)* between Muslims and Christians which lasted until the end of the fifteenth century, when the Moriscos began to develop their literature—selecting from the Arabic legacy the narratives which best met their needs.

The long coexistence of the Muslim and Christian communities at war and in peace with similar goals but different religious ideologies resulted in a common outlook—notwithstanding the differences separating them. Thus, similarities between Arabic and Spanish could not have been altogether accidental. The Mozarabs, who lived under Muslim rule, and their counterparts, the Mudejars/Moriscos, who lived under Christians, played no small part in the diffusion and transmission of Arabic literary genres, including epic narratives, didactic stories, aphorisms, and proverbs.

Epic narratives became the patrimony of Muslim and Christian societies alike and contributed to the formation of the institution of chivalry, which appears to have the same semantic value in Arabic, Spanish, and French, the sense of "horsemanship." The Arabic term *furūsiyyah* is derived from *faras* (horse), from which the term *fāris* (knight) is also derived. They correspond to the Spanish *caballería* and *caballero* and to the French *chevalérie* and *chevalier.* The tenth-century Ibn al-Nadīm[103] devotes a section to *furūsiyyah,* in which he lists books dealing with the bearing of arms, weapons, etiquette of wars, and the conduct of participants—all of which constitute the basic ingredients of the institution of chivalry.

The hero (Ar. *fāris*, Sp. *caballero*, Fr. *chevalier*, Alj. *kaballero*) is a horseman whose existence depends on a horse, a sword, a cause, and a situation in which he is able to demonstrate his prowess. These primary ingredients enable him to display superior human qualities of honor (*'irḍ*) and manliness (*murūwah*) embodying all the virtues of courage, magnanimity, generosity, and hospitality.[104] He is the personification of the pre-Islamic leader (*sayyid*) whose goal is to avenge humiliation and correct wrong.[105] His deeds alone are the only guarantee for his preeminent position and prestige, and allow him to assume sonorous surnames befitting his station such as *Ghālib* (Victorious) and *al-Sayyidi al-baṭṭāl* (My Lord and Maximum Hero)—two surnames that correspond to *Campeador* and *Mio Cid*.[106] He is often knighted in a solemn ceremony[107] and owes allegiance and loyalty to a king or a prophet.[108] His sword, which was ordinarily captured from the enemy, was also given a sonorous name: 'Alī's Dhū-l-fiqār, the Cid's Colada and Tizon, and Roland's Durandal and Almace.[109] His horse also receives a name.[110]

In the battlefield he engages his equal first; afterward he may fight the rank and file of the army—if and when needed.[111] He takes an oath to accomplish his mission by abstinence from washing or shaving until he triumphs.[112] However, he is not above deceit, craftiness, and even theft in the pursuit of the enemy.[113] He is self-assured and even boastful about his powess, invoking his name in an intimidating fashion[114] in elegant and poetical language. He is, above all, a lover who would invoke the name of his beloved before an enterprise that is ordinarily dedicated to her.[115] All in all, he was not a mythical being but a man of flesh and blood possessing very great qualities deserving of emulation and admiration.

Besides these features common to both Arabic and Spanish epic naratives, there is the question of structure. A narration which develops around separate episodes appears in the Cid and Aljamiado narratives and finds its best expression in *Don Quijote,* where the naration is often interrupted by dialogues that contribute to making the protagonist much alive. Cervantes's *Don Quijote,* though a parody of chivalry, not only brings out the elements of chivalry but also is structured in episodes without nexus. Cervantes witnessed the last days of the Moriscos and came into contact with some of them in Algiers and in Spain; he may be assumed to have known the literary taste of the Moriscos, for whom he had little sympathy, as evidenced by repeated unfavorable refferences to them. It is possible that he used his Don Quijote to redicule them as well as the society of his time. Whatever his motivation, Cervantes drew his material from the then numerous books on chivalry, following their content and structure. He calls his composition a narration[116] or "true history" (*verdadera historia)* as his Don Quijote perceives it,[117] and as the Arab compilers of old perceived such compositions. His "brainless" Don Quijote, who had read all the available books on chivalry, meticulously follows the norms of the institution. He displays his eloquence and "clarity of prose" befitting a knight who conceives chivalry as consisting of battles, duels, wounds, love, and torment and as aiming at undoing offenses, straightening myopy correcting wrong, mending abuses, and settling accounts.[118] Don Quijote undertook no adventure without first giving a name to his horse, Rocinante; for himself he chose Don Quijote de la Mancha from his original name Quijada or Quesada; and to his dame he gave "the musical, perfect and expressive name of Dulcinea del Toboso." Finally, Don Quijote asked the innkeeper to knight him in the manner of old.[119]

The didactics, fables, aphorisms, and proverbs, some traceable to India, Greece, and the Ancient Near East and prominent in classical Arabic literature, can be observed alike in early Spanish and Aljamiado literature. It may not be a mere coincidence that such genres, which remained pervasive until the time of the Moriscos in the sixteenth century, should have had wide currency in early Spanish literature, which drew heavily from Arabic works through translation and oral transmission. Already in the twelfth century, Pedro Alfonso, a convert from Judaism, wrote a collection of stories under the title of *Disciplina Clericalis,* which was a rendition from Arabic aimed at instructing his fellow clerics in the facts of life through unsavory and mundane stories. The *Disciplina* had an enormous inpact and was emulated by a number of authors. About the same time, the school of translation at Toledo gave impetus to the translation of Arabic works on a variety of subjects —including *Kalīlah wa-Dimnah,* a book of fables, and the *Sendebar,* known as *El libro de los engãnos e los asayamientos de las mugeres,* consisting of some twenty-six episodes or *enxenplos* (examples) which depict the deceit and cunning of women. These and other works served as models influencing Juan Manuel's *Conde Lucanor,* consisting of fifty-one examples related by the wise Patronio to his eager pupil, Count Lucanor. The didactic approach also is found in Juan Ruiz's *Book of Good Love,* consisting of edifying stories, fables, and aphorisms. One may add *The Book of the Twelve Wisemen,* dealing with the instruction of a young man in his duties; *The Book of One Hundred Chapters,* consisting of moral and political maxims; *The Book of Good Proverbs; The Book of Philosophy;* and *The Secret of Secrets*—all of which contain maxims and norms for guidance and upright living.[120]

In sum, didactic literature in the form of stories, fables, aphorisms, proverbs, and epic narratives had an unbroken continuity that began with classical Arabic literature and passed to Spanish and Aljamiado literatures, with much of its early modality, perspective, and purpose intact.

9

Morisco Poetry

Morisco poetry appears to have broken completely with Arabic classical poetry, as represented by the *Qaṣīdah*(Ode), considered the model of versification. Nowhere can the depth of latinization of the Moriscos be better seen than in their basically Spanish versification with occasional use of *zajal,*[1] a form common among Muslim Spaniards for centuries. Classical versification, as represented by the *Qaṣīdah,* requires a deep knowledge of Arabic, not to mention familiarity with Arabic meters and the ability of versification. Although Arabic versification died out as a result of de-arabization, the *zajal* and *Muwashshaḥ* forms of versification, which had become common among Arabic and Romance speaking people from about the eleventh century, endured among the Mudejars and , subsequently, the Moriscos, who perpetuated them in their songs, *zambras,* and other poems. This versification fitted quite well into Romance dialect, displacing the classical Arabic meters peculiar to Arabic. The use of the *zajal* in Spanish versification is demonstrated by the *Cantigas* of Alfonso X in the thirteenth century and by some of the Archpriest of Hita's poems in his famed *Book of Good Love* written in the fourteenth century.[2]

Morisco poetry also deviates from the classical tradition with respect to quantity and content. Arabic and Andalusion poetry occupied a prominent place in society and was used abundantly on festive and solemn occasions, in peace and war, to instruct, delight, and entertain the audience. Varied and flexible, it possessed the themes of love, praise, satire, elegy, war, asceticism, nature, cities, palaces, gardens, wine, and so on.[3] Poetical expression had cherished goals of both artistry and eloquence. In contrast, poetry constitutes a relatively small fraction of extant Morisco literature. That poetry is simple, and content is limited to religious matters or laments of the Morisco plight. Like prose writing, poetry was clandestine, sometimes bearing an author's name and sometimes remaining anomymous. Fewer than a dozen titles are extant: *The Poem of Joseph,*[4] *Praise and Exaltation of the Prophet Muhammad,*[5] *Couplets in Praise of God,*[6] *Couplet in Praise of Islam,*[7] *Couplets Invoking the Intercession of Prophets,*[8] *Couplets Praising the Prophet's Cloak,*[9] *Couplets of Lament,*[10] and *Couplet Exalting the Genealogy of 'Alī.*[11] In addition, there are the poems of the emigres Ibrahim Bolfad,[12] Juan Alfonso,[13] and Muhammad Rabadan,[14] the most celebrated Morisco poet.

Although Morisco Poetry is permeated with arabism and Islamic thought, it does bear a Spanish stamp and has an affinity with Spanish poetry of the period. After refering to *The Poem of Joseph* and Rabadan's poetry, the Spanish scholar Gayangos sees Morisco poetry as possessing a beauty and singular style which placed it on par with other Spanish Poetry and which added a new dimension not achieved by the initiators of the Italian model:

> The beauty and the singular style of these compositions, and especially of the last, make us regret that no more specimens are to be found of a school of poetry which, had it been more extensively cultivated, would without any doubt have materially affected Spanish literature, by leading poets of that nation to adopt the strong and vivid colouring of oriental fancy, instead of the hackneyed sentiments and verses introduced by Boscan and his imitators after the Italian fashion. Let any one compare a sonnet of Garcilaso, the Petrarch of Spain, with the true Morisco romances, and he will soon perceive the immense advantage which, in point of simplicity and feeling, these small compositions possess over the best contrivances of the Castilian poets.[15]

Such an assessment may be fully appreciated only with a sympathy for the Morisco poet, an understanding of his background, and familiarity with the subject matter within an Islamic context, where expressions and images acquire not only special meaning and coloring, but evoke a magnetic association with basically religious themes. This in itself placed Morisco poetry beyond the reach of Christian poets of the day, who could hardly be inspired by content that often conflicted with established Christian doctrine. Nevertheless, a modern reader can appreciate the profound sentiments found in most Morisco poetry.

As with Morisco prose writing, it is difficult on the basis of available material to ascertain the evolution of Mudejar/Morisco poetic compositions.

One may assume that such compositions may have started as early as the thirteenth century and evolved with the progressive decline of arabization and the superimposition of latinization that was almost completed in the course of the sixteenth century. The assumption that such poetical compositions may have existed at an early date in a Spanish dialect may be justified because of the long-standing bilingualism among Mudejars/Moriscos, even long before they had become subject people. Unfortunately, surviving compositions are difficult to date, as in the case of *The Poem of Joseph* which is believed by some to have been composed in the fourteenth century whereas others believe it to have been as late as the sixteenth century. The bulk of Morisco poetry, as can be deduced from internal evidence, was written during the sixteenth century—although some of it, such as *The Praise of Muhammed,* may have been composed during the fifteenth century.

All indications are that *The Poem of Joseph* was one of the earliest poems. It may have been written in the middle of the fourteenth century by an Aragonese, who appears to have been under Castilian influence. There are two manuscripts[16] of the poem belonging to different periods.[17] The poem is based on the Qur'ānic version of the biblical Joseph as expounded on by later Qur'ānic commentators and other Arabic writers; however, the poem was not written directly from the Arabic version, but more probably from an Aljamiado recension in prose[18] translated from the Arabic original. Joseph was loved by his father Jacob but hated by his jealous brothers, who threw him in a well and claimed that he had been eaten by a wolf. He was rescued by merchants, who sold him as a slave in Egypt, where he endured untold hardships but attained great success. This was marred by the attempted seduction of Zulaykhah or Zalifa, who accused him of trying to dishonor her when she had actually been rejected by Joseph. He went to jail, but was freed and regained his position. Finally, he was reunited with his father and family. The poet describes Joseph's vicissitudes in a skillful, moving language with a simplicity that evokes great sympathy for the protagonist. The poet brings out some of Joseph's great qualities and endowments: his dream, in which he saw the sun, the moon, and eleven stars doing homage to him, was meant as a sign for interpreting obscure things; when a black man injured Joseph, God sent a great tempest that subsided only after Joseph had forgive him; Joseph's beauty so dazzled the ladies of the palace that they cut their fingers while peeling oranges without feeling pain. The poem makes pleasant reading, and some of its passages have a poetic quality equal to the *Poema del Cid or the Milagros de Berceo.*[19] The poem was written in *cuaderna via* (four lines to the strophe), of which the following couplets are transliterated and translated:

1. Lowamiyento ada-Allāh e-lalto yes i verdadero
   Onrrado i qonpilido señor dereytorero
   Faranko i poderoso ordenador sertero.

2. Gharan yes el-su-poder todo el mundo abarqa
   Non sale enqubre cosa ke en-el-mundo nasqa

Si-qiyere on la mar ni-en-toda la komarqa
Ni-yen-la-tiyerra piriyeta ni-yenla balanqa.

3. Faghobos a saber oyades mis amados
Lo-ke kontesiyo en-los tiyenpos pasados
A jaqo [i a Y]ūsuf i-ya-sus diyes ermanos
Por kobdisiya [i enbi] diya obiyeron a seyer malos.

7. Komo iyera Yūsuf niño de poqos años
Enbisando el-padre non-se kobriyo de-los ermanos
Kontandoles el-suweño ke viyo en los altos
Pensaron le tarayisiyon i-y-andaron le en-nghano.

8. Diziyeron todos a una faghamos la-sertera
Rrueghemos a nuwestoro padre rroshariya verdadera
Por ke nos de a Yūsuf en komiyenda ver[dadera]
I mostarar le-mos mañas de muy buwenas maneras.[20]

1. Praise be to God, the High and the True
The Just, Self-Sufficient, and Guiding Lord,
Bountiful, True and Powerful Orderer.

2. Great is He; His power embraces all the world
No created thing is ever hidden from Him,
In the sea, in the borderline,
In all the earth and among the stars.

3. Hear my friends, I shall tell you
What happened in bygone times
To Jacob, Joseph, and his ten brothers,
Who through cupidity and envy turned bad.

7. As Joseph was a child but a few years old,
Favored of his father among his brothers,
He told them of the dream he saw on high
And they thought of treason and proceeded with deceit.

8. All said in unison, Let us be sure
And plead with our father stringently
To give Joseph to our protection,
Showing him good conduct in our cunning.

After the plot is set, the poetic narration develops smoothly. Suspense builds, leading the audience to share indignation, sadness, and rejoicing.[21] The poem concludes not only with the happy reunion, but with forgiveness of the brothers and of Zulaykhah, whom Joseph rejuvenated in her old age and married.

Also belonging to the fourteenth century is *The Praise and Exaltation of the Prophet Muhammad,* seventy-one couplets composed in zajal form.

Translated from an Arabic original, the poem may have had wide currency among the *Mudejars,* ancestors of the *Morriscos.* The poem has *sonority and musicality* and was sung to the accompaniment of musical instruments at festive and religious ceremonies. The following couplets in *cuaderna via* serve as an illustration:

	Aljamiado	*Translation*
	Yāḥabībī, yā Muḥammad	O my beloved, O Muḥammad
	Wa-alṣṣālatu 'alā Muḥammad	And prayer be upon Muḥammad.
1.	Debuwes de la loor a min señor ensalsado	After praising my exalted Lord
	Farre alṣṣala sobre alnnabi onrrado	I shall pray upon the honorable Prophet.
	Alṣṣala siyenbere seya alturado	May prayer always be raised
	Sobre nuwestoro alnnabī Muḥammad	Upon our Prophet Muḥammad.
	Yā ḥabībī, yāMuḥammad	O my beloved, O Muḥammad
	Wa-alṣṣalātu 'alā Muḥammad	And prayer be upon Muḥammad.
2.	Alṣṣala ke seya esbandesido	May prayer be widespread
	Ensiyelos i-yen tiyerras seya oyido	And heard in heavens and earth,
	Borke a nosotros seya meresido	So that we may deserve it
	E ayamos el-amor de Muḥammad	And find the love of Muḥammad.
	Yā ḥabībī, yāMuḥammad	O my beloved, O Muḥammad
	Wa-alṣṣalātu 'alā Muḥammad	And prayer be upon muḥammad.
3.	Alṣṣalāes ke no se puwedan kontar	Prayers that cannot be reckoned,
	Mas son ke la pulubiya i las arenas de la mar	For they are more than the rain and the sands of the sea,
	Borke bodamos biyen entarar	So that we may enter well
	En la roghariya de Muḥammad	In supplication of Muḥammad.
	Yā ḥabībī, yā Muḥammad	O my beloved, O Muḥammad
	Wa-alṣṣalātu 'alā Muḥammad	And prayer be upon Muḥammad.
4.	No podiriyan todos los korasones	All hearts cannot
	Lonparar todas las bendisiyones	Name all the benedictions,
	Ni kontar las donasiyones	Nor count the gifts
	Ke fuweron dadas a Muḥammad	That were bestowed on Muḥammad.
	Yā ḥabībī, yā Muḥammad	O my beloved, O Muḥammad
	Wa-alṣṣalātu 'alā Muḥammad	And prayer be upon Muḥammad.
5.	Diso el señor de la gharandiya	The Lord of greatness said

No kiriyariya a noche ni diya	That He would not create night or day,
Ni eskuredad ni luz no abriya	Nor darkness or light
Sino por el gharande amor de Muḥammad	Had it not been for the great love for Muḥammad.
Yā ḥabībī, yā Muḥammad	And prayer be upon Muḥammad
Wa-alṣṣalātu ‘alā Muḥammad	And prayer be upon Muḥammad.
6. Ni aljanna ni jahannam no terniya	There would be neither Paradise, nor Hell,
Ni al-‘arshi ni alkursi no fariya	Nor throne, nor chair
Ni siyels ni tieyrras no abriya	Nor Heaven, nor earth,
Sino por la onnor de Muḥammad	Had it not been for the honor of Muḥammad.
Yā ḥabībī, yā Muḥammad	O my beloved, O Muḥammad
Wa-alṣṣalātu ‘alā Muḥammad	And prayer be upon Muḥammad.[22]

Aljamiado	*Translation*
Yā ḥabībī, yā Muḥammad	O my beloved, O Muḥammad
Wa-alṣṣalātu ‘alā Muḥammad	And Prayer be upon Muḥammad.
43. Señor fazed alṣṣala sobrel	O Lord, pray upon him
I fejinos amor kon-el	And make us love him,
Sakanos en su torobel	Make us join his suite
Jus la seña de Muḥammad	At the sign of Muḥammad.
Yā ḥabībī, yā Muḥammad	O my beloved, O Muḥammad
Wa-alṣṣalātu ‘alā Muḥammad	And Prayer be upon Muḥammad.
44. Pazed alṣṣala de konosensiya	Make prayer with knowledge
Sobre la luz de la kereyensiya	Of the light of belief,
I selaldo kon rrebenensiya	Seal it with reverence
El-allasalām sobre Muḥammad	And peace on Muḥammad.
Yā ḥabībī, yā Muḥammad	O my beloved, O Muḥammad
Wa-alṣṣalātu ‘alā Muḥammad	And prayer be upon Muḥammad.
45. Tu palabra pelaghara luwegho	Your word will then come forth
I sera rresebido tu rruwegho	And your supplication will be heard
I fara el-assalām enteregho:	And you will have full peace:
Asi son los fechos de Muḥammad	Thus are Muḥammad's deeds.
Yā ḥabībī, yā Muḥammad	O my beloved, O Muḥammad
Wa-alṣṣalātu ‘alā Muḥammad	And prayer be upon Muḥammad.

46. Kiyen kiyera puwena bentura	Whoever wishes good fortune
I y-alkansar gharado de altura	And to attain great heights,
Pospongha la torpeza en la noche eskura	Stop impurity in the dark night
I fagha alṣṣala sobre Muḥammad	And utter prayer upon Muḥammad
Yā ḥabībī, yā Muḥammad	O my beloved, O Muḥammad
Wa-alṣṣalātu 'alā Muḥammad	And prayer be upon Muḥammad.[23]

The poem in *Praise [alabansa] of God* is written in the same vein, exalting God's power, attributes, His preeminent role in Creation, and in His relation to man. It concludes with a praise to Muḥammad:

Ada Allāh mi señor anoblesiyendo
E alabando
Fagho muchas lowasiyones
E santefikasiyones,
Akel ke fuwe pirimero sin pirimeriya
I y-asi sera saghero sin sagheriya
Akel ke no se le adelanto ora ni tiyenpo
Ni lo porbiyene keresimiyento ni menghuwamieynto,
El noble paresiyente sin paresensiya
El gharan sekretado sin eskondensiya
El fablante sin estormentes,
Muy alto ordenador sin pensamiyentos,
Perpetual sin fin en saber muy akabado,
Rrey durable, sobro toda cosa poderoso.
No ay lenghuwa ke senbalanse su gharandeza.
Tan bendito e alabado es en su alteza.
No lo toma kansansyo ni suweño ni dormir
El es aunado sin naser e sin morir,
Señor sin mudansa ni bolbimiyento.
No abe a el semesansa ni akostamiyento,
El gharande aunado señor de la nobleza
El rriko abastado sin menghuwa i sin falakeza
Es sin kuwerpo ni fighura ni desponimiyento,
Ante es kunpilido en todo su ordenamiyento.
Por su mersed aleghre nuwestoros korasones
E su gharasiya e senoriyo e oygha nuwestaras petisiyones.[24]

To God, my noble
And glorified Lord,
I make many Praises
And sanctification.
The one Who is the First without a beginning.
And thus He will be the Last without end,
The One neither hour nor time preceded

Nor growth nor diminution comes to,
Of noble countenance without resemblance,
The great Hidden without concealment,
The speaker without instruments,
The very lofty Orderer without pondering,
Eternal without end and with consummate knowledge,
Eternal King over all powerful things.
No language describes his greatness,
So blessed and praised is He in His Highness.
Fatigue, drowsiness, and sleep will not take Him;
He is One without birth or death,
Lord without mutation and change
Having neither resemblance nor proximity,
The great One, Lord of nobility,
The Self-Sustaining without diminution or frailty.
Incorporeal, without form and arrangement,
And Perfect above all in His ordinance.
By His grace our hearts rejoice
And our requests are heard by his grace and Lordship.

In the series of praises is the exaltation of Islam, probably sung along with the praises to God and Muḥammad. It is written in *zajal* form and in *cuaderna via* with an Arabic refrain:

Allāh yā rabī	O God my Lord,
Yā Muḥammad darabī	O Muḥammad, my guide,
Yā verdadero annabī	O True Prophet
de arabi de arabi.	Of the Arab and from the Arab.
Es Allāh solo i senero	God is One and Alone,
de sin ninghun aparsero	None resembling Him
Y Muḥammad su mensajero	And Muḥammad His messenger
Que todo fuwe verdadero.	That all was true.
i el-alislām mi adin	And Islam my religion
Allāh yā rabī	O God my Lord
Yā Muḥammad darabī	O Muḥammad, my guide
yāverdadero annabī	O true prophet
de arabi de arabi.[25]	Of the Arab and from the Arab.

Of interest also is the poem dealing with the noble genealogy of 'Alī, cousin and son-in-law of Muḥammad. It starts by affirming God's power over the fate of man, endowing some with benefits while condemning others to perdition:

Aljamiado

A lo que dios ordena
Y esta en su enternidad determinado
Si es para premio o pena,
Sin remedio a de ser executado;
Unos glorifcados
Y otros para la pena condenados
Siendo mi bisagūelo
Mensajero de Allāh el mas querido
Y siendo Alī mi agūelo
Ebnu Abitalib el que fuc escogido
Esposo de la madre
Y el hijo de los dos Hucain mi padre
Cumplase lo ordenado,
Salgamos de la carcel de esta vida
de el bien dell es prestado
Gocemos de los bienes sin medida
Y con labor entremos
Contra los enemigos que oy tenemos[26]

Translation

What God ordains
Is eternally determined,
Whether reward or punishment,
That will be inescapable executed;
Some are graced
And others condemned to pain.
Being my great grandfather
The most beloved messenger of God
And being ‘Alī my grandfather,
Ibn Abī Ṭālib, the chosen one
Husband of the mother
And my father the son of the two Ḥusayns,
Let what is ordained be fulfilled.
Let us leave the jail of this life
And the good in it that is borrowed;
Let us enjoy the good things without measure
And let us go earnestly
Against the enemies we have nowadays.

The preceding anonymous poems are probably derived from the Arabic. However, for a number of poems, the authors are known, among them Ibrāhīm de Bolfad, Juan Alfonso, and Muḥammad Rabadan—all emigrés to North Africa who wrote their poetry in Romance using the Latin script. Their poetry at times conveys deep bitterness toward their Christian oppressors who exiled them to an unfriendly environment. Ibrāhīm de Bolfad was an emigré "resident of Algiers, *blind of corporeal sight* but illuminated by the vision of the heart and by understanding."[27] He composed a treatise expounding Islamic dogma, based on the Qur'ān with reference to religious obligations and observances, the existence of God, free will, and other religious themes. Ibrāhīm uses the evidence of causation to prove the existence of God:

I el testimonio de aber	The evidence of having
Señor dios forcossamente,	Perforce Lord-God
es lo creado; y tener	Is Creation, and having
color, tiempo, y fallacer;	Color, time, and death;
Como el bibir de la gente.	As in the life of man.
Pues ya en lo creado bemos	Thus, we see in Creation
no ay obras sin causador;	No work without a maker;
de donde claro entendemos	Hence, it is clear that
que aqueste sser que tenemos	The existence we have
sin duda tiene obrador.[28]	Has without doubt a maker.

The question of free will versus predestination, controversial among Muslim religious scholars, is explained by Ibrāhīm with the rational approach that man is responsible for his action since God had shown the path to be followed and endowed man with understanding and discernment:

Y pues que dios el escoger te a dado,	For God gave you the choice,
aunque no te lo dio absolutamente	Though not quite absolutely,
pus con entendimiento te a creado	And created you with understanding
dandote natural tan excelente,	Giving you a natural gift so excellent;
mira a qual de los dos te as inclinado	Look at which one of two was attracting you,
qual te parece ques mas conbeniente:	The one most convenient to you:
gocar de bida eterna y bien eterno,	Enjoying eternal life and eternal well-being
o pensar para siempre en el infierno[29]	Or thinking always about Hell.

Of similar bent was Juan Alfonso, an Aragonese of Christian or Jewish ancestry, who turned Muslim and defended his new faith with zeal. He emigrated to Tunis and Tetuan in present-day Morocco, leaving a handsome inheritance in his native Spain.[30] He struggled for survival in north Africa as a laborer. Judging from his extant works,[31] mostly poetry, he appears knowledgeable in both Christian and Islamic theology. The tenor of his writing is mostly apologetic, marked by acid attacks not only on Christian persecutors for injustices to the Moriscos, but also on the whole of Christian doctrine and practice. He considers Christianity an adulterated and bankrupt religion:

No solo las traducciones	Not only the translations
pero aun lo que trasladaron	But also what they transmitted
los propios orixinales	Of the proper originals
an hecho de mano en mano	That passed from hand to hand
de las escritureas claras	making of the lucid scriptures
un laberinto yntricado	An intricate labyrinth.[32]

In another poem,[33] Juan Alfonso sees in Christianity contradictions, omissions, and additions that disfigure the whole religion as enunciated by Christ. The popes, following Paul, were responsible for the disfiguration. He also refutes the concept of Trinity and the divinity of Christ. He ridicules communion as an act of "eating" God:

Bosotros que en una ostia	You take a wafer
que dezis el Sagramento	Calling it sacrament,
teneis por fe queta Dios	Take on faith that it is God
y on comeis aquel Dios buestro.	And then you eat that God of yours.

He points to the legitimacy of Muḥammad, whose coming was foretold by Christ himself:

Pues el mismo Cristo dijo	Well, Christ himself said
ablando por su maestro	Speaking on behalf of his Lord
tras el bendria un paraclito	That a paraclete will come after him
que seria santo y bueno	Who will be holy and good.
Y este sabed ques Muḥammad	Know that this is Muḥammad,
de Dios santo y mensajero	The holy and Messenger of God
el que trujo el alcoran	The one who brought forth the Qur'ān,
libro sagrado y perfecto.	The holy and perfect book.

Unlike the Christians' treatment of scriptures, no one ever dared add anything to the Qur'ān:

Y no ay alarbo ni turko	There is neither Arab nor Turk,
ansi sabio como necio	Be he wise or stupid,
que ose añadir sobre el	Who ever dared to add to it
una silaba ni un verso	A single syllable or a verse.

Y buestra fe se sabe	And in your faith are known
dos mil enbustes y enredos,	A thousand lies and mischiefs,
Y si alguno lo descrube	And if someone discover them
lo labrays luego con fuego.	You will relegate him to the fire.

Confession was abhorrent to the Moriscos. Juan Alfonso sees it as a laughing matter:

A una cosa me rio	One thing makes me laugh
del otro quentra en el tenplo	The one taking place in the temple,
con mas culpas y pecados	With more offenses and sins
que canicula en enero	Than the Dog Star in January.
Y a los pies de un confesor	And at the feet of a confessor
le diga muy secreto	To whom you utter secretly
que le perdone sus culpas	To forgive your offenses
y el le diga: "Ego asuelbo."	And he will say, "I absolve you."

Juan Alfonso reiterates similar points in another poem,[34] pointing to Christian conception of God as "graying and fatigued like old people": "Cabellos y barbas blancas/como los viejos."

He argues that Christ himself said he was a prophet and a messenger, yet the popes made him God, each adding to the Christian doctrine and thus disfiguring it. He objects to the idea of original sin in that even prophets could end in Hell until saved by Christ. This and other conceptions lead Juan Alfonso to conclude that Christianity is a mass of lies and ridiculous practices:

O ley llena de mentiras	O religion full of lies,
gente de verdad desiertos	People sterile of truth
que el laberinto de Creta	Not even the labyrinth of Crete
no tuvo tanto enredos	Had so much ensnaring.
Establecida por onbres	Established by men
diziendo el mismo maestro	When the Lord himself says
que el que la ley de onbre siguiere	That the one who follows the law of man
seran en vano sus hechos.	Will have his deeds end in vain.[35]

He may have also composed the following verses ridiculing the Eucharist:

Bosotros que en la oración	You who in prayer
como golosoa exipgios	Like cupid Egyptians
adoráys buestro dios pan	Worship your God, the bread,
ahogándolo entre bino.[36]	Submerging it in wine.

Muḥammad Rabadan is the best-known Morisco poet and, perhaps, the greatest by virtue of the enormous poetical production that came down to us. A native of Rueda in Aragón, he settled in Tunis and put into verse the whole Islamic doctrine. All his poetry was based on the prose writings of his Morisco predecessors. His talent resides in his poetical gift and the facility with which he was able to explain and expound on the Islamic faith in an even flowing verse that remained faithful to both poetical form and content. Gayangos describes his poetry; "That this poem abounds in beautiful images, that the author's style is full of vigor as well as charming simplicity, and that in point of cadence and harmony some verses are to be found equal, if not superior, to those of the best Spanish poets has sufficiently appeared in the foregoing extract."[37] Rabadan's major work, *Discourse of Light—the Origin and Limpid Genealogy of Our Leader and Blessed Prophet Muḥammad,* is a veritable encyclopedia of Islamic doctrine, beginning with Muammad and ending with an exaltation of the ninety-nine names of God. It consists of three hundred fifty-one folios in twenty-four songs (*cantos*) written in free verse (*verse suelto*). This verse biography of Muḥammad relies on al-Bakrī's *Book of Light*, tracing the genealogy of Muḥammad to the Creation.[38] It starts with a dedication to God, Creator of all things, and proceeds to the Creation of the world, with songs devoted to Adam and his immediate descendants Seth, Noah, and Abraham. The narration traces the ancestry of Jews and Christians through the line of Isaac to Jesus. This section was intended to dispel confusion and ignorance by tracing the genealogy of Muammad through Ismā'īl, traditionally regarded as the true heir and beneficiary of God's gifts, making Jews and Christians mere pretenders to God's benefits.[39] He then narrates the history of the immediate ancestors of Muḥammad—Hāshim, 'Abd al-Muṭṭalib, and his father 'Abdallah—to whom he devotes various songs, bringing the account to the marvels attending the birth of Muḥammad, his qualities, the marvel of the Qur'ān, his ascent to the seven heavens (*Mi'rāj*), and his death. Thus, it is a complete biography of Muḥammad, whose coming was manifest from the time of Creation in the form of light that appeared on the persons of his ancestors beginning with Adam. Rabadan's indebtedness to al-Bakrī's *Book of Light* is clear in argument and content. However, Rabadan attached to the work other songs that dealt with three significant and popular items: *The Fright of the Day of Judgment*, based on Qur'ānic verses; *A Song to the Months [lunas] of the Year*, calling attention to the fasting, prayers, and other religious duties; and *The Ninety-Nine Names of His Divine Majesty*, often known as the "Beautiful Names of God"[40] that should be recited by the faithful.

In explaining the trajectory of Islam from the Creation to the Day of Judgment, Rabadan, like his Muslim predecessors including Mudejars/Moriscos, had two objects in mind: first, to defend the validity of Islam in the light of history through Ismā'īl so as to silence Christian and Jewish critics, and second, to instruct and guide his fellow Moriscos in the path of true belief. Rabadan points out that Muḥammad's prophecy was marked by a sign of clear light shown on God's chosen people from time immemorial:

Fué la clara luz pasando	A clear light passed
Siempre por estos varones	Always through these virtuous men
Más perfectos y estimados,	Most perfect and esteemed
Por el Señor escogidos,	By the Lord chosen,
Por su palabra avisados;	By his word advised;
Corriendo de padre en hijo,	Passing from father to son
De un honrrado en otro	And from pious to pious.[41]

Although he points to the astonishing success of Islam under Muḥammad's leadership and that of his immediate successors, Rabadan could not but lament the abject state of his fellow Moriscos in the Iberian Peninsula, persecuted and deprived of their books and scholars. Nevertheless, this would end in brighter days; it is no more than God's will and His punishment for past sins:

Allah dió lugar	God made possible
Que los Moros deste reyno,	That the Moors of this kingdom
Con tantas persecuciones,	With so many persecutions
Sean pugnidos y presos;	Would be punished and enslaved.
Perdiendo los alquitebes,	Having lost the books,
No quedado rastro dellos;	Without leaving a trace;
los alimes acabados,	Scholars are gone
Quales muertos, quales presos,	Some dead, others jailed,
La Inquisicion desplegada	The Inquisition rampant
Con grandes fuerzas y apremios,	With great force and pressures,
Haciendo con gran rigor	Implementing with rigor
Cruezas y desafueros,	Cruelty and excesses;
Que casi por todas partes	Almost everywhere
hacia temblar el suelo:	The earth is made to tremble:
Aqui prenden y alli prenden	They apprehend here and there
A los baptizados nuevos,	The newly baptized,
Cargándoles cada dia	Imposing on them every day
Galeras, tormento y fuego	Galleys, torment, and fire
Con otras adversaciones	Along with other calamities
Que a solo Allah es el secreto.[42]	For which God alone knows the secret.

Signs of the end of the world are pictured vividly, with horror afflicting man:

Qué vivir tan desabrido,	What a peevish living,
Qué inquietud, que sobresalto,	What restlessness and fear,
Qué llagas sin medicinas,	What infested wounds without remedy,
Qué suenos tan quebrantados.	What dreams so shattered,

Qué enfermedades tan solas,	What infirmities so pervasive,
Qué dolores sin amahos.[43]	What pain without relief.

This despair is followed by the plea of the condemned during the Day of Judgment, who pleaded for the intercession of the prophets on their behalf, but were ignored. Then they are rescued through the intervention of Muḥammad:

O Muḥammad, nuestro amparo	O Muḥammad, our refuge,
Nuestro muro y defensor,	Our fortress and defender,
Refugio de nuestras penas	Refuge of our sufferings
Y en muestras tinieblas sol:	And sun in our darkness:
Pues para nuestro remedio	Since for our remedy
Te creo nuestro Señor	Our Lord created you
Hoy de rogar por nosotros	To plead for us today,
Te toca la obligacion.	This is your obligation.
Hoy es el día que debes	Today is the time you must
Publicar tu gran valor,	Announce your great worth
Que quanto mayor la culpa	In that the greater the sin,
Es la clemencia mayor.	The greater is the clemency.
Ya sabes que te seguimos	You know we follow you
Sin verte ni oir tu voz,	Without seeing or hearing your voice,
Y anuque en las obras faltemos,	And though we falter in deed
Tu dicho afirmámoslo.	Your sayings we affirm.
Eschástenos en olvido	You removed us from oblivion
En la fortuna mayor,	In the great fortune
Al tiempo que no hay ninguno	At a time when there is none
Que quiera rogar por nos.	Who wanted to plead for us.
Solo a tí, Muḥammad, toca	It belongs to you alone, Muḥammad,
Qu'esta señalada empresa	This is the special enterprise
A tí solo se guardó.[44]	Which He preserved for you alone.

Muḥammad will intercede, of course, but only upon the confession of faith by all mortals:

Libertará su familia	He will set free his family
De tan grande perdición;	From so great a perdition;
No sólo a los pecadores;	Not only the sinners,
Mas a quien jamás obró	But also those who never performed
Obra buena en su provecho,	A good deed for his benefit,
Sólo porque pronunció	Only Because he uttered
La unidad de la creencia	The unity of belief

Una vez mientras vivió.[45]	Once in his lifetime.

The pilgrim Puey de Monçon also recorded his adventures in verse. After describing the hardships of his journey by sea and land, the poet arrives in Mecca, which he describes with awe and wonderment:

Ansi i bamos am Maka	Thus we went to Mecca,
Esa bendita sibdad	That blessed city,
Ke sus puwertas son al-baraka	Whose doors are benediction,
I sus paredos piyedad	And whose walls piety;
Sus tejados kalaredad	Its roofs are clarity
I-ya-ella toda es bendisiyon	And all of it is blessing.
Puwes kuwal kiyere ke	Thus, whoever wants
A elle ba tiyene ghanado el-perdon.	To go to it will gain reward.
Dezir o-se de la kasa	Saying as though of the house,
Ke de Maka se deziya	As used to be said about Mecca
I de la orden i kawsa	And about the order and cause,
Ke nesta kasa abiya	That this house there was
Kasa de tanta baliya	A house of so much worth,
Kasa de tanta nobleza	A house of so much nobility,
oro i palata i rrikeza	Gold, silver, and wealth
ke-stimar no se podriya.	That could not be valued.
Alli estan kuwatoro al-miḥrabes	There are the four *miḥrabs*
De las nuwestaras kuwatoro rreghlas;	Of our four canons;
Ay de rrikas asomo'as	There are rich minarets
Muy altas i rrikas i bellas	Very lofty, rich, and beautiful
A kuwanto las kuwatoro de-llas	Four of which correspond to
De nuwestoros kuwatoro doktores	Our four doctors,
A la kasa dan mil favores	Bestowing on the house one thousand favors
Kosas son de marabillas.[46]	That are marvellous things.

In conclusion, Morisco poetry is limited to religious and doctrinal matters, thus, aiming at instructing and keeping the faith in an adverse environment. This limitation with respect to themes, structure and variety of verbal expressions would place the poetry outside the realm of spontaneity making it utilitarian, aimed at a single purpose of responding to Morisco plight and future aspirations. As such, the poetry appears to be concerned more with conveying a message in a clear and simple manner than with aesthetics and poetical niceties. It is simply meant to reaffirm and defend the Islamic faith against outside attack by first reiterating and upholding Islamic faith, and secondly, by refuting and ridiculing Christian doctrine. Moreover, it has an edifying purpose, as in the poem of Joseph with which the Moriscos identified themselves in connection with Joseph's tribulations, and his ultimate triumph against overwhelming odds. In this the Morisco finds consolation and hope in his own ultimate deliverance at the hand of God from the injustices of his Christian oppressor. Similarly, the poems in praise of Muhammad and God evoke a great reverence and adulation, and express profound sentiment and unshakable conviction. Muḥammad is portrayed as God's tool and the cause behind the very existence of the world and behind the necessity of the existence of Paradise and Hell. He is the most favored of God's creatures. This unique position conforms to the will of God, Who is primeval, knowing, powerful , ordering, self-sustaining, and perfect. All in all, Morisco poetry conveys porfound religious sentiments and is expressed in a clear language—qualities that make it an effective and powerful tool for maintaining Morisco beliefs.

The English rendering of the poems follows a literal translation and, as such, does not do justice to the original. Despite its simplicity, Morisco poetry expresses intense feeling which no translation can properly convey. Only a feeling for the language and an awareness of Morisco plight could help measure the intense emotion that such a poetry is capable of producing in the audience.

10

Conclusion

Using insight gained from their own literature and from external evidence embodied in contemporary documentation of the Inquisition and historians, it is reasonable to say that the Moriscos were victims of church, state, and the Catholic populace owing to circumstances beyond their control and beyond that of their Catholic oppressors. Their plight has been acknowledged even by their most rabid opponents, who would justify the harsh treatment imposed on the Moriscos as dictated in the interest of achieving the unity of church and state. Further, opponents viewed the harsh measures imposed on the Moriscos as necessary and unavoidable in the light of Morscos' stubbornness and their propensity to rebellion, conspiracy, heresy, and treason. This propensity on the part of the Morsicos was not altogether imaginary, but owed its existence to complex factors that contributed to inflexible attitudes resulting from actions and reactions or challenges and responses.

This confrontation between Christian and Muslim societies had a long and complex history, culminating with the Moriscos in the sixteenth century. After the completion of the Reconquest in 1492, the Christian monarchs were faced with the problem of a heterogeneous population with disparate cultures and religions. They attempted to forge a monolithic society by all the means at their disposal, completely disregarding pacts and pledges entered into with their Muslim subjects, who constituted a good share of the population. They forced Catholicism upon the Moriscos and imposed numerous edicts limiting their human and civil liberties, creating an adversary relationship of mistrust, fanaticism, and fear which prevailed throughout the sixteenth century with no prospect of a viable solution. Abuses of all sorts were committed, often in the name of religion and national unity. This relentless method proved unproductive, and alienated the Moriscos, who responded to the challenge with passive resistence and occasional open revolt, fortified by the strong conviction of ultimate redemption.

Catholic concern for religious and national unity grew in urgency with increased Spanish involvement in the Mediterranean, where Spain had to contend with the ambitions of neighboring France and the ever-increasing Ottoman presence in the Mediterranean and North Africa, threatening Spain itself. The Ottomans were particularly feared as Muslims who would come to the rescue of their oppressed co-religionists, the Moriscos. Ottoman threat (whether real or imaginary), the rise of Protestantism, and rampant piracy in the Mediterranean exacerbated an already tense relation between Christians and Moriscos, influencing church and state to resolve the Morisco question as expeditiously as possible, regardless of the means—even if it meant total extermination. In their anxiety, church and state collaborated upon a solution through harsh measures, hoping thereby to speed results. These unreasonable and precipitious actions proved unworkable from the outset and no doubt strengthened the Moriscos' determination to uphold their beliefs and to practice their customs covertly. Polarization had taken place and widened as time went on, with no possible return to a life of tolerance and coexistence, let alone assimilation.

As a powerless minority, the Moriscos were exploited and deprived of elementary rights and opportunities, developing intense hatred for their oppressors and all they stood for—including Christianity, which was associated with unscrupulous bishops and greedy, ignorant clerics. Attempts were made by some statesmen and clerics, such as Talavera, to reach the Moriscos by the more humane method of persuasion through education, even if this meant the continued use of Arabic as the language of instruction and the preservation of many Morisco customs. Such men recommended the establishing of schools and seminaries, training priests, and publishing suitable materials. Though this path aimed at Christianization, zealots frowned upon it as too slow and lenient. And though such a method appeared sound when all other means failed, it required substantial financing which neither church nor state was willing to provide. As a result, the Moriscos remained largely ignorant of the fundamentals of Christianity, and for this they were severely punished when apprehended, their shortcomings being blamed on their stubbornness and evil ways.

For his part, the Morisco, preoccupied with survival and fear of harassment, could be neither receptive to the insatiable oppressors nor able to bridge on his own the gap separating him from his Christian neighbors. His situation worsened as time went on, and he was deprived of elementary civil rights with little or no protection from either church or state. In his enforced status as a new convert, he fell under the jurisdiction of the Inquisition, which had unlimited power to apprehend any person on the slightest pretext. The accused was considered guilty until proved innocent and was entirely at the mercy of the Inquisition, which often confiscated his property to defray the costs of the trial. The Inquisition was notorious for its abuses; no justice could be expected from it. The secular authorities were also notorious for breaking promises and pledges, replacing them with edicts that aimed at the total effacement of Morisco individuality and his right to exist in a Christian society. Under the circumstances, the Morisco came to mistrust and loathe both secular and ecclesiastical authorities, who often appeared more interested in his damnation than in the salvation of his soul. Thus, he was driven to despair and made to feel a stranger in his own homeland, living on the margin of a society that despised him. There was little he could do except fantasize and hope for better days.

The Moriscos were left with little choice but to live a dual life: a life of appearance conforming to the demands of the oppressor and a life of reality conforming to the deep-rooted traditions. Although they were told that they could emigrate, many obstacles were placed in their way, and most of the Moriscos lacked the means for undertaking such a risky venture. Thus, perhaps, their sole alternative was to seek an outlet in the traditions of their ancestors, relying heavily on an unshaken belief that Islam offered ultimate deliverance. Notwithstanding the harsh measures aimed at eradicating them, Islamic traditions were still much alive in daily life with respect to beliefs, rituals, food, dress, marriage, divorce, and a host of other transactions. The task of preserving Islamic traditions and handing them on to the next generation was undertaken by a body of devoted scholars who disseminated Islamic doctrine at the risk of their own lives. However limited their education may have been, these men knew the essentials of Islamic religion and codified it in Romance, the language of the people, relying frequently on Arabic materials which were either paraphrased or translated and avoiding long scholarly details that would confuse the initiates. This material, drawn from several Arabic genres, was carefully selected and written in simple language. It is essentially didactic and free from controversial items pertaining to dogma, rituals, and others observances. In this simplicity lies, perhaps, the greatest contribution of the Moriscos.

By this means, the Moriscos developed and maintained a strong religious perspective and an equally strong historical consciousness about their past and future role in the order of things. They resigned themselves that their fate was preordained, that their present tribulations were the result of past sins, and that their redemption would come from repentance and return to the true faith. How could this be otherwise when several prophecies give ample testimony not only about their deliverance from the oppressor but their ultimate triumph over him? The painful life of simulation (*taqīyah)* in which they gave lip service to Christianity but held Islam in the heart would pass without retribution, for the religious law itself condones such a dual posture under adverse conditions. Thus, they maintained the validity and superiority of the Islamic faith and defended it against their Christian adversaries in an extensive literature that is a monument to their courage and determination.

Morisco literature is an eloquent expression of belief, determination, and defiance. It is, at the same time, a source of strength against harassment, persecution, and arbitrary justice. Its strength lies in a set of beliefs and convictions that God's will would prevail in the end and that man and his deeds are always subordinated to it. This fatalist conception relying on Muḥammad and the Almighty permeates Morisco writings whatever the subject matter—love, epic narratives, history, poetry, and stories. It is essentially didactic literature, elucidating religious verities and God's designs in the order of things. The Moriscos had their relapses in a seeming overreliance on magic, talisman, and astrology—subjects that were marginal to both religion and science and often controversial among Christian and Muslim scholars. But it is doubtful that the Moriscos, who lacked sophistication, ever realized the religious implications of such practices.

Morisco's self-expression inspired by Islamic traditions convey an intense devotional feeling and great expectation of a promising future at the hands of the Almighty. Their vicissitudes, however traumatic at times, were relatively mild in contrast with those of the prophets, who never lost sight of God's presence and mercy. Even the greatest of the prophets had their tribulations: Abraham's struggle for establishing monotheism, Moses' trials, Job's suffering, Jesus' rejection, and Muḥammad's persecution and wars with indomitable enemies. All their tribulations were part of God's design and had the purpose of testing, punishing, and rewarding. Even His most favored religion, Islam, had difficult beginnings, but triumphed miraculously at the end with His intervention through the angel Gabriel and 'Alī, who heroically vanquished whole armies, giants, and even spirits and demons. Tamīm's journey into a strange world of demons and spirits and Carcayona's punishment and exile into the wilderness by her pagan father are lessons in the reaffirmation of the faith in face of enormous danger, resulting ultimately in handsome rewards.

Inasmuch as Islam and its prophet were under persistent attacks by Christian apologists, the Moriscos were the more preoccupied with establishing the validity of Islam for the dual purpose of maintaining the faith and refuting their adversaries. For this they invoked history and the Scriptures to demonstrate that Islam has been manifest from the Creation through a divine light that foretold the coming of Muḥammad. Prophets, Christ himself, acknowledged his coming, and some of them, including Moses, undertook long journeys in search of him. Though Islam emerged in history during the seventh century, it was believed to have been here at all times with Abraham, Jacob, Joseph, Moses, Job, Jesus, and even Alexander the Great as its most distinguished followers. In a word, Islam is the one and only universal religion, abrogating both Judaism and Christianity.

This posture of course had its counterpart among Christians. With each side claiming exclusive truth and religious verities, there was no room for accommodation, let alone genuine understanding. The intensity of the conflict was so great that it obscured much of the sociocultural interaction that had been going on from the time of the Arab conquest of Spain in 711. The process of change in demography, language, culture, and religion was influenced by the factors of military power, expansionism, durability, and a modicum of stability resulting first in arabization and Islamization under the Muslims and then in latinization and Christianization under the Christians. These changes were realized by force of circumstance, though the methods were different. All indications are that the Arab conqueror allowed history to take its course, with little or no attempt from above to impose religion or culture on the subject people. The Arabs instituted a policy of tolerance from the outset, allowing the subject people to practice their religion and to continue the use of their language and customs. On their part, judging from numerous treaties and pacts, the Christian conquerors at first emulated the Islamic example by allowing their subject people the freedom to practice their religion and to use their language and customs. However, they failed to follow up the spirit and letter of their pledges, rescinding them at will and replacing them by harsh edicts.

Nonetheless, there existed much interaction at all levels of society. It would be erroneous to suggest that the Moriscos lived in a complete isolation from Christian society. They remained an integral part of the social fabric, contributing their labor in agriculture, industry, communication, and even medicine. They dealt constantly with their Christian neighbors—transacting business, cultivating friends, engaging in marriages, participating in festivities, and sharing many of the customs of the day. This kind of participation was continuous but freer and more pronounced throughout the Reconquest from the eleventh century to the end of the fifteenth century, during which the Christian conquerors depended on the skill and technology of their subject people, the Mudejars, who were the true ancestors of the Moriscos. Only after the edict of forced conversion, followed by other restrictive measures, did this role diminish, not by the cessation of the hard labor of the Moriscos but by their estrangement in being exploited and burdened by responsibilities without the benefits that go with them. Arabism and Islam were being replaced by gradual latinization and Christianization. Arabic slowly gave way to Romance, which became almost the sole instrument of self-expression. Poetry was hispanized in form and content. Literary taste, though with a strong Arabic base, conformed in many ways to current literary themes despite its strong religious elements. This can be seen in epic narratives, stories of all kinds, proverbs, and wisdom sayings, not to mention the great propensity of both Moriscos and Christians for magic, sorcery, and astrology. All these forms of literature appear to follow similar if not identical traditions. Moriscos were not alien nor different from the mainstream of Spanish society except for the stigma attached to them of being associated with an ethnic group and a religion for which they were punished without regard to Christian charity.

Infidelity and disloyalty were the common charges in trials before the tribunals of the Inquisition, in which the accused victims had to prove their innocence at the cost of their individual liberties and properties. The Moriscos could not get relief from either church or state. There is no indication that the secular and ecclesiastical authorities seriously attempted to reach the Moriscos through persuasion or benign treatment that would eventually lead to the Moriscos' assimilation into Christian society. Their policy was consistent even toward Moriscos who had accepted Christianity willingly and given ample proof of their faith: these Moriscos were regarded as equally undesirable as the Morsicos who remained ignorant of Christian doctrine and rituals.

Intolerance knows no boundaries and flourishes in an atmosphere of lawlessness in which the powerful make and break laws at will. It is not much consolation to observe that such conditions still exist in the world and that little has been learned from the past. History is blamed for repeating itself; human and civil rights remain still in the eye of the beholder.

Notes

1. THE MORISCOS IN A HOSTILE ENVIRONMENT

1. For instance, Llorente, *Historia* and Lea, *Moriscos* and *History* point to the excesses and intolerances of the Inquisition. One may also mention the Spanish scholars Fernández y González, *Estado social*, and Janer, *Condición*, both of whom bring out the plight of the Moriscos. However, Janer considers the expulsion of the Moriscos both necessary and unavoidable in the light of the excesses of both Christians and Moriscos.
2. Contemporary historians such as Aguilar, Aznar, de Cardona, Bleda, Fonseca, Gualdaljara, Mármol, Rojas, Ripol, Zapata and others showed little sympathy for the Moriscos. They were followed in the nineteenth century by Sangrador, Monoz y Gaviera, Dánvila y Boronat. For one, Dánvila, *Expulsión*, who was followed by Boronat, *Moriscos*, produces ample documentation only to show that the Moriscos got what they deserved, and that their expulsion was overdue and justifiable for securing the unity and security of church and state. To them, the conflict of race and religion made the assimilation of the Moriscos impossible. Moreover, the Moriscos never responded to the overtures of tolerance and Christian charity and stubbornly remained attached to their beliefs and customs conti-

nuing to rebel and conspire with the enemies of Spain. Menéndez y Pelayo, *Historia*, II, 632, considers the expulsion not only a necessity but "an indispensible compliment of historical law; and it is only regretable that it took so long to achieve."

3. Mainly, Caro Baroja, Cardaillac, Cirac, Carrasco, Domínguez, Reglá, García-Carcel and Vincent. More significant still is the interest in the self-expression of the Moriscos as contained in their Aljamiado literature which has been brought to the fore by Gayangos, Saavedra, Guillén, Galmés and Harvey, among others.
4. The term Mudejar may also have been derived from the Arabic *dākhala*, meaning "to enter into contract with." Cf. Fernándezy González, *Estado social*, 3ff. and Cagigas, *Mudéjares*, I, 58ff. It should be added that the term Mudejar was hardly used until the fifteenth century, and was often superseded by designations of Moros, Sarracenos, Ismaelitas, Agarenos and Mahometanos—all of which were also applied to the Moriscos.

   On the Mudejars, see Circourt, *Histoire*; Ladero, *Muéjares*; López Martinez, *Mudéjares*; Macho Ortega, *Condición*; Pedregal, *Estado*; Roca Taver, *Un siglo*; Torres Fontes, *Mudéjares*; Gautier-Dolché, "Des Mudéjares"; y Torres Balbas, "Unos aspectos."
5. Fernández y González, *Estado social*, chapter X, suggests that it was through the Mudejars that Arabic elements infiltrated into the works of Alfonso X, Juan Manuel, Juan Ruíz and others. Besides, they made their contribution to the arts, architecture and agriculture. See also Cagigas, *Mudéjares*, I, 147.
6. The term Mozarab is derived from the Arabic *musta'rib*, meaining arabized. On the Mozarabs and their role as intermediaries between Muslims and northern Christians, see Cagigas, *Mozárabes*; Simonet, *Historia*; and González Palencia, *Mozárabes.*
7. Dánvila, *Expulsión*, 19ff.; Fernández y González, *Estado social*, 118ff. and 264ff.; Cagigas, *Mudéjares,* I, 144; Burns, *Islam*, 124ff. It may be added, however, that James I converted many mosques into churches contrary to pacts entered to with Muslims (Cf. Cagigas, *Mudéjares,* II 368).
8. Burns, *Islam*, 187.
9. Dánvila, *Expulsión*, 23. It should be added that the role of the papacy in Spanish affairs was constant and further enhanced by the activist intervention of the Monks of Cluny in southern France. See Cagigas, *Mudéjares*, 99ff., and Cantarino, *Monjes*, 156ff.
10. Cagigas, *Mudéjares*, I, 134ff., points out that the Cid left virtually the administration of Valencia in 1094 in the hands of Muslims establishing a model, followed by and large in Aragon but hardly in Castile, that pursued a course of gradual intolerance. Though Toledo surrendered peacefully in 1085 to Alfonso VI, who pledged to guarantee the freedom of worship and movement to Muslim subjects and the preservation of their institutions, such a policy was revoked in time and in 1102 the main mosque of Toledo was converted into a cathedral by its Cluniac Bishop while Alfonso was away.
11. These and similar measures led to a policy of segregation which was continued even with the institution of forced conversion. At the Fourth Council of Letran in 1215, it was decided to have Jews and Muslims wear distinctive clothing so as to distinguish them from the rest of the Christians. This was done at the behest of the papacy (Fernández y González, *Estado social, 83ff.).* Subsequently at the Council of Valladolid in 1408, it was decided that Moors should wear a yellow-

green clock and a crescent over their right shoulder (*Ibid.*, 212; cf. Dánvila, *Expulsión,* 47).

12. Dánvila, *Expulsión*, 54ff.
13. Lea, *History*, I, 369.
14. Dánvila, *Expulsión, 43*.
15. *Cabanelas, Juan de Segovia*, 110.
16. As quoted by Dánvila, *Expulsión*, 60.
17. Ibid., 68.
18. Mármol, *Historia*, 145–150; Garrido-Atienza, *Capitulanciones*; Gaspar Remiro, *Último pacto*; Ladero, *Mudéjares*, 29–53.
19. Alcalá, *Arte*. Attempts at reaching the Moriscos through education continued throughout the sixteenth century, but failed because of a lack of genuine support from either church or state. However, several manuals were written for that purpose, such as Ayala's *Catechim, Doctrina* and *Instructions.* Cf. Janer, *Condición,* 20ff.
20. Lea, *Moriscos*, 29ff. It appears obvious that Talavera was carrying out the Catholic kings' policy of conversion, notwithstanding the terms of capitulations. In 1500, Talavera complained to the monarchs: "Those people whom you sent to help me are a hindrance not because they intend bad, but because they believe they are right." As quoted by Boronat, *Moriscos*, I 112.
21. It is not clear whether this conversion included only the elches (Ar. *'ilj*), who were uncouth people of Spanish stock (Cf. Domínguez, *Historia*, 19). At any rate, Boronat, *Moriscos,* I 107ff., defends Cisneros' action and criticizes Talavera's method saying that it overlooks "the character of the Muḥammadan race."
22. Lea, *Moriscos*, 31.
23. Ladero, *Mudéjares*, 57-58. On their part the Granadans appealed to Egypt and the Ottomans asking for help. The Egyptian ruler made a strong representation to the papacy, which in turn communicated with the Catholic kings. Mindful of possible retaliation against Christians living in Egypt, the Spanish monarchs sent Pietri Martiri de Angleria to Egypt to reassure the Egyptian ruler that Muslim subjects will be treated with magnanimity. Pietri left record of his mission in his *Legatio Babylonica*.
24. The text of the edict is in Fernández y González, *Estado social*, 432. It should be noted that a provision calling for disarming the Moriscos was also included. This was of the utmost concern to the Moriscos in a country beset by insecurity. Such provision made the Moriscos defenseless. Lea, *Moriscos*, 190, states the problem: "The deprivation of arms was not only a humiliation but it left them defenseless at a time when violence was constant and to an Old Christian the blood of the deprived race was little more than that of a dog." Disarming the Moriscos became a general policy as reflected in the edicts of 1511, 1515, 1525, 1526, 1541, 1545, 1559 and 1563. See Dánvila, "Desarme."

    Those and other edicts also contained provisions forbidding the Moriscos to wear silken clothes, or mount horses and other restrictions—all of which were considered the prerrogatives of Old Christians.
25. For more details on the question of "purity of blood," see Sicroff, *Controverses*. Cf. Caro Baroja, *Moriscos*, 42ff; and Domínguez, *Historia*, 129-133. Caro Baroja appears to ignore the fusion of the several ethnic groups which has been going on for centuries, and is inclined to trace the origin of the Moriscos to Arabs, Berbers, Persians, and Jews. In this connection, it is relevant to point out that the

Moriscos, like their ancestors the Mudejars, were often designated in edicts, memoranda and correspondence as "nuevamente convertidos," "Moros," "Sarracenos," "Agarenos," and "Mohametanos." Cf. note 4. Only occasionally the term *morisco* was used. In his *Libro de Buen amor*, stanzas 1228 and 1230, the fourteenth-century poet Juan Ruíz refers to *moros* but uses *morisco* and *Morisca* as an adjectival form.

26. Castro, *España,* 57. Writing in the nineteenth century, Ferández y González, *Estado social,* pp. 1, says: "Heir to the glorious tradition of his race that dominated almost the entire Spanish soil, he (the Morisco) maintained a patriotic sentiment for the native country like the sailor, who prefers all sort of danger to the abandonment of his ship. No doubt, the Moriscos were Spaniards and no less so than the Castilians and Aragonese."
27. For specific cases before the tribunals of the Inquisition, see Dressendörfer, *Islam*; García-Arenal, *Inquisición*; Cirac, "Procesos"; Ubieto, "Procesos"; Pons-Boigues, "Inquisición."
28. On the nature and methods of the Inquisition, see Lea, *History*; Llorente, *Historia*; Kamen, *Spanish Inquisition*; Pinta Llorente, *Inquisición*; García-Carcel, *Orígenes*; La Riguardia, *Histoire*; Turben Ville, *Spanish Inquisition*. For one, Lea, *Moriscos*, 109ff., points to the excesses of the Inquisition saying that it operated in an impenetrable secrecy . . . no one calls in question its justice nor could he complain of its acts; witnesses remained anonymous and could not be cross-examined; the victim was represented by a staff member of the tribunal who often urged his client to confess and throw himself on the mercy of the court; and the whole inquisitorial process was based on the assumption that the accused was guilty at the time of arrest. Such arbitrary justice was of great concern to the Spanish monarchs, who often pleaded for restraint and moderation. In 1508, Ferdinand wrote to the inquisitors reproving them and warning them that no one should be converted or baptized by force (text in Lea, *Moriscos*, 407-408). In 1564, Philip II issued a plan of conciliation instructing the Inquisition to use its power with moderation. These and other appeals were ignored leaving the Moriscos at the mercy of the clergy: "Such was the condition of the Morisco question after seventy years of striving in which the designs, more or less sagacious, of the rulers had been wrecked by the supineness, the greed and the corruption of those whose duty it was to save the hundreds of thousands of souls confided to their charge." (Lea, *Moriscos*, 168).
29. Aznar Cardona, *Expulsión*, f. 132ff. as inserted in García-Arenal, *Moriscos*, 230ff., conveys, perhaps, the general feeling toward the Moriscos. Cardona displays contempt for all things connected with the Moriscos including their condition, way of life, vestment and food. He attributes all sort of vices to the Moriscos presenting them as a pestilence. He says that they are vile, careless, and enemies of letters and the sciences; they bring up their children as animals without any education or hygiene; they are dumb and crude in speech, barbarous in language and ridiculous in dress; they eat on the floor and live on vegetables, grains, fruits, honey and milk; they do not drink wine nor buy meat unless it is slaughtered by them; they love charlatanry, stories, dancing, promenading and other bestial diversions; they pursue jobs that require little work such as weaving, tailoring, shoemaking, carpentry and the like; they are peddlers of oil, fish, paste, sugar, eggs and other produce; they are inept at bearing arms and, thus, are cowards and effeminate; they travel in group only; they are sensual and disloyal;

they marry young and multiply like weeds (*malas hierbas*) overcrowding places and contaminating them. Cf. Caro Baroja, *Moriscos*, 131.

30. Ibid., 136.
31. Ibid., 218. The Morisco population shrank considerably from 1527 to 1563, after which it increased at a rapid pace, a fact which led Lapeyre, *Geógraphie*, 31, to remark that such proliferation was one of the causes of their ruin.
32. For instance, the charming novel, *Abencerraje* and Pérez de Hita's *Guerras civiles*. See Cirot, 'Maurophilie." It should be added that Juan Ruíz and Alfonso Alvárez de Villasandino admired Moorish qualities of generosity, pride, and beauty of Moorish ladies (Fernández y González, *Estado social*, 228) and that Lope de Vega used the theme of Christians and Moors in some of his plays depicting the Moor as gallant, enamoured, jealous and with a Christian soul (Carrasco Urgoiti, *El moro*, 83).
33. Caro Baroja, *Moriscos*, 229. See also Giner, "Cervantes"; González Palencia, "Cervantes"; Fradejas, "Musulmanes"; Labib, *Der Maure*' Harvey, *Moriscos*. Cervantes, *Coloquio*, 317, reproaches the Moors for lack of sincerity and for their propensity to treason. For copious details, see Carrasco Urgoiti, *El moro*, 77ff. 157ff.
34. Caro Baroja, *Moriscos*, 113ff.
35. Lincoln, "Prophecies"; see below chapter II, notes 61ff.
36. See Braudel, *Mediterranée*, 1047, and his "Les espagnols"; Hess, "Moriscos" and *The Forgotten Frontier*, 121-122; Sánchez Montes, *Franceses*; Reglá, *Estudios*, 72 and 83; Cardaillac, "Morisques et Protestants" and *Morisques et Chretiens*, 125ff.; Cabanelas, "Proyectos."
37. Schwoebel, *Shadow*, chapter I.
38. The appeal to the Turks was sent in 1501 in the form of an Ode (Ar. *Qaṣīdah*) translated into English by Monroe, "A Curious Appeal." See also Janer, *Condición*, 278-279; Temimi, "Une Lettre" and Hess, "Moriscos." Cf. note 23.
39. However, the Catholic kings' policy of forced conversion was hesitant since it met with little success. Both Dánvila, *Expulsión*, 41ff. and Boronat, *Moriscos*, I, 93ff, defend the new policy.
40. The controversy became heated among theologians and gained crescendo after the revolt of 1520 in Valencia between the Germanías (communes) and the nobility, in which the Moriscos remained loyal to their landlords, but ended victimized by the *agermenados* who killed many of them and forced a substantial number to take the sacrament of baptism at the point of the sword. See Dánvila, *Expulsión*, 87ff.; Boronat, *Moriscos*, I, 130ff.; Lea, *Moriscos*, and Piles, *Aspectos*.
41. Text in Gallego Gamir, *Moriscos*, 198ffe.; Janer, *Condición*, 26; The reaction of the Moriscos of Valencia was violent, resulting in the revolt of Espadan. On the revolt, see García-Arenal, "Revuelta" and Rull Villar, "Rebelión."
42. The text of revoking the measures is in Dánvila, *Expulsión*, 102-105. Cf. Boronat, *Moriscos*, I, 165, and Domínguez, *Historia*, 263.
43. Dánvila, *Expulsión*, 135. Cf. Janer, *Condición*, 27, who reiterates the same idea.
44. On Philip II's reign and policies, see Cabrera, *Felipe Secundo* and Braudel, *Mediterranée*.
45. Text in Dánvila, *Expulsi*ón, 167-169. It should be recalled that conversion through persuasion and instruction was initiated by Talavera, but failed for lack of schools, churchs, money, and available qualified and sincere clerics. Priests were more often than not ignorant and indulged in what Lea, *Moriscos*, 147, calls

"spoilation, embezzlement and malversation of every kind." These deficiencies were quite known and brought to the attention of the papacy. On their part, the Moriscos looked upon such edict of grace with mistrust and ignored it as they did in 1510, 1525, 1597 and 1599 when similar edicts were issued.

46. It should be recalled that the new edict is basically a reiteration of the one issued in 1526 and which was rescinded. Cf. note, 4. See Mármol, *Historia*, 161; Janer, *condición*, 31ff.; Ladero, *Mudéjares*, 318; Gallego et al., *Moriscos*, 170, and Caro Baroja, *Moriscos*, 152.
47. For the plea of the Morisco: Núñez Muley to rescind the edict, see chapter II, note 21.
48. On the revolt of the Alpujarras, see the contemporary works of Hurtado de Mendoza, *Guerras civiles*, and Mármol, *Historia*. The savagery of the revolt is described by Pérez de Hita, *Guerras*, 606ff.; see Garrad, *Causes*; Hitos, *Mártires*; Lea, *Moriscos*, 236ff., and Caro Baroja, *Moriscos*, chapter XI.
49. On the repatriation of the Granadans, see Mármol, *Historia*, 360ff.; Janer, *Condición*, 43-44; Lea, *Moriscos*, 259; and Vincent, "Expulsion."
50. Monfies (Ar. *Munfī*) means 'exiled,' or 'living in rural areas and mountains.' See Fernández y González, "Monfies"; Vincent, "Bandits," and García Martínez, "Bandolerismo." Cf. also, Janer, *Condición*, 56, and Domínguez, *Historia*, 57-71.
51. Turkish threat was a major and genuine concern to the Spanish monarchy in particular and Christendom in general. The Moriscos placed a great hope in that the Turks would eventually come to their rescue as part of prophecies (See chapter II, notes 61ff). For more details see, Mas, *Turks*; Braudel, *Mediterranée*, II, 480; Dánvila, *Expulsión*, 296-308; Bronat, *Moriscos*, II, 219-249; Sánchez Alvárez, "Aspectos," and Cabanelas, "Proyectos."
52. Braudel, *Mediterranée*, 586ff.; and Reglá, *Estudios*, 207.
53. Reglá, *Estudios*, 212.
54. Dánvila, *Expulsión*, 153-159.
55. Janer, *Condición*, 57; Dánvila, *Explusión*, 160; Domínguez, *Historia*, 141. These and similar views were common among clerics and bishops, mainly, Guerrero of Granada and Juan de Ribera of Valencia.
56. The Memorandum is by Bishop Marín Salvatierra is found in Boronat, *Moriscos*, I, 612-633, and García-Arenal, *Moriscos*, 157-175. There were numerous memoranda by other bishops, among which is one by Alonso Gutierrez dated September 6, 1588, reiterating the same feeling and labeling the Moriscos as enemies of the king and Spain (text in Boronat, *Moriscos*, I, 634-638). Bishop Juan Ribera of Valencia, who had hoped to indoctrinate the Moriscos, also issued a similar memorandum in 1601. Cf. Boronat, *Moriscos*, II, 35ff.
57. Boronat, *Moriscos*, II, 91-92.
58. For one, Bleda, *Crónica*, 948, and *Defensio*, 298ff., called for a general massacre. See Lea, *Moriscos*, 298ff., and Domínguez, *Historia*, 69ff.
59. Text in Boronat, *Moriscos*, I, 524-529. Cf. note 19.
60. Caro Baroja, *Moriscos*, 141.
61. Janer, *Condición*, 85, adheres closely to the views of contemporaries and maintains that the reasons for the expulsion were disloyalty, disobedience, conspiracy, heresy, murder and collusion with Turks. Cf. Boronat, *Moriscos*, II, 208, and Reglá, *Estudios*, 64.
62. The expulsion proceeded smoothly with little or no resistance—although there

were attempts at circumventing the order of expulsion through hiding and appeal to religious sentiments. However, the authorities were uncompromising and promised a reward of twenty *escudos* to anyone who would apprehend a Morisco, leading Janer, *Condición*, 83, to observe: "Greedy Christians would fetch escapees like cattle in the rugged sinuosity of the mountain ridges." Cf. Boronat, *Moriscos*, II, 305, and Reglá, *Estudios*, 63.

63. Boronat, *Moriscos*, II, 190ff., gives ample details about the manner of expulsion. Cf. Reglá, *Estudios*, 35. For Morisco flight into France see Cardaillac, "Passage" and "Morisques en Provence."
64. Reglá, *Estudios*, 103ff.
65. Ibid., 97ff. The number appears exaggerated. Lapeyre, *Géographie*, puts it at 3717.
66. Ibid., 14. Lapeyre, Ibid., 205, places it at 60818.
67. It is almost impossible to give precise figures on the number of Moriscos expelled. For the different estimates, see Janer, *Condición*, 279; Lea, *Moriscos*, 359; Dánvila, *Expulsión*, 337-338; and Domínguez, *Historia*, 90. Lapeyre, *Geógraphie*, 204, gives the several estimates and supplies his own based on statistical records:

Valencia	117,464
Cataluña	3,716
Aragón	60,818
Castile, Mancha and Extremaduras	44,625
Murcia	13,552
Andalucia	29,939
Granada	2,026
Total	272,140

68. As quoted by Reglá, *Estudios*, 49.
69. For one, Bleda, *Crónica*, 1021, deplores the fact that he will die without seeing the land purified from the evil seed. Cf. Caro, Baroja, *Moriscos*, 243ff.
70. Caro Baroja, *Moriscos*, 246-247.
71. As quoted by Caro Baroja, *Moriscos*, 247. In this connection, the gypsies occupied the bottom of the social ladder and were denigrated by virtue of their complexion, beliefs, and behavior. They were described as libertines, brigands, thieves, kidnappers and eaters of children (See Caro Baroja, *Vidas*, I, 59ff.).
72. Swinburne, *Travels*.
73. Townsend, *Journey*.
74. Ford, *Handbook*.
75. Irving, *Alhambra*. Boronat, *Moriscos*, II, 593-594, and Lapeyre, *Geógraphie*, Appendix XIII, insert a document indicating an alarming concern about the large number of exiled who had returned to the mainland.
76. Bleda, *Crónica*, chapter XXXVI, says that Moriscos could be seen in Rome. Janer, *Condición*, 319, says that a number of Moriscos settled in Venice. For Morisco exile into France, see Cardaillac, "Passages" and "Morisques en Provence."
77. Domínguez, *Historia*, 225ff.
78. Ibid., 238. Janer, *Condición*, 95, states the Morisco dilemma: "Moors and Turks persecuted them for what they had of Christian and Christians of France and Italy did the same for what they had of Muḥammadan." Cervantes, *Don Quijote*, II, chapter 54, who did not have much sympathy for the Moriscos, expresses their

plight: "Doquiera que estamos lloramos por España que en fin nacimos en ella y es nuestra patria natal; en ninguna parte hallamos el acogimiento que nuestra desventura desea, y en Berbería y en todas las partes de Africa donde esperabamos ser recibidos, acogidos y regalados, allí es donde nos ofenden y maltratan."

79. Morisco presence in Tunisia has been the object of several studies: Epalza, *Études*, "Moriscos", "Recherches" and "Trabajos"; Latham, "Toward the Study"; Abdulwahab, "Coup d'oeil"; Pieri, "L'acueil"; Penella, *Moriscos*; and Salvador, "Emigración."
80. Braudel, *Mediterranée*, 592-597.
81. Lapeyre, *Geógraphie.*
82. Caro Baroja, *Moriscos.*
83. Reglá, *Estudios.*
84. Danvila, *Expulsion.*
85. Ibid., 344. Janer, *Condición*, 120, condemns the excesses on both sides and laments the intolerance and the implacable hatred. However, he dismisses the possibility of conciliation between Christians and Moriscos as due to the great disparity between Islam and Christianity. He argues (Ibid., 122) that national unity brought Spain to the European family rather than leaving it under the oppressive weight of an Oriental civilization. He considers (Ibid., 102) the consequences of the expulsion on Spain as minimal, arguing that the depopulation of the country was going on long before the expulsion and was due to internal and international wars, emigration of people, pestilence, drought and hunger. He concludes (Ibid., 113) that the expulsion was beneficial in securing national unity and putting an end to the strife between the two races.
86. Dánvila, *Expulsión*, 340. Boronat, *Moriscos*, I, 53ff., reiterates similar feeling saying that the Moriscos always responded to magnanimity with vindictiveness, treachery and fanaticism; he concludes wondering why the expulsion did not take place much earlier.
87. Domínguez, *Historia.*
88. Ibid., 225.
89. Ibid., 223.

2. MORISCO REACTION: A SELF-IMAGE

1. Caro Baroja, *Moriscos,* 8: "*El vasallo moro era un poco menos que un esclavo.*" Janer, *Condición*, 31, says that the Moriscos had to endure many offenses in addition to heavy taxes, violence, rapacity of tax collectors and to disorderly soldiers. Lea, *Moriscos*, 178ff., points to the lamentable conditions of the Moriscos, citing the constant friction with Christian neighbors often resulting in bloodshed and massacres; serfdom; disregard of pledges made to them; and enforced conversion with no compensatory privileges. "They were Christians as regard duties and responsibilities and subjection to the Inquisition, but remained Moors as respect liabilities and inequality before the Law." (ibid., 183). They were exploited by the nobility and terrorized by the officials of the Inquisition. "In short they were defenseless and every one, cleric and layman, pillaged them systematically." (ibid., 186). They were restricted in their movement and emigration, forbidden to possess arms, hold offices and benefices, or enter colleges and universities.
2. Castro, *España*, 57: "*El moro trabajaba y produc*ía, y el cristiano señ*oreaba en un extasis de magnificencia personal.*" As a result, the landlords, who depended

on Morisco labor and know-how, often interceded on behalf of Moriscos to a point of allowing them to practice their religion in their estates. Several noblemen were tried for favoring or defending heretics among whom was Sancho de Cardona, admiral of Aragón, who was brought before the Inquisition on charges of protecting Moriscos. See boronat, *Moriscos*, I, 443-469.

3. Aznar, *Expulsión*, 33. Caro Baroja, *Moriscos*, 73, gives the text of an ordinance of 1552 containing some seventy-four skills or professions practiced by the Moriscos. Cf. Domínguez, *Historia*, 109ff. It is significant to note that the Moriscos were expert farmers who excelled in the cultivation of sugar, cotton, silk, rice and other produce. Besides, they were excellent craftsmen excelling in leather work, fabrication of textiles, porcelains, and other crafts. See also Janer, *Condición*, 47.
4. Burns, *Islam*, 72.
5. Caro Baroja, *Moriscos*, 49.
6. Ibid., 159.
7. Mármol, *Historia*, II, 157.
8. Caro Baroja, *Moriscos*, 51.
9. Hurtado de Mendoza, *Guerras*, 107; Mármol, *Historia*, II, 178.
10. Helpers (Ar. *anṣār*) were Medinese who gave refuge to Muḥammad after his flight from Mecca in 622, a date that marks the beginning of the Muslim calendar (*Hijrah*).
11. Emigrés (Ar. *Muhājirūn*) were early Muslims who joined Muḥammad in his flight from Mecca to Medina.
12. ‘Abd Manāf was the ancestor of Muḥammad and the guardian of the Holy Shrine of the Ka‘bah in pre-Islamic times.
13. As quoted by Saavedra, *Discurso*, 138.
14. See chapter V, note 74.
15. Harvey, "El Mancebo," 25.
16. Ticknor, *Historia*, IV, 420; cf. Saavedra, *Discurso*, 144.
17. Cf. chapter I, note 45.
18. Boronat, *Moriscos*, I, 651-665. Weidits, *Trachtenbuch*, who traveled in Spain in 1529, left precious drawings of Morisco clothing. For more details on the clothing, furnishing, and festivals of the Moriscos see Arié, "Traje musulmán"; Bernis, "Modas"; Martínez Ruíz, "Almohadas"; Credilla, "Ceremonias"; Granja, "Cocina," "Fiestas," and "Milagros."
19. Munzer, *Viaje*.
20. The text of Núñez's Memorandum is in Mármol, *Historia*, 161ff., and García-Arenal, *Moriscos*, 47-56. See also Foulché-Delbose, "Memorial," and Garrad, "The Original Memorial."
21. See chapter I, note 5.
22. The full text of the poem in English translation is in Lea, *Moriscos*, 434-437. The poem was composed in 1568 aiming at securing help from fellow Muslims from within and outside of the Peninsula.
23. Caro Baroja, *Moriscos*, 168.
24. Domínguez, *Historia*, 49.
25. Umayyah refers to the ancestors of the Umayyads, who ruled in Damascus (661-750) and later in Spain (756-1031). Cf. Hurtado de Mendoza, *Guerra*, 25-26.
26. Caro Baroja, *Moriscos*, 159ff.
27. Mármol, *Historia*, II, 157.

28. García Martínez, "Bandolerismo."
29. Janer, *Condición*, 36ff.
30. Ibid., 39ff.
31. Mármol, *Historia*, II, 178; Hurtado de Mendoza, *Guerra*, 107.
32. Janer, *Condición*, 52.
33. Mármol, *Historia, II, 157.*
34. *Ibid.*
35. *See EI, Ṭaḳiya.*
36. For more details, see Dressendörfer, *Islam*, 131ff., and Cardaillac, "Aspectos."
37. Text in Longás, *Vida*, 305-307; Harvey, "Crypto—Islam."
38. Cantineau, "Lettre"; cf. RAH T13.
39. Mones, *Asnā'*. Al-Wansharīshī gives his legal opinion, arguing that Muslims could not possibly feel free to exercise their religious duties under non-Muslim rule; thus, it is a sin to remain under such conditions. Other jurists maintain that fleeing the land of the infidels to the land of belief (Islam) is a religious duty incumbent on every Muslim until the Day of Judgment.
40. Boronat, *Moriscos*, II, 619, Cf. Cardaillac, *Morisques et Chrétiens*, 92ff.
41. BNM 245 as quoted by Saavedra, *Discurso*, 156.
42. BNM 9067, f. 212r; cf. Saavedra, *Discurso*, 170.
43. Saavedra, *Discurso*, 108. Queen Isabella is said to be in Hell under all the Jews (Cardaillac, *Morisques et Chrétiens*, 101).
44. Saavedra, *Discurso*, 159. A Morisco refugee in Tunis thanks the Lord for having escaped the tyranny of the Inquisition (RAH S2, f.52).
45. RAH T13, f.137r: "*Adoradores del ṣalib* (Ar. ṣalīb) *i los comedores delpuwerko.*"
46. *BNM 9653, f. 9v; cf. Cardaillac, Morisques et Chrétiens*, 100.
47. RAH S2, f.8v; cf. Cardaillac, *Morisques et Chrétiens*, 100.
48. BNM 9653, f. 16r; cf. Cardaillac, "Aspectos."
49. Junta 3, f. 134v =Kontzi, *Aljamiado*, II, 458.
50. BNM 9074, f.41r; cf. Cardaillac, "Aspectos."
51. Morgan, *Mohamedanism*, II, 295.
52. BNM 4944, f. 73v-74r. Cf. chapter V, notes 135ff. and note 176. Reference to scriptural material attesting to the veracity of Islam and the legitimacy of Muḥammad's prophecy is also contained in the story of Sarjīl Ibn Sarjūn (BNM 4953, f. 2v-16r; cf. below chapter VI, note 82).
53. Junta 3e, f. 215v-216r. = Kontzi, *Aljamiado*, II, 633.
54. Junta 3, f. 222v. = Kontzi, *Aljamiado*, II, 656-647.
55. BNM 5300: *Libro de las suwertes*, a portion of which appears in Gil, *Colecci*ón, 3-32.
56. Gil, *Colección, 7.*
57. *Ibid., 11.*
58. *Ibid., 14.*
59. Lincoln, *"Prophecies."*
60. Mármol, *Historia*, 169-174, inserts three prophecies which were reproduced by García-Arenal, *Moriscos, 57-62. Cardaillac, Morisques et Chr*étiens, 49-52, reproduces one.
61. BNP 774, f. 411-415 = Lincoln, "Prophecies," 638-641.
62. The use of the word Allāh by a Spanish Christian is significant.
63. BNP 774, f. 415-422.

64. BNP 774, f. 417.
65. Text in Mármol, *Historia*, 171-172, and García-Arenal, *Moriscos*, 57-62.
66. RAH T13, f.172v-173r; cf. BNP 774, f.400ff. and Lincoln, "Prophecies," 634-638.
67. RAH T13, f.173r: "*i por esto senbaran mucho i-koseran poko i-tarabajaran mucho i-abaran poko porovecho.*"
68. Ibid., f. 173v: "*ke sera poka la-verghuwensa e-alzine (Ar. al-zinā') i-norrakonosera el-ermano a su ermano.*"
69. Ibid., f. 173r: "*abra discordiya enetere los dos rreyes adoradores del ṣalib (Ar, ṣalīb) i-los komedores del puwerko.*"
70. Ibid., f. 173v: "*a-de-ser señor de -la-tiyerra i-de-la-mar.*"
71. Ibid., f. 176r.
72. Ibid., f.176v: "*Puwes tened buwen esperansa kel-tiyenpo se aserca.*" In this connection, it is relevant to mention the testament of the Grand Turk (RAH T18/, Cardaillac, *Morisques et Chrétiens*, 401-406) in which the ruler counsels his son and predicts that he will, with Allāh's help, have victory over the Christian infidels and will enter Rome shattering the house of Peter and Paul and destroying the Gods and idols made of gold, silver and marble, and where he will give barely to his horses on the altars (RAH T18, f.132). Cf. Deny, 'Pseudo-Propheties."
73. Cardaillac, *Morisques et Chrétiens*, 52ff.; cf. Domínguez, *Historia*, 59ff.
74. BNM 9067, as quoted by Galmés, "Interés literario," 196.
75. Andrés, *Opera*.
76. Cf. above, note 21.
77. Cabanelas, *El morisco granadino*, 15.
78. Luna, *Historia*.
79. Monroe, *Islam*, 11.
80. Cabanelas, *El morisco granadino*.
81. Alcántara, *Historia*; cf. Cabanelas, *op.cit.*, 173ff.
82. Cabanelas, *op. cit.*, 235ff.

3. MORISCO EDUCATION AND LITERATURE

1. Ibn Khayr (1180), al-Ḍabbī (1203), Ibn al-Khaṭīb (d. 1374), and al-Maqqarī (d. 1632), among others, give an impressive list of talented people who came from the East and settled in al-Andalus, and of Andalusians who settled in North Africa and the East. See Makkī, *Ensayo*; Chejne, *Muslim Spain*, 148.
2. Rāqilī, *Ta'yīd al-dīn*; see Asín, "Tratado" and chapter V, notes 74ff. below.
3. Al-Qaysī, BNM 4944; See Asín, "Polémica," and chapter V, notes 83ff.
4. Turmeda, *Tuḥfah*. See chapter V, notes 89ff.
5. See chapter V, notes 113ff.
6. See chapter VI, notes 2ff.
7. Codera, "Almacén." The manuscripts found in the Almonacid were catalogued by Ribera *et al., Manuscritos,* and are currently housed in the Asín Palacios Institute of Arabic Studies in Madrid. The collection covers the gamut of Aljamiado literature and consists of religious items, legends, stories and numerous magical and astrological material. It appears that the Inquisition was aware of the existence of Arabic and Aljamiado books, which were used as evidence against accused Moriscos. Unfortunately, reference to such books by the tribunals of the Inquisition was more often than not laconic, labeling them as dealing with the Muḥammadan sect or the Qur'ān. See Labarta, "Libros." It should be added that the collection of the Almonacid and the extant Aljamiado manuscripts

reflect the content of Morisco education. For more details on education in Muslim Spain, see Ribera, "Ensananza."

8. On the religious significance of Arabic, see Chejne, *Arabic*, 8ff.
9. García-Arenal, *Inquisición*, 108.
10. Ibid., 108-109.
11. Manuscript of BUB, f. 176v, as quoted by Penella, "Sentimiento," 458-459.
12. Junta 6, f. 1. Cf. Ribera et al., *Manuscritos*, 35.
13. Chejne, *Arabic*, 10.
14. BNM 5380. See Solá-Solé, "Textos," and Hoenerbach, "Moriscos," 53, plate 7.
15. Junta 8, f. 50. Cf. RAH V13.
16. RAH T20.
17. BNM 5238 and Junta 25.
18. Junta 39, f. 38-42 and f. 166-181.
19. He is Abū Isḥāq Ibn al-Sarī al-Zajjāj (d.923; he studied under the famous belletrist al-Mubarrad (d. 898), the author of the *Perfect Book (al-Kāmil)*.
20. He is Abū 'Abdallāh Muḥammad Ibn Dāwūd Ibn 'Ajurrūm al-Sanhājī (d. 1323).
21. Junta 59, f. 104-175, and Junta 12, f. 160-187.
22. RAH T5.
23. Ibid., f. 118r-118v; cf. Junta 4, RAH T12 contains an explanation of some expressions found in the works of the famous theologican al-Ghazālī (d.1111).
24. García-Arenal, *Inquisición*, 26.
25. Ibid.
26. Junta 3, f. 119v = Kontzi, *Aljamiado*, II, 418.
27. Junta 8, f. 182 = Gil, *Clección*, 1.
28. Ibid.
29. Ibid. It may be added that BNM 5452 contains a valuable document in Arabic exalting the importance of the religious scholar *(faqīh)*. Text in Hoenerbach, *Urkunden*, 264ff.
30. Ibn 'Abd Rabbih, *'Iqd*, II, 206-215. Cf. Chejne, *Muslim Spain*, 166ff.
31. González Palencia, *Mozárabes*, produces copious documents showing the prevalent use of Arabic by the Mozarabs of Toledo to the beginning of the fourteenth century.
32. Fernández y González, *Estado social*, 232. Casiri, I, 260, 284, 292, 295, 297, etc. It should be noted that the Granadans maintained the use of Arabic throughout the sixteenth century, as attested by the testimony of Núñez Muley (See above, chapter II, note 21). It may be added that the many edicts issued during the sixteenth century contained provisions forbidding the use of Arabic.
33. Harvey in *EI*, s.v. *'Adjamiyya*.
34. Ticknor, *Historia*, IV, 420; Saavedra, *Discurso*, 144. Although the consensus of opinion is that Arabic is eminently important in the religious life of every Muslim, a Morisco refugee in North Africa reasoned that using Arabic at all cost among people who do not understand it would lead to the same error of Christians, who have their scriptures in Latin so that people could not read or understand them, thus, perpetuating ignorance about the true Christian doctrine (BNM 9653, f.118r; Cardaillac, *Morisques et Chrétiens*, 179). Though not knowing Arabic is tantamount to a sickness, it was considered expedient to render the Qur'ān into a foreign language so that the mute and the inflicted will have access to it (Ibid., f. 7).

35. Samarqandī is Abū Layth Ibn Muḥammad Ibn Ibrāhīm (d. 985). Al-Bakrī is Aḥmad Ibn Muḥammad Abū-l-Ḥasan (d. 1545). Al-Quḍā'i is Abū 'Abdallāh Muḥammad Ibn Salām Ibn Ja'far Ibn 'Alī (d. 1062); cf. *GAL*, I, 418, and S. I, 584.
36. BNM 5252, f. 3. In 1568, a Morisco of Valencia maintained that he was able to read and write Arabic, but could not understand the Qur'ān (Boronat, *Moriscos*, I, 553).
37. Junta 1, f. 2; Gayangos, *Memorial*, 247-248.
38. Junta 62, f. 1-3. Writing in Aragón at the time of the expulsion Muḥammad Dovera attributes the neglect of the religious law to the loss of the Arabic language, which was suppressed by the Christians (Cardaillac, *Morisques et Chrétiens*, 153-154).
39. Dánvila, *Expulsión*, 170.
40. Ibid., 174ff., gives a list of those alfaquíes with reference to their place of residence and professional competence.
41. Published by Gayangos, *Memorial*. The *Brevario* is extant in four manuscripts: Junta 1, written in Arabic characters; and BNM 2026, BNM 6016, and Junta 55 written in Latin characters. Cf. RAH S3.
42. Cabanelas, *Juan de Segovia*, 142ff.
43. The word Ikshadil is, according to Cabanelas (above, note 42) a corruption of 'Isā de Jābir.
44. Junta 1, f.216r.
45. On the Mancebo, see Saavedra, *Discurso*, 150-155, and Harvey, "Mancebo."
46. Translated from Saavedra, *Discurso*, 155.
47. Junta 62, f. 440-442.
48. Harvey, "Mancebo."
49. BNM 245.
50. Saavedra, *Discurso*, 150ff.
51. *Guía de la salvación* as quoted by Gayangos, "Language," 79-80.
52. Saavedra, *Discurso*, 144.
53. Hegyi, "Uso."
54. Millás Vallicrosa, "Albaranes," produces three Arabic documents in Hebrew characters dated 1378; and Bosh, "Escrituras," produces six documents. The use of Hebrew script for writing Arabic goes back to much earlier date. For instance, Maimonides (d. 1204) made profuse use of Hebrew script for writing Arabic.
55. For instance RAH S1. Cf. Fernández y González, *Estado social*, 238.
56. This statement is based on the author's observations while living in Colombia, S. A., during 1938-1945.
57. Junta 3, f. 228r = Kontzi, *Aljamiado*, II, 658-659.
58. Ibn Khaldūn, *Muqaddimah*, III, 171ff.
59. See note on Transliteration.
60. Saavedra, *Discurso*, 145ff.
61. Ibid., 365.
62. Gayangos, "Language."
63. Gayangos, *Leyes*.
64. Gayangos, *Suma*.
65. *Ticknor, Historia*, IV, 247.
66. Fernández y González, *Estado social*, 237; see also 438 and 441.
67. Müller, *Morisco Gedichte*.

68. Mörf, *Poema*.
69. Stanley, "Poetry."
70. Saavedra, *Discurso*, 187.
71. Ibid., 171. On the other hand, Boronat, *Moriscos*, II, 384ff., minimizes the value of Aljamiado literature with respect to form and content; he was followed by Menéndez y Pelayo, *Historia*, 64ff.
72. Summerized in Chejne, *Muslim Spain*, 383ff.
73. Guillén, *Leyendas*, I, 13; cf. Chejne, *Muslim Spain*, 376-377.
74. Guillén, *Leyenda de José*.
75. Gil, *Colección*.
76. Gil, "Manuscritos."
77. Pano y Ruata, *Coplas* and his "Recontamient."
78. Codera, "Almacén."
79. Ribera et al., *Manuscritos*. Ribera wrote incisive articles: "Colección," "Supersticiones," and "Vida religiosa."
80. Menéndez Pidal, *Poema*.
81. Meneu, "Literatura."
82. Zettersteen, *Handbuch*, "Notice," and "Some Chapters."
83. González Palencia, "Noticias"; see also his "Cervantes," and "Curandero."
84. Longás, *Vida*.
85. Asín, "Original," "Polémica," and "Tratado."
86. Nykl, *Rrekontamiento*, which includes an introduction to Aljamiado Literature.
87. Lincoln, "Prophecies."
88. Lincoln, "Aljamiado Texts."
89. Harvey, "Yusé Banegas."
90. Harvey, *Literary Culture*.
91. Harvey, see Bibliography for titles.
92. Pareja, "Relato."
93. Hoenerbach, *Urkunden*.
94. Hoenerbach, "Moriscos."
95. Manzanares, "Dos manuscritos," "Capítulo,' "Notas," and "Textos."
96. Vernet, "Exégesis," "Traducciones," and "Alcoran."
97. Moraleda, "Edición."
98. López Lillo, "Transcripcion."
99. Galmés, *Épica, Historia,* "Influencia del árabe," "Influencias," "Interés," "Interés literario," *Libro*.
100. Published in Madrid, 1978.
101. Labib, "Spanish Lautenwicklung," "papel," and *Der Maure*.
102. Hegyi, *Edicion*, "Uso," and "Observaciones."
103. L. Cardaillac, "Aspecto," "Morisques en Provence," *Morisques et Chretiens*, "morisques et Protestants," "Passage," and "Probleme."
104. D. Cardaillac, *Polémique* and "Algunos problemas."
105. Kontzi, *Aljamiado*, "Aspectos," and "Calcos."
106. Klenk, "Tasdīd" and *Leyenda*.
107. Chejne, *Muslim Spain*, chapter 20, and "Plegaria."
108. The tendency toward gradual latinization can be seen in BNM 4907; RAH T18; RAH T13; RAH V11; RAH V2, among others.
109. The tendency of preserving Arabic appears in materials containing the Qur'ān and traditions as in RAH T1; RAH T2; and RAH T3.

110. Bilingualism can be seen in Qur'ānic Commentaries (Junta 47 and Junta 51); in the seven capital prayers (Junta 44); in Ibn 'Ajurrum, *'Ajurrumiyah*, and al-Zajjāj, *Taqrīb* (Junta 59, f. 104-130 and 176-216), and in al-Quḍā'ī, *Kitāb al-Shihāb* (Junta 29 and Junta 39).
111. Mainly, RAH T5.
112. There is a number of manuscripts by Moriscos written in Latin script: BNM 5043; BNM 9067; BNM 9655; RAH S4, and others.
113. For more detailed information, see the several editions of Aljamiado texts that include lengthy introduction bearing on linguistic matters, mainly, Galmés, *Historia*, 218ff, and his *Libro*, II, 26ff; Nykl, "Rrekontamiento"; Kontzi, *Aljamiado*, I, 60ff; Hegyi, *Edición*.
114. For more details on arabisms in Aljamiado texts, see Nykl, "Rrekontamiento," 448ff.; Galmés, "Influencias," *Libro*, II, 66ff., and *Historia*, 234ff.; Kontzi, *Aljamiado*, I, 69ff., and "Calcos"; D. Cardaillac, *Polémique*, I, 60ff.; Hegyi, *Edición*, 1ff.; and "Observaciones"; Floriano, "Algunos Problemas." On arabism in the Spanish language, see Neuvonen, *Arabismos*; Fernández y González, "Influencia"; Eguilaz, *Glosario*; Dozy et al., *Glossaire*.
115. The area of interaction between Islam and Christianity in Spanish soil needs further and careful research and the Aljamiado literature has great potential in this connection and may serve as starting point. Galmés, "Interés literario," 204, recognizes the close interdependence of Aljamiado literature and early Spanish literature in the area of didactic, epic, and even mysticism. He gives the interesting suggestion that the great Spanish mystic Juan de la Cruz may have been a Morisco himself.

4. RELIGION, BELIEFS, AND OBSERVANCES

1. Ladero, *Mudéjares*, 318; Codera, "Almacén."
2. Junta 3, f. 229r = Kontzi, *Aljamiado*, II, 661.
3. BNM 4953, f. 162.
4. Chejne, *Arabic*, 9.
5. Kritzeck, *Peter*, 51ff.; cf. below, chapter V, note 11.
6. Alverny, "Deus traductions."
7. Vernet, "Exegésis," 128; and his "Traducciones."
8. See chapter V, note 212.
9. See chapter V, note 212.
10. See López Lillo, "Transcripción"; López Morilla, "Etimologías"; Moraleda, "Edición"; Vernet, "Exégesis" and "Traducciones"; Zettersteen, "Some Chapters."
11. Mainly, BNM 4907; BNM 4938; BNM 5078; BNM 5081; BNM 5313; BNM 5378; BNP 290; BNP 1844; Junta 12; Junta 18; Junta 24; Junta 28; Junta 39; Junta 40; Junta 41; Junta 42; RAH T1; RAH T3; RAH T5; RAH T6; RAH T8; RAH T10; RAH T12; RAH T13; RAH T19; RAH V8; RAH V10; RAH V13; RAH V17; and RAH V26.
12. BNM 4983; BNM 5378, f. 79ff.
13. BNM 5267.
14. BNM 5081; Junta 12.
15. Particularly the chapter entitled *al-Qadr* (Q 97). See RAH T10.
16. BNM 5228; RNM 5313; BNM 5378.

17. Junta 3, f. 110 = Kontzi, *Aljamiado*, II, 400.
18. BNM 5228 and BNM 5313.
19. BNM 9653.
20. BNM 9067.
21. BPT 9 and RAH S3.
22. For instance RAH T5. Other commentaries: Junta 18; Junta 25; Junta 51; and Junta 62; RAH T12; f. 77ff. and RAH T13, f. 35-125.
23. RAH T5, f. 1, where the term *sharḥe* is used.
24. Gil, *Colección*, 153, where the Aljamiado appears in small letters above the Arabic, written in bold characters.
25. RAH T5, f. 1.
26. RAH T5, f. 1: *Este es sharḥe i-deklarasion de las alwaraqas* (Ar. *al-waraqah*). *Waraqah* means folio or paper.
27. Gil, *Colección*, 163, where Aljamiado and Arabic are used.
28. The expression *el-ḥadīth* is used in Aljamiado to mean not only a prophetic tradition, but "a narration" and "story."
29. The Six Canonical Books (*al-kutub al-sittah*) are those of Bukhārī (d. 870), Muslim (d. 875), Abū Dāwūd (d. 888), Tirmidhī (d. 892), Ibn Mājah (d. 886), and Nisā'ī (d. 915). For further information on each one and their works, see the articles in the *EI.*
30. Particularly those traditions relating to Spanish Islam, such as Muḥammad's prophecy regarding the future of al-Andalus (See chapter II, note 65), or befriending a Christian for forty days (See chapter II, note 49).
31. 'Abdallāh Ibn al-'Abbās (d. ca. 688) was a relative of Muḥammad and one of the early traditionists.
32. 'Abdallāh Ibn Mas'ūd (d. ca. 653) was also an early traditionist.
33. Abū Hurayrah was a companion of the Prophet and transmitter of prophetic traditions.
34. Anas Ibn Mālik was a companion of the Prophet and father of Mālik, the founder of the renowed Mālikite school of law that remained for a long time the sole legal school in al-Andalus.
35. The four Orthodox caliphs, who were also companions of the Prophet, were: Abū Bakr (r. 632-634), 'Umar (r. 634-644), 'Uthmān (r. 644-656) and 'Alī (r. 656-661).
36. For instance, BNM 5223; BNM 5305, and RAH S1.
37. The Arabic title of the work is: *Tanbīh al-ghāfilīn wa-iḍāḥ sabīl al-muridīn*. Cairo , 1326 A. H.
38. The Arabic title is: *Kitab al-tafrī 'fī-l-fiqh*, of which there are the following Aljamiado manuscripts: Junta 33; BPT 336; and BNM 4870. Cf. Saavedra, *Discurso*, 247ff., and Gonźalez Palencia, 'Noticias," 139.
39. On the *Brevario Sunni*, see chapter 3, note 41.
40. Junta 62.
41. Junta 62, f. 105-110.
42. *Castighos para las jentes.*
43. Junta 53.
44. BNM 5252, BNM 5273, and BPT 1.
45. Mainly, BNM 5943; BNM 5374; BNM 5377; and BNM 5378.
46. BNM 9067.
47. The Beautiful names of God (Ar. *al-asmā' al-ḥusnā*; Alj. *nonberes fermosos*)are

found in: BNM 5223; BNM 5378; BNM 5380; BNM 5385; Junta 44; RAH T1; RAH T3; RAH T6; RAH T13; RAH T19; and RAH V26.

48. God unity (Ar. *tawḥīd*) is a basic tenet of Islam to which the Moriscos adhered, deriving the necessary evidence from thirty-seven passages of the Qur'ān. See BNM 5374; BNM 5378; BNM 5385; RAH T1; RAH T3; and RAH V17.
49. The Moriscos followed the traditional conception of Christ and Christianity, devoting ample material to them. See BNM 5305, f. 14r-22v; BNM 5313, f. 177r-180r; BNM 5223, f. 240r-241r; BNM 9067, f. 182r-205r; RAH S1, f. 992-128v (see Vespertino, "Figuras"), dealing with Christ's birth, his time, and falsity of the Christian doctrine and other aspects of Christ's life.
50. Some of the heated controversies against Christianity can be found in BNM 4944; BNM 5302; RAH T12; RAH V6; and RAH V7. See Cardaillac, *Morisques et Chretiens;* D. Cardaillac, *Polemique*; and below, chapter V.
51. Junta 3, 178v = Kontzi, *Aljamiado*, II, 546. Mālik is the founder of the Mālikite legal school and author of the legal code, *al-Muwaṭṭa'*.
52. Ibid.
53. In addition to the comprehensive works of Samarqandī Ibn Jallāb, Jābir, and the Mancebo already mentioned, there are BNM 5354; BNM 5374; BNM 4953; BNM 4238; BNP 774; Junta 64; and others dealing with one or more aspects of the religious duties. Cf. Longás, *Vida*, Ribera, "Vida," and Zettersteen, "notice" and *Handbuch*.
54. Junta 3, f. 148r = Kontzi, *Aljamiado*, II, 483.
55. See Junta 1 and Gayangos, *Suma*. Credilla, "Ceremonias," gives a good summary of Morisco rites as they were known to the Inquisition.
56. Junta 62.
57. 'Īsa de Jābir, *Brevario (MHE*, 253). Cf. Mancebo, *Tafsira* (Junta 62, f. 1).
58. 'Īsā de Jābir, *Brevario*, MHE, 254-260.
59. Junta 3, f. 205v-206r = Kontzi, *Aljamiado*, II, 611-612.
60. See above, note 47.
61. BCM 1420, f. 38-47 = Chejne, "Plegaria."
62. For instance, RAH T13.
63. Ibid.
64. See above, note 48.
65. See chapter VI, notes 18ff.
66. Junta 64, f. 14v = Kontzi, *Aljamiado*, 760-762.
67. See above, note 53.
68. Junta 3, f. 233v = Kontzi, *Aljamiado*, II, 673.
69. Ibid.
70. Junta 3, f. 124 = Kontzi, *Aljamiado,* II, 429. Also BNM 4953, f. 54v-61v = Hegyi, *Edición*, 44-49, where prayer is discussed at some details.
71. Junta 3, f. 124 = Kontzi, *Aljamiado*, II, 429. For detailed discussion of ablution, see Longas, *Vida*, 16ff. and BNM 4870; BNM 5306; RAH T3; RAH T13.
72. Junta 3, f. 124v = Kontzi, *Aljamiado*, II, 430.
73. Junta 64/21, f. 8r-9r = Kontzi, *Aljamiado*, II, 756. Cf. RAH T4, f. 52ff.
74. Junta 64/21, f. 10r = Kontzi, *Aljamiado*, II, 757.
75. RAH T4, f. 64v.
76. BNM 5306, f. 52.
77. Junta 3, f. 119v = Kontzi, *Aljamiado*, II, 418; RAH T4, f. 68.
78. The Imām could be any Muslim, but he must, first and above all, be

knowledgeable and upright Muslim (BNM 4870).

79. The recitation of the Qur'ān was done ordinarily in Arabic. The most commonly recited chapters (sūras) of the Qur'ān, or verses thereof (*āya,* Pl. *āyāt*) appear to be the following: Q3: 16 and 24; Q87; Q91; Q97; Q110; Q113; and Q114.
80. The seven major prayers are found in BNM 5377; BNM 5378; BNM 5325; Junta 44; RAH T2; and RAH T3.
81. Junta 3, f. 122 = Kontzi, *Aljamiado*, II, 423.
82. RAH T19, f. 214ff. Cf. Longas, *Vida*, 81ff.
83. RAH T17, f. 136ff. BNM 4953, f. 40r-54r = Hegyi, *Edición*, 32-43.
84. For this kind of invocations, see BNM 5301; see BNM 5301; BNM 5377; 4953, f. 154v-161r = Hegyi, *Edición,* 142-246.
85. BNM 5223, f. 24ff.
86. RAH V12 and RAH V15.
87. On *azake,* see Ibn Jallāb, *Tafria* (BPT 7, Book 3); 'Isā de Jābir, *Brevario, MHE,* 320ff.; and Longás, *Vida,* 231ff.
88. Junta 64/21, f. 4v Kontzi, *Aljamiado,* II, 752.
89. Longás, *Vida,* 246-249.
90. Junta 3, f. 162v Kontzi, *Aljamiado,* II, 513.
91. On fasting, see Ibn Jallāb, *Tafria* (BPT 7, Book 4); 'Isā de Jābir, *Brevario, MHE,* 303-305; BNM 4953, f. 30v-32r. Cf. Longás, *Vida,* 214ff.
92. RAH T4, f. 20v.
93. Junta 64/21, f. 11r-12r Kontzi, *Aljamiado,* II, 758.
94. Junta 3, f. 128v Kontzi, *Aljamiado,* II, 442.
95. On pilgrimage, see Ibn Jallāb, *Tafria* (BPT 7, Book 6); 'Isā de Jābir, *Brevario, MHE,* 32ff.; and Longās, *Vida,* 250ff.
96. On Jihād (Holy War), See Ibn Jallāb, *Tafria* (BPT 7, Book 7).
97. On *Fada,* see Ibn Jallāb, *Tafria* (BPT 7, Book 10); 'Isā de Jābir, *Brevario, MHE,* 381-382; Junta 3, f. 141v Kontzi, *Aljamiado,* II, 470.
98. Junta 3, f. 189r Kontzi, *Aljamiado,* II, 571.
99. Longás, *Vida,* 262.
100. On marriage, see Ibn Jallāb, *Tafria* (BPT 7, Book 20); RAH T8; Longás, *Vida,* 270-283.
101. Junta 3, 197v Kontzi, *Aljamiado,* II, 589
102. 'Isa de Jābir, *Brevario, MHE,* 299-300; *Long*ás, Vida, 284, 302.
103. Carcía-Arenal, *Inquisición,* 62-63, points to the practice of burying the belongings of the dead among some Moriscos of Cuenca.
104. The importance of the letter of the dead can be surmised by its occurrence in Aljamido manuscripts, mainly, Junta 3, f. 215r Kontzi, *Aljamiado,* II, 632; Junta 8; Junta 24; RAH T1 and RAH T13.
105. Junta 3, f. 198v Kontzi, *Aljamiado,* II, 593. Also BNM 4953, f. 62ff. Hegyi *Edición,* 50ff.
106. On dietary law, see BNM 5306, 63ff; 'Isā de Jābir, *Brevario, MHE,* 330ff; Longas, *Vida,* 264-270.
107. Junta 3, f. 208v Kontzi, *Aljamiado,* II, 616.
108. Junta 3, f. 128r-128v Kontzi, *Aljamiado,* II, 442-443.
109. Junta 3, f. 119v Kontzi, *Aljamiado,* II, 417.
110. Junta 3, f. 134 Kontzi, *Aljamiado,* II, 458.
111. Junta 3, f. 97r-97v Kontzi, *Aljamiado,* II, 375-376.
112. *El-ḥadīth del bebdor de vino* Junta 8, no. 4 Gil, *Colección,* 52-64.

113. Gil, *Colección,* 132. It may be relevant to mention that the fourteenth century Juan Ruīz, *Libro,* stanzas 528ff., emphasizes the evil effect of wine. While he condones drinking in moderation, he illustrates its evil effect on a devout hermit, who, after indulging in wine at the behest of the devil was robbed of his body and soul through raping a girl and murdering her afterward (stanzas 539-541). Moreover, Ruíz maintains that wine blinds people, shortens life, saps power, causes limbs to tremble, makes the breath smell bad and the mouth foul, burns the entrails and eats the liver (stanzas 544-545).
114. Junta 3, f.119r Kontzi, *Aljamiado,* II, 416. It is equally relevant to mention that Juan Ruíz, *Libro,* stanzas 555-556, condemns gambling as evil and considers profit accruing therefrom as usury, which is forbidden by the religious law (*Sharī'ah*).
115. Junta 3, f. 184 Kontzi, *Aljamiado,* II, 556.
116. Junta 3, f. 141r Kontzi, *Aljamiado,* II, 469
117. Junta 3, f. 132r Kontzi, *Aljamiado,* II, 453.
118. Junta 3, f. 163v Kontzi, *Aljamiado,* II, 516.
119. Junta 3, f. 133r Kontzi, *Aljamiado,* II, 455.
120. See above note 49, and chapter VI, notes 104ff. See also, Abd al-Jalil, *Marie;* Hayek, *Christ* and *Mystère*; Michaud, *Jésus*; Parrinder, *Jesus*; Matteo, *Divinitá*; Pareja, "Relato"; and Vespertino, "Figuras." (See also Junta 9 and BNM 5302)
121. BMN 4944, f. 88; and chapter V, notes 149ff.
122. BMN 4944, f. 23r; chapter V, notes 177 and 198.
123. BMN 4944, f.1ff; cf. chapter V, notes 117ff.
124. BMN4944, f. 35v; cf. chapter V, notes 140ff.
125. BNM 4944, f. 55r
126. Q4 : 71. Jesus ('Isā) is mentioned sometwenty-nine times in the Qur'ān and is referred to as "'Isā Ibn Maryam" (Jesus the son of Mary).
127. Q5 : 109, 110, 116.
128. Q4 : 147.
129. See Ibn Ḥazm, *Fiṣal*, II, 170; III, 41. BNM 4944, 41v , 62r, 68r, 81r. Cf. chapter V, notes 149 and 166ff.
130. BNM 4944, f. 67r-67v. In his *Libro*, Juan Ruíz makes, perhaps, some suggestive remarks regarding the problem surrounding Christian ceremonies and sacraments, and he does it in an irreverent way. In the Fable of the Burstard, a cleric is represented by a wolf, who was asked to baptize little pigs so that they may die as Christians : "bautizat a mis fijuelos porque mueran cristianos", (stanza 776). He also points to the theological aspects of confession and penance, maintaining that they are not codified in writing (stanzas 1130-1131). As such, they can be made directly to God, thus conforming to Islamic view. However, Juan Ruíz makes the concession that they can be made to the high echelon of the church, but not to simple and untutored clerics, who would certainly fall in error for things they cannot do. In fact, they would be like the blind leading the blind:

    En esto yerran mucho, que lo non pueden fazer
    de o que fazer no pueden non se deben entremeter;
    si el ciego al ciego adiestra o lo quier traer
    en la foya dan entreambos e dentro van caer (stanza 1145).

    This evaluation does conform to Morisco sentiment which expresses the general Islamic conception in that God alone is the Confessor. Cf. chapter V, note 98.
131. BNM 4944, f. 89v.

5. THE POLEMICS OF THE MORISCOS

1. A listing of Arabic polemical literature is found in Steinschneider, *Polemische*; Anawati, "Polémique"; Epalza 'Notes." One may single out Ibn Ḥazm of Cordova, who refuted world religions including Judaism and Christianity showing the superiority of Islam over all of them; see his *Fiṣal*, II, 42ff. One may add Turmeda, *Tuḥfah*, who launched a bitter attack against Christianity. On some Christian polemicists, see Daniel, *Islam* and *Arabs*; and Southern, *Views*.
2. The most incisive work on the building of an image is Daniel, *Islam*.
3. As quoted by Hitti, *Islam*, 50.
4. The attacks of al-Kindī were refuted by 'Abadallāh Ibn Ismā'īl al-Hāshimīin his *Risālah*.
5. The Martyrs of Cordova were zealot Christians who insulted Islam and its founder in public knowing that such a conduct would lead to the death penalty. On their revolt, See Colbert, *Martyrs*; Simonet, *Historia*, 413ff; and Waltz, "Significance."
6. The writings of Alvaro and Euglogio constitute the main Latin documentary evidence of that period. For details on their writings see Simonet, *Historia*, 399ff. and 457ff.
7. Daniel, *Arabs,* chapter 2.
8. *La Chanson de Roland*, 98.
9. Daniel, *Arabs*, 232ff.
10. See below, notes 51ff.
11. Kritzeck, *Peter*, 32ff.
12. Ibid., 115ff. and 155 ff. In addition to the translation of the Qur'ān, Peter also secured a translation of the biography of Muḥammad and the text of al-Hāshimī's *Risālah* defending Islam.
13. Alverny, "Deux traductions."
14. Jiménex de Rada (1176-1247) wrote his *Historia Arabum* (Madrid, 1793) in which he included a biography of the Prophet.
15. Alfonso X (1252-1284) also included a biography of Muḥammad in his *Crónica general*. Cf. Chejne, *Muslim Spain*, 1255ff.
16. Peter Pascual wrote: *Sobre el Seta mahometana* and *Contra los fatalistas mahometanos*. Cf. Daniel, *Islam*, 19, and Index.
17. Ramón Martin is the author of *Explanatio Symboli Apostolorum et Pugio Fidei* in which he uses primary sources in his refutation of both Judaism and Islam. Cf. Daniel, *Islam*, 48-49 and Index.
18. Raymond Lull was an accomplished Arabist with great missionary zeal; he wrote numerous works dealing with doctrinal matters. Cf. Daniel, *Islam,* 66, and Index.
19. Alfonso X, *Primera crónica general*, 116ff.
20. Alfonso X, *Antología*, 92; cf. Chejne, *Muslim Spain*, 125ff.
21. Bacon, *Opus Majus*, where his indebtedness to Arab thinkers is often recognized.
22. Dante, *Divine Comedy*, Inf. xxviii.
23. Schwoebel, *Shadow*, 4ff.
24. As cited by Hitti, *Islam*, 54ff.
25. Lydgate, *Fall of Princes*, 921; of. Hitti, *Islam*, 55.
26. Shakespeare, *Henry VI*, I, ii, 140ff.
27. Shakespeare, *Romeo and Juliet*, V, 184; *Henry IV*, iii, 84.
28. Hitti, *Islam*, 56.
29. See above, note 8.

30. See Ibn al-Khaṭīb, *A'māl*, 12, 23, 196. The term Rūm, meaning Roman, was applied ordinarily to the Byzantines, whereas Ifranj meant "French" or "Westerner," particularly from the time of the Crusades in the eleventh century. Christians were often referred to as the "Worshipers of the Cross" in the connotation of idol worship to which the Moriscos added the label, "Eaters of Pork" (Cf. chapter II, note 45).
31. Ibn al-Abbār, *Ḥullah*, II, 126; Ibn al-Khaṭīb, *A'māl*, 203. It is important to note that both Ibn al-Abbār and Ibn al-Khaṭīb were Andalusians who lived at a critical period of Andalusian history.
32. For *kāfir*, *dār al-ḥarb, dār al-islām* and *Djihād*, see *EI.*
33. Ibn Khaldūn, *Muqaddimah*, I, 119.
34. Ibid, I, 163.
35. Ibid., I, 158ff.
36. Ibid., I, 167.
37. Mas'udī, *Murūj*, 34.
38. Ṣā'id, *Ṭabaqāt,* 8f.
39. Bakrī, *Jughrāfiyah*, 81, as quoted by Chejne, *Muslim Spain*, 286.
40. Ibid.
41. Ibn Munqidh, *An Arab Syrian Gentleman,* 161ff.
42. See above, note 1.
43. Q2 : 62.
44. Q2 : 111.
45. Q2 : 113.
46. Q5 : 19.
47. Q5 : 51.
48. For *ahl al-dhimmah* or *ahl al-kitāb*, see *EI.*
49. Ibn Ḥazm, *Fiṣal.* Asín's translation, *Abenházam*, is being used here.
50. Ibn Ḥazm, *Radd*, 45.
51. Ibn Ḥazm, *Fiṣal*, III, 9ff.
52. Ibid., III, 13-14.
53. Ibid., III, 15ff.
54. Ibid., III, 16.
55. Ibid., III, 17ff.
56. Ibid., III, 19.
57. Ibid., III, 21.
58. Ibid., III, 22ff.
59. Ibid., III, 26.
60. Ibid., IV, 1-12.
61. Ibid., IV, 31.
62. Ibid., IV, 32.
63. Ibid., III, 36.
64. Ibid., III, 37ff. The question of abrogation (*al-nāsikh wa-l-mansūkh*) is accepted in Islamic doctrine not only vis-à-vis Judaism and Christianity but within the Qur'ān itself.
65. Ibid., III, 42.
66. Ibid., III, 43.
67. Ibid., III, 68ff.
68. See above, notes 11 and 13.
69. Chejne, *Muslim Spain*, 127ff.

70. On the correspondence of al-Bājī and the French monk, see Cutler, "Who was the Monk of France." 'Iyāḍ's work has the interesting title, *Kitāb al-shifā' wa-ta'rīf ḥuqūq al-muṣṭafa* (*The Book of Cure and Determination of the Rights of the Pure One*).
71. Cf. Cardaillac, *Morisques et Chrétiens*, 215.
72. He is Aḥmad Ibn 'Abd al-Ḥaqq al-Khazrajī (d. 1187). Cf. Granja, "Milagros."
73. Cf. Cardaillac, *Morisques et Chrétiens*, 216.
74. Steinschneider, *Polemische,* 34. The treatise is analyzed by Asín, "Tratado," on the basis of Gayangos' manuscript, no. 31.
75. Asín, "Tratado," 251ff. Gayangos 31, 4-15.
76. Cardaillac, *Morisques et Chrétiens*, 53.
77. See BNM 4944, f. 1ff; and below, notes 117ff.
78. Asín, "Tratado," 254-255 Gayangos 31, f. 15-16.
79. Ibid., 255-256 = f. 16ff.
80. See BNM 4944; below, notes 134ff.
81. Asín, "Tratado," 256-285 f. 21-30 Cf. BNM 4944, below, note 137.
82. Asín, "Tratado," 258-261 f. 30-54. Cf. BNM 4944, below, note 132.
83. BNM 4944, f. 59v and f. 74v Cardaillac, *Polémique,* II, 99 and 15.
84. Qaysī's Arabic text is analyzed by Asín, "*Polémia.*"
85. *BNM 4944 f. 59.*
86. *Epalza, Tuḥfah*, has a good introduction about Turmeda and his works.
87. Asín, 'Polémica," 306. Cf. BNM 4944, below, note 188.
88. Ibid., 301-302. Cf. BNM 4944, below, note 174.
89. Epalza, *Tuḥfah*, 218. Cf. BNM 4944, below, note 161.
90. Ibid., 219.
91. Ibid., 227.
92. Ibid., 276-295. Cf. BNM 4944, below, note 192.
93. Ibid., 285. Cf. BNM 4944, below, note 149.
94. Ibid., 287.
95. Ibid., 289.
96. Ibid., 292ff.
97. Ibid., 297-304. Cf. BNM 4944, below, note 144.
98. Ibid., 309-361. Cf. BNM 4944, below, note 206.
99. Ibid., 369-381. Cf, BNM 4944, below, notes 187ff.
100. Ibid., 382-403. Cf. BNM 4944, below, notes 156ff.
101. Ibid., 404-429.
102. Ibid., 450-468.
103. Ibid., 453.
104. Ibid., 455.
105. Ibid., 457.
106. Ibid., 463.
107. Ibid., 469
108. Ibid., 470-497. Cf. BNM 4944, below, notes 134, 161 and 170.
109. See above, note 84.
110. BNM 4944, below notes 177ff.
111. Epalza, *Tuḥfah,* 487.
112. BNM 4944, f. 49v and 59v.
113. Ibid., f. 59v.
114. Ibid., f. 1-35v.

115. Ibid., f. 36r-101v [5] Cardaillac, *Polémique*, II, 4-267. In addition to BNM 4944, one may add the following polemical treatises: BNM 9074; BNM 9655; Junta 8; Junta 9; RAH T12; RAH V6; and RAH V7.
116. BNM 4944, f. 1r; Cf. above Rāqilī, *Ta'yīd*, above, notes 74ff.
117. Ibid., f. 2v.
118. Ibid., f. 3r.
119. Ibid., f. 3v.
120. Ibid., f. 3r.
121. Ibid., f. 4-5.
122. Ibid., f. 6r.
123. Ibid., f. 7r.
124. Ibid., f. 7v.
125. Ibid., f. 74: *"puwes no es sino los muslimes fijos de Ismā'il. . . ke-elleos no seran erederos de la tiyerra.*
126. Ibid., 7v-8r: *"Ke la su onrra i-bondad no ubo neguna menwa nidefalimento por ella seye siyerba o-katiba de Ibrāhīm."*
127. Ibid., 8v.
128. Ibid., 11r-11v.
129. Ibid., f. 16r.
130. Ibid., f. 18r.
131. Ibid., f. 18v.
132. Ibid., f. 20r.
133. Ibid., 22v.
134. Ibid., 27r.
135. Ibid., f. 23r-23v.
136. Ibid., f. 25r-29v.
137. Ibid., f. 30r-30v.
138. Ibid., f. 32r-34v.
139. Ibid., f. 35v: *"i-yel-muslim ke tiyene seso i-leye lo-ke dize en este libro debepensa en-todo esto i-yaghradeser al -kiriyador porke no-lo fizo deskereyido i-maldicho i-lo-fizo muslim kereyente en el kiriyador e-yen-su al-nnabī Muḥammad."*
140. Ibid., f. 36r.
141. Ibid., f. 36r-101v = Cardaillac, *Polémiques,* II, 4-267.
142. Ibid., f. 36v-41v = Cardaillac, op cit., 5-27.
143. Ibid., f. 42r-58v = 29-93.
144. Ibid. f. 59r-82r = 97-185.
145. Ibid., f. 83v-83v = 187-191.
146. Ibid., f. 84 r = 193.
147. Ibid., f. 84v-101v = 195-267.
148. Ibid., f. 36 = 93. Cf. Ibn Ḥazm, *Fiṣal*, II, 170, and III, 40.
149. Ibid., f. 40r = 21.
150. Ibid., f. 44v = 39 : *"Vuwestoro kiriyador vos veye i vos oye . . . . yo vos veyo i vos oygho."*
151. Ibid., f. 45r = 41 : *"Puwes ke seghamiyento es este tan gharande ke leyen i-no entiyenden asi komo el-lasno ke liyeba libros."*
152. Ibid., f. 45v-46r = 43-45.
153. Ibid., f. 46r = 45.
154. Ibid., f. 46v-47v = 47-51.
155. Ibid., f. 49v-49r = 55-57.

156. Ibid., f. 49v = 59.
157. Ibid., f. 52r = 71.
158. Ibid., f. 52v = 71.
159. Ibid., f. 53v = 75.
160. Ibid., f. 54r-54v = 77-79.
161. Ibid., f. 56r = 85.
162. Ibid., f. 56v = 87.
163. Ibid., f. 57r = 89.
164. Cf. above, notes 85ff.
165. bnm 4944, f. 60r-60v = 101-103.
166. Ibid., f. 62r = 105.
167. Ibid., f. 62v = 107.
168. Ibid., f. 63v = 111.
169. Ibid., f. 65r = 117.
170. Ibid., f. 68r = 129.
171. Ibid., f. 68v = 131.
172. Ibid., f. 69r = 133.
173. Ibid., f. 69v = 135.
174. Ibid., f. 71r = 141.
175. Ibid., f. 73v-74r = 151-153.
176. Ibid., f. 74v = 155.
177. Reference is made here to Q5:64 and Q51:47.
178. BNM 4944, f. 76v = 163 : *"Puwes a vosotros seya vuwestara ley i-ya-mi la-miya."* (Q6:109).
179. Ibid., f. 78v = 171.
180. Ibid., f. 79r = 173.
181. Ibid., f. 79v = 175.
182. Cf. above, note 85.
183. BNM 4944, f. 81v = 183.
184. Cf. above, note 106.
185. BNM 4944, f. 82v = 187. Cf. above, note 98.
186. Ibid., f. 83r = 189. Cf. Ibn Ḥazm, *Fiṣal*, II, 158.
187. Ibid., f. 83v = 191.
188. Ibid., f. 84r = 193.
189. Ibid., f. 84v = 195. Cf. Ibn Ḥazm, *Fiṣal,* II, 155.
190. 'Umar Ibn 'Abd al-'Azīz was the Umayyad caliph of Damascus (717-720).
191. BNM 4944, f. 87r = 209.
192. Ibid., f. 87v = 211.
193. Ibid., f. 88v = 211.
194. Ibid., f. 88v = 215.
195. Ibid., f. 89v = 219.
196. Ibid., f. 91r = 225.
197. Ibid., f. 92v-93r = 231-233.
198. Ibid., f. 93v-94v = 235-237.
199. Ibid., f. 95r-97r = 241-249.
200. Ibid., f. 98r-99v = 253-259.
201. Ibid., f. 99v-100r = 259-261.
202. Ibid., f. 100r-100v = 261-263.
203. RAH V7 consists of five folios and was transcribed by Cardaillac, *Polémique*, II,

269-285.

204. Ibid., f. 3v = II, 277.
205. BNM 4944, f. 67r-67v = Cardaillac, *Polémique*, II, 125-127.
206. RAH V7, f. 4r = Cardaillac, op; cit., 279.
207. Q3 : 129: of. Turmeda, note 98.
208. Daniel, *Arabs,* 310-312.
209. Cabanelas, *Juan de Segovia,* 110ff.
210. Ibid., 155ff.
211. Martin García, *Sermones,* often cites the Qur'ān, so does Ribera Florit in his *Polémica.* Cf. Sanz, *Tratado* and Cardaillac, *Morisques et Chrétiens,* 387.
212. Andrés, *Opera*, f. 21ff; cf. Cardaillac, *Polémique*, I, 165.
213. Péez de Chinchón, *Antialcorán,* f. 89f.
214. Ibid., f. 100r.
215. Cardaillac, *Morisques et Chrétiens,* 310ff.
216. See chapter VI, notes 31ff.
217. Cf. BNM 4944, f. 93r; BNM 9067, f. 7r; BNM 9653, 10r; BNM 9654, f. 3r.
218. BNM 9067, f. 205ff.
219. See above, notes 86ff. As stated in chapter IV, note 49; the space devoted to Christ in Aljamiado literature is considerable. See BNM 9067, f. 175r ; BNM 9074, f. 19r; BNM 9654, f. 3r; BNM 9655, f. 39r; and others.
220. BNM 9653, f. 177; BNM 9654 f. 7.
221. BNM 9067, f. 196r; BNM 9074, 40r; BNM 9654,13r; and BNM 9655, f. 39r.
222. BNM 9653, f. 178r; BNM 9074, 59v, BNM 4944, f. 67r, and RAH V7, 4r.
223. See Turmeda, notes 98ff above. For more details, see Cardaillac, *Morisques et Chrétiens*, 310ff.
224. Cf. Turmeda note 105 above. BNM 9655, f. 16r.
225. BNM 9067, f. 64r; BNM 9655, f. 179r. Turmeda note 98 above.
226. BNM 9067, f. 206r; BNM 9074, f. 55v; BNM 9654, f. 14r. Cf. Turmeda, note 98 above.

6. HISTORY, LEGENDS, AND TRAVEL

1. BNM 4908; Junta 64/21. Hoenerbach, *Urkunden*, 181ff; 185ff; 203ff.; 221ff. This work is edited and translated into German a good number of documents.
2. BNM 5452 = Hoenerbach, *Urkunden*, 176ff.; 227ff.; 35ff.; and 352ff.
3. BNM 5073; BNM 5228; Junta 64/21, where similar items are found. Cf. Hoenerbach, *Urkunden*, 134ff., 151ff., 161ff., and 168ff.
4. BNM 5228, no.7.
5. BNM 4908, no.3.
6. BNM 5267, no. 2.
7. BNM 5073, no. 2.
8. BNM 5073, no. 3.
9. BNM 5073, no.6.
10. BNM 5073, nos. 8, 9, 10, and 11, were transcribed by Lincoln, "Textos."
11. BNM 5073, no. 12, published by Hoenerbach, *Urkunden,* 252ff.
12. BNM 5073, no. 14, published by Hoenerbach, *Urkunden,* 236ff., 240ff., and 246ff.
13. Saavedra, *Discurso,* no. 123.
14. Gil, *Colección,* 134-138; Junta 64/10 and Junta 100 published by Hoenerbach, *Urkunden,* 34ff. and 354ff.

15. Gil, *Colección, 139-150.*
16. *See Hoenerbach, Urkunden.*
17. Saavedra, *Discurso,* no. 127.
18. *Libro de las luces,* translated from the Arabic *Kitāb al-anwār.* The work appeared to have been popular among the Moriscos, and is one of the very few works of which we have more than one manuscript, mainly, BNM 4955; PR 3225; RAH T18; and BPT 9, described by González Palencia, "Noticias," 140-143. Guillén, *Leyendas,* II, 29-93, transcribed the portion on the birth of Muḥammad on the basis of BNM 4955, f. 108-148, and Kontzi, *Aljamiado,* II, 800-837, transliterated another portion of the same, f. lv-41r.
19. Rabadan's *Discourse* was translated into English by Morgan, *Mohametism.* Cf. Stanley, "Poetry" and Ticknor *Historia,* IV, 275ff., and Saavedra, *Discurso,* 172ff.
20. BUB D565, f. 115ff.; Junta 8; RAH T8; RAH T12; and RAH T13.
21. BNP 290; RAH T12; and RAH T18.
22. BNM 5053 = Guillén, *Leyendas,* II, 269-300. Cf. BNP 263 and Junta 9, no. 3.
23. PR 3226, f. 91ff. and BNM 5354.
24. Escorial 1880, no. 10, and PR 3226.
25. BMN 5374, no. 9; BNP 290, no. 7; and RAH T13, no. 25.
26. RAH T12.
27. BNM 5378 and RAH T18. The praise of the cloak is probably based on a poem composed by al-Buṣīrī (d. 1294), a manuscript of which is in the Escorial; 248.
28. Guillén, *Leyendas,* II, 159-164.
29. RAH T18, f. 120-125 = Guillén, *Leyendas,* II, 145-158, Cf. BNM 5337 and chapter VIII, notes 11ff.
30. PR 3226, no. 12.
31. PR 3226, no. 13; RAH T12, no. 9; and BNP 290.
32. BNM 4955, f. 3v.
33. Ibid., f. 46ff.
34. Ibid., f. 93ff.
35. Ibid., f. 103v.
36. Ibid., f. 108.
37. Ibid., f. 110.
38. Ibid., f. 112.
39. Ibid., f. 114.
40. Ibid., f. 118.
41. Ibid., f. 118ff.
42. Ibid., f. 121ff.
43. Ibid., f. 119.
44. Ibid., f. 124ff.
45. Ibid., f. 128ff.
46. Ibid., f. 129.
47. Ibid., f. 131ff.
48. Ibid., f. 136.
49. Q9: 1-5
50. See chapter VIII, notes 6ff.
51. Mainly, RAH T17, f. 161-179; transcribed by Guillén, *Leyandas,* II, 269-300; and BNM 5053, f. 1-18, transliterated by Kontzi, *Aljamiado,* II, 839-876. See also BNP 263 and Junta 9.

52. Asín, *Escatología.*
53. RAH T17 and BNM 5053 differ in some details. For instance, while RAH T17, f. 161v, has "a dark night in which neither a rooster sang nor a dog barked," BNM 5053, f. lr, has "a dark night with great thundering and lightening."
54. RAH T17, f. 161. BNM 5053, f. 1, has: "six hundred wings on which are inscribed pearls and rubies, each having one hundred years journey *(andadura).*
55. RAH T17, f. 163.
56. Ibid., f. 164; cf. BNM 5053, f. 3.
57. Ibid., f. 165.
58. RAH T17, f. 165 : *"yuzghado es el fecho,"* while BNM 5053, f. 3r, reads: *"pagha el feyto akel ke es en la madre del alkitāb."*
59. RAH T17, f. 165. BNM 5053, f.3v, has: "Thou art the most honored of God's creatures" *(Ke tu es el mas onrrado de los formados de-Allāh).*
60. RAH T17, 165. BNM 5053, f. 3v, refer to different precious stones.
61. RAH T17, f. 166; BNM 5053, f. 4r. 'Praising the Lord" is a rendition of the arabism *"ke attasbiḥan kon atasbiḥes"* (literally, "praise with praises"). Cf. Kontzi, *Aljamiado,* II, 846.
62. RAH T17, f.166: *"El mas onrrado de los formados de las jentes."*
63. Ibid., f. 167; BNM 5053, f. 5r.
64. RAH T17, f. 170, has Idris while BNM 5053, f. 6v, has Moses as the central figure. From this point on, both manuscripts have different central figures.
65. BNM 5053, f. 8r, lists Adam as a major known figure who is also mentioned in the first heaven. RAH T17, f. 171, simply mentions the ascention to the fifth heaven with reference to the opening of a gate that overlooked the abyss of earth where cheaters and imbibers of wine could be seen suffering damnation of Hell.
66. RAH T17, f. 172-179, deals with the sixth heaven where Muḥammad is introduced to the angels Michael and Israfil and where Muḥammad had a dialogue with God with Moses in attendance. BNM 5053, f. 8r-10r, does not mention any particular figure.
67. BNM 5053, f. 14r.
68. Ibid., f. 15r.
69. Ibid.
70. Ibid., f. 15v-16r.
71. Ibid., f. 18r.
72. RAH T17, f. 177.
73. See chapter VIII, notes 6ff.
74. BNM 4953, no. 12, f. 63vff, (*el-alḥadith del al-'arabe y la Doncella*). Guillén, *Leyendas*, II, 217-232.
75. BNM 9067, no. 14 (*Historia de un Profeta y una Profetisa). Guillén*, *Leyendas*, II, 159-166.
76. RAH T18, f. 1-4 (*El milagro de la luna: el-alḥadith del annabī Muḥammad con el rey Ḥabīb*). Guillén, *Leyendas*, II, 259-265.
77. RAH T18, f. 4v-20v; Guillén, *Leyendas*, II, 359-388. Account of Muḥammad's death also appears in BNP 290; BNP 774; PR 3226, no. 13; Junta 9, no. 4; Junta 13; RAH T12, no. 9; and RAH T19.
78. RAH T18, f. 12v.
79. Ibid., f. 16ff.
80. Junta 8, f. 156-160. It is interesting to note that the Eastern scholar al-Tha'ālibī, *Qiṣaṣ,* 182, says that the Ten Commandments given to Moses on Sinai were

meant for Muḥammad's community.

81. Junta 8, f. 80-108. Al-Tha'ālibī, *Qiṣaṣ*, 315-322, devotes ample space to Balūqīyaš search. He is said to have found a large number of people reciting the confession of faith (*shahādah*) in which Muḥammad's name is included.
82. BNM 4953, f. 2v-16r; transliterated by Hegyi, *Edición*, 2-13.
83. See chapter V, notes 75ff.
84. RAH V3.
85. Junta 4.
86. Junta 43, no. 6.
87. Junta 4, f. 180; Gil, *Colección*, 97-98.
88. BNM 4953, f. 184r-187; transliterated by Hegyi, *Edición*, 167-169.
89. BUB D565.
90. BNM 4953, f. 78v-90; Guillén, *Leyendas*, III, 65-82.
91. BNM 4953, f. 86vff.
92. Guillén, *Leyendas, III, 187.*
93. BNM 4953, f. 77r-78r; *transliterated by Hegyi, Edición*, 64-65.
94. See chapter VIII, notes 9ff.
95. See chapter VIII, notes 11ff.
96. RAH T18, f. 114; cf. chapter VIII, note 31.
97. Guillén, *Leyendas*, II, 217ff. Cf. above, note 74.
98. BNM 5337, no. 4.
99. See chapter VIII, notes 24ff.
100. See chapter VIII, notes 16ff.
101. RAH S1 and RAH T18.
102. Guillén, *Leyendas*, III, 278-286.
103. Junta 8, f. 73-81.
104. Mainly, BNM 5378.
105. Abraham (Ibrāhīm) is mentioned some sixty-five times in the Qur'ān. Al-Tha'ālibī, *Qiṣaṣ*, 63-87, deals with various aspects of his life: his birth; the danger that faced him in establishing monotheism; his travel to Egypt where Hagar was given to his wife Sarah as slave; Ismā'īl's birth from Hagar and his wandering in the desert where the Zamzam well was dug by Gabriel (p. 72); Abraham's journey to Mecca where he built the Ka'bah assisted by Ismā'īl; and other details. His qualities are described as "friend of God"; "father of hospitality"; "the Imām (leader) of those who believe in one God"; and "the one whom God named the first true Muslim." See Moubarak, *Abraham*. It is for this reason that Abraham occupies a prominent place in Aljamiado literature as attested by the following manuscripts: BNM 5313, no. 9; Junta 3, no. 8; Junta 9, f. 73-77; PR 3226, no. 8; RAH T12, no. 2.
106. Ismā'īl was particularly important to the Moriscos as the true ancestors of Arabs and Muslims, in view of the fact that the Moriscos were labeled Agarenos. That is, they were considered descendants of Hagar and Abraham; and Ismā'īl was viewed as a bastard by Judeo-Christian polemicists. Thus, the circumstances surrounding his birth and his role as the true heir of mankind were defended against the charges of illegitimacy (see BNM 4944, f. 1-35; cf. chapter V, notes 117ff.). Though Ismā'īl may not be as important as Abraham in the Islamic tradition, he is mentioned some twelve times in the Qur'ān and al-Tha'ālibī *Qiṣaṣ*, 88-90, considered him important enough to include him among the major prophets treated by him.

107. Cf. Guillén, *Leyendas*, III, 287-306.
108. BNM 5305, no. 6; Guillén, *Leyendas*, I, 225-266. Cf. al-Tha'ālibī, *Qiṣaṣ*, 135-144, where he gives a moving account of Job's suffering and final rejuvenation.
109. Al-Tha'ālibī, *Qiṣaṣ*, 94-125, says that the story of Joseph has been regarded as the best story by virtue of conveying a good conduct, patience, forgiveness, continence, unity (of God), knowledge of biographies, and interpretation of dreams. This popularity, no doubt, was kept alive by the Moriscos, who preserved much of the Oriental version as contained in al-Tha'ālibī's work. See BNM 5292 and RAH T12.
110. BNM 247; Morf, *Poema*; Menéndez Pidal, *Poema*. See also Guillén, *Leyenda de José*, and Klenk, "Leyenda."
111. BNM 5305, no. 1; Guillén, *Leyendas,* , I, 315-381. Moses appears more than one hundred and thirty times in the Qur'ān and is highly regarded in Muslim traditions. Al-Tha'ālibī, *Qiṣaṣ*, 148-221, devotes ample space to him and deals with his birth, youth, exodus from and return to Egypt, miracles and commandments. His importance among the Moriscos may be gauged by the extant Aljamiado manuscripts dealing with various aspects of his life: BPT 10, no. 7; Junta 4; Junta 9; Junta 40; RAH T8; RAH T13; and RAH T19.
112. BNM 6061, no. 1, and RAH T13, no. 23.
113. RAH T19, no. 3, f. 6ff.
114. BNM 5305, no. 1, f. 1ff.; Guillén, *Leyendas*, I, 315-322.
115. BNM 5223, f. 273. PR 3226, no. 5.
116. BNM 5305, f. 64-103; Guillén, *Leyendas*, I, 281-311. Cf. RAH T9, no. 2. Solomon appears some seventeen times in the Qur'ān and al-Tha'ālibī, *Qiṣaṣ*, 257-293, mentions several of his extraordinary powers and his association with demons. The Moriscos regarded him highly at the religious and magical level. Cf. chapter VII, notes 117ff.
117. BNM 5305, no. 6.
118. BNM 5254; Guillén, *Leyenda de Alejandro*, and Nykl, *Rerkontamiento*. Alexander the Great is mentioned in the Qur'ān under Dhū-l-Qarnayn (The Two Horned). As such, he was the object of commentaries and elaborate stories. In the Arabic version as given by al-Tha'ālibī, *Qiṣaṣ*, 322-332, Alexander is considered not only a believer (*mu'min*, Ibid., 63), but a prophet—though not a messenger (*rasūl*). In a tradition, Muḥammad is reported to have said: "I do not know whether or not Dhū-l-Qarnayn (Alexander) was a prophet." (Ibid., 324). However, when he established his kingdom in a wide area of the world, God revealed Himself to him saying: "I have sent you to all creatures of East and West and made you my proof." (Ibid., 324). Moreover, the Angel Raphael is said to have been his friend. (Ibid., 329). It is significant to note that the legend was known in Western Islam (See García Gómez, *Texto*) and that it had its Spanish counterpart in the *Libro de Alexandre*.
119. Q18: 83.
120. See chapter V, notes 86ff., and notes 149ff. It should be mentioned that Jesus ('Īsā) appears twenty-five times in the Qur'ān as a prophet and a man created from dust. Al-Tha'ālibī, *Qiṣaṣ*, 342-466, gives a straightforward account about Christ who is looked upon with reverence—reverence that continued unabated among the Moriscos despite the heated controversies between them and their Christian neighbors.

121. Gil, *Colección*, 33-35.
122. Samarqandī (BNM 4871, f. 328-335 ; Guillén, *Leyendas*, III, 321-347.
123. BNM 4953, f. 90v-100v; Guillén, *Leyendas*, II, 131-144; Hegyi, *Edición*, 79-89.
124. Samarqandī (4871, f. 328-335); Guillén, *Leyendas*, III, 321-347.
125. Samarqandī (BNM 4871, f. 139-160); Guillén, *Leyendas*, III, 351-388. Cf. Junta 4, no. 2.
126. BNM 5301, f. 1-8; Guillén, *Leyendas*, III, 307-317. Cf. Lincoln, "Textos," based on BNP 774.
127. See above, notes 51ff.
128. Gil, *Colección*, 61-71.
129. Ibid., 70-72.
130. Junta 64/21, f. 1r-4v = Kontzi, *Aljamiado*, II, 750-752.
131. Gil, *Colección*, 73-76.
132. See chapter III, notes 45ff.
133. BNP 290, no. 4, contains information for the traveler (avisos para el caminante) about provisions, routes, places, etc.
134. RAH T16, no. 2.
135. Junta 13, f. 179-219; Pano y Ruata, *Coplas*; Gil, *Colección*, 78-96.
136. Gil, *Collección*, 89.
137. Lincoln, "Itinerary."
138. BNP 290, no. 4.
139. See chapter VIII, notes 9ff.
140. Ibn Hishām, *Sīrat rasūl Allāh*.
141. See chapter VIII, notes 11ff.
142. Ibid., notes 80ff.
143. Tha'ālibī, *Qiṣaṣ*, 86.
144. Ibid., 94.
145. Ibid., 260ff.
146. See chapter VII, notes 117ff.

7. SORCERY, TALISMAN, AND THE SCIENCES

1. On the extent of transmission of the Arabic sciences in the West, see Sarton, *Introduction*; Haskins, *Studies;* Mieli, *Science*; Dunlop. *Arabic Science*; Millás Vallicrosa, *Estudios*; Vernet, *Cultura*. It must be emphasized that Spain played an important role in the process of transmission and offered a fertile ground for acculturation and cross-fertilization. See Chejne, "Islamization" and "Role."
2. At a meeting of bishops in 1335 at Salamanca, Christians were urged not to use the services of malicious Jews and Saracens (Fernández y González, *Estado social*, 207). This kind of prohibition excluded Jews and Moors from engaging in jobs such as grocers, surgeons, and apothecaries (Ibid., 213). Cf. García Ballester, *Historia*, 51.
3. Ribera, Enseñanza," 248.
4. Fernández y González, *Estado social*, 386.
5. Cardoner, "Seis mujeres."
6. On the general subject of magic and sciences, see Thorndike, *History* and Malinowski, *Magic*. For Islam, see Fahd, *Divination*.
7. *On the superstitions of the Moriscos, see Ribera, "Supersticiones"; Garrido Atienza, "Moriscos grandinos"; for Spain in general, see Cirac, Procesos* and Caro Baroja, *Vidas*.

8. Ibn Khaldūn, *Muqaddimah*, III, 156.
9. Ibid., III, 158f.
10. Ibid., III, 161ff.
11. Ibid., III, 171ff. It must be emphasized, however, that Muslims had been ambivalent with respect to sorcery, talismans, and astrology, and there were heated controversies, in which some supporting them while others disavowing them. Already in the tenth century, Ibn al-Nadīm, *Fihrist*, 308-314, included them among the sciences. He was followed, among others, by the seventeenth-century Ḥajjī Khalīfah, *Kashf*, I, 33-35, who listed them along with works written on them. In the section devoted to the magical arts and to works written on them, Ibn al-Nadīm says that sorcerers and magicians claim that devils, genies, and spirits obey them and comply with their commands. He recognizes a variety of such "sciences": incantations (*'az̄'im*), which are achieved through a compact with the devil; magic (*siḥr*); white magic (*al-nirjiyāt); tricks (ḥiyal*); talismans (*Ṭilasmāt*) that are based on the observation of the stars; knowledge of the merit of God's names, prayers, and numbers (*'ilm al-khawāṣṣ*); making oneself invisible *('ilm al-khafā')*; help with the qualities of drugs *(isti'ānah bi-khawāss al-adwiyah)*; physiognomy *(firāsah)*; palmistry *(ikhtilāj)*; chiromancy *('ilm al-asāir)*; detection of mines *('ilm istinbāṭ al-ma'adin)*; forecasting rain *('ilm nuzūl al-ghayth)*; predicting the future *('ilm al-'irāfah)*; omens *(fa'l)*; prevention of future happenings *(zajir)*; lot casting *(qur'ah)*; geomancy *('ilm al-raml)*; and knowledge of good or bad days *('ilm al-ikhtiyārāt)*.
12. Astronomy and astrology often appear as "twin sisters" in Muslim scholarship. However, their intimiate relationship was questioned in the course of time, engendering a heated controversy with regard to their respective merit, some dissavowing astrology altogether while others recognizing its merit and validity. See Vernet, *Astronomía*. Cf. Chejme, *Ibm Hazm*, chapter IX.
13. On Arabic medicine in Europe, see Schipperges, *Assimilation*.
14. On medicine among the Moriscos, see the penetrating studies of García-Ballester, *Historia* and *Medicina*. Cf. below, notes 66ff.
15. BNM 4937, Memoria de los quartos del año, f. 1-6.
16. BNM 5267, f. 66ff. contains similar treatise.
17. Junta 22. Cf. Ribera, *Manuscritos*, 98-106, where it is described. Gil, *Colección*, 115-130, has an excerpt and Ribera made use of it in his "Supersticiones." It should be noted that *The Book of Marvellous Sayings (El libro de dichos maravillosos*) contains almost all the items mentioned in Ibn al-Nadīm, *Fihrist*, 308-314. See above, note 11.
18. BNM 5373.
19. Junta 59, f. 216-224v, and f. 228-233r = Kontzi, *Aljamiado*, 717-747.
20. *Alkitāb de suwertes* (BNM 5300).
21. Junta 22, f. 291-331.
22. Gil, *Colección*, 3.
23. Ibid., 3ff.
24. Ibid., 6ff.
25. Ibid., 8.
26. Ibid., 9.
27. Ibid., 11.
28. *Letanía para pedir agua* (Junta 23) and *El alkitāb del rogar por agua* (Junta 30).
29. *Los meses del año* (BNM 4955, f. 1-13; BNM 5306; BNM 5306; BNM 6064, n. 64;

BNP 290, no. 11; RAH T4, no. 1; RAH T13, no. 15).

30. BNM 5354, f. 91-104r. It should be noted that the month of Ramaḍān and others often receive special treatment in treatises and general works. See BNM 5223; Junta 9; RAH S1; RAH T13. Cf. Samarqandi (4871, chapter 43).
31. See Ribera, "Supersticiones," 493ff. Such notions of good and bad days were common among ancient Near Eastern people. Cf. Fahd, *Divination*, 468ff.
32. Suárez, "Días," transliterated and analyzed BNP 1163. Discerning the good and bad days is known in Arabic as *ilm al-ikhtiyārāt* (cf. above, note 11).
33. Ibid., 177; cf. PR 3226, f. 94ff.
34. Gil, *Colección*, 12-14; cf. RAH T13, f. 1ff.
35. Ibid., 12.
36. Ibid., 13-14.
37. Ibid., 14.
38. Several spells or incantations could be found in BNM 4937, f. 3-16; BNM 5267, f. 65ff; 5380, f. 143, among others.
39. Mainly, RAH T13, f. 150ff., and RAH V26, no. 3.
40. BNM 4937, f. 3ff.
41. RAH V25.
42. BNM 5385, f. 74; BNM 5377, nos. 7 and 23; RAH T1, no. 5; RAH T3, no. 9; RAH T9; RAH V24; and RAH V27.
43. RAH T11.
44. Junta 59, f. 228v = Kontzi, *Aljamiado*, II, 743.
45. Gil, *Colección*, 115.
46. Ibid., 116.
47. Ibid.
48. Ibid., 117.
49. Ibid., 130.
50. An arabism from *khatim*, pl. *khawātim.*
51. *Junta 59, f. 218v* = Kontzi, *Aljamiado*, II, 724-725.
52. Ibid., f. 223r = 738.
53. Gil, *Colección*, 121ff.
54. Ibid., 125.
55. Ibid., 125-126.
56. RAH T8, no. 10; cf. RAH V25.
57. Junta 59, f. 217v = Kontzi, *Aljamiado*, II, 721.
58. BNM 4953, f 152r = Hegyi, *Edición*, 140.
59. Junta 59, f. 223v = Kontzi, Aljamiado, II, 739ff. Cf. Junta 22, f. 122v.
60. BNM 5300.
61. Junta 59, f. 223ff. = Kontzi, *Aljamiado*, II, 739-740. *Atado* is a calque of the Arabic *marbūt* or *ma'qūd* meaning "bound" or "tied up," in a state of impotency as a result of magic, spirit, or birth defect. Thus the formula is meant to free the individual from this bondage. See Suyūṭī, *Raḥmah*, 111ff. and 121ff.
62. Ibid.
63. Ibid., f. 217 = 720.
64. Ibid., f. 216v = Kontzi, *Aljamiado*, II, 719.
65. Ibid., f. 216 v = 718.
66. BNM5273.
67. *Tratado muy noble de los cinco sabios doctores de medicina* (BNM 4937, f. 25-39).

68. *Tratado muy noble* (BNM 5267, f. 73-111 = Hoenerbach, *Urkunden*, 317ff.), is similar to BNM 4937 of the preceding note.
69. BNM 5078 = Hoenerbach, *Urkunden*, 368ff. and 375ff.) contains medical prescriptions.
70. BNM 5452, nos. 16, 18, and 19.
71. BNM 5238.
72. RAH T15 contains "practica de medicina" and is trilingual: Castilian, Latin, and Arabic.
73. Ibn Zuhr belonged to a distinguished family of Andalusian physicians. He was probably Marwān 'Abd al-Malik Ibn Abī 'Alā' (d. 1162), known to the West as Avenzoar.
74. RAH T16.
75. Ibid., f. 70.
76. Ibid., f. 40.
77. Ibid., f. 48.
78. Ibid., f. 51.
79. Ibid., f. 77. Other prescriptions (*rrecebtas*) appear in Junta 37; Junta 59; RAH V28; RAH V29; and RAH V31.
80. Ribera, "Supersticiones," 512-513.
81. Ibid., 508-509.
82. García Ballester, *Historia*, 182.
83. The granting of *ijāzah* (certificate) was a common practice in classical Islam; it was often issued by established scholars to students studying a particular work. Thus, a student could have as many certificates as the number of teachers.
84. The text of the *ijāzah* was published by Seco de Lucena, "Titúlo."
85. Cabanelas, "El morisco granadino."
86. *Actas Cortes de Castilla* (Madrid, November 13, 1607), XXIII, 583ff., as quoted by García Ballester, *Historia*, 111.
87. Ibid., 587; García Ballester, *Historia*, 112.
88. Ibid.
89. García Ballester, *Historia*, 120ff.
90. Ibid., 133. Cf. Gonzālez Palencia, "Curandero."
91. Ibid., 120.
92. Carboner, "Seis mujeres."
93. García Ballester, *Historia*, 125.
94. Ibid., 147.
95. Ibid., 160.
96. Ibid., 156.
97. Ibid., 159.
98. Ibid., 14ff.
99. Ibid., 122.
100. Cirac, *Procesos*.
101. See chapter VIII, notes 8ff.
102. Ibn Ḥazm, *Fiṣal*, V, 147ff. and 168ff. For a more detailed account of the occult sciences, see Chejne, *Ibn Ḥazm*, chapter IX.
103. Ibn Ḥazm, *Fiṣal*, II, 164ff. and 186ff. Cf. Chejne, *Muslim Spain*, 172.
104. Ibn Khaldūn, *Muqaddimah*, III, 116ff.
105. Caro Baroja, *Moriscos*, 132-133.
106. Caro Baroja, *Vidas*, II, 157.

107. Ibid., I, 107ff.
108. Such pacts with the Devil appear in Juan Manuel, *Conde Lucanor*, Ejemplo XLV, and Juan Ruíz, *Libro*, stanzas 1454-75.
109. Juan Ruíz, *Libro,* stanzas 123-152.
110. Ibid., stanza 140.
111. Ibid., stanzas 152, 576-632.
112. Caro Baroja, *Vidas*, II, 163.
113. Ibid., II, 173.
114. Lea, *History*, IV, 192.
115. Caro Baroja, *Vidas*, II, 176.
116. Ibid., I, 191, has such fórmulas:
De lugar en lugar
de orilla en orilla
sin Dios ni Santa María.
117. See chapter VI, note 116. The tenth-century Ibn al-Nadīm, *Fihrist*, 309-311, says that incantations (*'azā'im*) can be laudable or blameworthy; they are laudable in that Solomon was the first one who enslaved and employed spirits and demons, contracting a pact with seventy of them who complied with his wishes. On the other hand, incantations are blameworthy if they are performed by way of magic in which the magician becomes subservient to the Devil for accomplishing his goal. Moreover, the eleventh-century al-Tha'ālibī, *Qiṣaṣ*, 257-293, says that God himself had endowed Solomon with extraordinary traits and gifts such as making the wind subservient to him so that he could use it as a form of transport; having the devils weave him a carpet in the middle of which was placed a throne of gold and surrounded by three thousands chairs; having an army made up of spirits, genies, beasts, and birds; knowing the language of birds; and building a flying city and marvellous edifices. Besides, he had his magical ring with which he performed extraordinary feats.
118. *The Clavicula Salomonis* was extant in both Hebrew and Latin versions. English edition, ed. S. L. McGregor Mathers (London, 1899).
119. See chapter VII, note 17.
120. Caro Baroja, *Vidas*, I, 135ff.
121. In his *Vidas*, Caro Baroja gives the profiles of several sorcerers—mostly Old Christians—who appeared before the tribunals of the Inquisition and about whom there is ample information regarding the nature of the charges against them. The case of Velasco, I, 267ff., offers insightful information regarding the practice of sorcery.
122. Ibid., I, 283: "Y vien puede ser aya yo sido como los gitanos que hacen los hurtos los vecinos y echansele a ellos.
123. Ibid., I, 295-297.
124. Ibid., I, 209.
125. Ibid., I, 219ff. The case of Dr. Torralba is in many respects similar to that of the Morisco Román Ramírez. Cf. above, note 90ff.
126. See chapter VIII, note 45.
127. See chapter VIII, note 16.
128. See chapter VIII, note 29.
129. See chapter VIII, note 27. This and the above extraordinary occurrences bring to mind similar extraordinary marvels as found in the *Arabian Nights*. In the *Story of the Merchant and the Genie*, a sorcerer converts a woman into a hind, and a

slave and her child into a cow and a calf, respectively. In the *Story of the Prince Aḥmad,* there is a magic carpet that flies, an ivory tube that allows to see the desired object from enormous distances, and an apple that cures all maladies. Finally, in the *Story of Aladdin*, there is the wonderful lamp by means of which all desires beyond one's dreams are fulfilled on simple request.

130. Caro Baroja, *Vidas*, II, 17.
131. Ibid., II, 18.
132. Ibid., II, 47.
133. Ibid., II, 131.

8. SECULAR LITERATURE

1. Saavedra, *Discurso*, 187.
2. Ibid., 189. There is a great deal of arabism in aljamiado literature, particularly in religious texts. The Moriscos saw special meaning to some of the religious expressions.
3. Galmés, "Interés literario," 190.
4. Ibid., 202.
5. On Arabic epic literature, see Hammer-Purgstall, "Chevalerie"; Heller, "Sīrat 'Antar"; Conrad, "Delhemma"; "Delhemma Sayyid al-Battal"; "Principaus personnages"; and "Ḏāt al-Himma." See also Ribera, "Épica"; Menéndez Pidal *Epopeya*. But the most comprehensive and penetrating studies on the subject are: 'Abd al-Badī', *Épica*; Marcos, *Poesía*; and Galmés, *Épica* and his edition of the Aljamiado work, *El libro de las batallas.*
6. *El libro de las batallas* (BNM 5337) was first transcribed by Guillén, *Leyendas*, and recently published in a scholarly transliteration by Galamés, *Libro.*
7. For more details, see Marcos, *Poesía*, 225ff. and 269ff.
8. See Heller, "Sīrat 'Antar."
9. Junta 3, f. 154r-154v = Kontzi, *Aljamiado*, II, 495-496.
10. See below, note 31, *The Legend of 'Ali and the Forty Girls.*
11. *The Battle of Ḥunayn* deals with the conquest of Mecca and exists in two manuscripts: *Esta es la batalla de Badri i Ḥunayn* (BNM 5337, f. 48r-61r = Galmés, *Libro,* I, 184-212); and *¾Esta es la estoriya de la konkista de la kasa de la Makka onrrada* (RAH T18, f. 120r-125r = Galmés, *Libro*, I, 184-212, and Guillén, *Leyendas*, II, 145-158).
12. BNM 5337, f. 59r = Galmés, *Libro*, I, 207.
13. *Esta es la batalla de al-Asiyad i los de Makka kon l-annabī* (BNM 5337, f. 1r-13v = Galmés, *Libro*, I, 103-121, and Guillén, *Leyendas*, II, 233-258).
14. BNM 5337, f. 7v = Galmés, *Libro*, I, 112.
15. Ibid., f. 9r = Galmés, *Libro*, I, 115.
16. *Este es el rrekontamiyento del rrey al-Muhalhal ibnu āl-Fayadi kon Khalid Ibnu al-Walid al-Makhzumiyu* (BNM 5337, f. 61r-86r = Galmés, *Libro*, I, 213-244, and Guillén, *Leyendas*, II, 167-216.
17. *Esta es la batalla del vali Yarmūq i su konkista gharande* (BNM 5337, f. 95r-148v = Galmés, *Libro*, I, 257-325, and Guillén, *Leyendas*, III, 83-186.
18. Ibid., f. 95v = Galmés, *Libro*, I, 256.
19. BNM 5337, f. 14r-31v = Galmés, *Libro*, I, 122-145, and Guillén, *Leyendas*, II, 325-358.
20. Ibid., f. 28v = Galmés, *Libro*, I, 140.
21. Ibid., f. 26v = Galmés, *Libro*, I, 138.

22. *Esta es la batalla de al-Ashyab ibnu Ḥanqar* (BNM 5337, f. 86r-95r = Galmés, *Libro*, I, 245-256).
23. Ibid., 86v = Galmés, *Libro*, I, 245.
24. *El alḥadith del alkathar del oro i la estoriya de la kuluwebra kon 'Alī Ibnu Abi Ṭālib* (PR 3226, f. 1r-39r = Galmés, *Libro*, I, 326-344, and Guillén, *Leyendas*, III, 201-230.
25. Ibid., f. 10v-11r = Galmés, *Libro*, I, 331.
26. Ibid., f. 19v = Galmés, *Libro*, I, 335.
27. Ibid., f. 35v = Galmés, *Libro*, I, 343.
28. *La batalla de khuzaymata al-Bāriqiyyah i de al-Ākhwāṣ ibnu Mukhāḍ* (BNM 5337, f. 31v-36r = Galmés, *Libro*, I, 146-151).
29. *El alḥadīth de Wara il-Ḥujurati* (BNM 5337, f. 36r-46v = Galmés, *Libro,* I, 152-183.) There is another version (BNM 5313, f. 81r-111v = Galmés, *Libro*, I, 152-183).
30. Ibid., 44v = Galmés, *Libro*, I, 176.
31. *Leyenda de 'Ali y las cuarenta doncellas* (RAH T18, f. 114r-120r = Galmés, *Libro*, I, 345-355, and Guillén, *Leyendas*, III, 231-246).
32. Ibid., 119r = Galmés, *Libro,* I, 353.
33. Ibid., f. 119v = Galmés, *Libro*, I, 354.
34. Galmés, *Épica*, 21. For Maghāzī literature, see Paret, *Maghāzī.*
35. *'Abd al-Badī', Épica.*
36. Marcos, *Poesía.*
37. Galmés, *Épica*, and his incisive introduction to the *Libro*. Cf. above, note 5.
38. Edited and transliterated by Galmés, *Historia*, on the basis of RAH V1. Cf. Saavedra, "Historia," who rendered it into Latin characters but without following a rigorous system of transliteration.
39. *El baño de Zarieb*, is found in two manuscripts (Junta 4 and RAH T12) and was reproduced by Gil, *Colección*, 97-114, on the basis of Junta 4. See Saavedra, "El alhadith."
40. Asín, "original."
41. *La donzella Carcayona* is extant in BNM 5313 f. 134ff.; BNM 9067, no. 11; Junta 3, f. 75ff.; Junta 57; and RAH, V4. Guillín, *Leyendas*, I, 181-224, transcribed it on the basis of BNM 5313, f. 134-181v.
42. Gil, *Colección*, 46-51.
43. Ibid., 51.
44. *Rrekontamiyento muy buweno ke kontesiyo a partida de unos sabiyos ṣāliḥes* (BNM 5313, f. 66-76, transcribed by Guillén, *Leyendas*, I, 267-280).
45. *Rrekontamiyento de Tamīm al-Āddar* (BNM 4953, f. 100v-128r = Hegyi, *Edición*, 90-117, and Guillén, *Leyendas*, II, 97-127). On the Arabic version of the story, see Basset, "Aventures."
46. Except for one occasion in which Muḥammad is pictured to have smashed the idols with his sword.
47. Transcribed by Guillén, *Leyendas*, II, 159-166.
48. *Este es el relato del l-annabī Muḥammad kon el rrey Ḥabīb (RAH T18, f. 1-4 =* Guillén, Leyendas, II, 259-265).
49. *Este es el alḥadīth del al'arabī i la donzella* (BNM 4953, f. 128v-140r = Hegyi, *Edición*, 118-129, and Guillén, *Leyendas*, II, 217-230).
50. Arabic wisdom sayings in the form of aphorisms and proverbs formed an important part of Arabic belles/lettres (*adab*). This is also the case for medieval Spanish

literature as attested by the *Libro de Alixandre, Libro de los buenos proverbios, Libro de los doce sabios*, and others.

51. *Libro de las mil y doscientas sentencias de Muḥammad* (BNM 5354, f. 1-85. Cf. Junta 8, nos. 13, 16, 18, 20, and 23).
52. See *GAL,* I, 418, and S, I, 584. 'Abdallah al-Quḍā'ī was an Eastern scholar who wrote several works, among which is the *Kitāb al-shihāb (Book of the Stars*), which contains *The One Thousand and Two Hundred Sayings of the Messenger of God (Alf wa-mi'atā kalimah min ḥadīth rasūl Allāh).*
53. BNM 5354, f. 3v.
54. Ibid.
55. Ibid.
56. Ibid., f. 4r.
57. Ibid.
58. Ibid.
59. Ibid. Most probably this is a rendition from the Arabic: *ra'su al-ḥikmati makhā fatu allāhi* (lit., the beginning of wisdom is the fear of God). Observe that *ra's* has the dual meaning of "head" and "beginning" and the Morisco translator used the calque *kabesa* for *ra's*.
60. Ibid., f. 4v. *Sayṭān* (devil) is a arabism.
61. Ibid.
62. Ibid., 5r. *Jahannam* (Hell) is an arabism.
63. Ibid. *Jāhiles* (ignorant) is an arabism of *Jāhil*, pl. *jāhilūn*. It is relevant to note that the Moriscos disregarded the Arabic plural formation and simply added an *s* to the Arabic singular for the formation of the plural as is often the case for Spanish.
64. Ibid. *Azine* (adultery) is an arabism of *al-zinā'.*
65. *Ibid., f. 5v.*
66. *Ibid., f. 7v. Lajanna* is an arabism of *al-jannah* (Paradise).
67. Ibid. *Khalaqados* (created) is an arabism from the roots kh-l-q meaning "to create," on the basis of which the Moriscos formed the verb *khalaqar* and the participle *khalaqados*. This is one of many examples.
68. Ibid. Again *kabesa* is a calque of *ra's* meaning "head" or beginning.
69. Ibid., 8r.
70. Ibid. *El-wazir* is an arabism of *al-wazīr* (vizier).
71. Ibid.
72. Ibid., f. 71r.
73. Ibid.
74. *Libro i-taraslado de buwenas doktrinas i-kastighos i-buwenas kostumeres* (BNM 5267, 1ff.) that in part deals with acting "with science and knowledge" and the rewards accruing from glorifying God, acknowledging His unity, asking His forgiveness.
75. *Alkitāb de preicas i esemplos i doktrinas para medicinar al alma i amar otra vida i aborrecer este mundo* (Junta 53).
76. *Kastighos para las jentes* (Junta 8).
77. *Los kastighos de 'Alī* (RAH T13, f. 221v-233).
78. *Los kastighos de alḥakīm a su hijo* (BNM 5313, f. 51-60).
79. *Los kastighos de Dukama el-alḥakīm a su hijo* (BNM 4953, f. 72r–74r = Hegyi, *Edición*, 59–63). Dukama cannot be identified and may refer to Luqmān or other pre-Islamic legendary figure.

80. In fact, Luqmān appears in the Qur'ān (Chapter 31: 12–13) as a man whom God endowed with the gift of wisdom (*ḥikmah*) and as admonisher. Tha'ālibī, *Qiṣaṣ*, 312–315, says that he may have been an Israelite or a Black Nubian, who was a carpenter or tailor by trade, but endowed with wisdom. See *El* and Basset, *Loqman*.
81. BNM 4953, f. 72r.
82. Ibid.
83. Ibid., 73r.
84. Ibid., 73v.
85. Ibid., 74r.
86. Ibid.
87. Ibid., 74v.
88. Ibid., 75r.
89. Ibid., 75v.
90. Ibn al-Nadīm, *Fihrist*, 304–308.
91. A summary of *The Unique Necklace* appears in Chejne, *Muslim Spain*, 204–208.
92. Dozy, *Histoire,* I, 9ff.
93. Cf. Galmés, *Épica*, 18.
94. Hammer-Purgstall, "Chevalerie."
95. See Heller in the *EI* and 'Abd al-Badī', *Épica*, 52.
96. Canard, "Delhemma" and "principaus personnages."
97. 'Abd al-Badī', *Épica*, 43.
98. Galmés, *Épica*, 133f.
99. *Mío Cid*, verses 405ff; cf. Marcos, *Poesía*, 292.
100. See above, note 23ff.
101. Ribera, "Épica."
102. For the Arabic text, see Ibn 'Abd Rabbihi, *'Iqd*, IV, 501–572; Spanish translation in Marcos, *Poesía*, 107–137; and English translation by Monroe in *JAOS, 91 (1971), 67#95.*
103. *Ibn al-Nadīm, Fihrist*, 314. One may refer to Ibn 'Abd Rabbihi, *'Iqd*, I 99–179, who devotes a whole book to war, describing the warrior's qualities of perseverance, audacity, courage and others; he delves into the qualities of horses, their names, and description of weapons. Cf. Juan Manual, *Libro del caballero*, describing the art of chivalry.
104. Fares, *L'honneur*, 31ff.
105. Ibid., 72; cf. Marcos, *Poesía*, 249.
106. Galmés, *Épica,* 54ff., suggests that *Campeador* and *Mío Cid* are mere renditions from the Arabic *ghālib* and *sayyidi*, respectively.
107. Ibid., 21.
108. In the Aljamiado texts, 'Alī appears to owe his allegiance and loyalty to Muḥammad and is motivated by a strong commitment to Islam.
109. According to Galmés, *Épica*, 66, Roland's Durandal and Almace are renditions from the Arabic *dhu-l-andar* (possessor of brilliance) and *almās* (diamond), respectively.
110. Endowing a horse with a name was a common practice among pre-Islamic Arabs. Cf. Marcos, *Poesía*, 232.
111. This procedure is quite common in Aljamiado texts in which 'Ali always appears to have engaged his equal first and the rank and file of the army afterward. Cf. above, note 32.

112. Cf. Marcos, *Poesía*, 263.
113. Craftiness and deceit in combating the enemy do not appear to constitute blameworthy qualities and are found in both Arabic, Spanish, and Aljamiado. Cf. Galmés, *Épica*, 68ff. Ibn 'Abd Rabbihi, *'Iqd*, I, 127, cites a prophetic tradition that says: "War is deceit (khud'ah)." He adds that the Prophet himself would appear to adopt one strategem while intending to follow another.
114. Galmés, *Épica*, 90ff.
115. Ibid., 98ff.
116. Cervantes, *Don Quijote*, chapter I, 23.
117. Ibid., chapter 2, 28.
118. Ibid.
119. Ibid., chapter III.
120. For more details and bibliographical data on these works, see Alborg, *Historia*, 150ff, Cf. Chejne, *Muslim Spain*, 407 ff., and "Role." See bibliography under *Libro*. In a recent work, Lacarra, *Cuentística,* gives ample details to the presence of *Kalīlah wa-Dimnah*, the *Sindbar*, and *Barlaam* in such medieval Spanish works.

9. MORISCO POETRY

1. *Zajal* (Sp. zejél) is essentially a strophic composition in colloquial Arabic starting ordinarily with a refrain and ending with the same, or something rhyming with it, which is called *kharjah*. For a full description of the structure of *zajal* and its kindred *muwashshaḥ*, which is written in classical Arabic, see Chejne, *Muslim Spain*, chapter XIII.
2. Cf. Saavedra, *Discurso*, 183ff.
3. For a general view of classical poetry, see Chejne, *Muslim Spain*, chapter XII.
4. BNM 247 = Morf, *Poema*, RAH T12 = Menéndez Pidal, *Poema*. Cf. Ticknor, *Historia,* IV, 422ff.; and Saavedra, *Discurso*, 162.
5. *Almadha de alabandsa al-annabi Muḥammad* (Escorial, 1880, f. 16–30) which is a translaiton from Arabic into Aljamiado consisting of seventy-one coplas. See Miller, *Drei Morisco Gedichte*. Cf. *Estas son las loblas del annabī Muḥammad* (Junta 13, f. 188r-192r and 244v–249r = Kontzi, *Aljamiado*, II, 679–699). Also, Junta 9, f. 16ff.
6. *Alabansa ada Allāh* (Escorial, 1880, f. 37vff.). *Koblas as Allah* (Junta 37, f. 272–275); and *Una suplica a Allāh* (RAH T7, no. 1).
7. *Coplas in alabansa del adīn del alislām i del annabī Muḥammad* (Junta 52, f. 375ff).
8. *Poesía pidiendo misericordia por la intercesion de todos los profetas* (Escorial, 1880, 40ff.) consisting of fifteen couplets and published by Müller, *Drei Morisco Gedichte.*
9. *El poema alburda* (BNM 5377), consisting of sixteen folios.
10. BNM 9067, no. 1; which also contains *Un romance contra la religion cristiana*, no. 20; and another romance by Juan Alfonso, no. 23, f. 205r–208v, which is reproduced by Cardaillac, *Morisques et Chrétiens*, 480–483, who also has another romance by the same author (BNM 9067, 212r–215v = 484–488). These romances are written in Latin script.
11. *Coronica y relation de la esclarecida descendencia Sharifa* (BUB D565, f. 1ff.).
12. *Comentacion sobre un tratado que conpuso Ibrāhīm de Bulfad* (BNM 9653),

written in Latin script.

13. BNM 9067; cf. above, note 10.
14. *Discorso de la luz y descendencia y linaje claro de nuestro caudillo y bien aventurado anabī Muḥammad (British Museum, Harl. 7501), which consists of 351 folios and thirty cantos written in Latin script. See Morgan, Mahometism*; Stanley, "Poetry"; and Ticknor, *Historia*, IV, 275, which contains some excerpts.
15. Gayangos, "Language," 83.
16. The so-called manuscript B refers to BNM 247 and manuscript A to RAH T12. Cf. above, note 4.
17. Morf, *Poema*, believes that ms. B was written in the fifteenth century while Menéndez Pidal, *Poema*, places part of ms. A in the fourteenth century and the remainder in the sixteenth century.
18. *Rrekontamiyento de Jakob i de su fijo Yūsuf* (BNM 5292). CF. Guillén, *Leyenda de José*.
19. Galmés, "Interés literario," 199.
20. Alḥadīth de Yūsuf (RAH T12, f. 1 = Mendéz Pidal, *Poema*, 15–16).
21. Poem A (RAH T12) is incomplete and concludes with Joseph's relation with Zulaykhah. For the whole story, see the prose version in BNM 5292 = Guillén, *Leyenda de José*, of which Gayangos, "Language," 85–90, gives and excellent summary.
22. *Koblas del annabī Muḥammad* (Junta 1882–188v = Kontzi, *Aljamiado*, II 679–681). Cf. Manzanares, "Textos."
23. Ibid., f. 246r–246v. = 691–692. Cf. Junta 9 = Manzanares, "Textos," 315–316. It must be observed that the whole refrain: "Yā habībī, yā Muḥammad/ wa alṣṣalatu 'alā Muḥammad" is in Arabic and is repeated after each couplets according to the best tradition of *Zajal* or *muwashshaḥ*.
24. *Alabansa ada Allāh* (Escorial, 1880, 36v–38v = Kontzi, Aljamiado, II, 766–767). Cf. Müller, *Drei Morisco Gedichte*, 238–242.
25. *Coplas en alabansa del adīn del alislām i del annabī Muḥammad* (Junta 52, f. 575–578v and Junta 17, f. 272–276 = Manzanares, Textos").
26. BUB D565; cf. above, note 11, and Saavedra, *Discurso*, 287–288.
27. Saavedra, *Discurso*, 168, and Galmés, "Interés literario," 200–201.
28. BNM 9653, f. 66. Cf. Saavedra, *Discurso*, 169, and Galmés, "Interés literario," 201.
29. BNM 9653, f. 234r. Cf. Saavedra, *Discurso*, 169, and Galmés, "Interés literario," 201.
30. BNM 9653, f. 12.
31. Mainly, BNM 9067; BNM 9653; BNM 9655; and RAH S2. Cf. Cardaillac, *Morisques et Chrétiens*, 184.
32. As quoted by Saavedra, *Discurso*, 170–171.
33. BNM 9067, f. 205r–208v = Cardaillac, *Morisques et Chrétiens*, 480–483.
34. BNM 9067, f. 212r–215 = Cardaillac, *Morisques et Chrétiens*, 484–488.
35. Saavedra, *Discurso*, 171, quotes the first part of the poem.
36. BNM 9654, f. 10r = Saavedra, *Discurso*, 172, and Cardaillac, *Morisques et Chrétiens*, 181.
37. Gayangos, "Language," 92.
38. See chapter VI, notes 19ff. Also note 14.
39. See chapter V, notes 75ff. and 117ff.

40. See chapter IV, note 61.
41. As quoted by Saavedra, *Discurso,* 173.
42. Ibid., 176.
43. Ibid., 178.
44. Ibid., 179.
45. Ibid, 180.
46. Gil, *Colección*, 89–90 (Junta 13, f. 179–219). Cf. Pano y Ruata, *Coplas*.

List of Abbreviations

AHDE.	*Anuario de Historia del Derecho Español*
AHN.	*Archivo Kistórico Nacional*
AHR.	*American Historical Review*
AIC.	*Archivo Inquisitorial de Cuenca*
AR.	*Archivum Romanicum*
BAE.	*Biblioteca de Autores Españoles*
BAH.	*Biblioteca Arábico-Hispana*
BAS.	*Bibliotheca Arabo-Sicula*
BCB.	*Biblioteca Central de Barcelona*
BEA.	*Bulletin des études arabes* (Algiers)
BELOV.	*Bibliothèque de l'École des langues Orientales Vivantes*
BEO.	*Bulletin d'études orientales*
BH.	*Bulletin Hispanique*
BHS.	*Bulletin of Hispanic Studies*
BNM.	*Biblioteca Nacional de Madrid*
BNP.	*Bibliothèque Nationale de Paris*
BPT.	*Biblioteca Provincial de Toledo*

BRABl.	*Boletín de la Real Academia de Buenas Letras de Barcelona*
BRAE.	*Boletín de la Real Academia Española*
BRAH.	*Boletín de la Real Academia de Historia*
BUB.	*Biblioteca de la Universidad de Bolonia*
BUG.	*Boletín de la Universidad de Granada*
Byzantium.	*Byzantium.*
Casiri.	M. Casiri, *Biblioteca Arabico-Hispana Escurialensis*
CEM.	*Cuadernos de Estudios Medievales*
CHE.	*Cuadernos de Historia de la medicina española*
CT.	*Cahiers de Tunis*
EI.	*Encyclopedia of Islam*
CAI.	C. Brockelmann, *Geschichte der arabischen Literatur*
HR.	*Hispanic Review*
JA.	*Journal asiatique*
JAOS.	*Journal of the American Oriental Society*
IJMES.	*International Journal of Middle Eastern Studies*
JNES.	*Journal of Near Eastern Studies*
JRAS.	*Journal of the Royal Asiatic Society*
Junta.	J. Ribera, et al., *Manuscritos árabes y aljamiados de la Biblioteca de la Junta*
MAO.	*Mélanges africans et orientaux.*
MCV.	*Mélanges de la Casa de Velázquez.*
MEAH.	*Miscelánea de Estudios Árabes y Hebraicos*
MHE.	*Memorial Históric Español*
MO.	*Le Monde Oriental*
MRAH.	*Memorias de la Real Academia de la Historia*
MW.	*Muslim World*
NBAE.	*Nueva Biblioteca de Autores Españoles*
OE.	*Obras Escogidas de Historia y Filolgía árabe*
PIHEM.	*Publications de L'Institut de Hautes Études Marrocaines*
PR.	*Palacio Real*
RABM.	*Revista de Archivos, Bibliotecas y Museos*
RAH.	*Real Academia de Histori*
RCEH.	*Revista del Centro de Estudios Históricos de Granada y Su Reino*
RDTP.	*Revista de Dialectología y Tradiciones Populares*
RE.	*Revista de España*
REI.	*Revue des Études Islamiques*
RFE.	*Revista de Filología Española*
RH.	*Revue Hispanique*
RIEEI.	*Revista del Instituto Egipcio de Estudios Islámicos*
RIEI.	*Revista del Instituto de Estudios Islámicos*
RO.	*Revista de Occidente*
RT.	*Revue Tunisienne*
RPh.	*Romance Philology*
SEI.	*A Shorter Encyclopedia of Islam*
SI.	*Studia Islamica*
ZDMG.	*Zeitschrift der Deutschen Morgenländischen Geselschaft*

Bibliography

‘Abd al-Badī‘, L. *La épica árabe y su influencia en la épica castellana*. Santiago (Chile), 1954.

‘Abd al-Bāqī, M. F. *Mu‘jam al-mufahras li-alfāz al-Qur’ān al-karīm*. Cairo, A.H. 1378.

Abd el-Jalil, J. M. *Marie et l’Islam*. Paris, 1949.

Abdulwahab, H. H. “Coup d’oeil général sur les apports ethniques étrangers en Tunisie.” *RT*, 24(1917),305-316 and 371-373.

Actas del coloquio internacional sobre literatura aljamiado y morisca, Madrid, 1978.

Aguilar, Gaspar. *Expulsiónde los moros de España por la S. C. R. Magestad del Rey don Felipe Tercero*. Valencia, 1610.

Ajo G. y Sainz de Zuñiga, C. M. *Historia de las universidades Hispánicas*. Madrid, 1967.

Alborg, J. L. *Historia de la literatura española*. 2d ed. Madrid, 1970.

Alcalá, Pedro de. *Arte para ligeramente saber la lengua ar*ábiga. Granada, 1505.

______. *Vocabulista arábigo en letra castellana*. Granada, 1505.

Alcalá Veceslada, A. *Vocabulario andaluz*. Andujar, 1933.

Alcántara Godoy, J. *Historia de los falsos cronicones*. Madrid, 1868.

Alfonso, Pedro. *Disciplina Clericalis*, ed. A. Gonzáles Palencia. Madrid, 1948.

Alfonso X (el sabio). *Antología de Alfonso X el sabio*, ed. A.G. Solalinde, 4th ed.

Madrid, 1960.

______. *Primera crónica general de España*, ed. V. J. Filgueira. Madrid, 1949.

Alguazir, Muh. *Apología contra los artículos de la ley cristiana* (BNM 9074).

Alfonso, Juan. BNM 9067 and B NM 9655.

Alverny, Marie Thérèse D'. "Deux traductions latines du Coran au Moyen Age." *Archives d'histoire doctrinaire et littéraire de Moyen Age*, 23 (1948), 69-131.

Anawati, G. "Polémique, Apologie et Dialogue islamo-chrétien." *Euntes Docete*, 22 (1969), 375-452.

Andrés, Juan. *Opera chiamata confusione della seta machumetana.* Seville, 1537.

Arié, R. "Acerca del traje musulmán en España desde la caída de Granada hasta la expulsión de los moriscos." *RIEI*, 13 (1965), 103-117.

______. "Les études sur les morisques en Espagne a la lumière des travaux récents." *REI, vol. 35 (1967), 225-229.*

______. "Remarques sur l'alimentation des musulmans d'Espagne au cour de bas Moyen Âge." *CEM* 35. (1974-75), 299-312.

Armstead, S. C. "Existió un romancero de tradición oral entre los moriscos?" *Actas del coloquio*, 211-232.

Arocena González, D. *El manuscrito aljamiado 9067 de la Biblioteca Nacional de Madrid.* Las Palmas (n. d.)

Asín Palacios, M. *Abenházam de Córdoba y su historia crítica de las religiones.* 5 vols., Madrid, 1928-1932.

______. "El original árabe de la novela aljamiada, El baño de Zarieb'. In *Homenaje de Men*éndez Pidal, Madrid, 1924, I: 378-388.

______. "La polémica anticristiana de Muhammad AlCaise." *OE* (Madrid, 1948), 295-319; also in *RH*, 21(1909), 339-361.

______. "Un tratado morisco de polémica contra los judíos." *OE*, 245-275.

Ayala, Martin de. *Catechism para instrucción de los nuevamente convertidos de los moros.* Valencia, 1599.

______. *Doctrina christiana en lingua aráviga y castellana.* Valencia, 1566.

______. Les instructions e ordinations per als novament convertits del regne de Valencia festes per les autoritats apostolica y real M. de A. archebispe de Valencia ha manat se guarden en est archepispat de Valencia. Valencia, 1566.

Aznar, Jeronimo. *Expulsión justificada de los moriscos españoles.* Zaragoza, 1612.

Aznar Cardona, Pedro. *Expulsión justificada de los moriscos españoles y suma de las excelencias christianas de nuestro Rey D. Felipe el Cathólico Tercero deste nombre.* Huesca, 1612.

Bacon, R. *Opus Majus*, ed. J. H. Bridges. London, 1900.

Bakrī, Abū 'Ubaydallah al-. *Jughrāfiyat al-Andalus wa-Urubbā.* E. 'Abd al-Raḥmān al-Ḥajjī. Beirut, 1968.

Bakrī, Aḥmad Ibn Muḥ. *Kitāb al-anwār (Libro de las luces).* BNM 4995; PR 3225, and RAH T-17 and TAH T18.

Basset, Renê, ed. "Les aventures merveilleuses de Temim el-Dāri." *Giornale della societa Asiatica Italiana* 5 (1891), 3-26.

______. *Loqmān Berbère.* Paris, 1890.

Bataillon, M. "Les nouveaux Chrètiens de Segovie en 1510." *BH* 58 (1956), 208-231.

______. "L'arabe a Salamanque au temp de la Renaissance." *Hespéris* 21 (1935), 1-17.

Bauer y Landauer, I. *Relaciones y manuscritos (moriscos).* Madrid (n. d.)

Bautista Vilar, J. "Los moriscos de la gobernación y obispado de Orihuela." *Al-Andalus* 43 (1978), 323-368.

Bermudez de Pedraza, F. *Antiguèdad y excelencia de Granada.* Madrid, 1908.
______. *Historia eclesiástica de la ciudad de Granada.* Granada, 1638.
Bernis, C. "Modas moriscas de la sociedad cristiana española del siglo XV y principio del XVI." *BRAH*, 144 (1959), 199-228.
Bleda, B. J. *Crónica de los moros de España.* Valencia, 1618.
______. *Defensio fidei in causa neophytorum, sive Morischorum Regni Valentiae.* Valencia, 1610.
Bofarull y Mascaro, P. d. *Colección de documentos inéditos del archivo general de la Corona de Aragón.* 41 vols. Barcelona, 1847-1920.
Bolfad, Ibrāhīm de. BNM 9653.
Boronat y Barrachina, P. *Los moriscos españoles y su expulsión.* 2 vols. Valencia, 1901.
______. *El beato Juan de Ribera y el colegio de Corpus Cristi.* Valencia, 1904.
Bosch Vila, J. *"Dos nuevos manuscritos y papeles sueltos de moriscos aragoneses." Al-Andalus* 32 (1957), 463-470.
______. "Escrituras oscenses en aljamía hebraico árabe." In *Homenaje a Millás* Vallicrosa. Barcelona, 1954, I: 183-214.
______. "Los documentos árabes del archivo catedral de Huesca." *RIEI* 5 (1957), 1-48.
Braudel, F. "Conflicts et refus de civilisation; espagnols et morisques au XVI siècle." *Annales, Economies, Societés Civilisations* 2 (1947), 397-410.
______. "Les espagnols et l'Afrique du Nord de 1492 à 1577." *Revue Africaine* 49 (1968), 184-233 and 351-428.
______. *La Mediterranéen a l'êpoque de Philippe II.* Paris, 1949.
______. *La Mediterranée et le monde mediterranéen* a l'*époque de Philippe II.* Paris, 1949.
Brockelmann, C. *Geschichte der arabischen Literatur.* 2 vols. and 3 suppls. Weimar and Leiden, 1898-1942.
Burns, R. *The Crusader Kingdom of Valencia.* Princeton, 1975.
______. *Islam and the Crusaders: Colonial Survival in Thirteenth Century Valencia.* Princeton, 1973.
______. *Medieval Colonialism.* Princeton, 1975.
______. "Social Riots on the Christian-Moslem Frontiers (Thirteenth-Century Valencia)." *AHR* 66 (1961), 378-400.
Cabanelas Rodríguez, D. "Cartas del morisco granadino Miguel de Luna." *MEAH* 14/15 (1965-66), 31-47.
______. "Juan de Segovia y el primer Alcorán trilingue." *Al-Andalus*, 14 (1949), 149-174.
______. *Juan de Segovia y el problema islámico.* Madrid, 1952.
______. *El morisco granadino Alonso del Castillo.* Granada, 1965.
______. "Proyecto de alianza entre los sultanes de Marruecos y Turquía contra Felipe II." *MEAH* vol. 6 (1957), 57-76.
Cabezudo Astrain, J. "Noticias y documentos sobre los moriscos aragoneses." *MEAH* 5 (1956), 105-118.
______. "Los conversos aragoneses." *Sefarad*, 18 (1959), 272-282.
Cabrera de Cordoba, L. *Felipe secundo, rey de España.* 4 vols. Madrid, 1876-1877.
Cabrillana Ciezar, N. "Esclavos moriscos en la Almería del siglo XVI." *Al-Andalus* 40 (1975), 53-128.
Cagigas, I. de las. "Una carta aljamiada granadina." *Arabica* 1 (1954), 271-275.
______. *Los mozárabes.* Madrid, 1947.
______. *Los mudèjares.* 2 vols. Madrid, 1948-49.

______. "Problemas de minoría y el caso de nuestro medievo." *Hispania* 10 (1950), 506-538.

Canard, M. "Delhemma, épopée arabe des guerres arabo-byzantines." *Byzantium* 10 (1935), 283-300.

______. "Delhemma, Sayyid Battal et Omar al-No'man." *Byzantium* 12 (1937), 183-188.

______. "Les principaux personnages du roman de chevelarie arabe Dat al-Himma. wa-l-Baṭṭāl." *Arabica* 7 (1965), 158-173.

Cantarino, V. *Entre monjes y musulmanes. El conflicto que fué España.* Madrid, 1978.

Cantineau, Jean. "Lettre du moufti d'Oran aux Musulmans d'Andalousie." *JA* 210 (1927), 1-17.

Cardaillac, Denise. *La polémique anti-chrétienne du manuscript no. 4944 de BNM.* 2 vols. Montepellier, 1972.

______. "Algunos problemas linguísticos." *Actas del coloquio*, 413-422.

Cardaillac, Louis. "Un aspecto de relaciones entre moriscos y cristianos: polémica y taqiyya." *Actas del Coloquio*, 107-122.

______. "Morisques en Provence." *Les Langues Romanes* 79 (1971), 297-316.

______. *Morisques et Chrêtiens. Un affrontment polèmique (1492-1640).* Paris, 1977.

______. "Morisques et Protestants." *Al-Andalus* 36 (1971), 29-63.

______. *Le passage des Morisques en Languedoc.* Montepelleir, 1970.

______. "Le probleme Morisque en Amérique." *MCV* vol. 10 (1976), 283-306.

Cardoner, A. "Seis mujeres hebreas practicando la medicina en el reino de Aragón." *Sefarad* 9 (1949), 441-445.

Caro Baroja, J. *Los Moriscos del Reino de Granada.* Madrid, 1957.

______. "Los Moriscos aragoneses según un autor de comienzo del siglo XVII." *Razas, Pueblos y Linajes.* Madrid, 1957, 81-96.

______. *Vidas mágicas e Inquisición.* 2 vols. Madrid, 1962.

Carrasco Urgoiti, M. S. *El moro de granada en la literatura del siglo XV al XVIII. Madrid, 1956.*

______. *El problema morisco en Aragón al comienzo del reinado de Felipe II.* Valencia, 1969.

Casiri, M. *Bibliotheca Arabico-Hispana Escurialensis.* 2 vols. Madrid, 1760-1770.

Castaneda, V. "Manifestaciones de los hijos de moriscos que quedaron en Onteniente." *BRAH* 82 (1923), 421-427.

Castillo, Alonso del. *Inscriptions of the Alhambra. Letters.* and *Catalogue of the Escorial Arabic manuscripts.*

Castro, Américo. *España en su historia: Cristianos, moros y judíos.* Buenos Aires, 1948.

______. *La realidad histórica de España.* 6th ed. Mexico, 1975.

Cervantes S. M. *Don Quijote.* Madrid, 1967.

______. *El coloquio de los perros.* Madrid, 1952.

Chanson de Roland.

Chaplyn, M. A. *Le Roman mauresque en France.* Paris, 1928.

Chejne, A. *The Arabic Language: Its Role in History.* Minneapolis, 1969.

______. *Ibn Hazm of Cordova and His Conception of the Sciences.* Chicago, 1982.

______. "Islamization and Arabization in al-Andalus." In *Islam and Cultural Change in the Middle Ages.* Wiesbaden, 1975, 59-86.

______. *Muslim Spain: Its History and Culture.* Minneapolis, 1974.

______. "The Role of al-Andalus in the Transmission of Ideas." In *Islam and the Medieval West*, Albany, 1980, 110-133.

______. *Plegaria bilingué arabe-aljamiado de un morisco* (in press).

Cirac Estopinan, S. *Los procesos de hechicería en la Inquisiciín de Castilla la Nueva (Tribunales de toledo y Cuenca).* Madrid, 1942.

______. *Registro de los documentos del Santo Oficio de Cuenca y Sigúenza.* Cuenca-Barcelona, 1965.

Circourt, Comte de. *Histoire de Maures, Mudéjares et Morisques.* 3 vols. Paris, 1845-1848.

Cirot, Georges. "La maurophilie littéraire en Espagne au XVI eme siecle." *BH* 40 (1938-44), 150-157 and 46 (1944), 5-25.

Codera F. "Almacén de un librero morisco descubierto en Almonacid de La Sierra." *BRAH* 5 (1884), 269-276.

Colbert, E. P. *The Martyrs of Cordova (850-859).* Washington, 1962.

Colin, Georges. "Projet de traité entre les morisques de la Casba de Rabat e le roi d'Espagne en 1631." *Hespéris* 42 (1955), 17-25.

Colonge, Chantal. "Reflet littéraire de la question morisque entre la guerre des Alpujarras et l'expulsion." *BRABLB* 33 (1969-70), 137-243.

Corominas, J. *Diccionario crítico de la lengua castellana.* 4 vols. Madrid-Berna, 1954-1957.

Corral y Rojas, Antonio de. *Relación de la rebelión y expulsión de los moriscos del reyno de Valencia.* Valladolid, 1613.

Coseriu, E. *Arabismos o Romanismos?* Montevideo, 1961.

Credilla, C. P. "Ceremonias de moros que hacen los moriscos." *RABM* 1874, 165-169.

Cueva, Luis de la. *Diálogos de las casas notables de Granada.* Seville, 1603.

Cutler, A. "Who was the Monk of France and When Did He Write." *Al-Andalus* 28 (1963), 249-270.

Daniel, N. *The Arabs and Medieval Europe.* London, 1975.

______. *Islam and the West: The Making of an Image.* Edinburgh, 1966.

Dante, A. *La divina comedia.* Span. trans. A. Aranda. Sanjuan-Barcelona, 1958.

Dánvila y Collado, M. "Ajuar de una morisca de Teruel en 1583." *BRAH* 6(1885), 410-439.

______. "Desarme de los moriscos en 1563." *BRAH* 10(1887), 275-306.

______. *La expulsión de los moriscos españoles.* Madrid, 1889.

Derenbourg, H. et al. *Manuscripts arabes de l'Escurial.* 3 vols. Paris, 1884-1941.

Deny, J. "Les pseudo-propheties concernant les Turks au XVI siecle." *REI* 10 (1936), 201-220.

De Sousa. *Vestigios de la lingua arabica en Portugal.* Lisbon, 1789.

Dioscorides. *Materia Medica.*

Documents relatifs a la guerre de Grenade. ed. R. Foulché-Delbose *RH* 31 (1914), 486-523.

Dollfus, L. "Morisques et chrétiens de 1492 a 1570." *Revue d'Histoire des Religions* 20(1889).

Domínguez Ortiz, A. "Algunos documentos sobre Moriscos granadinos." *Miscelánea de Estudios dedicados al profesor Antonio Marin Ocete.* Granada, 1974, I: 247-254.

______. "Los cristianos nuevos." *BUG* 21 (1949), 249-297.

______. "Felipe IV y los moriscos." *MEAH* 7 (1959), 55-65.

______. "Los moriscos granadinos antes su definitiva expulsión." *MEAH* 12/13 (1963-64), 113-129.

______. "Notas para una sociología de los moriscos españoles." *MEAH* 11 (1962),

39-54.
______. *Política y hacienda de Felipe IV*. Madrid, 1960.
______. and B. Vincent. *Historia de los moriscos*. Madrid, 1978.
Dozy, R. *Histoire des musulmans d'Espagne jusqu'à la conquête de l'Andalousie par les Almoravides, ed. E.* Lévi-provencal. 2d. ed. 3 vols. Leiden, 1932.
______. *Supplement aux dictionnaries arabes*. 2 vols. Leiden, 1881.
______. and H. W. Englemann. *Glossaire des mots espagnols et portugais dérives de l'arabe*. Leiden, 1869.
Dressendorfer, P. *Islam unter der Inquisition; die Morisco-prozesse in Toledo 1575-1610*. Wiesbaden, 1971.
______. "Crypto-musulmanes en la Inquisición de la Nueva España." *Actas del coloquio*, 447-473.
Dunlop, D. M. *Arabic Science in the West*. Karachi, 1958.
Eguilaz, D. L. de. *Glosario etimológico de las palabras españolas de origen oriental*. Granada, 1886.
Encyclopedia of Islam (EI).
Epalza, M. de. "Moriscos y andalusíes en Tunez durante el sigl XVII." *Al-Andalus* 34 (1969), 247-327.
______. "Notes pour une histoire des polémiques antichrétienne dans l'occident musulman." *Arabica* 18 (1971), 99-105.
______. "Recherches récentes sur les emigrations des 'Moriscos' en Tunisie." *CT* 18 (1970), 139-147.
______. "Sobre un posible autor español del Evangelio de Bernabe." *Al-Andalus* 28 (1963), 479-481.
______. "Trabajos actuales sobre la comunidad de moriscos refugiados en Tunis desde el siglo XVII a nuestros días." *Actas del coloquio*, 427-444.
______. *La Tuḥfa, autobiografía y polémica islámica contra el cristianismo de 'Abdállah al-Tarjuman (Fray Anselmo Turmeda)*. Rome, 1971.
______. and R. Petit. *Études sur les moriscos andalous en Tunisie*. Madrid-Tunis, 1974.
Escolano, Diego. *Memorial a la Reina N. S. cerca de las muertes que en odio de la fé y religion christiana dieron los moriscos*. Granada, 1671.
Estebanez Calderón, S. *Discurso. Seminario pintoresco español* 46 (1848).
Fahd, Toufic. *La divination arabe*. Leiden, 1966.
Fares, Bichr. *L'honneur chez les arabes avant l'Islam*. Paris, 1932.
Fernández y González, F. *Estado social y político de los mudéjares de Castilla*. Madrid, 1866.
______. *La influencia de las lenguas y literaturas orientales en la nuestra*. Madrid, 1894.
______. "De los moriscos que permanecieron en España despues de la expulsión." *RE* 19 (1871), 103-114 and 20 (1871), 363-376.
Fernández y González, M. *Los monfíes de las Alpujarras*. Madrid, 1856.
Fernández Guerra, A. *Reflexiones sobre la rebelión de los moriscos y censo de población*. Granada, 1840.
Floriano, L. "Algunos problemas del lexíco jurídico en la literatura aljamiado-morisca." *Actas del coloquio*, 373-397.
Fonseca, Damián. *Justa expulsión de los moriscos de España, con la instrucción, apostasía y traición dellos*. Rome, 1611.
Ford, R. *A Handbook for Travellers in Spain*. 2d ed. London, 1847.
Foulché-Delbose, R. "Memorial de Francisco Nunez Muley." *RH* (1899), 205-239.
Fradejas, J. "Musulmanes y moriscos en el teatro de Calderón." *Tamuda* 5 (1967),

185-228.

Fuster, Joan. *Poetas, Moriscos y Curas*. Madrid, 1969.

Gallego y Burín, A. and Gamir Sandoval. *Los moriscos del reino de Granada según el sínodo de Guadíx de 1554,* ed. D. Cabanelas Rodriguez Granada, 1968.

Galmés de Fuentes, A. *Colección de literature española aljamiado-Morisco*. Madrid, 1970.

______. *Épica árabe y épica castellana*. Barcelona, 1978.

______. *Historia de los amores de Paris y Viana*. Madrid, 1970.

______. "Influencia del árabe en la prosa medieval española." *BRAE* 35/36 (1955-56).

______. *Influencias sintácticas y estilísticas del 'arabe en la prosa medieval castellana.* Madrid, 1956.

______. "Interés en el orden linguístico de la literatura española aljamiado-morisca." *Actes du X congres International de Linguistique et Philologie Romanes.* Paris, 1965.

______. "Interés literario de los escritos aljamiado-moriscos." *Actas del coloquio,* 189-208.

______. *El libro de la batallas.* 2 vols. Madrid, 1975.

Gamir Sandoval, A. *Organización de la defensa de la costa del Reino de Granada desde su reconquista hasta finales del siglo XVI.* Granada, 1947.

García-Arenal, M. "Los censos de moriscos de 1589 a 1594 establecids por el tribunal de la Inquisición de Cuenca." *Hispania*, (1978).

______. *Inquisición y moriscos. Los procesos del Tribunal de Cuenca.* Madrid, 1978.

______. *Los Moriscos.* Madrid, 1975.

García Ballester, L. *Historia social de la medicina en la España de los siglos XIII al XVI.* Madrid, 1976.

______. *Medicina, ciencia y minorías marginadas: Los Moriscos.* Madrid, 1977.

______. and J. López Pinero. "Galenismo arabizado y humanismo en la España renacentista." *CHME*, 15 1976.

García Carcel, R. *Orígenes de la Inquisición spañola. El Tribunal de Valencia 1478-1530.* Barcelona, 1976.

______. "La revuelta morisca del Espadan." *Al-Andalus* 41 (1976), 121-146.

García Gómez, E. *Un Texto arabe occidental de la leyenda de Alejandro*. Madrid, 1929.

García Martínez, S. "Bandolerismo, piratería y control de los moriscos en Valencia durante el reinado de Felipe II." *Estudis* Vol. 1 1972, 85-167.

Garrad, K. *The Causes of the Second Rebellion of the Alpujarras* (1568–1571). Ph.D. dissertation, 1955.

______."La Inquisición y los moriscos granadinos." *BH 67 (1965), 63#77.*

______. "The Original Memorial of Don Francisco Núñez Muley." *Atlante* 2 (1954), 198–226.

Garrido Atienza, M. *Capitulaciones para la entrega de Granada.* Granada, 1910.

______. "Los moriscos granadinos. Agúeros, hechizos, encantamientos y otros maleficios." *La Alhambra* 2 (1889), 349–350.

Gaspar Remiro, M. *Granada en poder de los católicos (1492–94).* Granada, 1912.

______. *Últimos pactos y correspondiencias entre los reyes católicos y Boabdil sobre la entrega de Granada.* Granada, 1910.

Gautier-Dolché, J. "Des mudéjares aux morisques." *Hespéris* 45 (1958), 271–289.

Gayangos, Pascual de. "Glosario de las palabras aljamiadas y otras que se hallan en dos tratados y en algunos libros de moriscos." *MHE* 5 (1853), 423-449.

______. "Language and Literature of the Moriscos." *British and Foreign Review* 8

(1839), 63–95.
______. *Leyes de Moros. MHE* 5 (1853), 11–246.
______. *Suma de los principales madamientos y devedamientos de la ley yçunna. MHE* 5(1853), 247–422. Cf. Jābir.
______. "Sumario e recopilación de todo lo romançado por el licenciado Alonso del Castillo." *MHE* 3 (1852).
Gil, Pablo. "Los manuscritos aljamiados de mi colección." *Homenaje a don Francisco Codera.* Zaragoza, 1904, 537–549.
______. and et al. *Colección de textos aljamiados.* Zaragoza, 1888.
Giner, Fr. "Cervantes y los moriscos valencianos." *Anales del Centro de Cultura valenciana,* 962, 131–149.
Gómez del Campillo. *Catálogo de las causas contra la fé* seguidas ante el tribunal del Santo Oficio de la Inquisició*2n de Toldeo.* Madrid, 1903.
González Palencia, A. "Cervantes y los moriscos." *BRAE 27 (1947#48), 107#122.*
______. *"El curandero morisco del siglo XVI, Rom*án Ramírez." *Leyendas e Historias,* 1942, 215–284.
______. "Las fuentes de la comedia 'Quién mal anda mad acaba de Juan Ruíz de Alarcón'." *BRAE* 16 (1929), 199–222 and 10 (1930), 247–274.
______. *Moros y cristianos en España medieval.* Madrid, 1945.
______. "Noticias y extractos de algunos manuscritos árabes y aljamiados de Toledos y Madrid." *Miscelénea de Estudios y Textos árabes.* Madrid, 1915, 117–145.
Granja, F. de la. *La cocina araábigo-andaluza según un manuscrito inédito.* Madrid, 1960.
______. "Fiestas cristianas en al-Andalus." *Alandalus* 34 (1949), 1–53.
______. "Milagros españoles en una obra de polémica musulmana." *Al-Andalus* 33 (1968), 311–365.
Guadalajara y Javier, M. *Memorable expulsión y justísimo destierro de los moriscos de España.* Pamplona, 1613.
______. *Prodición y destierro de los moriscos de Castilla hasta el valle de Ricote.* Pamplona, 1614.
Guillén Robles, F. *Catálogo de los manuscritos árabes existentes en la Biblioteca Nacional de Madrid.* Madrid, 1889.
______. *Leyenda de José y de Alejandro Magno.* Zaragoza, 1888.
______. *Leyendas moriscos.* 3 vols. Madrid, 1885–86.
Ḥajji Khaliifah. *Kashf al-ẓunūn*, ed. G. Flügel. 7 vols. Leipzig-London, 1835–1856.
Halperin Donghi, T. "Un conflicto nacional: moriscos y cristianos viejos en Valencia." *CHE* 24 (1955), 5–155 and 26 (1957), 83–250.
Hammer-Purgstall, J.B. "La chevaléria des arabes, antérieure á celle de l'Europe." *JA 4a ser. 13, 8#10.*
Harvey, L.P. "Aljamiado" in *EI.*
______. "Crypto-Islam in Sixteenth Century Spain." *Actas,* Madrid, 1964, 163–178.
______. *The Literary Culture of the Moriscos (1492–1609).* Ph.D. dissertation, Oxford University, 1958.
______. "El mancebo de Arévalo y la literatura aljamiada." *Actas del Coloquio,* 21–41.
______. "Un manuscrito aljamiado en la biblioteca de la Universidad de Cambridge." *Al-Andalus* 23 (1958), 49–74.
______. *The Moriscos and Don Quijote.* London, 1974.
______. "A morisco manuscript in the Godolphin Collection at Zatham College, Oxford." *Al-Andalus* 27 (1962), 461–465.

______. "Yusé Banegas un moro noble de Granada bajo los Reyes Católicos." *Al-Andalus* 21 (1956), 297-302. BNM 245.

al-Hāshimī, 'Abdallah. *Risālat 'Abdallah Ibn Ismā'īl al-Hāshimī ilā 'Abd al-Misīḥ Ibn Isḥāq al-Kindī wa-risālat al-Kindī ilā al-Hāshimī*. Cairo, 1912.

Haskins, C.H. *Studies in the History of Medieval Science. 2d. ed. Cambridge, Mass., 1927.*

Hayek, Michel. le Christ de l'Islam. Paris, 1959.

______. Le mystére *d'Ismaël.* Paris, 1964.

Hegyi, Ottmar. *Edición y estudio del manuscrito aljamiado no. 4953 de la Bibloteca Nacional de Madrid.* Ph.D. dissertation, University of Toronto, 1969. Madrid, 1981.

______. "Observaciones sobre el Léxico árabe en los textos aljamiados." *Al-Andalus* 43 (1978), 303-322.

______. "El uso del alfabeto árabe por minorías musulmanas." *Actas del coloquio,* 147-163.

Heller, B. "Sīrat 'Antar." in *EI.*

Hess, A.C. *The Forgotten Frontier. A History of the Sixteenth Century Ibero-African Frontier.* Chicago, 1978.

______. "The Moriscos: An Ottoman Fifth Column in Sixteenth-Century Spain." *IAHR* 74 (1968), 1-25.

Hitos, Francisco. *Martīres de la Alpujarra en la rebelió*n de los moriscos. Madrid, 1935.

Hitti, P.K. *Islam and the West.* Princeton, 1962.

Hoenerbach, Wilhelm. "Los moriscos a la luz de sus documentos." *Actas del coloquio,* 49-69.

______. *Spanish islamischen Urkunden aus der Zeit der Nasriden und Moriscos.* Los Angeles, 1965.

Hurtado de Mendoza, D. *Guerra de Granada hecha por el rey de Espaã don Felipe II. BAE,* 21, 1946, 65-122.

Ibn al-Abbār. *al-Ḥullas al-siyarā',* ed. H. Mu'nis. 2 vols., Cairo, 1963.

Ibn 'Abd Rabbihi. *al-'Iqd al-farīd,* ed. A. Amīn et al. 7 vols. Cauto, 1948-1953.

Ibn 'Ajurrūm. *al-'Ajurrūmiyyah.* Cairo (n.d.)

Ibn Ḥazm. *al-Fisal fī-l-milal wa-l-niḥal.* Cairo, A.H. 1347-1348. Spanish translation M. Asīn palacios. 5 vols. Madrid, 1927-1932.

______. *Marātib al-'ulūm in Rasā'il Ibn Ḥazm,* ed. I. 'Abbās. Cairo, 1952; and Chejme, in *Ibn Ḥazm.*

______. *al-Radd 'alā Ibn Naghrīlah,* ed. I. 'Abbās. Cairo, 1960.

______. Ṭawq al-ḥamāah, ed. D.K. Petrof, Leiden, 1914.

Ibn Hishām. *Sīrat Rasūl Allāh.* Cairo (n.d.)

Ibn jallāb. *kitāb al-tafrī' fī-l-fiqh* (*Tafria,* Junta 33, BPT 336 and BNM 4870).

Ibn Khaldūn. *Al-Muqaddimah.* English trans. F. Rosenthal. 3 vols. New york, 1958.

Ibn al-Khaṭīb. *A 'māl al-a'lām,* ed. L. Lévi-Provençal. Rabat, 1934.

Ibn Munqidh, U. *An Arab Syrian Gentleman and Warrior.* English trans. P.K. Hitti. New York, 1929.

Ibn al-Nadīm. *Al-Fihrist,* ed. G. Flügel. Leipzig, 1871-1872.

Ibn Sīnā. *al-Qānūn fī-l-ṭibb.*

Ibn Zuhr. *Taysīr.*

Jābir, 'Isā. *Brevario Sunni* in *MHE* 5 (1853), 247-422 (Cf. Gayangos; BNM 2076, BNM 6016; Junta 1 and Junta 60).

Janer, F. *Condición social de los moriscos.* Madrid, 1857.

Jean Leon de Granada. *Diccionario árabe español* (Escorial, 598).

Johnson, Wm. W. *The Poema de José. A Transcription and Comparison of Extant Manuscripts*. University of Mississippi, 1974.

kamen, H. *The Spanish Inquisition*. New York, 1965.

al-Khazrajī, A. *Kitāb maqāmi' al-ṣulbān* (Cf. Granjas in Al-Andalus 33 (1968), 311-365.

Klenk, U. *"La Leyenda de Yūsuf" ein Aljamiadotext.Zeitschrift fur romanische Philologie*. Tübingen, 1972.

______. "El 'tasdīd' en la 'Leyenda de Yūsuf'." *Actas del coloquio*, 399-412.

Kontzi, von Reinhold. *Aljamiado Texte*. 2 vols. Wiesbaden, 1974.

______. "Aspectos del estudio de textos aljamiados." *Thesaurus*, 25 (1970), 3-20.

______. "Calcos semánticos en textos aljamiados." *Actas del coloquio*, 315-335.

Kritzeck, James. *Peter The Venerable*. Princeton, 1964.

Labarta, A. "Los libros de los moriscos valencianos." *Awraq* 2 (1979), 72-80.

Labib, Gisela. *Der Maure in dem dramatischen Werk Lope de Vega*. Hamburg, 1961.

______. "El papel de la literatura aljamiado en la transmisión de algunos aspectos estructurales de la lengua árabe sobre el aragonés." *Actas del coloquio*, 337-359.

______. "spanish Lautentwicklung un arabisch-islamischen-Geist in einem Aljamiado-Manuskipt des 16 Jarhunderts." (Ms. 5301 der Biblioteca Nacional de madrid). *Vox Romana* 26 (1967), 37-107.

Lacarra, María J. *Cuentistica medieval en España*. Zaragoza, (n.d.)

Ladero Quesada, M.A. *Granada, historia de un paiís isliíco*. Madrid, 1969.

______. *Los Mudéjares de Castilla en tiempo de Isabel I.* Villadolid, 1969.

Lapesa, R. *Historia de la lengua española*. 6th ed. New York, 1965.

Lapeyre, Henri. *Géographie de l'Espagne morisque*. Paris, 1959.

La Riguardia, E. *Histoire de persecutions religiouses d'Espagne: Juifs, Mores et protestants*. Paris, 1860.

Latham, J.D. "Towards a Study of Andalusion Immigration and Its Place in Tunisian History." *CT* vol. 5, 1957, 203-252.

Latrie, Le Comte de Mas. *Relations et commerce de l'Afrique septentrionale au Magreb avec les nations chrétiénne au Moyen Age*. Paris, 1886.

Lea, Charles H. *A History of the Inquisition of Spain*. 4 vols. New York, 1906-07.

______. *The Moriscos of Spain*. London, 1901.

Leclerc, J. *Histoire de la tolérance au siécle de la Reforme*. Paris, 1955.

Libro de Alexandre, ed. R.S. Willis, Princeton, 1934.

Libro de buenos proverbios. Attributed to Greek, Latin and Arab philosophers and attributed to Ḥunayn Ibn Isḥāq.

Libro del caballero et del escudero.

Libro del cavallero Zifar, ed. Ch. Philip Wagner, Ann Arbor, 1929.

Libro de cien capitulos, ed. A. Rey. Bloomingron, 1960.

Libro del consejo y de los consejeros. Zaragoza, 1962.

Libro de los doce sabios, ed. J.K. Walsh in *BRAE* 29 (1975).

Libro de los engaños et los asaymiento de las mugeres (Sindbar), ed. J.E. Keller. Chapel Hill, N.C., 1953.

Libro de los estados (Juan Manuel), ed. R.B. Tate. Oxford, 1974.

Libro de los exemplos.

Libro de flores de filosofiía, ed. H. Knust in *Dos Obras didacticas y do leyendas*. Madrid, 1878.

Libro de los gatos

Libro infinido (by Juan Manuel), ed. J.M. Blecua. Granada, 1952.

Libro de Kalīlah wa-Dimnah, ed. J.E. Keller and R. White Linker. Madrid, 1967.

Libro del secreto de los secretos (Poridat de proidades), ed. H. Knust in *Dos obras didacticas y doy leyendas*. Madrid, 1878.

Libro del Sindbar (cf. *Libro de los engaños*).

Lincoln, Joseph N. "Aljamiado Prophecies." *PMLA* 52 (1937), 631–644.

______. "Aljamiado Texts, legal and Religious," *HR* 13 (1945), 102–124.

______. "An Itinerary for Morisco Refugees from Sixteenth-Century Spain." *Geographic Review* 29 (1939), 483–487.

Llorente, J.A. *Historia criitica de la inquisición de España*. Barcelona, 1835.

Longás, Pedro. *Vida religiosa de los moriscos*. Madrid, 1915.

Lópes, David. *Textos en aljamía portuguesa*. Lisbon, 1897.

López-Baralt, L. "Cronica de la destrucción de un mundo: la literatura Aljamiada-Morisca." *BH* 87 (1980), 16–58.

López Lillo, C. "Transcripción y notas a un manuscrito morsco del Corán." (Ms. 18, Junta). M.A. thesis, University of Barcelona, 1966.

López Marínez, C. *Mudéjares y moriscos sevillanos*. Seville, 1935.

López-Morillas, C. "Etimologías escodias del Corán aljamiado (Ms. 4938 BNM)." *Actas del coloquio*, 365–371.

Loupias, Bernard. "La pratique secrète de l'Islam dans les évechés de Cuenca et de Sigüenza en XVI et XVII siècles." *Hespéris* 6 (1965), 115–132.

Luna, Miquel de. *Historia verdadera del Rey don Rodrigo en la cual se trata de la causa principal de la pérdida de España*. Granada, 1592–1600. English trans. under the title of *The Hisotyr of the Conquest of Spain by the Moors*. London, 1687.

Lydgate, J. *Fall of Princes*, ed. first name Bergen. Washington, 1923.

Macho y Ortega, F. *Condición social de los mudéjares aragoneses*. Zaragoza, 1923.

Makki, Maḥmud A. *Ensayo sobre las aprotaciones orientales en la España musulmana*. Madrid, 1968.

Malinowski, B. *Magic, Science and Religion and Other Essays*. New York, 1955.

Mālik Ibn Anas. *Muwaṭṭa'*. Cairo, A. H. 1349.

Mancebo de Arévalo. BNM 245; *Tafsira* (Junta 47; Junta 62 and Junta 73).

Manuel, Juan. *El Conde Lucanor*. 4th ed. Madrid, 1968.

______. *Libro del caballero et del escudero*.

Manzanares de Cirre, M. "El capítulo de racontaciones del Libro de Samarkandi." *Actas del coloquio*, 237-257.

______. "Dos manuscritos aljamiados inéditos. *Modern Philology* 62(1964-65), 130-136.

______. "El otro mundo en la literatura aljamiado-morisca." *HR* 41(1973), 599-608.

______. "Notas sobre la aljamía." *Anuario de Estudios Medievales* 5(1968), 479-483.

______. "Textos aljamiados- poesía religiosa morisca." *BH* 72(1970), 323-372.

Maqqarii. *Nafḥal-ṭīb*, ed. I. 'Abbās. 8 vols. Beirut, 1968.

Marcais, Georges. "Testour et sa grande mosquéée. Contribution a l'étude des Andalous en Tunisie." *RT* vol. (1942), 147-169.

March, José M. "Sobre la conversión de los moros del reino de Granada. Nuevos documentos." *Razón y Fé* 79(1927), 338-348.

Marcos Marin. F. *Poesía narrativa árabe y* épica hispán*ica*. Madrid, 1971.

Mármol Carvajal, Luis del. *Historia del rebelión y castigo de los moriscos del Reyno de Granada*. 2 vols. Madrid, 1797, and *BAE* (1946)

Martínez Ruíz, J. "Escritura bilingue en el reino de Granada (siglo XVI) según

documento inédito del Archivo dela Alhambra. *Actas del primer Congreso Internacional de de Hispanistas* (Oxford, 1964), 371-374.
______. "Almohadas y calzados moriscos." *RDTP* 23 (1967), 289-313.
______. "Fuentes inéditas del léxico-hispano-árabe." *RFE* 48(1965), 421-435.
______. *Inventario de los bienes moriscos del reino de Granada (siglo XVI)*. Madrid, 1972.
______. "Léxico de origen árabe en documentos del siglo XVI." *RFE* 48(1965), 121-133.
______. "Un nuevo texto aljamiado: el recetario de Sahumarios en uno de los manuscritos árabes de Ocana." *RDTP* 30 (1974), 3-19.
______. "Siete cartas de dote y arras del Archivo de la Alhambra (1546-1609)." *RDTP* 22 (1966), 41-72.
______. and J. Albarracín. *Libros árabes, aljamiado-mudéjares y bilingues descubiertos en Ocana.* Toledo, 1969.
Marty, P. "Folkore tunisien: l'onomastique des noms propres de personne." *REI* 10 (1936), 363-434.
Mas, A. *Les Turks dans la littérature espagnole de Siecle d Or.* 2 vols. Paris, 1967.
Mas'ūdī. *Murūj al-dhahab.* Cairo, 1948.
Matteo, Ignacio di. *Un codice espagnolo inedito de secolo XVII di Ibrāhīm Taylibī.* Palermo, 1912.
______. *La divinitá di Cristo e la dottrina della trinitá in Maometto e nei polemisti musulmani.* Rome, 1938.
______. "Il taḥrīf ad alterazione della Biblia secondo i musulmani." *Bessarione* 21 (1922), 64-111 and 223-260.
Mekinassi, A. *Léxico de las palabras espanolas de origen árabe.* Tetuan, 1963.
Mendoza, Diego de. *Historia de Granada. BAE*, vol. 21. Madrid, 1852.
Mendoza y Bobadilla. *El tizón de la nobleza española y sambenitos de sus linajes.* Barcelona, 1880.
Menéndez y Pelayo, M. *Historia de los heteredoxos españoles.* 7 vols. Madrid, 1933.
Menéndez Pidal, R. *Poema de Yūsuf.* Granada, 1952; also in *RABM*, 8 (1902).
Meneses García, E. *Correspondencia del Conde de Tendilla (1508–1513).* 2 vols. Madrid, 1973.
Merchan Fernández, A. *Los Judíos de Valladolid.* Valladolid, 1976.
Michaud, H. *Jésus selón le Corán.* Neuchatal, 1960.
Michel, Francisque. *Histoire des races maudites de la France et de l'Espagne.* Paris, 1847.
Mieli, A. *La science arabe et son role dans l'évolution scientifique mondiale.* Leiden, 1966.
Millás Vallicrosa, L. "Albaranes mallorquines en aljamiado—hebraico-árabe." *Sefarad* 4 (144), 275-286.
______. *Estudios sobre la historia de la ciencia española.* Barcelona, 1949.
Monés, H. "Asnā'-l-matājir fī bayān aḥkām man ghalaba 'alā waṭanih al-naṣārah wa-lam yuhājir." *RIEEIM* 5 (1975), 129-191.
Monneret de Villard, U. *Lo studio dell'Islam in Europa nel XII e XIII secolo.* Vatican, 1944.
Monroe, James. "A Curious Morisco Appeal to the Ottoman Empire." *Al-Andalus* 31 (1966), 281-303.
______. *Islam and the Arabs in Spanish Scholarship.* Leiden, 1970.
Moraleda Alvārez, L. "Edición de un manuscrito del Corn." (Junta 25). M. A. thesis, University of Barcelona, 1965.

Morf,H. "Poema de José." *Gratulationschrisft der Universitat Bern.* Leizig, 1883.
Morgan, J. *Mahometism Fully Explained.* London, 1723,
Moubarak, Y. *Abraham dans le Coran.* Paris, 1958.
Müller, M. J. "Drei Morisco Gedichte." *Sitzungberichte der Kongl. Bayerischen Academie der Wissenchaften zu Munchen* 1860, 201-253.
Munoz y Gaviria, J. *Historia del alzamiento de los moriscos, su expulsión de España y sus consecuencias en todas las provincias.* Madrid, 1861.
Munzer, J. *Viaje por España y Portugal, 1944-1495.* Trans. J. Lopez Toro. Madrid, 1951.
Neuvonen, E. K. *Los arabismos del español en el siglo XIII.* Helsinki, 1941.
Núnez Muley, Fr. (See Garrad).
Nykl, A. R. "El rrekontamiento de Alisandre." *RH* 77 (1929), 409-611.
______. *Hispano-Arabic Poetry.* Baltimore, 1946.
Oliver Asín, J. "Un morisco de Túnes, admirador de Lope." *Al-Andalus* 1 (1933), 413-418.
______. "Origen árabe de rebato, arrobda y sus homónimos." *BRAE* 15 (1928), 347-395 and 496-542.
______. *El Quijote de 1604.* Madrid, 1948.
Palenco Romero, J. *Aben-Humeya en la historia y en la leyenda.* Granada, 1915.
Pano y Ruata, Mariano de. *Coplas del peregrino de Puey Moncon viaje a la Meca en el siglo XVI.* Zaragoza, 1897.
______. "Recontamiento de Almiced y /Almayesa." *Homenaje a don F. Codera.* Madrid, 1904, 35-50.
Pareja, Félix M. "Un relato morisco sobre la vida de Jesús y María." *Estudios Eclesiásticos* 34 (1960), 859-871.
Paret, Rudi. *Die legendare Maghāzi-Literatur.* Tubingen, 1930.
Parrinder, G. *Jesus in the Qur'ān.* London, 1965.
Paz, Ramón. *Papeles de Inquisición.* Madrid, 1947.
Pelorson, Jean M. "Recherches sur la comedia Los moriscos de Hornachos'." *BH* 74 (1972), 5-42.
Penella Roma, J. *Los moriscos españoles emigrados al norte de Africa después de la expulsión.* Ph. D. dissertation, University of Barcelona, 1971.
______. "El sentimiento religioso de los moriscos españoles emigrads." *Actas del coloquio*, 447-473.
Pedregal y Fantini, J. *Estado social y cultura de los mozárabes y mudéjares españoles.* Seville, 1878.
Pérez Bustamante, C. "El pontífice Paulo V y la expulsión de los moriscos. "*BRAH* 129 (1951), 219-233.
Pérez de Chinchón, B. *Libro llamado antialcorán, que quiere dezir contra el alcorán de Mahoma.* Valencia, 1932.
Pérez de Culla, Vicente. *Expulsión de los moriscos rebeldes de la Sierra y Muela de Cortes.* Valencia, 1965.
Pérez de Hita, Ginés. *Guerras civiles de Granada.* Cuenca, 1619 and *BAE*, vol. 3, Madrid, 1944.
Phillips, Carla Rahn. "The Moriscos de la Mancha 1570-1614." *The Journal of Modern History* (Abstracts) 50 (1978), D1067-D1095.
Pieri, H. "L'accueil par les Tunisiens aux morisques expulsés d'Espagne: un témoignage morisque." *Ibla* 118 (1968), 63-70.
Pignon, J. "Une géographie de l'Espagne morisque." *CT* 14 (1966), 286-300.

Pike, Ruth. "An Urban Minority: The Moriscos of Seville." *JMES* 2 (1971), 368-377.

Piles, L. *Aspectos sociales de las germanías de Valencia.* Madrid, 1952.

Pinta Llorente, M. de la. *La inquisición española y los problemas de la cultura e intolerancia.* Madrid, 1953.

Pita Merce, R. *Lérida morisca.* Lerida, 1977.

Planella, J. "Judíos y moriscos españoles." *Razón y Fé* 1 (1901), 496-506.

Pons Boigues, Fr. "La Inquisición y los moriscos de Valencia." *El Archivo* 2 (1887), 251-258 and 309-314.

Ponsot, P. "Les morisques, la culture irriguée du blé et le probleme de la décadence de l'agriculture espagnole au XVII siècle." *MCV* 7 (1971), 237-262.

Puey de Moncon. *Coplas* (See Pano y Ruata).

Qāḍī 'Iyāḍ. *Kitāb al-shifā' bi-ta'rīf ḥuqūq al-muṣtafā.*

al-Qaysī. BNM 4944 (cf. Asín, "Polémica").

al-Quḍā'ī, Abūh Muḥ. *Kitāb al-shihāb.* Baghdad (n. d.). (BNM 5354, Junta 29 and Junta 39).

Rabadan, Muḥ. Bristish Museum: Harl. 7501 (See Morgan).

Rāqilī, Muḥ. *Ta'yīd al-millah* (Gayangos 31; Asín, "Tratado.")

al-Rāzī. *al-Ḥāwī fī-l-ṭibb.*

Reglá, J. "La cuestión morisca y la coyuntura internacional en tiempo de Felipe II." *Estudios de Historia Moderna* 3 (1953), 217-234.

______. "La expulsión de los moriscos y sus consecuencias." *Hispania* vol. 109 (1953), 215-267 and 447-461.

______. *Estudios sobre los moriscos.* 3d. ed. Barcelona, 1974.

______. "Los moriscos: estado de la cuestión y nuevas aportaciones documentales." *Saibati* 10 (1960) (1960), 106ff.

Ribera, Juan de. *Instancias para la expulsión de los moriscos.* Barcelona, 1612.

Ribera, Julián. "Una colección de manuscritos árabes y aljamiados." in *Diser. y op.* I, 417-433.

______. *Disertaciones y opúsculos (Diser y Op.).* 2 vols. Madrid, 1928.

______. "La enseñanza entre los musulmanes españoles." *Diser.y Op.* I, 229-359.

______. "Épica andaluza romanceada." *Diser. y Op.* 93-150.

______. "Superticiones moriscas." *Diser. y Op.* I, 493-527.

______. "Vida religiosa de los moriscos. " BRAH 1918.

______. et al. *Manuscritos árabes y aljamiados en la biblioteca de la Junta.* Madrid, 1912.

Ribera Florit, J. M. *La polémica cristiano-musulmana en los sermones del maestro Inquisidor don Martín García.* Barcelona, 1967.

Ricard, Robert. "Les morisques et leur expulsion vue de Mexique." *BH* 33 (1931), 252-254.

Rincon, Juan del. *Buía de la salvación compuesto por Abdekarim Juan del Rincon pra uso de sus hermanos los muslimes.* (Cf. Gayangos, "Language," 79.)

Ripol, Juan *Diálogo de consuelo por la expulsión de los moriscos de España.* Pamplona, 1912.

Roca Traver. F. A. *Un siglo de vida mudéjar en la Valencia bajomedieval (1238-1338).* Zaragoza, 1952.

Rochau, A. L. *Die Moriscos in Spain.* Leipzig, 1853.

Rodríguez Rivero, A. "Un documento relativo al alzamiento de los moriscos, 1570." *Mauritania* 182 (1943), 22-24.

Rojas, J. L. *Relaciones de algunos sucesos célebres, nuevos y postreros de Berbería y salida de los moros de España*. Lisbon, 1613.

Romano, D. "Un texto en aljamía hebraico-árabe." *Sefarad* 29 (1969), 313-318.

Ron de la Estrada, C. "Manuscritos árabes en la Inquisición granadina, 1582." *Al-Andalus* 23 (1958), 210-211.

Ruíz, Juan. *Libro de buen amor,* ed. A. Zahareas and English trans. S. R. Daly. University Park and London, 1978.

Rull Villar, B. "La rebelión de los moriscos en la Sierra de Espandán y sus castillos." *Anales del Centro de Cultura Valenciana* 44 (1960), 54-71.

Saavedra, E. "El alhadiz del bano de Zarieb." *Mundo Ilustrado* 88 (1881).

______. *Discurso. MRAE* 6 (1889), 141-328.

______. "La historia de la ciudad de Alatón." *Revista Hispano Americana* 44 (1882).

______. "Historia de los amores de Paris y Viana." *Revista Historica* 22 (1867).

Ṣā'id of Toledo. *Ṭabaqāt al-uman*, ed. L. Cheikho, Beirut, 1912.

Ṣalvador, Emilia. "Sobre la emigración mudéjar a Berbería." *Estudis* 4 (1975), 39-68.

Samarqandī. *Kitāb tanbīh al-ghāfilīn*. Cairo, A. H. 1326 (*Elkitāb de Samarqandi*, BNM 4871).

Sanahuja, P. *Lérida en sus luchas por la fé. Judíos, moros conversos, inquisición, moriscos.* Lérida, 1946.

Sánchez Alvarez, M. "Algunos aspectos sobre los turcos en la literatura aljamiado-morisca." *Actas del coloquio,* 295-311.

Sánchez Montes, J. *Franceses, Protestantes, Turcos, Espanoles.* Madrid, 1951.

Sangrador y Vitores, M. *Memoria histórica sobre la expulsión de los moriscos de España en el reinado de Felipe III.* Valadolid, 1858.

Sanz, Manuel. *Tratado breve contra la secta Mahometana.* Seville, 1693.

Schiaparelli, C. *Literaturgeschichte der Araber, von ihrem Beginne bis zu Ende des swolften Jahrhunderts der Hidschret.* 7 vols. Vienna, 1850-1856.

Schipperges, H. *Die Assimilation der Medizin durch lateinische Mitteralter.* Wiesbaden, 1964.

Schwoebel, R. *The Shadow of the Crescent, the Renaissance Image of the Turks (1453-1517).* Nieuwkoop, 1967.

Seco de Lucena, L. "El título profesional de un médico del sigl XV." *MEAH* 3 (1954), 23-40.

______. *Documentos arábigo granadinos.* Madrid, 1961.

Semaen, K. I. ed. *Islam and the Medieval West.* Albany, N.Y. 1980.

Sicroff, A. *Les controverses de status de pureté de sang en Espagne au XVIème et XVIIème siècles.* Paris, 1960.

Simonet, Francisco. *El cardenal Jiménez de Cisneros y los manuscritos arábigo-granadinos.* Granada, 1885.

______. *Glosario de voces ibéricas y latinas usadas entre los mozárabes.* Madrid, 1888.

______. *Historia de los mozárabes de España.* Madrid, 1860.

Solá-Solé, J. M. "El artícuo 'al' en los arabismos del iberorománico." *RPh* 21 (1968).

______."Un texto aljamiado sobre la articulación de los signos hispano-árabes." *RPh* 24 (1970), 86-89.

Solomon (King). *Clavicula Salomonis*, ed. S. L. McGregor Mathers. London, 1899.

Soulah, M. *Une élegie andalouse sur la guerre de Grenade.* Algiers, 1914.

Southern, R. W. *Western Views of Islam in the Middle Ages.* Cambridge, Mass., 1962.

Spivakosky, Erika. "Un episodio de la guerra contra los moriscos." *Hispania*, vol. 126 (1971), 399-431.

Stanley, H. E. J. "The Poetry of Mohamed Rabadan." *JRAS*, vol. page 5 (1867-1872).

Steiger, A. *Contribución a la fonética del hispano-árabe y de los arabismos en el ibero-románico y el siciliano.* Madrid, 1932.

______. *Origin and Spread of Oriental Words in European Languages.* New York, 1963.

Steinschneider, M. *Die hebraischen uebersetzungen des Mittelalters.* Berlin, 1893.

______. *Polemische und apologetische Literatur in arabischen Sprache.* Leipzig, 1877.

Súarez, Pedro. *Historia del Obispado de Guadix y Baza.* Madrid, 1696.

Súarez Pinera, R. "Días fastos y nefastos en las creencias de los muslimes." *Actas del coloquio,* 165-185.

Suyutī. *AP-Raḥmah fī-l-ṭibb wa-l-ḥikmah.* Cairo (n. d.).

Swinburne, H. *Travels Through Spain in the Years 1775-1776.* London, 1779.

Ṭaylibī, Ibrāhīm. RBC 1976 (See Matteo,*Codice).*

Ṫemimi, A. "Une lettre des morisques de grenade au Sultan Suleimān al-kānūnī en 1541." *Revue d'Histoire Maghrebine* 3 (1975), 100-105.

Teres, E. "El dictionario español latino-arábigo del P. Canes." *Al-Andalus* 21 (1956), 255-276.

al-Tha'ālibī. *Qiṣaṣ alj-anbiyā'.* Cairo (Cairo, n. d.).

Thorndike, L. *A History of Magic and Experimental Science.* 8 vols. New York-London, 1964.

Ticknor, George. *History of Spanish Literature.* ed ed. Boston, 1866. Spanish trans., Madrid, 1856.

Torres Balbás, L. *Algunos aspectos del mudejarismo urbano medieval.* Madrid, 1954.

Torres Fontes, J. "El alcalde mayor de los aljamas de moros en Castilla." *AHDE* 1962, 131-182.

______. "Moros, judíos y conversos en la regencia de don Fernando de Anteguera." *CHE* 31/32 (1960), 60-97.

______. "Los mudéjares murcianos en el siglo XIII." *Murgetana* 17 (1961), 59-90.

Torres Morera. *Repoblación del reino de Valencia después de la expulsión.* Valencia, 1969.

Townsend, J. *A Journey Through Spain in the Years 1786-1787.* London, 1792.

Trend, J. B. *The Language and History of Spain.* London, 1953.

Turben Ville, A. S. *The Spanish Inquisition.* London, 1932.

Turmeda, Fray Anselmo. *Tuḥfah* (See Epalza, *Tuḥfa*).

Ubieto Arteta. "Procesos de la Inquisición de Aragón." *RABM* 67 (1959), 549-559.

Valencia, P.de. *Tratado acerca de los moriscos de España* (BNM 8.888).

Valera, Cipriano de. *Los dos tratados del papa y de la misa.* Madrid, 1851.

Verdu, Fray Blas. *Engaños y desengaños del tiempo con un discurso de la expulsión de los moriscos de España.* Barcelona, 1612.

Vernet, Juan. *Astrología y astronomía en el renacimiento. La revolución copérnicana.* Barcelona, 1974.

______. *La cultura hispano-árabe en Oriente y Occidente.* Barcelona, 1978.

______. "La exégesis musulmana tradicional en los coranes aljamiados." *Actas del coloquio,* 123-144.

______. *Literatura árabe.* 3d. ed. Barcelona, 1972.

______. "Traducciones moriscas del corán." *Der Orient in der Forschung, Festschrift fur Otto Spies.* Wiesbaden, 1967, 686-705.

______. and L. Moraleda. "Un Alcorán fragmentario en aljamiado." *BRABBL* 33 (1969-1970), 43-75.

Vespertino Rodríguez, A. "Las figuras de Jesús y María en la literatura aljamiado-morisca." *Actas del coloquio,* 259-292.

Villanueva Rico, C. *Habices de las mezquitas de la ciudad de Granada.* Madrid, 1961.
Vincent, B. "L'albaicin de Grenade au XVIème siècle." *MCV* 7 (1971), 187-222.
———. "Les bandits morisques en Andalousie au XVIème siècle." *Revue d'Histoire Moderne et Contemporaine* 21 (1974), 389-400.
———. "Combien de morisques ont été expulsé du royaume de Grenade." *MCV* 8 (1971), 397-399.
———. "La expulsion des morisques du royaume de Grenade et leur repartition en Castille." *MCV* 6 (1970), 210-246.
———. "Les morisques d'Extremadure au XVIème siècle." *Annales de Démographie Historique*, 1974, 431-448.
Vinas Mey, C. *El problema de la tierra en España en los siglos XVI y XVII.* Madrid, 1941.
Waltz, J. "Significance of the Voluntary Martyrs of Ninth Century Cordova." *MW* 1970.
Weiditz, C. *Das Trachtenbuch des Christoph Weiditz von seinen Reisen nach Spanien (1529) und den Niederlanden* (1531/32), ed. T. Hampe. Berlin-Leipzig, 1927.
al-Zajjāj. *Taqrīb.*
Zapata, S. *Expulsión de los moriscos rebeldes de la Sierra y y Muela de Cortes.* Valencia, 1635.
Zbiss, S. M. *Présence espagnole a tunis,* 1969.
Zettersteen, K. V. "Ein Handbuch der religiosen Pflichten der Mohammedaner in Aljamia." *MO* 15 (1921), 1-174.
———. "Notice sur un ritual musulman en langue espagnole en caracteres arabes et latin." *Centenario della nascitá di Michele Amari*, I, 277-291.
———. "Some Chapters of the Coran in Spanish Transliteration." *MO* 5 (1911), 39-41.

ALJAMIADO MANUSCRIPTS

Aljamiado manuscripts are, for the most part, described by Saavedra, *Discurso*; Guillén Robles, *Catálogo*; Ribera et. al., *Manuscritos*; and González Palencia, "Noticias." Most manuscripts are multiple consisting of various items and lack titles. They are listed here as to their content insofar as they are mentioned in the text. Reference to editions or transliterations is given in abbreviated form after each item. Titles are given for the most part in modern Spanish spelling.

BCB. Biblioteca Central de Barcelona

BCB 680. Consists of miscellanea: bilingual invocations and traditions; a portion of which was edited and transliterated by Chejne, *Plegaria.*

BM. British Museum

BM: Harlow 7501 (Saavedra 68; cf. Morgan, *Mahometism*; Stanley, "Poetry." BNP 8162).

BNM. Biblioteca Nacional de Madrid.

BNM 245 = Saavedra 13. *Sumario de la relación y ejercicio espiritual por el Mancebo de Arévalo.* Also, Junta 73.
BNM 2076 = Saavedra 2. *Brevario Sunni.* Also, BNM 6016; Junta 1; RAH MS 3.
BNM 4238 = Saavedra 48. *Miscelánea de papeles sueltos.*
BNM 4870 = Saavedra 11. *Alkitāb de la tafria* por Abū-l-Qāsim 'U aydallāh Ibn

al-Ḥusayn Ibn Shihā. Also, González Palencia, "Noticias," 8; Junta 33.

BNM 4871 = Saavedra 10. *Kitāb al-Samarqandi.* Also Junta 6.

BNM 4907 = Saavedra 34. *Fragmentos* (Qur'ānic chapters in Arabic and Aljamiado).

BNM 4908 = Saavedra 24. *Documentos y fragmentos varios aljamiados, Castellanos y árabes.* (Hoenerbach, *Urkunden,* 180-193, 203-226, and 377-384).

BNM 4934. *Documentos varios en latín, árabe, Catellano y lemosin.*

BNM 4937 = Saavedra 20. *Memoria de los cuartos del ano.*

BNM 4938 = Saavedra 22. *Alcorán abreviado.*

BNM 4944 = Saavedra 23. *Disputa contra loss judíos y disputa contra los cristianos.* Photocopy and transliteration of folios 36r-100v by D. Cardaillac, *Polémique;* and transliteration of folios 36r-59 by Kontzi, *Aljamiado,* II, 777-789.

BNM 4953 = Saavedra 21. *Alhadīl Ibn Sarjūn* (castigos de 'Umar, Dukama, Luqman; rey Tabi'a; Tamīm al-Addār; el árabe y la doncella). Transliterated by O. Hegyi, *Edición.*

BNM 4955 = Saavedra 27. *Kitāb al-anwār (libro de las luces).* Transliterated, Kontzi, *Aljamiado,* II, 799-838. Cf. González Palencia, "Noticias," 9.

BNM 4897. *Tratado jurídico.*

BNM 5043 = Saavedra 12. *Papel suelto* (contains a letter to a religious scholar).

BNM 5052. *Inventario de los bienes matrimoniales de dona mayor Alváez.*

BNM 5053 = Saavedra 37. *Recontamiento que recontó el-annabí Muḥammad cuando subió a los cielos y las maravillas que Allah le dió ver.* Transliterated Kontzi, *Aljamiado,* II, 839-876.

BNM 5073 = Saavedra 38. *Documentos varios en castellano, árabe y aljamía* (Litigation and contracts; Lincoln, "Aljamiado Texts"; Hoenerbach, *Urkunden,* 135-175, 236-258, 276-283, 318-325, and 334-342.

BNM 5078 = Saavedra 39. *Fragmentos de un alcorán abreviado.* Recetas (Hoenerbach, *Urkunden,* 368-370 and 375-376).

BNM 5081 = Saavedra 39. *Del Fablimiento del alcorán y del bien que se hace con el.*

BNM 5098. *Novelas árabes.*

BNM 5223 = Saavedra 36. *Miscelánea* (The Beautiful Names of God; prayers, lunar months, advices, Day of Judgment, etc.).

BNM 5223, 5346, 5377, 5378, 5384, 5385 and 5389. *Devocionario musulman.*

BNM 5228 = Saavedra 17. *Memoria a mi Miguel de Zeyne; Alcorán; oraciones,* etc.

BNM 5238. *Documentos en árabe y aljamía.*

BNM 5252 = Saavedra 26. *Tratado y declaración y guía para seguir y mantener el adin de alislam.* Transliterated Kontzi, *Aljamiado,* II, 877-886.

BNM 5254 = Saavedra 16. *Recontamientos del Rey Alixandre.* Transliterated, Nykl, *Aljamiado Literature.*

BNM 5267 = Saavedra 25. *Libro y traslado de buenas doctrinas y castigos y buenas costumbres.* Hoenerbach, *Urkunden,* 197-198 and 271-374.

BNM 5292 = Saavedra 47. *Recontamiento de Yacob y de su fijo* Yucof (Morf, *Poema*; Menéndez Pidal, *Poema*).

BNM 5300 = Saavedra 42. *Alkitāb de suertes.*

BNM 5301 = Saavedra 41. *Alhadīth de dos amigos* (Guillén, *Leyendas,* III, 307-317; Lincoln, "Aljamiado Texts"; Labib, "Spanish").

BNM 5302 = Saavedra 40. *La historia de 'Isā.*

BNM 5305 = Saavedra 45. *Alhadīth de Musa, 'Umar, 'Isa, Ayyūb, Sulaymān.* (Guillén, *Leyendas*).

BNM 5306. Soler Ali Ibn Muḥammad Ibn Muḥammad. *Brevario*. (Cf. Junta 1).

BNM 5313 = Saavedra 15. *Alcorán abreviado; los castigos del alḥakīm;* La docella Carcayona (Guillén, *Leyendas,* I, 181-224; cf. Junta 3, no. 2), etc.

BNM 5319 = Saavedra 18. *Comentario canónico moral de Abū Muḥammad 'Abdallah Ibn Abī Zayd.*

BNM 5337 = Saavedra 33. *Batallas de los primeros tiempos del islamismo.* Guillén, *Leyendas,* II, 145ff; Galmés, *Libro,* I.

BNM 5354 = Saavedra 44. *La Alfaḍīla de los alṣalaes; los nombres de las lunas.*

BNM 5373. *Libro de moriscos.*

BNM 5374 = Saavedra 49. *Prácticas religiosas musulmanas usadas entre los moriscos* (Ablution, prayer, fasting, etc.).

BNM 5377 = Saavedra 32. *El poema alburda; los siete alhaykales; oraciones, etc.*

BNM 5378 = Saavedra 29. *Miscelánea: tahlīl alcorán; los siete alhaykales; los treinta y siete lugares del alcorán en que se nombra la unidad de Alláh,* etc.

BNM 5380 = Saavedra 50. *Alhaykales y otros documentos moriscos* (manner of pronouncing the Arabic letters and the Beautiful Names of God).

BNM 5385 = Saavedra 31. *Los 37 lugares del alcorán donde se proclama la unidad de Dios; los nombres de Allāh; los siete alhaykales.*

BNM 5452 = Saavedra 35. *Documentos various* (Hoenerbacn, *Urkunden,* 199-202, 227-229, 326-333, and 352-253).

BNM 6016 = Saavedra 3. *Un memorial y sumario de los principales mandamientos* (In Latin script) by 'Isā de Jābir. Cf. Gayangos, *Suma*; BNM 2076; Junta 1 and Junta 55.

BNM 9067 = Saavedra 9. (In Latin script). *Explicación de téminos religiosos y legales; tratado de la doctrina Islámica según el rito de Mālik; resena sobre las principales herejías Islámicas; Historia de la doncella Caracyona; historia de un profeta y una profetisa; discusión contra la divinidad de Cristo; contra la Trinidad; la falsedad de la religion cristiana; y romances contra la religion cristiana por* Juan Alfonso (L. Cardaillac, *Morisques*, 481-488). Ed. Arocena, *Manuscrito.*

BNM 9074 = Saavedra 4. (In Latin script). *Apologia contra la ley cristiana* by Muḥammad Alguazir.

BNM 9534 = Saavedra 6. *Explicación de la ley Islámica.*

BNM 9653 = Saavedra 5. *Comentación sobre un tratado que compuso Ibrāhim de Bolfad.* (In Latin script).

BNM 9655 = Saavedra 8. (In Latin script). *Apología contra la la religion cristiana.*

BNM 9656 = Saavedra 7. *Artículos de la ley mahometana y explicación de ella en Castellano.*

BNP. Bibliotheque Nationale de Paris.

BNP 1844 = Saavedra 59. *Capítulos de alcorán y oraciones.*

BNP 774 = Saavedra 60. *Historia de la muerte del annabī; rogaria; oraciones; demandas de judíos; los cinco aṣalaes; messes y fiestas; escándalos; profecía de San Esidoro; profecía de Muḥammad sobre Espana* (Lincoln, "Aljamiado Prophecies").

BNP 263 = Saavedra 64. *Alfaḍīla del dīa de 'ashūra y del al-jum'ah; alḥadīth del annabī cuando puyó a los cielos; alsuṭbas; meses del ano.*

BNP 1163 = *Los escojidos días de la luna* (Súarez, "Días").

BNP 8162 = Saavedra 61. *Discurso de la luz* by Muḥammad Rabadan (BM: Harlow 7501).

BPT. Biblioteca Provincial de Toledo

BPT 1 = Saavedra 54. *Materia religiosa.*

BPT 7 = Saavedra 55. *Alkitāb de la tafria* (BNM 4870 and Junta 33).

BPT 9. *Kitāb al-anwār* by al-Bakrī (BNM 4955 and PR 3225).

BUB. Biblioteca de la Universidad de Bolonia.

BUB D565 = Saavedra 69. *Crónica y relación de la esclerecida descendencia Sharīfah, los que vinieron de 'Alī Ibn Abī Ṭālib.*

Escorial 1880 = Saavedra 53. *Aljuṭba de Ramaḍān; alabanza al anabi; alabanza ad Allāh;* Poesía (Muller, "Drei MoriscoGedichte"; Kontzi, *Aljamiado*, II, 765-776).

Junta. Manuscritos árabes y aljamiados en la biblioteca de la Junta (Ribera et al. *Manuscritos*).

Junta 1. *Brevario Sunni* de 'Isā de Jābir (BNM 2076; BNM 6016; RAH S3; cf. Gayangos, *Suma*).

Junta 3. *Capítulos del alcorán; casos de derecho* (Kontzi, *Aljamiado*, II, 347-667).

Junta 4. *Códice de miscelánea: el waṣīya de 'Alī; dīa de juicio; Mūsā con Allāh; aldu'a; aguado (wuḍū') aṣala; el waṣīyah del gran turco* (Sánchez, "Turcos"); *bano de Zarieb* (Saavedra, "Alhadiz").

Junta 6. *Kitāb al-Samarqandī* (BNM 4871).

Junta 8. *Castigos para las gentes; nacimiento de Muḥammad; Alḥadīth de Ibrāhīm; alḥadīth de Mūsā; alfadilas de laylat al-qadr; días del Ḥajj; la carta de la muerte; cuentos de los sabios; ventaja del pobre sobre el rico; derecho; tratado polémico contra los judíos; máximas morales.*

Junta 9. *Miscelānea: Nacimiento y genealogía del profeta; coplas (Muller); ascension de Muḥammad; muerte de Muḥammad; rituals; alḥadīth de Ibrāhīm* (Junta 8); *nacimiento de 'Īs; alfaḍilas de los meses; alḥadīth de Mūsā; libro de polémica.*

Junta 12. *Modo de leer el alcorán según Nāfi; el al-'ajurrimiyah; rituals.*

Junta 13. *Fé casos sobre materia religiosa; ejercicios caligráficos; rogativas; dichos del profeta; las coplas del annabī* (Kontzi, *Aljamiado*, II, 678-710); *coplas del alhijante de Puey Moncon* (Pano); *muerte del'annabī.*

Junta 18. *Azoras alcoránicas* (Vernet, "Coranes aljamiados").

Junta 20. *Miscelanea: oraciones y sermones.*

Junta 22. *Libro de dichos maravillosos* (recetas mágicas; formulas *y signos cabalísticos; amulets (Gil, Textos, 115ff.); conjuros; nombres mágicos*).

Junta 23. *Letanía para pedir agua.*

Junta 24. *Cuentas; oraciones; azoras alcoránicas; carta de la muerte; ventajas de los días de la semana.*

Junta 25. *Fragmentos de gramítica árabe; azoras alcoránicas; aljutbas;*

Junta 26. *Alkiīb questá en él el conto de Dhu-l-Qarnaya; sortilegios y pronó*sticos.

Junta 28. *Miscelánea: alzoras alcoránicas; preceptos religiosos; oraciones.*

Junta 29. *Kitāb al-shihāb* by Abū 'Abdallā Muḥammad Ibn Salam Ibn Ja'far Ibn 'Alī al-Quḍā'i (texto arabe con traducción aljamiada interlinear). Junta 39. Also BNM 5354.

Junta 30. *El alkitāb del rogar por agua.*

Junta 33. *El alkitāb de la tafria* (BNM 4870).

Junta 37. *Miscelánea: alḥadith de la calabera; alḥadīth del rey Muhalhal; fragment de gramática árabe; tratado de medicina; cuentos; coplas a Dios.*

Junta 39. *Miscelánea: Kitāb al-shihāb; azoras alcoránicas; ḥadīth* (bi-lingue).

Junta 40. *Miscelánea: Azoras alcoránicas; alḥadith de Mūsā.*
Junta 41. *Miscelánea: azoras alcoránicas; rogaria del agua* (Kontzi, *Aljamiado*, II, 712-716).
Junta 42. *Miscelánea: azoras alcoránicas; adu'a.*
Junta 43. *Miscelánea: Amuletos; alburda; futūḥ al-Andalus.*
Junta 44. *Miscelánea: Nombres de Allāh; los siete alhaykales; oraciones.*
Junta 47. *Comentario (Tafsira)* por el Mancebo de Arévalo. (BNM 245).
Junta 52. Traduccion del arabe- Coplas.
Junta 53. *Alkitab de preicas y ejemplos y doctrinas para medicinar el alma y amar la otra bida y aborrecer este mundo.*
Junta 55. *Devocionario musulman.*
Junta 56. *Devocionario musulman.*
Junta 59. *Recetas medicinales; talismanes* (Kontzi, *Aljamiado,* II, 718-748).
Junta 60. *Brevario Sunni de 'Isā de Jābir* (In Latin script; cf. Jābir).
Junta 62. *Tafsira del Mancebo de Arevalo* (cf. Mancebo).
Junta 64. *Dichos de Jesús; paraíso and diálogo con Jesús* (Kontzi, *Aljamiado,* II, 750-764).
Junta 73. *El Mancebo de Arévalo* (BNM 245; cf. Mancebo).

PR. Palacio Real.

PR 3225 = Saavedra 51. *Libro de las luces (Kitāb al-anwār* by al-Babkrī; cf. al-Bakrī).
PR 3226 = Saavedra 52. *El alḥadīth del alcázar; alḥadīth del annabī; el alḥadīth de los milagros.*

RAH. Real Academia de Historia.

RAH S1 = Saavedra 70. *Gualardón del ayuno y del aṣala; alḥadīth de la muerte de Bilāl; alḥadīth de un rey de al-Yaman; alḥadīth del nacimiento de'Isā; alfaḍīla del ayuno y del mes Ramadān.*
RAH S3 = Saavedra 72. *Brevario sunni de'Isā de Jābir* (cf. Jābir).
RAH S4 = Saavedra 73. *Leyes de moros.*
RAH S5 = Saavedra 74. *El hundidor de cismas y erejías.*
RAH T1 = Saavedra 75. *Los 37 lugares del alcorán donde se enuncia la unidad de Dios; los 99 nombres de Allāh; la carta de la muerte.*
RAH T2 = Saavedra 76. *Los siete alhaykales; adu'as.*
RAH T3 = Saavedra 77. *Los 37 lugares del alcorán en que se dice la unidad de Dios; os 99 nombres de Allāh; los siete alhaykales.*
RAH T4 = Saavedra 78. *La orden y la regla de las lunas; rituals.*
RAH T5 = Saavedra 79. *Traducción de azoras alcoránicas* (Q 5:1, Q 11 : 158, Q 59: 18-24).
RAH T6 = Saavedra 80. *Azoras alcoránicas; los nombres de Allāh; du'as; tahlīl.*
RAH T7 = Saavedra 81. *Una súplica a Allāh en verso.*
RAH T8 = Saavedra 82. *Alcorán abreviado; la orden y regla de las lunas; los cinco aṣalaes; las demandas de Mūsā; predicación en el nacimiento del annabī; capítulos para la mujer que no puede parir.*
RAH T9 = Saavedra 83. *Formulario matrimonial; historia de Solomón; alḥirz para la alḥabība.*
RAH T10 = Saavedra 84. *Un comentario del Zanati sobre la sūra 97 (Sūrat al-Qadr).*
RAH T11 = Saavedra 85. *Un ḥirz con palabras griegas y hebreas; incovaciones a las cuatro estaciones del ano; ángeles de cada dí; alḥirz alqāsim.*

RAH T12 = Saavedra 86. *Alḥadīth de Yūsuf; alḥadīth de Ibrāhīm; historia del nacimiento de Muḥammad; historia de un solitario Israelita; el castigo de 'Umar a su hijo; alḥadīth del legarto; alḥadīth de Bilāl; la disputa con los cristianos; alḥadīth del bano de Zarieb; alḥadīth de Tamīm; explicación de unas palabras de una obra de al-Ghazzāli; dos juṭbas; texto y traducción del capítulo 36 del alcorán.*

RAH T13 = Saavedra 87. *Pronósticos acerca del ano; desenganacion que izo el-ashayṭān al annab̄ Muḥammad; respuesta del Mufti de Oran; Los cuartos del ano; alcorán con taducción comentada; aljuṭba; adu'a para decir cada manana; la carta de la muerte; recetario; nombres de las lunas; alnushra de Muḥammad; alfaḍīla de los meses de Rayab y de Sha'bān; los cinco aṣalaes; los escándalos; los cinco almalakes; las demandas que hizo Sarjīl; recontamiento de cuando Mūsā fabló con Allah; los castigos de 'Alī; las demandas de los judíos; historia del nacimiento del annabī; historia del fundamento del adīn del alislām.*

RAH T15 = Saavedra 89. *Práctica de medicina.*

RAH T16 = Saavedra 90. *Colección de recetas; itinerario de Venecia a Espana.*

RAH T17 = Saavedra 91. *El libro de las luces* (cf. al-Bakrī); *historia del día del juicio; historia del puyomiento del annabī.*

RAH T18 = Saavedra 92. *El alḥadīth del annabī con el rey Ḥabīb; muerte de Muḥammad; libro de las luces (cf. al-Bakrī); alḥadīth de 'Alī con cuarenta doncellas; historia de la conquista de la casa de Meca; el waṣīya del gran turco llamado Muḥammad 'Uthmān* (Sánchez, "Turcos"); *alḥadīth de la muerte de Bilāl; traducción de una oración; poema en alabanza de Muḥammad.*

RAH T19 = Saavedra 93. *El castigo de 'Umar; alḥadīth de 'Umar; alḥadīth de Mūsā; los día nozientes y aprovechantes; las lunas del ano; las fadas buenas; los nombres fermosos de Allāh; alcorán; rituals; alkitāb de las suertes; alkitāb de suenos; preguntas de unos judíos a Muḥammad; Allāh y Mūsā; muerte de Muḥammad; derechos de familia.*

RAH V1 = Saavedra 94. *Fragmentos de Paris y Viana* (Guillén, "Historia"; Galmés, *Historia*).

RAH V2 = Saavedra 95. *Fragmento de un alḥadīth de Muḥammad.*

RAH V3 = Saavedra 96. *Fragmentos de una historia de al-Ḥayyay Ibn Ibn Yūsuf.*

RAH V4 = Saavedra 97. *Fragmento de la historia de la doncellaa Carcayona.*

RAH V6 = Saavedra 99. *Fragmentos de la disputa de los muslimes con los cristianos sobre la unidad de Allāh.*

RAH V7 = Saavedra 100. *Diputacion de los muslimes con los judíos; fragmentos de la disputación de los muslimes con los cristianos (*D. Cardaillac, *Polémique*, II, 269-285).

RAH V8 = Saavedra 101. *Fragmentos de alcorán.*

RAH V9 = Saavedra 102. *Fragmentos de alcorán.*

RAH V10 = Saavedra 103. *Fragmentos d alcorán; ángeles y genios; conjuros.*

RAH V11 = Saavedra 104. *Oraciones.*

RAH V12 = Saavedra 105. *Aljutba*

RAH V13 = Saavedra 106. *Unos ataṣbiḥes; versículos de alcorán; oración; ejercicio de escritura.*

RAH V14 = Saavedra 107. *Lo que se dice después de la aliqāma.*

RAH V15 = Saavedra 108. *Dos aljutbas.*

RAH V17 = Saavedra 110. *Los 37 lugares del alcorán en que se afirma la unidad de*

Allāh; azoras y oraciones.

RAH V21 = Saavedra 114. *Catálago en columna de los vocablos correspondientes a unas aljuṭbas.*

RAH V24 = Saavedra 117. *Valor de un hirz.*

RAH V25 = Saavedra 118. *Cédulas mágicas para varias enfermedades.*

RAH V26 = Saavedra 119. *Nombres cabalísticos de Allāh; anushara; rituals; los nombres de Allāh.*

RAH V27 = Saavedra 120. *Fórmulas cabalísticas.*

RAH V28 = Saavedra 121. *Receta latina.*

RAH V29 = Saavedra 122. *Receta.*

RAH V30 = Saavedra 123. *Litigio.*

RAH V31 = Saavedra 124. *Recetas.*

Index